CONTENTS

The Business Environment

Ian Worthington and Chris Britton

De Montfort University, Leicester

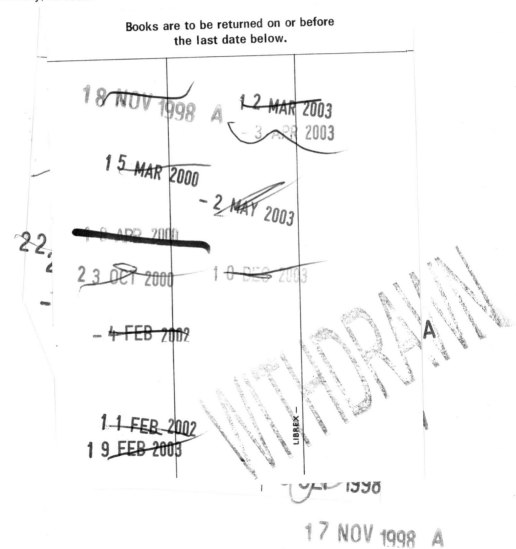
PITMAN
PUBLISHING

For Lindsey, Tom and Georgina and for
Rachael, Philip and Nick, with our love

PITMAN PUBLISHING
128 Long Acre, London WC2E 9AN

A Division of Longman Group Limited

First published in 1994

© Ian Worthington and Chris Britton, 1994

A CIP catalogue record for this book can be obtained from the British Library.

ISBN 0 273 60275 6

Typeset by Land & Unwin (Data Sciences) Ltd, Bugbrooke, Northamptonshire
Printed and bound in Great Britain by Page Brothers, Norwich, Norfolk

The Publishers' policy is to use paper manufactured from sustainable forests.

PREFACE

Interest in business studies has never been greater; witness, for example, the spectacular growth in the number of business schools in British universities and institutes of higher education over the last ten years and the rapidly increasing number of courses at degree and sub-degree level in which business is an important, and frequently dominant, element. Accompanying this growth in institutional provision has been an equally impressive growth in the number of books and journals devoted to the various aspects of business – including texts on management principles and practice, organisation theory, strategic management, marketing, human resource management, business economics, accounting and finance, and so on. Whilst such contributions have invariably been welcomed and have augmented our knowledge of the business world, the overwhelming preoccupation of scholars with the internal aspects of organisational life has tended to mean that the external influences on business activity have received little attention. This book is an attempt to redress the balance.

It should be stated at the outset that our central aim is to provide a study *of* business, rather than a study *for* business – a text for students rather than practitioners, although hopefully the latter will find much of the material useful and informative. In embarking on this study, we recognise that our perspective has been conditioned by years of teaching students on business studies courses in a variety of institutions, as well as our own interests and specialisms, and consequently the choice of subject matter and the ordering of material will not suit all tutors teaching on Business Environment courses. We have, however, attempted to discuss all the mainstream areas found on degree and HND-level courses in the large number of institutions with which we are familiar, as well as exploring some newer topics which are beginning to receive prominence in a growing number of Business Schools (e.g. corporate responsibility). In addition, whilst adopting a UK perspective, we have also drawn a substantial amount of our material from European and international sources – something often promised but not always delivered!

Each chapter in the book follows a common format, which includes objectives, a case study, review questions and assignments, and a guide to further reading. A comprehensive review of data and information sources is included in Chapter 16 and we would strongly encourage students to make regular use of these sources, particularly the quality newspapers and journals which contain a wealth of information and analysis on the changing business environment.

In carrying out this study, we have received considerable help from numerous organisations to whom we extend our thanks. These have included the Department of Trade and Industry, the Department of the Environment, the Cabinet Office, the Monopolies and Mergers Commission, the European Commission, the European Information Centre (Leicester City Council), Business in the Community, and the Confederation of British Industry.

Our gratitude also goes to the students and staff of Leicester Business School who have unwittingly helped us to gather information and to formulate our ideas over more years than we would care to mention. In particular we would like to acknowledge the considerable help and encouragement given to us by Gary Cook, Andy Rees, Professor Derrick Ball, Professor John Coyne and the staff of De Montfort University Library. To Janice Cox, who typed the majority of the script under demanding circumstances, goes our special thanks and admiration – she never once complained and always met the deadlines.

We would also like to acknowledge the considerable help, support and encouragement given to us by Dr Penelope Woolf of Pitman Publishing who has retained faith in us throughout the project. To her go our special thanks.

Our greatest debt, however, is owed to our families who have paid the highest price in terms of lost time, boring conversations, tetchiness and a general lack of consideration. Despite all this they have remained encouraging, supportive and loving. It is to them that we rightly dedicate this book.

Ian Worthington
Chris Britton
February 1994

CONTRIBUTORS

Authors

Ian Worthington, BA (Hons), PhD, is Principal Lecturer in the Department of Corporate Strategy, Leicester Business School, De Montfort University, where he specialises in business environment. He has published both in Britain and the USA and is co-author of a recent book on marketing.

Chris Britton, BA (Hons), MSc, is Senior Lecturer in the Department of Economics, De Montfort University. Her teaching and research interests lie in the field of industrial economics and labour markets where she has contributed to several publications, including co-authorship of a book on executive recruitment for *The Economist*.

Contributors

Diane Belfitt, BA (Hons), has taught Law at a number of institutions, including Leicester Polytechnic and Leicester University. She currently works at Charles Keene College in Leicester and examines for the Joint Matriculation Board.

Zena Cumberpatch, BA (Hons), MSc, is Senior Lecturer in the Department of Corporate Strategy, Leicester Business School, De Montfort University. Her main research interests include teaching and learning strategies and gender issues, and she has given conference papers on these topics. She is currently engaged in doctoral research in this area.

Dean Patton, BA (Hons), PGCE, is Senior Lecturer in the Department of Corporate Strategy, Leicester Business School, De Montfort University. His teaching and research interests centre on small firms and environmental policies within business. He has published in both these areas.

PART 1

Introduction

CHAPTER 1

Business organisations: the external environment

Ian Worthington

Business organisations differ in many ways, but they also have a common feature: the transformation of inputs into output. This transformation process takes place against a background of external influences which affect the firm and its activities. This external environment is complex, volatile and interactive, but it cannot be ignored in any meaningful analysis of business activity.

OBJECTIVES

1 To understand the basic features of business activity.
2 To portray the business organisation as a system interacting with its environment.
3 To recognise the range and complexity of the external influences on business activity.
4 To survey the central themes inherent in the study of the business environment.

INTRODUCTION

Business activity is a fundamental and universal feature of human existence and yet the concept of 'business' is difficult to define with any degree of precision. Dictionary definitions tend to describe it as being concerned with buying and selling or with trade and commerce, or the concern of profit-making organisations, and clearly all of these would come within the accepted view of business. Such a restricted view, however, would exclude large parts of the work of government and its agencies and the activities of non-profit-making organisations – a perspective it would be hard to sustain in a climate in which business methods, skills, attitudes and objectives are being increasingly adopted by these organisations. It is this broader view of business and its activities which is adopted below and which forms the focus of an investigation into the business environment.

THE BUSINESS ORGANISATION AND ITS ENVIRONMENT

A model of business activity

Most business activity takes place within an organisational context and even a cursory investigation of the business world reveals the wide variety of organisations involved, ranging from the small local supplier of a single good or service to the multibillion $ international or multinational corporation producing and trading on a global scale. Given this rich organisational diversity, most observers of the business scene tend to differentiate between organisations in terms of their size, type of product and/or market, methods of finance, scale of operations, legal status and so on. Nissan, for example, would be characterised as a major multinational car producer and distributor trading on world markets, whilst a local builder is likely to be seen as a small business operating at a local level with a limited market and relatively restricted turnover.

Whilst such distinctions are both legitimate and informative, they can conceal the fact that all business organisations are ultimately involved in the same basic activity, namely, the transformation of inputs (resources) into output (goods or services). This process is illustrated in Figure 1.1.

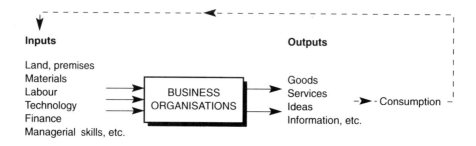

Fig. 1.1 The business organisation as a transformation system

In essence, all organisations acquire resources – including labour, premises, technology, finance, materials – and transform these resources into goods or services required by their customers. Whilst the type, amount and combination of resources will vary according to the needs of each organisation and may also vary over time, the simple process described above is common to all types of business organisation and provides a useful starting point for investigating business activity and the environment in which it takes place.

A more detailed analysis of business resources and those internal aspects of organisations which help to transform inputs into output can be found in Chapters 2 and 5 below. The need, here, is simply to appreciate the idea of the firm as a transformation system and to recognise that in producing and selling output most organisations hope to earn sufficient revenue to allow them to maintain and replenish their resources, thus permitting them to produce further output which in turn produces further inputs. In short, inputs help to create output and output creates inputs. Nor should it be overlooked that the output of one organisation may represent an input for another, as in the case of the firm producing capital equipment or basic materials or information or ideas. This interrelationship between business organisations is just one example of the complex and integrated nature of business activity and it helps to highlight the fact that the fortunes of any single business organisation are invariably linked with those of another or others – a point clearly illustrated in many of the examples cited in the text.

The firm in its environment

The simple model of business activity described above is based on the systems approach to management (see Chapter 2). One of the benefits of this approach is that it stresses that organisations are entities made up of interrelated parts which are intertwined with the outside world – the 'external environment' in systems language. This environment comprises a wide range of influences – economic, demographic, social, political, legal, technological, etc. – which affect business activity in a variety of ways and which can impinge not only on the transformation process itself, but also on the process of resource acquisition and on the creation and consumption of output. This idea of the firm in its environment is illustrated in Figure 1.2.

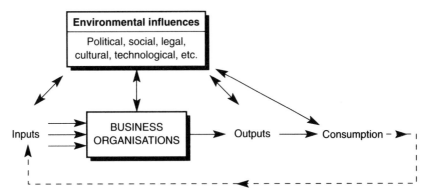

Fig. 1.2 The firm in its environment

In examining the business environment, a useful distinction can be made between those external factors which tend to have a more immediate effect on the day-to-day operations of a firm and those which tend to have a more general influence. Figure 1.3 makes this distinction.

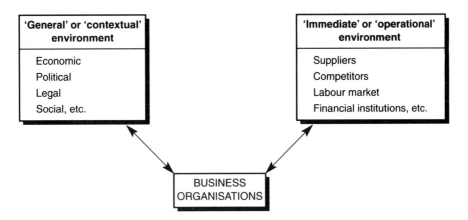

Fig. 1.3 Two levels of environment

The immediate or operational environment for most firms includes suppliers, competitors, labour markets, financial institutions and customers, and may also include trading organisations, trade unions and possibly a parent company. In contrast the general or contextual environment comprises those macroenvironmental factors such as economic, political, socio-cultural, technological and legal influences on business which affect a wide variety of businesses and which can emanate not only from local and national sources but also from international and supranational developments.

This type of analysis can also be extended to the different functional areas of an organisation's activities such as marketing or personnel or production or finance, as illustrated in Figure 1.4. Such an analysis can seen to be useful in at least two ways. First, it emphasises the influence of external factors on specific activities within the firm and in doing so underlines the importance of the interface between the internal and external environments. Second, by drawing attention to this interface, it highlights the fact that whilst business organisations are often able to exercise some degree of control over their internal activities and processes, it is often very difficult, if not impossible, to control the external environment in which they operate.

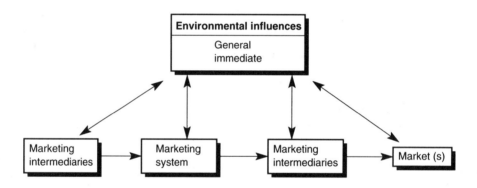

Fig. 1.4 Environmental influences on a firm's marketing system

THE GENERAL OR CONTEXTUAL ENVIRONMENT

Whilst the external factors referred to above form the subject matter of the rest of the book, it is useful at this point to gain an overview of the business environment by highlighting some of the key environmental influences on business activity. In keeping with the distinction made between general and more immediate influences, these are discussed separately below.

The political environment

A number of aspects of the political environment clearly impinge on business activity. These range from general questions concerning the nature of the political system and its institutions and processes (Chapter 3), to the more specific questions relating to government involvement in the working of the economy (Chapter 4) and its attempts to influence market structure and behaviour (Chapters 8, 12, 14). Government activities, both directly and indirectly, influence business activity and government can be seen as the biggest business enterprise at national or local level (Chapter 10). Given the trend towards the globalisation of markets and the existence of international trading organisations and blocs, international politico-economic influences on business activity represent one key feature of the business environment (Chapters 3, 5, 13). Another is the influence of public, as well as political, opinion in areas such as environmental policy and corporate responsibility (Chapter 15).

The economic environment

The distinction made between the political and economic environment – and, for that matter, the legal environment – is somewhat arbitrary. Government, as indicated above, plays a major role in the economy at both national and local level (Chapter 4 and 10) and its activities help to influence both the demand and supply side (e.g. see Chapter 11). Nevertheless there are a number of other economic aspects related to business activity which are worthy of consideration. These include various structural aspects of both firms and markets (Chapters 7, 8, 9, 12) and a comparison of economic theory and practice (e.g. Chapters 11, 12, 13).

The legal environment

Businesses operate within a framework of law which has a significant impact on various aspects of their existence. Laws usually govern, amongst other things, the status of the organisation (Chapter 7), its relationship with its customers and suppliers and certain internal procedures and activities (Chapter 6). They may also influence market structures and behaviour (e.g. Chapter 12). Since laws emanate from government (including supranational governments) and from the judgments of the courts, some understanding of the relevant institutions and processes is desirable (e.g. Chapters 3 and 6).

The socio-cultural environment

Both demand and supply are influenced by social and cultural factors. Cultural factors, for example, may affect the type of products being produced or sold, the markets they are sold in, the price at which they are sold and a range of other variables. People are a key organisational resource and a fundamental part of the market for goods and services. Accordingly, socio-cultural influences and developments have an important effect on business operations, as do demographic changes (Chapter 5).

The technological environment

Technology is both an input and output of business organisations as well as being an environmental influence on them. Investment in technology and innovation is frequently seen as a key to the success of an enterprise and has been used to explain differences in the relative competitiveness of different countries (Chapter 5). It has also been responsible for significant developments in the internal organisation of businesses in the markets for economic resources.

THE IMMEDIATE OR OPERATIONAL ENVIRONMENT

Resources and resource markets

An organisation's need for resources makes it dependent to a large degree on the suppliers of those resources, some of whom operate in markets which are organised to a considerable extent (e.g. Chapter 5). Some aspects of the operation of resource markets or indeed the activities of an individual supplier can have a fundamental impact on an organisation's success and upon the way in which it organises its internal procedures and processes. By the same token, the success of suppliers is often intimately connected with the decisions and/or fortunes of their customers, as the decline of the UK coal industry demonstrates. Whilst some organisations may seek to gain an advantage in price, quality or delivery by purchasing resources from overseas, such a decision can engender a degree of uncertainty, particularly where exchange rates are free rather than fixed (Chapter 13). Equally, organisations may face uncertainty and change in the domestic markets for resources as a result of factors as varied as technological change, government intervention or public opinion (e.g. conservation issues).

Customers

Customers are vital to all organisations and the ability both to identify and meet consumer needs is seen as one of the keys to organisational survival and prosperity – a point not overlooked by politicians who are increasingly using business techniques to attract the support of the electorate. This idea of consumer sovereignty – where resources are allocated to produce output to satisfy customer demands – is a central tenet of the market economy (Chapter 4) and is part of an ideology whose influence has become all pervasive in recent years. Understanding the many factors affecting both individual and market demand and the ways in which firms organise themselves to satisfy that demand is a vital component of a business environment that is increasingly market-led.

Competitors

Competition – both direct and indirect – is an important part of the context in which many firms operate and is a factor equally applicable to the input as well as the output side of business. The effects of competition, whether from domestic organisations or from overseas firms (e.g. see Chapter 13), is significant at the macro as well as the micro level and its influence can be seen in the changing structures of many advanced industrial economies (Chapter 9). How firms respond to these competitive challenges (e.g. Chapter 8) and the attitudes of governments to anti-competitive practices (Chapter 14) is a legitimate area of concern for students of business.

ANALYSING THE BUSINESS ENVIRONMENT

In a subject as all-encompassing as the business environment it is possible to identify numerous approaches to the organisation of the material. One obvious solution would be to examine the various factors mentioned above, devoting separate chapters to each of the environmental influences and discussing their impact on business organisations. Whilst this solution has much to recommend it – not least of which is its simplicity – the approach adopted below is based on the grouping of environmental influences into four main areas, in the belief that this helps to focus attention on key aspects of the business world, notably contexts, firms and their markets and issues of significance to entrepreneurs and to society as a whole.

In Part 2 consideration is given to the political, economic and legal contexts within which businesses function. In addition to examining the influence of political and economic systems, institutions and processes on the conduct of business, this section focuses on the macroeconomic environment and on influences affecting key organisational resources, particularly labour, technology and raw materials. The legal system and the influence of law in a number of critical areas of business activity is also a primary concern and one which has links with Part 3.

In Part 3, attention is focused on three central structural aspects: legal structure, size structure and industrial structure. The chapter on legal structure examines the impact of different legal definitions on a firm's operations and considers possible variations in organisational goals based on legal and other influences. The focus then shifts to how differences in size can affect the organisation (e.g. access to capital, economies of scale) and to an examination of how changes in scale and/or direction can occur, including the role of government in assisting small-business development and growth. One of the consequences of changes in the component elements of the economy is its effect on the overall structure of industry and commerce – a subject which helps to highlight the impact of international competition on the economic structure of many advanced industrial economies. Since government is a key actor in the economy, the section concludes with an analysis of government involvement in business and in particular its influence on the supply as well as the demand side of the economy at both national and local level.

In Part 4, the aim is to compare theory with practice by examining issues such as pricing, market structure and foreign trade. The analysis of price theory illustrates the degree to which the theoretical models of economists shed light on the operation of business in the 'real' world. Similarly, by analysing basic models of market structure, it is possible to gain an understanding of the effects of competition on a firm's behaviour and to appreciate the significance of both price and non-price decisions in the operation of markets.

The analysis continues with an examination of external markets and the role of government in influencing both the structure and operation of the marketplace. The chapter on international markets looks at the theoretical basis of trade and the development of overseas markets in practice, particularly in the context of recent institutional and financial developments (e.g. the Single Market, the Exchange Rate Mechanism). The section concludes with an investigation of the rationale for government intervention in markets and a review of government action in three areas, namely, privatisation and deregulation, competition policy and the operation of the labour market.

Finally, in Part 5, consideration is given to two aspects of business which are of increasing importance. One of these – corporate responsibility towards the natural environment – raises fundamental questions about the moral dimension of business activity, a subject often overlooked by writers and commentators on the business scene. Against a background of increasing national and international concern over the environmental impact of business, the chapter examines the idea of corporate social responsibility and the different forces which impact on an organisation in this area. The chapter concludes with an analysis of the benefits which derive from an environmentally responsible approach by businesses and illustrates some of the ways in which such an approach has been implemented by large organisations.

The concluding chapter in this section – and appropriately, in the book as a whole – emphasises the continuing need for organisations to monitor change in the business environment and examines a number of frameworks through which such an analysis can take place. In seeking to make sense of their environment, businesses need access to a wide range of information, much of which is available from published material, including government sources. Some of the major types of information available to students of business and to business organisations – including statistical and other forms of information – are considered in the final part of this chapter.

CENTRAL THEMES

A number of themes run through the text and it is useful to draw attention to these at this point.

Interaction with the environment

Viewed as an open system, the business organisation is in constant interaction with its environment. Changes in the environment can cause changes in inputs, in the transformation process and in outputs and these in turn may engender further changes in the organisation's environment. The internal and external environments should be seen as interrelated and interdependent, not as separate entities.

Interaction between environmental variables

In addition to the interaction between the internal and external environments, the various external influences affecting business organisations are also frequently interrelated. Changes in interest rates, for example, may affect consumer confidence and this can have an important bearing on business activity. Subsequent attempts by government to influence the level of demand could exacerbate the situation and this may lead to changes in general economic conditions, causing further problems for firms. The combined effect of these factors could be to create a turbulent environment which could result in uncertainty in the minds of managers. Failure to respond to the challenges (or opportunities) presented by such changes could signal the demise of the organisation or at best a significant decline in its potential performance.

The complexity of the environment

The environmental factors identified above are only some of the potential variables faced by all organisations. These external influences are almost infinite in number and variety and no study could hope to consider them all. For students of business and for managers alike, the requirement is to recognise the complexity of the external environment and to pay greater attention to those influences which appear the most pertinent and pressing for the organisation in question, rather than to attempt to consider all possible contingencies.

Environmental volatility and change

The organisation's external environment is further complicated by the tendency towards environmental change. This volatility may be particularly prevalent in some areas (e.g. technology) or in some markets or in some types of industry or organisation. As indicated above, a highly volatile environment causes uncertainty for the organisation (or for its subunits) and this makes decision-making more difficult.

Environmental uniqueness

Implicit in the remarks above is the notion that each organisation has to some degree a unique environment in which it operates and which will affect it in a unique way. Thus, whilst it is possible to make generalisations about the impact of the external environment on the firm, it is necessary to recognise the existence of this uniqueness and where appropriate to take into account exceptions to the general rule.

Different spatial levels of analysis

External influences operate at different spatial levels – local, regional, national, supranational, international. There are few businesses, if any, today which could justifiably claim to be unaffected by influences outside their immediate market(s).

Two-way flow of influence

As a final word, it is important to recognise that the flow of influence between the organisation and its environment operates in both directions. The external environment influences firms, but by the same token firms can influence their environment and this is an acceptable feature of business in a democratic society which is operating through a market-based economic system. This idea of democracy and its relationship with the market economy is considered in Chapters 3 and 4.

SYNOPSIS

In the process of transforming inputs into output, business organisations operate in a multifaceted environment which affects and is affected by their activities. This environment tends to be complex and volatile and comprises influences which are of both a general and an immediate kind and which operate at different spatial levels. Understanding this environment and its effects on business operations is of vital importance to the study and practice of business.

CASE STUDY: NATIONAL POWER

The privatisation of the electricity industry in England and Wales in 1990/91, split the former public utility into three parts: electricity generation, electricity distribution and the national grid. Responsibility for electricity distribution was given to 12 regional electricity companies, each of which became a shareholder in the privatised national grid company which they control through a holding company called Gridco. Electricity generation – with the exception of the nuclear power plants – was vested in two new generating companies, National Power and Power Generation which replaced the old Central Electricity Generating Board.

As the larger of the two generating companies which sell their electricity to the regional distributors, National Power is in a strong position in the UK energy market and its purchasing policies have a fundamental impact on the UK coal industry. Despite this influence the company has faced a number of important challenges since privatisation which have required it to look for new market opportunities beyond its initial sphere of operations. For a start, a succession of mild winters has reduced the domestic demand for electricity and this cut in consumption has been made worse by a recession which affected the UK economy in the early 1990s causing a decline in industrial usage. Added to this, pressure from the regional electricity companies who are independently developing generating capacity – particularly through gas-fired power stations – has limited the possibilities for growth for National Power and its rival PowerGen, both of whom have joined the 'dash for gas' which is seen as more environmentally friendly.

Faced with these problems in its main markets, National Power has embarked on a strategy of international expansion in selected overseas locations. In July 1993, for example, the company announced the acquisition of a subsidiary of the Texas-based Transco Energy gas pipeline company as part of its £1 billion investment programme. The business, known as Transco Energy Ventures (TEVCO), has interests in power generation in the south-east of the United States and is to be run by a newly established holding company called National Power America Inc.

REVIEW AND DISCUSSION QUESTIONS

1 In what senses could a college or university be described as a business organisation? How would you characterise its 'inputs' and 'output'?

2 Taking examples from a range of quality newspapers, illustrate ways in which business organisations are affected by their external environment.

3 Give examples of the ways in which business organisations can affect the external environment in which they operate.

4 With regard to the case study, explain how National Power's competitive environment has changed since privatisation.

ASSIGNMENTS

1 Assume you are a trainee in a firm of management consultants. As part of your induction process you have been asked to collect a file of information on an organisation of your choice. This file should contain not only information on the structure of the organisation and on its products, but also on the key external influences which have affected its operations in recent years.

2 Using newspapers and periodicals, produce a short report on the reasons for the government's recent decision to close a substantial number of pits in the UK coal industry.

FURTHER READING

Daniels, J.D., and Radebough, L.H., *International Business: Environments and Operations*, 5th edition, Addison-Wesley, 1989.

Palmer, A., and Worthington, I., *The Business and Marketing Environment*, McGraw-Hill, 1992.

CHAPTER 2

Business organisations: the internal environment

Ian Worthington and Zena Cumberpatch

The systems approach to the study of business organisations stresses the interaction between a firm's internal and external environments. Key aspects of the internal context of business include the organisation's structure and functions and the way they are configured in pursuit of specified organisational objectives. If the enterprise is to remain successful, constant attention needs to be paid to balancing the different influences on the organisation and to the requirement to adapt to new external circumstances. This responsibility lies essentially with the organisation's management which has the task of blending people, technologies, structures and environments.

OBJECTIVES

1 To outline the broad approaches to organisation and management, paying particular attention to the systems approach.
2 To examine alternative organisation structures used by business organisations.
3 To discuss major aspects of the functional management of firms.
4 To illustrate the interaction between a firm's internal and external environments.

INTRODUCTION

The internal features of business organisations have received considerable attention by scholars of organisation and management and a large number of texts have been devoted to this aspect of business studies.[1] In the discussion below, the aim is to focus on three areas of the internal organisation that relate directly to a study of the business environment: approaches to understanding organisations, organisation structures, and key functions within the enterprise. Further insight into these aspects and into management and organisational behaviour generally can be gained by consulting the many specialists books in this field, a number of which are mentioned at the end of this chapter.

A central theme running through any analysis of the internal environment is the idea of 'management', a concept which has been subjected to a wide variety of definitions. As used in this context, management is seen both as a system of roles fulfilled by individuals who manage the organisation (e.g. entrepreneur, resource manager, co-ordinator, leader, motivator, organiser) and as a process which enables an organisation to achieve its objectives. The essential point is that management should be seen as a function of organisations, rather than as a controlling element, and its task is to enable the organisation to identify and achieve its objectives and to adapt to change. Managers need to integrate the various influences on the organisation – including people, technology, systems and the environment – in a manner best designed to meet the needs of the enterprise at the time in question and be prepared to institute change as and when circumstances dictate.

APPROACHES TO ORGANISATION AND MANAGEMENT

An important insight into the principles which are felt to underlie the process of management can be gained by a brief examination of organisational theories. These theories or approaches – some of which date back to the late nineteenth century – represent the views of both practising managers and academics as to the factors that determine organisational effectiveness and the influences on individuals and groups within the work environment. Broadly speaking, these approaches can be broken down into three main categories: the classical approach, the human relations approach, and the systems approach.[2] Since the last of these encompasses the model presented in Chapter 1, particular attention is paid to this perspective.

The classical approach

Classical theories of organisation and management mostly date from the first half of the twentieth century and are associated with the work of writers such as Taylor, Fayol, Urwick and Brech. In essence, the classicists basically viewed organisations as formal structures established to achieve a particular number of objectives under the direction of management. By identifying a set of principles to guide managers in the design of the organisational structure, the proponents of the classical view believed that organisations would be able to achieve their objectives more effectively. Fayol, for example, identified fourteen principles which included the division of work, the scalar chain, centralisation and the unity of command – features which also found expression in Weber's notion of 'bureaucracy'. Urwick's rules or principles similarly emphasised aspects of organisation structure and operations – such as specialisation, co-ordination, authority, responsibility and the span of control – and were presented essentially as a code of good management practice.

Within the classical approach special attention is often given to two important sub-groupings, known as 'scientific management' and 'bureaucracy'. The former is associated with the pioneering work of F.W. Taylor (1856–1915) who believed that scientific methods could be attached to the design of work so that productivity could be increased. For Taylor, the systematic analysis of jobs (e.g. using some form of work study technique) was seen as the key to finding the best way to perform a particular task and thereby of achieving significant productivity gains from individuals which would earn them increased financial rewards. In Taylor's view, the responsibility for the institution of a scientific approach lay with management under whose control and direction the workers would operate to the mutual benefit of all concerned.

The second sub-group, bureaucracy, draws heavily on the work of Max Weber (1864–1920) whose studies of authority structures highlighted the importance of 'office' and 'rules' in the operation of organisations. According to Weber, bureaucracy – with its system of rules and procedures, specified spheres of competence, hierarchical organisation of offices, appointment based on merit, high level of specialisation and impersonality – possessed a degree of technical superiority over other forms of organisation, and this explained why an increasing number of enterprises were becoming bureaucratic in structure. Nearly 50 years after Weber's studies were first published in English, bureaucratic organisation remains a key feature of many enterprises throughout the world and is clearly linked to increasing organisational size and complexity. Notwithstanding the many valid criticisms of Weber's work, it is difficult to imagine how it could be otherwise.

The human relations approach

Whereas the classical approach focuses largely on structure and on the formal organisation, the human relations approach to management emphasises the importance of people in the work situation and the influence of social and psychological factors in shaping organisational behaviour. Human relations theorists have primarily been concerned with issues such as individual motivation, leadership, communications and group dynamics and have stressed the significance of the informal pattern of relationships which exist within the formal structure. The factors influencing human behaviour have accordingly been portrayed as a key to achieving greater organisational effectiveness, thus elevating the 'management of people' to a prime position in the determination of managerial strategies.

The early work in this field is associated with Elton Mayo (1880–1949) and with the famous Hawthorne Experiments, conducted at the Western Electric Company (USA) between 1924 and 1932. What these experiments basically showed was that individuals at work were members of informal (i.e. unofficial) as well as formal groups and that group influences were fundamental to explaining individual behaviour. Later work by writers such as Maslow, McGregor, Argyris, Likert and Hertzberg continued to stress the importance of the human factor in determining organisational effectiveness, but tended to adopt a more psychological orientation, as exemplified by Maslow's 'hierarchy of needs' and McGregor's 'Theory X and Theory Y'. Maslow's central proposition was that individuals seek to satisfy specific groups of needs, ranging from basic physiological requirements (e.g. food, sleep, sex) through safety, love and esteem, to self-actualisation (i.e. self-fulfilment); progressing systematically up the hierarchy as each lower level need is satisfied (see Figure 2.1). To McGregor individuals at work were seen by management as either inherently lazy (Theory X) or committed to the organisation's objectives and often actively seeking responsibility (Theory Y). These perceptions consequently provided the basis for different styles of management, which ranged from the coercive to the supportive.

McGregor's concern with management styles is reflected in later studies, including Ouichi's notion of 'Theory Z'.[3] According to Ouichi one of the key factors in the success of Japanese manufacturing industries was their approach to the management of people. Theory Z organisations were those which offered workers long-term (often

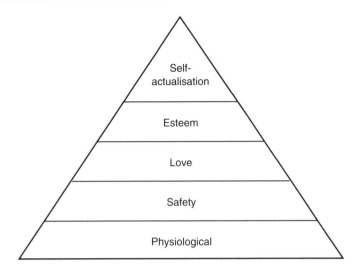

Fig. 2.1 A hierarchy of needs

lifetime) employment, a share in decision-making, opportunities for training, development and promotion, and a number of other advantages which gave them a positive orientation towards the organisation. For Ouichi, the key to organisational effectiveness lay in the development of a Japanese-style Theory Z environment, adapted to western requirements.

The systems approach

More recent approaches to organisation and management have helped to integrate previous work on structures, people and technology, by portraying organisations as socio-technical systems interacting with their environment. Under this approach – that became popular in the 1960s – organisations were seen as complex systems of people, tasks and technologies that were part of and interacted with a larger environment, comprising a wide range of influences (see Chapter 1). This environment was frequently subject to fluctuations, which on occasions could become turbulent (i.e. involving rapid and often unpredictable change). For organisations to survive and prosper, adaptation to environmental demands was seen as a necessary requirement and one which was central to the process of management.

The essence of the systems approach has been described in Chapter 1, but is worth repeating here. Organisations, including those involved in business, are open systems, interacting with their environment as they convert inputs into output. Inputs include people, finance, materials and information, provided by the environment in which the organisation exists and operates. Output comprises such items as goods and services, information, ideas and waste, discharged into the environment for consumption by 'end' or 'intermediate' users and in some cases representing inputs used by other organisations.

Systems invariably comprise a number of sub-systems through which the process of conversion or transformation occurs. Business organisations, for example, usually have sub-systems which deal with activities such as production, marketing, accounting and human resource management and each of these in turn may involve smaller sub-systems (e.g. sales, quality control, training) which collectively constitute the whole. Just as the organisation as a system interacts with its environment, so do the sub-systems and their component elements, which also interact with each other. In the case of the latter, the boundary between sub-systems is usually known as an 'interface'.

Whilst the obvious complexities of the systems approach need not be discussed, it is important to emphasise that most modern views of organisations draw heavily on the work in this area, paying particular attention to the interactions between people, technology, structure and environment and to the key role of management in directing the organisation's activities towards the achievement of its goals. Broadly speaking, management is seen as a critical sub-system within the total organisation, responsible for the co-ordination of the other sub-systems and for ensuring that internal and external relationships are managed effectively. As changes occur in one part of the system these will induce changes elsewhere and this will require a management response that will have implications for the organisation and for its sub-systems. Such changes may be either the cause or effect of changes in the relationship between the organisation and its environment, and the requirement for managers is to adapt to the new conditions without reducing the organisation's effectiveness.

Given the complex nature of organisations and the environments in which they operate, a number of writers have suggested a 'contingency approach' to organisational design and management (e.g. Lawrence and Lorsch, Woodward, Perrow, Burns and Stalker).[4] In essence, this approach argues that there is no single form of organisation best suited to all situations and that the most appropriate organisational structure and system of management is dependent upon the contingencies of the situation (e.g. size, technology, environment) for each organisation. In some cases a bureaucratic structure might be the best way to operate, whilst in others much looser and more organic methods of organisation might be more effective. In short, issues of organisational design and management depend on choosing the best combination in light of the relevant situational variables; this might mean different structures and styles coexisting within an organisation.

ORGANISATION STRUCTURES

Apart from the very simplest form of enterprise in which one individual carries out all tasks and responsibilities, business organisations are characterised by a division of labour which allows employees to specialise in particular roles and to occupy designated positions in pursuit of the organisation's objectives. The resulting pattern of relationships between individuals and roles constitutes what is known as the organisation's structure and represents the means by which the purpose and work of the enterprise is carried out. It also provides a framework through which communications can occur and within which the processes of management can be applied.

Responsibility for establishing the formal structure of the organisation lies with management and a variety of options is available. Whatever form is chosen, the basic need is to identify a structure which will best sustain the success of the enterprise and will permit the achievement of a number of important objectives. Through its structure an organisation should be able to:

● achieve efficiency in the utilisation of resources;
● provide opportunities for monitoring organisational performance;
● ensure the accountability of individuals;
● guarantee co-ordination between the different parts of the enterprise;
● provide an efficient and effective means of organisational communication;
● create job satisfaction, including opportunities for progression; and
● adapt to changing circumstances brought about by internal or external developments.

In short, structure is not an end in itself, but a means to an end and should ideally reflect the needs of the organisation within its existing context and taking into account its future requirements.

The essence of structure is the division of work between individuals and the formal organisational relationships that are created between them. These relationships will be reflected not only in individual job descriptions, but also in the overall organisation chart which designates the formal pattern of role relationships and the interactions between roles and the individuals occupying those roles. Individual authority relationships can be classified as line, staff, functional and lateral and arise from the defined pattern of responsibilities, as follows:

● *Line relationships* occur when authority flows vertically downward through the structure from superior to subordinate (e.g. managers – section leader – staff).
● *Staff relationships* are created when senior personnel appoint assistants who normally have no authority over other staff but act as an extension of their superior.
● *Functional relationships* are those between specialists (or advisers) and line managers and their subordinates (e.g. when a specialist provides a common service throughout the organisation but has no authority over the users of the service). The personnel or computing function may be one such service that creates a functional relationship. (Note that specialists have line relationships with their own subordinates.)
● *Lateral relationships* exist across the organisation, particularly between individuals occupying equivalent positions within different departments or sections, (e.g. committees, head of departments, section leaders).

With regard to the division of work and the grouping of organisational activities, this can occur in a variety of ways. These include:

● By *function or major purpose*, associated particularly with departmental structures.
● By *product or service*, where individuals responsible for a particular product or service are grouped together.
● By *location*, based on geographical criteria.
● By *common processes* (e.g. particular skills or methods of operation).
● By *client group* (e.g. children, the disabled, the elderly).

In some organisations a particular method of grouping will predominate; in others there will tend to be a variety of types and each has its own particular advantages and disadvantages. In the discussion below, attention is focused on five main methods of grouping activities in business organisations. Students should attempt to discover what types of structure exist within their own educational institution and the logic (!) which underlies the choices made.

Functional organisation

The functional approach to organisation is depicted in Figure 2.2. As its name indicates, in this type of structure activities are clustered together by common purpose or function. All marketing activities, for example, are grouped together as a common function, typically within a marketing department. Similarly, other areas of activity, such as production, finance, personnel and research and development have their own specialised sections or departments, responsible for all the tasks required of that function.

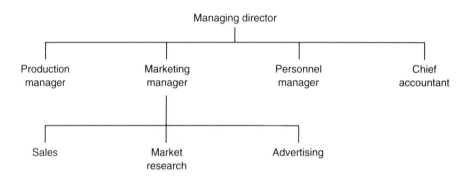

Fig. 2.2 A functional organisation structure

Apart from its obvious simplicity, the functional organisation structure allows individuals to be grouped together on the basis of their specialisms and technical expertise, and this can facilitate the development of the function they offer as well as providing a recognised path for promotion and career development. On the downside, functional specialisation, particularly through departments, is likely to create sectional interests which may operate to the disadvantage of the organisation as a whole, particularly where inequalities in resource allocation between functions becomes a cause for interfunction rivalry. It could also be argued that this form of structure is most suited to single-product firms and that it becomes less appropriate as organisations diversify their products and/or markets. In such circumstances, the tendency will be for businesses to look for the benefits which can arise from specialisation by product or from the divisionalisation of the enterprise.

Organisation by product or service

In this case the division of work and the grouping of activities is dictated by the product or service provided (see Figure 2.3), such that each group responsible for a particular part of the output of the organisation may have its own specialist in the different functional areas (e.g. Marketing, Finance, Personnel). One advantage of this type of structure is that it allows an organisation to offer a diversified range of products, as exemplified by the different services available in National Health Service hospitals (e.g. maternity, orthopaedic, geriatric, and so forth). Its main disadvantage is the danger that the separate units or divisions within the enterprise may attempt to become too autonomous, even at the expense of other parts of the organisation, and this can present management with problems of co-ordination and control.

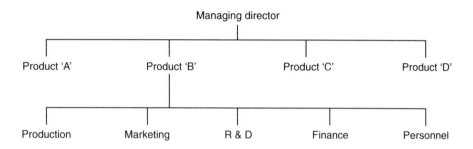

Fig. 2.3 A product-based structure

The divisional structure

As firms diversify their products and/or markets – often as a result of merger or take-over – a structure is needed to co-ordinate and control the different parts of the organisation. This structure is likely to be the divisional (or 'multidivisional') company.

A divisionalised structure is formed when an organisation is split up into a number of self-contained business units, each of which operates as a profit centre. Such a division may occur on the basis of product or market or a combination of the two, with each unit tending to operate along functional or product lines, but with certain key functions (e.g. finance, personnel, corporate planning) provided centrally, usually at company headquarters (see Figure 2.4).

The main benefit of the multidivisional company is that it allows each part of what can be a very diverse organisation to operate semi-independently in producing and marketing its products, thus permitting each division to design its offering to suit local market conditions – a factor of prime importance where the firm operates on a multinational basis. The dual existence of divisional profit centres and a central unit responsible for establishing strategy at a global level can, however, be a source of considerable tension, particularly where the needs and aims of the centre appear to conflict with operations at the local level or to impose burdens seen to be unreasonable by divisional managers (e.g. the allocation of central overhead costs).

Much the same kind of arguments apply to the holding company, though this tends to be a much looser structure for managing diverse organisations, favoured by both UK and Japanese companies. Under this arrangement, the different elements of the organisation (usually companies) are co-ordinated and controlled by a parent body

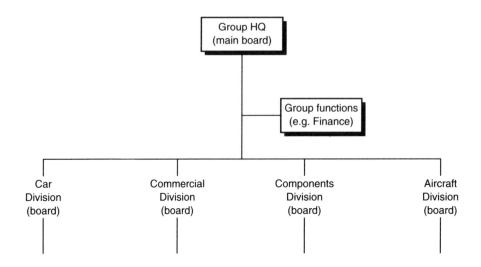

Figure 2.4 A divisional structure

which may be just a financial entity established to maintain or gain control of other trading companies (e.g. Lonhro). Holding companies are associated with the growth of firms by acquisition which gives rise to a high degree of product or market diversification. They are also a popular means of operating a multinational organisation.

Matrix structures

A matrix is an arrangement for combining functional specialisation (e.g. through departments) with structures built around products, projects or programmes (see Figure 2.5). The resulting grid (or matrix) has a two-way flow of authority and responsibility. Within the functional elements, the flow is vertically down the line from superior to subordinate and this creates a degree of stability and certainty for the individuals located within the department or unit. Simultaneously, as a member of a project group or product team, an individual is normally answerable horizontally to the project manager whose responsibility is to oversee the successful completion of the project, which in some cases may be of very limited duration.

Matrix structures offer various advantages, most notably flexibility, opportunities for staff development, an enhanced sense of ownership of a project or programme, customer orientation and the co-ordination of information and expertise. On the negative side, difficulties can include problems of co-ordination and control, conflicting loyalties for staff and uncertain lines of authority. It is not uncommon in an organisation designed on matrix lines for project or programme leaders to be unsure of their authority over the staff from the contributing departments. Nor is it unknown for functional managers to withdraw their co-operation and/or support for projects located outside their immediate sphere of influence.

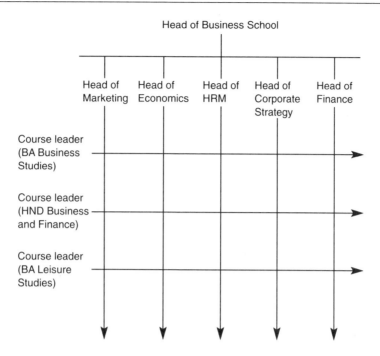

Fig. 2.5 A matrix structure in a Business School

Project teams

Despite its flexibility, the matrix often has a degree of permanence; in contrast, the project team is essentially a temporary structure established as a means of carrying out a particular task, often in a highly unstable environment. Once the task is complete, the team is disbanded and individuals return to their usual departments or are assigned to a new project.

Fashioned around technical expertise rather than managerial rank and often operating closely with clients, project teams are increasingly common in high-technology firms, construction companies and in some types of service industry, especially management consultancies and advertising. Rather than being a replacement for the existing structure, they operate alongside it and utilise in-house staff (and in some cases, outside specialists) on a project-by-project basis. Whilst this can present logistical and scheduling problems and may involve some duplication of resources, it can assist an organisation in adapting to change and uncertainty and in providing products to the customer's specifications. Project teams tend to be at their most effective when objectives and tasks are well defined, when the client is clear as to the desired outcome and when the team is chosen with care.

ASPECTS OF FUNCTIONAL MANAGEMENT

Most organisation structures reflect a degree of functional specialisation, with individuals occupying roles in departments, units or sections which have titles such as

Production, Finance, Marketing, Personnel and Research and Development. These functional areas of the internal organisation, and the individuals who are allocated to them, are central to the process of transforming organisational inputs into output. The management of these functions and of the relationships between them will be a key factor in the success of the enterprise and in its ability to respond to external demands for change.

The interdependence of the internal functions can be demonstrated by a simple example. Providing goods and services to meet the market's needs often involves research and development which necessitates a financial input, usually from the capital market or the organisation's own resources. It also requires, as do all the other functions, the recruitment of staff of the right quality, a task which is more often than not the responsibility of the Personnel department. If research and development activities lead to a good idea which the Marketing department is able to sell, then the Production department is required to produce it in the right quantities, to the right specifications and at the time the market needs it. This depends not only on internal scheduling procedures within the Production department, but also on having the right kind of materials supplied on time by the Purchasing department, an appropriate system of quality control and work monitoring, machinery that is working and regularly serviced, the finished items packed, despatched and delivered and a multitude of other activities, all operating towards the same end.

The extent to which all of these requirements can be met simultaneously depends not only on internal factors, many of which are controllable, but also on a host of external influences, the majority of which tend to be beyond the organisation's control. To demonstrate this interface between the internal and external environments, two key areas of functional management are discussed briefly below – marketing and human resource management. An examination of the other functions within the organisation would yield very similar findings.

Human resource management (HRM)

People are the key organisational resource; without them organisations would not exist or function. All businesses need to plan for and manage the people they employ if they are to use this resource effectively and efficiently in pursuit of their objectives. In modern and forward-looking organisations this implies a proactive approach to the management of people which goes beyond the bounds of traditional personnel management and involves the establishment of systems for planning, monitoring, appraisal and evaluation, training and development and for integrating the internal needs of the organisation with the external demands of the marketplace. Such an approach is associated with the idea of human resource management.

As in other areas of management, HRM involves a wide variety of activities related to the formulation and implementation of appropriate organisational policies, the provision of opportunities for monitoring, evaluation and change, and the application of resources to the fulfilment of organisational ends. Key aspects of 'people management' include:

- recruitment and selection;
- working conditions;

- training and career development;
- job evaluation;
- employee relations;
- manpower planning; and
- legal aspects of employment.

In most, if not all, cases these will be affected by both internal and external influences (e.g. size of the firm, management style, competition, economic and political developments), some of which will vary over time as well as between organisations.

The provision of these activities within an organisation can occur in a variety of ways and to different degrees of sophistication. Some very small firms may have little in the way of a recognisable HRM function, being concerned primarily with questions of hiring and firing, pay and other working conditions, but not with notions of career development, staff appraisal or job enrichment. In contrast, very large companies may have a specialist HRM or Personnel Department, often organised on functional lines and responsible for the formulation and implementation of personnel policies throughout the organisation. Such centralisation not only provides some economies of scale, but also a degree of standardisation and consistency across departments. To allow for flexibility, centralised systems are often combined with an element of decentralisation which permits individual departments or sections to exercise some influence in matters such as the recruitment and selection of staff, working conditions, training and career development.

To illustrate how the different aspects of HRM are influenced by external factors, one part of this function – recruitment and selection of staff – has been chosen. This is the activity within the organisation which seeks to ensure that it has the right quantity and quality of labour in the right place and at the right time to meet its requirements at all levels. To achieve this aim, the organisation initially needs to consider a large number of factors, including possible changes in the demand for labour, the need for new skills and likely labour turnover, before the processes of recruitment and selection can begin. These aspects in turn will be conditioned by a variety of factors such as changes in the demand for the product, the introduction of new technology and social, economic and demographic changes, some of which may not be anticipated or expected by strategic planners.

Once recruitment and selection is ready to begin, a further raft of influences will impinge upon the process, some of which emanate from external sources. In drawing up a job specification, for example, attention will normally need to be paid to the state of the local labour market, including skill availability, competition from other employers, wage rates in comparable jobs and/or organisations and socio-demographic trends. If the quality of labour required is in short supply, an organisation may find itself having to offer improved pay and working conditions simply to attract a sufficient number of applicants to fill the vacancies on offer. Equally, in fashioning its job advertisements and in drawing up the material it sends out to potential applicants, a firm will need to pay due attention to the needs of current legislation in areas such as equal opportunities, race discrimination and employment protection, if it is not to infringe the law.

Amongst the other external factors the enterprise may need to take into consideration in recruiting and selecting staff will be:

- the relative cost and effectiveness of the different advertising media;
- existing relationships with external sources of recruitment (e.g. job centres, schools, colleges, universities);
- commitments to the local community;
- relationships with employee organisations (e.g. trade unions, staff associations); and
- opportunities for staff training and development in local training and educational institutions.

Ideally, it should also pay some attention to possible future changes in the technology of the workplace, in order to recruit individuals either with appropriate skills or who can be retrained relatively easily with a minimum amount of disruption and expense to the organisation.

The marketing function

The processes of human resource management provide a good illustration of the interactions between a firm's internal and external environments. An even better example is provided by an examination of its marketing activities which are directed primarily, though not exclusively, towards what is happening outside the organisation.

Like 'management', the term 'marketing' has been defined in a wide variety of ways, ranging from Kotler's essentially economic notion of an activity directed at satisfying human needs and wants through exchange process, to the more managerial definitions associated with bodies like the Chartered Institute of Marketing.[5] A common thread running through many of these definitions is the idea that marketing is concerned with meeting the needs of the consumer in a way which is profitable to the enterprise. Hence strategic marketing management is normally characterised as the process of ensuring a good fit between the opportunities afforded by the marketplace and the abilities and resources of an organisation operating in it.

This notion of marketing as an integrative function within the organisation – linking the needs of the consumer with the various functional areas of the firm – is central to modern definitions of the term and lies at the heart of what is known as the 'marketing concept'. This is the idea that the customer is of prime importance to the organisation and that the most significant managerial task in any enterprise is first to identify the needs and wants of the consumer and then to ensure that its operations are geared to meeting these requirements profitably. Though it would be true to say that not all organisations subscribe to this view, it is generally accepted that the successful businesses are predominantly those with a customer rather than a production or sales orientation. Equally, the evidence suggests that the need to adopt such a customer-centred approach applies not only to private sector trading organisations, but also increasingly to public sector enterprises and to bodies not established for the pursuit of profits but for other purposes (e.g. charities, political parties, trade unions).

When viewed from a customer perspective, marketing can be seen to comprise a range of activities that go beyond the simple production of an item for sale. These include:

- Identifying the needs of consumers (e.g. through marketing research).
- Designing different 'offerings' to meet the needs of different types of customers (e.g. through market segmentation).

- Choosing products, prices, promotional techniques and distribution channels that are appropriate to a particular market (i.e. designing a 'marketing mix' strategy).
- Undertaking market and product planning.
- Deciding on brand names, types of packages, and methods of communicating with the customer.
- Creating a marketing information system.

As already indicated, in carrying out these activities the firm is brought into contact with a range of external influences of both an immediate and indirect kind. As Palmer and Worthington have shown, this external marketing environment can have a fundamental impact on the degree to which the firm is able to develop and maintain successful transactions with its customers and hence on its profitability and chances of survival.[6]

To illustrate how a firm's marketing effort can be influenced by external factors, the following brief discussion focuses on 'pricing', which is one of the key elements of the 'marketing mix': that is, the set of controllable variables which a business can use to influence the buyer's response, namely, product, price, promotion and place – the 4Ps. Of all the mix elements, price is the only one which generates revenue, whilst the others result in expenditures. It is therefore a prime determinant of a firm's turnover and profitability and can have a considerable influence on the demand for its products and frequently for those of its competitors (see Chapter 11).

Leaving aside the broader question of a firm's pricing goals and the fact that prices will tend to vary according to the stage a product has reached in its life cycle, price determination can be said to be influenced by a number of factors. Of these, the costs of production, the prices charged by one's competitors and the price sensitivity of consumers tend to be the most significant.

In the case of cost-based pricing, this occurs when a firm relates its price to the cost of buying or producing the product, adding a profit margin or 'mark-up' to arrive at the final selling price. Such an approach tends to be common amongst smaller enterprises (e.g. builders, corner shops) where costs are often easier to estimate and where likely consumer reactions are given less attention than the need to make an adequate return on the effort involved. The essential point about this form of price determination is that many of the firm's costs are influenced by external organisations – including the suppliers of materials, components, and energy – and hence pricing will often vary according to changes in the prices of inputs. Only larger organisations, or a group of small businesses operating together, will generally be able to exercise some influence over input prices and even then not all costs will be controllable by the enterprise.

Organisations which take an essentially cost-based approach to pricing will sometimes be influenced by the prices charged by competitors – particularly in markets where considerable competition exists and where the products are largely homogeneous and a buyer's market is evident (e.g. builders during a recession). The competitive approach to pricing, however, is also found in markets where only a few large firms operate and where the need to increase or maintain market share can give rise to virtually identical prices and to fierce non-price competition between the market leaders (see Chapter 12). A big cross-Channel ferry operator, for instance, will normally provide the service to customers at the same price as its rivals, differentiating its offering in terms of additional benefits (e.g. on-board entertainment) rather than price. Where this is the case, the external demands of the market rather than costs constitute the primary influence on a firm's decisions, and changes in market conditions (e.g. the actual or potential entry of new firms; changes in a competitors prices; economic recession) will tend to be reflected in price changes.

This idea of market factors influencing pricing decisions also applies to situations where firms fix their prices according to the actual or anticipated reactions of consumers to the price charged for a product – known in economics as the price elasticity of demand (see Chapter 11). In this case, the customer rather than a firm's competitors is the chief influence on price determination, although the two are often interrelated in that consumers are usually more price sensitive in markets where some choice exists. Differential levels of price sensitivity between consumers of a product normally arises when a market has distinct segments based on factors such as differences in income or age or location. In such cases a firm will often fix its prices according to the segment of the market it is serving, a process known as 'price discrimination' and one which is familiar to students claiming concessionary fares on public transport.

Whilst the above discussion has been oversimplified and does not take into account factors such as the price of other products in an organisation's product portfolio (e.g. different models of car), it illustrates quite clearly how even one of the so-called controllable variables in a firm's marketing mix is subject to a range of external influences that are often beyond its ability to control. The same argument applies to the other elements of the marketing function and students could usefully add to their understanding of the internal/external interface by examining how the external environment impinges upon such marketing activities as promotion, distribution or marketing research.

SYNOPSIS

The internal dimension of business organisations constitutes an extensive field of study and one to which students of business devote a considerable amount of time. In seeking to illustrate how a firm's internal organisation is influenced by its external environment, emphasis has been placed on a selected number of aspects of a firm's internal operations. Of these, its structure and functions were seen to provide a good illustration of the interface between the internal and external environments. Appreciating the existence of this interface is facilitated by adopting a systems approach to organisational analysis.

CASE STUDY: THE RENAULT–VOLVO MERGER

The market for cars is a global market, dominated by a relatively small number of European, Japanese and American companies. By the early 1990s many of these companies had began to experience difficult trading conditions brought about by overcapacity in the industry, depressed world markets and increasingly fierce competition as individual car producers struggled to maintain their market share. Large Japanese multinational organisations such as Nissan, Honda and Toyota entered into joint ventures with other car producers and began to establish

---

production facilities in overseas markets to overcome actual or potential trade barriers (see Chapter 4 case study). European rivals, including Renault and Volvo, similarly began to form strategic alliances to protect themselves from Japanese and American competition and from the fallout from the inevitable restructuring of Europe's over-crowded car industry – a process which looks set to continue to the end of the decade.

The formal links between Renault (France) and Volvo (Sweden) first began to take shape in 1990 with the signing of a co-operation accord. By 1991 the two companies had entered into a cross-share arrangement and had started to draw up a strategic programme for establishing a number of joint structures, including joint production-line planning, joint purchasing arrangements and a common assembly platform. Consequently the announcement in September 1993 that Renault and Volvo were finally to merge – to form the world's sixth largest car company and its twentieth largest industrial concern, with 200,000 employees and 12 per cent of the European car market – came as no surprise to industry observers.

The details which have emerged so far indicate that, at least in the short term, the new operating company, Renault–Volvo Automotive (RVA), will be responsible for the car, truck and financial subsidiaries of the two enterprises and will be answerable to its initial shareholders: Renault, Volvo and a holding company RVC, owned jointly by Renault SA and AB Volvo. RVC will be presided over by a board of directors drawn equally from France and Sweden and will oversee all stock decisions, including capital injections for RVA, thus protecting French interests once the full-scale privatisation of Renault has begun. RVA will be run by a five-member management board, chaired by the French who will provide three of the members. It will also be overseen by a 14-member supervisory board, under the chairmanship of Volvo's current chairman and including representatives of the workforce.

There seems little doubt that the new complex structure has been designed to ensure that Renault remains the dominant partner after the French company has been privatised (probably in 1994/5) – a process likely to be made easier by the establishment of RVA. It should also help to prevent hostile take-overs once shares become fully available on the open market. In operational terms, it is expected that the streamlining of management in the new group will make it more responsive to market changes and that shared facilities will provide benefits for both parties who will keep their separate trademarks. Volvo, for example, will get access to Renault's extensive European sales and production network, whilst Renault should benefit from Volvo's market position and sales organisation in the Middle East, South East Asia and the United States. The consequent opportunities to maximise buying, marketing, production and distribution opportunities are likely to improve the group's ability to compete in the fiercely competitive global market for cars and to ensure that Renault–Volvo is able to hold its own against Peugeot–Citroën, Volkswagen, Vauxhall–Opel, Ford and the others operating in the European sector of the market.[7]

NOTES AND REFERENCES

1   See, for example, Mullins, L. J., *Management and Organisational Behaviour*, Pitman, 1993; Cole, G. A., *Management: Theory and Practice*, 3rd edition, DP Publications, 1990.
2   For a more detailed account of the three approaches see, *inter alia*, the texts referred to in n. 1.
3   Ouichi, W. G., *Theory Z: How American business can meet the Japanese challenge*, Addison-Wesley, 1981.
4   The contingency approach is discussed in Cole, *op. cit.*, chapter 13.
5   See, for example, Kotler, P. and Armstrong G., *Principles of Marketing*, 5th edition, Prentice Hall, 1991, chapter 3.
6   Palmer, A. and Worthington, I., *The Business and Marketing Environment*, McGraw-Hill, 1992.
7   The planned merger was turned down by Volvo shareholders in December 1993.

REVIEW AND DISCUSSION QUESTIONS

1 In the systems approach to organisations, reference is made to 'feedback'. What is meant by this term and how can feedback influence the process of transforming 'inputs' into 'output'?

2 Should a firm's internal structure be influenced by considerations of management or by the market it serves? Are the two incompatible?

3 Examine ways in which a firm's external environment can influence one of the following functional areas: Finance *or* Production *or* Research and Development.

4 Describe the structure of an organisation with which you are familiar (e.g. through employment or work experience), indicating why the organisation is structured in the way it is. Are there any alternative forms of structure the organisation could adopt?

ASSIGNMENTS

1 As a student on a business studies course, you have decided to get some practical experience of the business world by running a small venture with a number of colleagues which you hope will also earn you enough income to support you during your time at college or university. Your idea involves printing and selling customised t-shirts throughout the institution and possibly to a wider market.

   Design an appropriate organisational structure which you feel will achieve your objectives, indicating your rationale for choosing such a structure and the formal pattern of relationships between individuals.

2 In self-selecting groups of three or four, identify an organisation which you feel has a bureaucratic structure. Produce a report indicating:
   (a) those features of the organisation's structure, management and operations which best fit the idea of bureaucracy; and
   (b) the practical consequences of these features for the working of the organisation.
   Give examples to support your comments.

FURTHER READING

Cole, G. A., *Management: Theory and Practice*, 3rd edition, DP Publications, 1990.
Handy, C., *The Age of Unreason*, Arrow Books, 1990.
Kotler, P. and Armstrong, G., *Principles of Marketing*, 5th edition, Prentice Hall, 1991, chapter 1.
Mullins, L. J., *Management and Organisational Behaviour*, 3rd edition, Pitman, 1993.
Palmer, A. and Worthington, I., *The Business and Marketing Environment*, McGraw-Hill, 1992.
Pugh, D. S. and Hickson, D. J., *Writers on Organisations*, 4th edition, Penguin, 1989.

PART 2

Contexts

CHAPTER 3

The political environment

Ian Worthington

Politics is a universal activity which affects the business world in a variety of ways. Understanding political systems, institutions and processes provides a greater insight into business decisions and into the complexities of the business environment. Given the increasing globalisation of markets, this environment has an international as well as a domestic element and the two are closely interrelated. Appreciating some of the key aspects of this environment and its impact on business organisations is vital for students of business and for managers alike.

OBJECTIVES

1 To gain an insight into the political context within which business operates.
2 To appreciate the relevance of political values to the organisation of business activity.
3 To examine key political institutions and processes at a variety of spatial levels.
4 To recognise that business organisations can influence, as well as be influenced by, the political environment.

INTRODUCTION

In the late 1980s, following a period of difficult negotiations, the British government entered into a collaborative agreement with the governments of Germany, Italy and Spain, to develop and produce a European fighter aircraft (EFA), due to come into service in the later 1990s. This agreement, which involved the participants jointly funding research and development costs, was greeted with delight by firms in Britain's aerospace industry and by their suppliers who welcomed the prospects of a large order of aircraft at a time when defence spending was being restrained. For firms such as GEC Ferranti, BAe, Lucas Aerospace, Rolls–Royce and Smiths Industries, the collaborative venture offered the prospects of future profits and the opportunity to retain their technological edge. For the communities in which these firms were based, it promised to sustain and possibly create employment during a period of growing economic uncertainty.

Subsequent indications (in 1992) that the German government would pull out of the venture – on the grounds of escalating costs and a reduced military threat – sent shock waves through the British aerospace industry and threatened to sour relations between the participating governments the rest of whom wished to continue with the project. In the event, a compromise was reached under which the countries involved agreed to continue with research and development in an effort to produce a cheaper aircraft, to be known as the Eurofighter 2000. Given the problems of German reunification, the German government has reserved the right to make a final decision on production at some time in the future. As a result, the aircraft is unlikely to enter service – if at all – before the year 2000.

What this simple example illustrates is that business activity takes place both within and across state boundaries and frequently involves governments, whether directly or indirectly. Consequently the political and economic arrangements within the state in which a business is located and/or with which it is trading can have a fundamental impact on its operations – even to the extent of determining whether it is willing or, in some cases, able to trade at all. It is this politico-economic context within which businesses function and the philosophical foundations on that it is based that are the focus of this and the following chapter.

As a prelude to a detailed analysis of the political environment, it is necessary to make a number of general observations regarding political change and uncertainty and its impact on business activity. First, the nature of a country's political system – including its governmental institutions – tends to reflect certain underlying social values and philosophies which help to determine how decisions are made, including decisions about the allocation of resources. Thus, whilst governments may come and go, the values on which their decisions are based tend to be more enduring and as a result disputes normally centre around 'means' (e.g. sources of revenue), rather than 'ends' (e.g. controlling inflation). Whilst this gives a certain degree of stability to the business environment, this stability cannot be taken for granted, as events in eastern Europe have readily demonstrated. In short, the political environment of business is a dynamic environment, containing both elements of continuity and change, and students and practitioners of business alike need to be constantly aware of developments in this area, if they are to gain a greater insight into the background of business decision-making.

Secondly, changes in the political environment also emanate from a country's institutional arrangements. The tendency in democratic states, for example, to have regular elections, competing political parties offering alternative policies, and a system of pressure groups, all help to generate a degree of discontinuity, which renders predictions about the future more uncertain. For a business, such uncertainty can create not only opportunities but also a degree of risk which will often be an important influence on its decisions. Moreover, given that perceptions of such risks (or opportunities) are also normally reflected in the attitudes and behaviour of a country's financial and other markets, this represents a further variable which at times can be critical for an organisation's future prospects. For many businesses, taking steps to maximise opportunities (or to minimise risk) may ultimately make the difference between short-term failure and long-term survival.

Thirdly, it is important to emphasise that political influences are not restricted to national boundaries – a point emphasised by the increasing importance of international and supranational groupings such as the G7 nations, the European Community and GATT (the General Agreement on Tariffs and Trade) all of which are discussed below. These external politico-economic influences form part of the environment in which a country's governmental institutions take decisions and their impact on domestic policy and on business activity can often be fundamental. No discussion of the business environment would be complete without an analysis of their role and impact, particularly in shaping international political and economic relationships.

Fourthly, the precise impact of political factors on a business tends to vary to some degree according to the type of organisation involved. Multinational corporations – operating on a global scale – will be more concerned with questions such as the stability of overseas political regimes than the small local firm operating in a localised market, where the primary concern will be with local market conditions. That said, there will undoubtedly be occasions when even locally based enterprises will be affected either directly or indirectly by political developments in other parts of the globe – as in the case of an interruption in supplies or the cancellation of a foreign order in which a small business is involved as a subcontractor. In short, whilst some broad generalisations can be made about the impact of global (or domestic) political developments on an individual organisation, each case is to some extent unique in both space and time, and observers of the business scene need to be cautious and open-minded in their analysis if they are to avoid the twin dangers of over-simplication and empiricism.

Finally, lest it should be supposed that businesses are merely reactive to changes in the political environment, it is essential to recognise that through their economic and other activities they can help to shape the political context in which they operate and to influence government decision-makers, often in a way which is beneficial to their own perceived needs. One of the hallmarks of democracy is the right of individuals and groups to seek to influence government, and businesses – both individually and collectively – have been active in this sphere for centuries. It would be a mistake to underestimate their impact on government policy or on the shaping of values in the established capitalist nations of Western Europe and elsewhere.

POLITICAL SYSTEMS

The nature of political activity

All social situations at certain times require decisions to be made between alternative courses of action. Parents may disagree with their offspring about the kind of clothes they wear or how late they stay out at night or how long they grow their hair. Students may challenge lecturers about a particular perspective on an issue or when they should submit a piece of work. The members of the board of directors of a company may have different views about future investment or diversification or the location of a new factory. In all these cases, some solution needs to be found, even if the eventual decision is to do nothing. It is the processes involved in arriving at a solution to a problem, where a conflict of opinion occurs, that is the very essence of political activity.

Politics, in short, is concerned with those processes which help to determine how conflicts are contained, modified, postponed or settled and as such can be seen as a universal social activity. Hence, individuals often talk of 'office politics' or the 'politics of the board room' or the 'mediating role' played by a parent in the event of a family dispute. For most individuals, however, the term 'politics' tends to be associated with activities at state level, where the resolution of conflict often involves large numbers of people and may even involve individuals in other states. Political activity at this level is clearly qualitatively different from the other social situations mentioned, and given the scale and complexity of the modern state, the problems requiring solutions can often be acute and chronic. Solving those problems tends to be seen, at least in part, as the function of government.

Government as a process is concerned with the pursuit and exercise of power – the power to make decisions which affect the lives of substantial numbers of people, be it at local, regional, national or even international level. Government may also refer to the institutions through which power tends to be formally and legitimately exercised, whether they be cabinets, parliaments, councils, committees or congresses. Whereas the pursuit and exercise of power tends to be an enduring feature of any society, governments are normally transitory, comprising those individuals and/or groups who, at a particular time, have the responsibility for controlling the state, including making laws for 'the good of society'. How governments exercise their power and the ideological foundations on which this is based, helps to indicate the nature of the political system and its likely approaches to the resolution of conflicts.

Authoritarian political systems

Broadly speaking, political systems can be seen to range across two extremes, on the one hand 'authoritarian' and on the other 'democratic'. In an authoritarian political system the disposition is to settle conflicts through the enforcement of rules, regulations and orders by an established authority. This authority may be an individual (e.g. a monarch or other powerful individual) or a group of individuals (e.g. a political party or military junta) who may have assumed political power in a variety of ways (e.g. by birth, election or coup). Once in power, the individual or group will tend to act so as to limit the degree of participation by others in the process of decision-making, even to the extent of monopolising the process altogether and permitting no opposition to occur. Where this is the case, a society is often described as being 'totalitarian' and is perhaps best exemplified by Nazi Germany and Stalinist Russia.

Democratic political systems

In contrast, in a democratic political system, the assumption is that as far as possible conflicts should be resolved by rational discussions between the various parties concerned, with the final solution being accepted voluntarily by all participants, even if they disagree. At one extreme, such consultation may involve all individuals, who have – in theory at least – equal influence over the final outcome (e.g. as in referendums or plebiscites). Given the scale and complexity of modern states, however, such examples of 'pure' or 'direct' democracy tend to be rare and it is invariably the case that the democratic solution to conflict resolution is achieved 'indirectly' through a system of political representation and responsibility. Under such a system, the wishes and views of individuals are said to be represented in an established authority (e.g. a government) that has normally been chosen by the people and which is accountable (responsible) to them at regular intervals through a variety of mechanisms, including regular and free elections (see Figure 3.1). Implicit in this, of course, is the requirement that individuals are able to change this authority and select another individual or group to represent them. Monopolisation of political power by any one individual or group can only occur, therefore, with the expressed consent of the people.

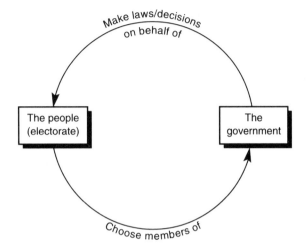

Fig. 3.1 Representative democracy

Democratic institutions and processes

The spread of democracy to many of the former authoritarian regimes in eastern Europe, and its implications for the organisation of business activity, makes it important to understand the key features of a democratic system of government. From the outset, it is vital to emphasise that democracy is far more than just popular government or a system of regular elections. The democratic approach to government implies the existence of a complex array of institutions and processes through which the wishes of the people are articulated and carried out. Foremost amongst these would normally be:

- A system of competing political parties.
- A system of regular and free elections based on universal adult suffrage.
- An independent judiciary.
- Mechanisms for the articulation of sectional interest (e.g. pressure groups).
- A powerful and elaborate system of political communications, independent of government control.
- Habitual processes of consultation, bargaining, explanation, education, compromise, and so on.
- Freedom of opinion, expression, organisation, movement, and so on.
- Respect for minority views.

Needless to say, no state is consistently and entirely democratic in the terms outlined above and all democratic societies at certain times tend to exhibit authoritarian characteristics – as when governments make and enforce decisions against the wishes of the people. Nor for that matter are all authoritarian societies totally devoid of democratic processes. These 'imperfections', however, should not be allowed to mask the essential point: authoritarian governments tend to limit the element of consultation and consent to the minimum they can get away with, whereas democratic governments generally try to maximise the element of consent and uphold the existence of certain basic individual freedoms, including the freedom to engage in entrepreneurial activity with a view to personal gain.

Political institutions in democratic states

In a democratic political system, then, one would expect to find institutional arrangements which not only reflected this ideal of government by consent, but which were also linked to the people by systems of representation and responsibility. Typically such arrangements would include:

- An electoral system which provided for the popular election of part, if not all, the government.
- Competing political parties seeking to win power in government by providing candidates for election by the people.
- A representative legislative assembly, responsible for making laws and for exercising some control over the executive branch of government.
- An executive, usually with one person at the head, responsible for the formulation and implementation of government policies and laws.
- An independent judicial system to interpret the law and to adjudicate in the event of dispute.
- Groups and individuals organised to bring pressure to bear on governments or parties or the people in pursuit of particular ideas or interests.

An illustration of how some of these elements can combine to provide a democratic approach to government is shown by the simplified model of the UK political system in Figure 3.2. Every few years, the people vote at a general election for candidates of competing political parties who are seeking to form the national government. Successful candidates are elected to the legislature (Parliament) and the majority party in the legislature forms the government, with individuals in government being allocated specific responsibilities for particular areas of work. The work of government is scrutinised by Parliament which acts as the people's representative and which is responsible for accepting, rejecting or amending proposals for laws made to it by the executive. Should the electorate wish to change the government, this is within its power at the next general election. Equally, between elections individuals are free to seek to influence government by joining pressure groups or other types of organisation (e.g. political parties) and by making their views known to their representatives or to the media.

Other democratic countries have similar institutional arrangements, usually dictated by history, custom and constitutional developments. Japan's legislature, the Diet, comprises representatives from the country's various political parties, the majority of whom are directly elected by the people at four-yearly intervals. Like Parliament, the

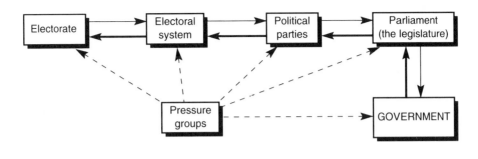

Key:

⟶   Flow of representation

⟵   Flow of responsibility

- - ⟶   Pressure group influence

Fig. 3.2 The UK political system

Diet consists of two houses, the House of Representatives and the House of Councillors, and legislation must pass through both houses prior to becoming law. Similarly, in France, Germany and the United States, direct elections of party candidates to the key part (or parts) of the legislature forms the basis of the democratic system and provides the link with the executive branch of government, the head of which is either directly elected by the people (e.g. in the US and France) or selected in some other way (e.g. in Germany and Japan).

What these examples clearly illustrate is how representation basically flows from people to government, whilst responsibility flows from government to people. Moreover they indicate the importance of the electoral system as a primary means of achieving representative government; indeed, in some countries – including the United States – the executive is elected separately from the legislative branch of government and is not – as in the United Kingdom's case – predominantly part of it. Implicit in the model, too, is the idea that democracy tends to incorporate a system of 'checks and balances' which prevent an elected government from exercising complete authority over every aspect of daily life. Such limits on government action are seen in a wide variety of institutional arrangements (e.g. the electoral system, a bicameral legislature, government, opposition, and so on) and are invariably mirrored in the pluralistic economic system which exists in democratic states. This system, with its elements of both private and state enterprise, is discussed more fully in Chapter 4.

A DEMOCRATIC POLITICAL SYSTEM IN ACTION: UK GOVERNMENT

A more detailed view of how a democratic system of government works can be gained by examining the roles and functions of the three main elements of the UK government: the legislature, the executive and the judiciary. This approach can equally be applied to governments in other democratic states and such an analysis could be useful to both students of international business and to firms involved in overseas trade, although space precludes it here. Suffice to say that differences in constitutional arrangements, together with different patterns of historical and cultural development, create some important distinctions between states that need to be taken into account when examining how a particular political system operates. In France, for example, the elected head of state (the President of the Republic) wields considerable political power and influence and can dissolve parliament, order referenda on certain issues and can send bills back to the National Assembly and Senate for further debate. In contrast, the British monarch, as head of state, is not elected and has largely ceremonial and symbolic functions and very little real political power under the British system of government.

The legislative branch of government

An indicated above, a directly elected legislature – representative of the people and responsible for making laws – is an important component of a democratic system of government. In the United Kingdom this function is carried out by Parliament, which comprises a non-elected upper chamber (the House of Lords) and an elected lower chamber (the House of Commons) whose members (currently 651 MPs) are elected by universal suffrage by the majority of citizens aged 18 and over. Whilst it is true to say that the Lords still retains some important powers – including the power to delay government legislation – it is generally accepted that the House of Commons is by far the most important part of the UK legislature, particularly since it contains key members of the political executive, including the Prime Minister and most of the Cabinet. For this reason the discussion below focuses on the role of the House of Commons.

As far as political representation and responsibility are concerned, this is achieved in a number of ways. For a start, Members of Parliament (MPs) are directly elected by their constituents and one of the MP's main roles is to represent the constituency for the period between general elections. Apart from holding regular surgeries at which individuals (including businessmen and women) can discuss their problems and views with their representative, MPs also speak on constituency matters in Parliament, frequently raise questions which require answers from government ministers, and generally scrutinise government proposals for any potential effects they may have on the constituency, including key groups within the local electorate (e.g. local businesses). Needless to say, there will be occasions on which the views of the elected member may differ from those of his or her constituents, particularly those who voted for candidates of an opposing political party; but this does not negate the idea of representation under the British system of parliamentary democracy. MPs represent their constituents first and foremost by having been elected ·by them and hence they provide a direct link between the electorate and the government of the day which is essentially drawn from the senior members of the majority party in Parliament.

Parliament also provides opportunities for the people's representatives to scrutinise and, where necessary, to criticise and challenge the decisions of government. In addition to such parliamentary mechanisms as question time and the adjournment debate, Parliament provides for a system of Select Committees of backbench MPs whose primary role is to scrutinise the work of government departments and other State agencies. Such committees – chaired by both government and opposition backbenchers – are able to question ministers and civil servants, call for departmental papers, cross-examine experts from outside government, and generally investigate the work of the executive, prior to reporting to Parliament on their findings. In bringing their views before Parliament and the public generally (especially through the media), Select Committees provide a check on government activity and hence form one of the strands by which governments remain answerable to the electorate in the period between elections.

Another significant strand is provided by the Opposition who not only represent an alternative choice of government, but also a means of scrutinising and criticising the work of the incumbent administration. Fundamental to this role is the ability of opposition MPs to publicise the decisions of government and to present alternative views to the public via party political broadcasts or promotional literature or debates in parliament, or by general media coverage. Such free and open discussions of issues and policies is a necessary condition for democracy and is an important element in the political education of the nation. Even where governments have large and relatively enduring majorities – as in the Thatcher era – the role of opposition parties remains a vital component of democracy and helps to provide a curb on unlimited government action.

Turning to its role as a legislative body, there is little doubt that the UK Parliament is largely a legitimising institution, giving formal authority to the wishes of the majority party. Through its control of the process of legislation, the parliamentary timetable, the flow of information and the vote of its members, the government is able to ensure that its legislative proposals not only come before Parliament, but are also almost invariably accepted, even if some delay occurs from time to time in enacting the government's programme (e.g. the Maastricht bill). Opportunities for individual MPs to sponsor legislation (e.g. through private members' bills) are few and far between and the outcome of such proposals depends ultimately on government support (or reluctant acquiescence), if the legislation is to get through its various stages in Parliament. Not surprisingly, this effective stranglehold by the government on the legislative process has led some commentators to talk of an 'elective dictatorship' and to question the true extent of democratic decision-making, particularly when modern governments are invariably elected by less than 50 per cent of the electorate.

The executive branch of government

Putting laws and policies into effect is formally the work of the executive. In the UK this role is carried out by a wide variety of institutions and agencies that are part of the machinery of government. These include the Cabinet, government departments, local authorities, nationalised industries, health authorities and a large number of other quasi-autonomous national government agencies, often referred to as 'quangos'.[1] In the discussion below attention is focused initially on the key institutions at central level since these are fundamental to the process of decision-making in Britain. Discussion of some of the other agencies can be found in subsequent sections of this chapter.

Under the British system of government, the core of the executive is the Cabinet, headed by the Prime Minister, an office of crucial importance given the absence of an elected head of state with effective political powers. British Prime Ministers not only have a number of significant political roles – including leader of the governing party, head of the government and head of the Cabinet – but they also have a formidable array of political powers, including the power to:

- choose members of the Cabinet;
- choose other non-Cabinet ministers;
- promote, demote or dismiss ministers;
- appoint individuals to chair Cabinet committees;
- appoint top civil servants;
- confer certain appointments and titles; and
- determine the date of the general election within the five-year term of office.

Whilst the existence of such rights and responsibilities does not infer that Prime Ministers will inevitably be all-powerful, it is clear that holders of the office have a key role to play in the decision-making process and much will depend upon how an individual interprets that role, upon their personality, and upon the constraints they face (both 'real' and 'imagined') in carrying it out. As Mrs. Thatcher found to her cost, retaining the office of Prime Minister is not only dependent on the electorate, but also on maintaining the support and confidence of parliamentary colleagues in the period between elections.

As indicated above, as head of the Cabinet the Prime Minister chairs the committee of senior ministers that is the overall directing force – or board of management – within British central government. Comprising about 25 to 30 ministers who have been appointed by the Prime Minister to head the various government departments (or to fulfil some other important functions), the Cabinet is responsible for directing and co-ordinating the work of the whole executive machine. Its functions include:

- Making decisions on the nature and direction of government policy, including public expenditure, economic policy, defence, foreign relations, industrial policy, and so on.
- Overseeing and co-ordinating the administration of government.
- Arbitrating in the event of disputes between ministers or departments (e.g. between the Treasury and the spending departments over levels of public expenditure during the annual round of negotiations).
- Discussing, deciding and generally directing the government's legislative programme, including laws relating to business.

A large part of this work, of course, is carried out using a system of committees and subcommittees, which are comprised of individuals chosen by the Prime Minister (including the chairperson) and which are supported by a small but powerful secretariat, headed by the Cabinet Secretary (a civil servant). Apart from providing an opportunity for more detailed discussions of issues and policies prior to full consideration by the Cabinet, the committee system has the advantage of allowing non-members of the Cabinet (including non-Cabinet ministers and civil servants) to participate in discussions in which they may have an interest. In this way, the system helps to provide a mechanism for communication and co-ordination between government departments and serves as a training ground for junior ministers, many of

Table 3.1 Selected cabinet committees, 1992/3

Committee name	Designation	Chairperson
Economic and Domestic Policy	EDP	Prime Minister
Overseas and Defence Policy	ODP	Prime Minister
Ministerial Committee on Nuclear Defence Policy	OPDN	Prime Minister
Ministerial Committee on Industrial Commercial & Consumer Affairs	EDI	Lord Privy Seal
Ministerial Committee on the Environment	EDE	Lord Privy Seal
Ministerial Committee on Legislation	LG	Lord President of the Council
Ministerial Subcommittee on European Questions	OPD(E)	Foreign Secretary
Ministerial Subcommittee on co-ordination of Urban Policy	EDH(U)	Environment Secretary
Ministerial Subcommittee on Women's Issues	EDH(W)	Employment Secretary

whom will subsequently achieve full Cabinet responsibilities. A selected list of cabinet committees for 1992/3 is shown in Table 3.1.

Much of the day-to-day work of central government is carried out in vast and complex administrative structures called government departments – a selected list of which, together with their basic responsibilities, is shown in Table 3.2. Most government departments are headed by Cabinet ministers (usually called the Secretaries of State) and include other ministers outside the Cabinet (e.g. Ministers of State, Parliamentary Under Secretaries of State) who have been appointed by the Prime Minister. Together these ministers constitute the political executive. As the head of a department, the Secretary of State has ultimate responsibility for its work and is answerable to Parliament through the various mechanisms referred to above.[2] In addition, he or she is expected to give overall direction to the work of the department – within the policy of the government as a whole – and to represent its interest in the Cabinet (e.g. over the size and use of its budget), in Parliament (e.g. in steering through legislation) and in the outside world (e.g. in the media). Large areas of this work are delegated to the Ministers of State who assume responsibility for specific areas of departmental work and they in turn will tend to delegate some duties to the department's junior ministers. Such an arrangement ensures not only coverage of the different aspects of a department's responsibilities, but also provides invaluable experience and training for ambitious young MPs appointed to a ministerial post.

Ministers are assisted in their work by permanent officials, known as civil servants or (more pejoratively) as 'bureaucrats', many of whom have spent a large part of their working lives in the government machine and hence are familiar with how it works and how to manipulate it in order to achieve particular objectives. Whereas ministers are politicians, civil servants are administrators vested formally with the task of carrying out the policies of the incumbent government, irrespective of their own political views and preferences. Perhaps not surprisingly, as key advisers to ministers on policy

Table 3.2 Key government departments, 1993

Department	Main responsibilities
HM Treasury	Government economic policy, including fiscal and monetary matters, privatisation, EC budget, public sector pay.
Foreign and Commonwealth Office	Foreign and Commonwealth issues, including EC and overseas development.
Home Office	Criminal policy and criminal justice, crime-related issues, immigration.
Environment	Environmental issues, housing and planning, local government.
Trade and Industry	Overseas trade and relations, Single Market, regional policy, innovation, corporate affairs, and so on.
Energy	Energy policy, energy sources, international energy matters.
Employment	Employment issues, including training, industrial relations, health and safety.
Education	Education policy and administration (including curriculum reform).
Health	Health matters, personal social services, health reforms.
Social Security	Social security policy and administration, including pensions and national insurance.
Northern Ireland Office	Law and order, security and other matters, including the Anglo-Irish Agreement.
Scottish Office	Wide range of functions, including education, justice, health, industry and agricultural matters.
Welsh Office	Various interests, including Welsh development, health and environment, tourism, culture.
Ministry of Agriculture, Fisheries and Food	Food, farming, fisheries and countryside issues (e.g. land use).
Transport	Public transport, roads, marine and aviation matters, Channel fixed link.

formulation and implementation, senior civil servants can exercise considerable influence over the nature and shape of government policy and legislation – a point amusingly emphasised in the popular British television programme *Yes Minister*[3]. For this reason, individuals or groups seeking to shape government thinking on an issue or piece of legislation frequently 'target' senior departmental officials in the hope of gaining influence in the policy process.

This potential for influence by senior civil servants is, of course, enhanced by the scope and complexities of modern government and by the fact that government ministers have a wide range of non-departmental as well as departmental responsibilities (e.g. as constituency MPs). Ministers consequently rely heavily on their officials for information and advice and civil servants are normally entrusted, under ministers, with the conduct of the whole gamut of government activities, including filling in the details of some legislation. Added to this, the need for policy co-ordination between departments requires regular meetings between senior officials, in groups which mirror the meetings of Cabinet subcommittees. Since these meetings of officials help to provide the groundwork and briefing papers for future discussions by ministers, they permit civil servants to influence the course of events, especially when a particular line or policy option is agreed by the senior officials in a number of departments.

Criticism of the influence of the senior civil service and of its secrecy and reluctance to change has led to a number of inquiries into how to improve its efficiency and *modus operandi*. In 1979, the new Conservative government appointed Sir Derek

Rayner of Marks & Spencer to introduce private sector management methods into the service and this was continued by his successor Sir Robin Ibbs of ICI who produced a report called *The Next Steps* (1988). This report led to many civil service responsibilities being 'hived off' to 'executive agencies', which operate semi-independently of government ministers, with their own budgets and performance targets and with a greater degree of independence over pay, financial and staffing matters, despite remaining formally part of the civil service. More recently, the government under John Major has announced its intention of implementing a scheme under which a proportion of the work of each department and agency would have to be put out to competitive tender. Under this proposal, bids can be made by in-house staff and outside contractors for a wide range of civil service functions, with Treasury rules insisting that 'value for money' must be the predominant concern in determining the outcome of the bidding process. This effective 'privatisation' of parts of the civil service is expected to affect up to 130,000 jobs in ministries as diverse as Education, Defence, Social Security, the Foreign Office and the Scottish Office.[4]

It is perhaps worth noting at this point that, however pervasive its influence, the civil service is not the only source of policy advice for governments. Apart from traditional bureaucratic channels, ministers often turn to specially appointed bodies for help and guidance in making policy choices. Some of these sources are permanent (or relatively permanent) and would include the various advisory bodies set up by past and present governments to assist in the policy process in specific functional areas (e.g. the Arts Council). Others are temporary, having been specially constituted by government to consider a particular problem and to report on their findings prior to going out of existence (e.g. public inquiries, Royal Commissions). Whilst the appointment of these advisory sources does not oblige the government to follow their advice, they can be regarded as useful sources of information, ideas and advice from outside the formal bureaucratic machine. Moreover the fact that they tend to have a membership representing a wide cross-section of interests (including representatives of particular pressure groups, industrialists, trade unionists, MPs, academics and others drawn from the list of 'the great and the good') helps to widen the scope of consultation and thus to enhance the democratic process.

The last generation has also seen governments turning increasingly to special advisers and policy planning units for help with policy development. Whereas advisers are individuals appointed by ministers (including the Prime Minister), usually from outside the civil service (e.g. Professor Walters was Mrs Thatcher's economic advisor), policy planning units and/or research units are groups of individuals generally recruited from and located within the government machine, with the aim of providing a range of policy and programme advice to both policy-makers and administrators. Often comprised of young and highly qualified individuals seconded to a unit from a wide range of occupational categories and disciplines (including statisticians, social scientists, economists, and general administrators), policy units are a valuable source of information and advice, and their operation at both central and local government level provides policy-makers with detailed research and analysis with which to support their policy judgements.

The judicial branch of government

The third arm of government, the judiciary – comprising the judges and the courts – is formally separate from and independent of Parliament and the government, despite the fact that the head of the judiciary, the Lord Chancellor, is both a member of the government and a member of the House of Lords, where he or she presides as Speaker. In essence the role of the judiciary is to put into effect the laws enacted by Parliament and to keep the government within the limits of its powers as laid down in statutes and in common law, as interpreted by the judiciary. Since 1973, it has also been responsible for interpreting European Community law. Given the complexities of the legal system and its relevance to the world of business, it is important to examine this aspect of government in more detail. This is undertaken in Chapter 6.

The role of political parties and pressure groups

Democratic government in the United Kingdom and elsewhere is founded on a party system, although the nature of the system and the influence of political parties in government varies from country to country, as well as over time. As indicated above, in the accepted model of democratic politics, parties compete for political power in an election-based representative system. To do this they must attract members, choose political candidates, produce leaders, establish a structure and develop a programme of policies which they hope will appeal to voters in sufficient numbers to allow the party to form part, and preferably the whole, of the elected government. Between elections, parties engage in a wide range of activities designed to sustain the organisation and its members, to seek or maintain public support and to influence government policies, both from inside and outside the legislative and executive branches of government. To achieve these aims, modern parties invariably require a complex bureaucratic organisation which tends to be organised at various spatial levels (e.g. local, regional, national, even supranational) and which comprises both a governmental (e.g. the parliamentary party) and an extra-governmental (e.g. the constituency party) element and a supporting secretariat. Perhaps not surprisingly, in the eyes of the general public the term 'political party' tends to connote that part of the organisation most frequently in view, namely the party as represented in Parliament through its MPs. In reality, of course, the parliamentary party represents the apex of a pyramid that is much larger and more complicated than this perception indicates.

Whilst the complexity of party organisation is beyond the scope of this book, it is worth emphasising that in terms of both organisation and philosophy, parties in democratic states are normally far from monolithic and that in the struggle for political power a party has to try to reconcile its own internal differences with the need to attract sufficient popular support. In effect, parties by nature tend to be coalitions of individuals and/or groups who, whilst sharing broadly similar views and objectives, may diverge in their thinking from time to time (e.g. 'Europhiles' and 'Eurosceptics' within the Conservative party) and may even engage in fierce battles over party organisation, policy-making or ideology – as in the case of the Labour party under Neil Kinnock. Accordingly, the evolution of party policy and its subsequent translation into governmental action tends to be the outcome of a complex process of political communication and brokerage between different parts of the organisation with differential levels of political power and influence.

Unlike political parties, pressure groups do not formally seek political office, although this distinction is to some extent open to question. They are, in effect, groupings of like-minded people who have voluntarily joined together to try to influence government thinking and policies and to represent the interests of their members. Traditionally, such groups (called 'lobbies' in America) tend to be divided into two main kinds:

1 *Interest groups* or *protective groups*, which protect the interest of a particular section of the community, such as trade unions or professional associations.
2 *Cause groups* or *issue groups*, which promote a particular cause, such as animal rights, penal reform, nuclear disarmament or civil liberties.

In practice, of course, it is often difficult to make such a clear-cut distinction, given that some interest groups such as unions often associate themselves with particular causes and may campaign vigorously alongside other groups in support of or against the issue concerned.

This ability of individuals to join together in an attempt to influence decision-makers – whether in pressure groups or political parties – is usually seen as a key indicator of democracy and an aid to efficient and representative government. Pressure groups provide governments with detailed information on specific areas of everyday activity without which rational decision-making would be difficult, if not impossible. They also fulfil a number of other important functions in a democratic system, including:

● Helping to defend minority interests.
● Providing for continuity in communications and consultation between the governors and the governed between elections.
● Assisting in the implementation of government policies and legislation.

The introduction of Health Service reforms, for example, relies on support from the various arms of the medical profession and on support from organisations such as the British Medical Association (BMA) and the other bodies representing the various interests of health service workers. Similarly, the effectiveness of government economic policies and their subsequent impact on business may rely to a certain extent on the reactions of such groups as employers' federations, chambers of commerce and trade unions, as well as on the responses of individual entrepreneurs and consumers (see Chapter 10).

Given this relative interdependence between government and pressure groups, it is common in democratic systems for certain groups to be consulted at some stage during the policy process. Such consultation may be 'formal' (e.g. when representatives of a group serve on advisory bodies, committees of enquiry, or Royal Commissions, and when consultation takes place on a government Green and/or White Paper) or 'informal' (e.g. off the record meetings between the pressure group and a government minister and/or civil servant), and may involve a group in hiring the services of a 'professional lobbyist' – often an ex-MP, minister or civil servant familiar with the structure of decision-making in a particular policy area or department. A group which is regularly consulted and whose opinion is readily sought by government may acquire 'insider status' and may even be incorporated into the formal decision-making process – prizes which are highly valued since they imply that the group has a legitimate right to be consulted by government prior to deciding on a particular course of action or inaction. In comparison, 'outsider groups' often find if difficult to make their voice heard in decision-making circles and for this reason may be forced to use different forms of direct action in order to publicise their views in the wider community and thereby gain public sympathy and support.

As this distinction between 'insider' and 'outsider groups' indicates, pressure groups can use a variety of methods to attract support for their cause or to protect the interests of their members. These range from direct consultation, negotiation and bargaining with decision-makers, to marches, strikes, disruption and other forms of demonstrative action designed to attract media attention in the hope of gaining public support (e.g. the French lorry drivers' blockade of motorways and major roads in July 1992 in protest against new motoring laws) – although frequently such action may have the opposite effect. In addition, some of the larger and better-organised groups have research facilities (e.g. CBI, TUC, RSPCA) and/or may employ 'experts' to advise on policy matters, and they are often able to mobilise substantial resources (including finance, influence, support, and access) in their attempts to get their voice heard.

What method a group employs at any one time tends to vary from issue to issue and from group to group, and generally reflects not only differences in group status and resources but also the structure of decision-making within the policy community concerned. In the United States, for instance, direct lobbying of Congressmen is a common tactic used by pressure groups, given the relative weakness of the party system and the tendency for an individual's electoral fortunes to be tied up with the support given to key groups within the constituency. In contrast in the United Kingdom, pressures of party discipline, the domination of the executive and the key role played by senior civil servants tends to make direct appeals to key actors in the government machine a more effective method of achieving political influence.

Because of the complexity of the political system, groups often find it both necessary and advantageous to operate at a variety of levels in the hope of building a coalition of support (see Figure 3.3). Public campaigns, for example, help to create public awareness of an issue or group and may affect the attitude of legislators and/or members of the executive, as well as possibly winning a group increased membership, support and finance. Groups also lobby political parties, MPs, government departments and agencies and are increasingly turning their attention to supranational institutions, such as the various bodies within the European Community, the International Monetary Fund, the United Nations and the G7 nations. As the locus of decision-making in key areas of policy (e.g. the world economy, the environment, world peace and order) increasingly shifts towards these bodies, pressure groups have been forced to adopt a more global approach to influence and this has encouraged interaction with similar groups in other countries. Hence at the Earth Summit in Rio in 1992, national and international leaders were lobbied by a wide range of nationally and internationally based groups, representing various sides of the environment debate (e.g. industry, development, energy, green issues) and often working in tandem with fellow groups.

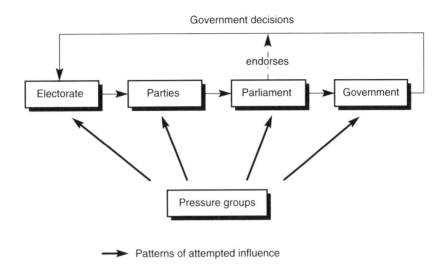

Fig. 3.3 Pressure groups and the democratic system

SUBNATIONAL GOVERNMENT

Democratic government occurs at subnational as well as national level and takes a wide variety of forms. In addition to the local branches of central government departments and public utilities, many states have local agencies for the administration of justice, local special purpose authorities (e.g. in the health service) and a system of regional and/or local government. Such decentralisation and deconcentration of political authority is generally seen as beneficial, since it brings the formulation and administration of policy 'nearer to the people' and is said to provide for decisions which are more sensitive to local needs and aspirations. Concomitantly, however, it also raises the question as to the degree of autonomy of local agencies within a centralised system of government and as recent history has demonstrated this is a controversial and perennial source of debate and dispute in many parts of the world.

In this context, a useful distinction can be drawn between 'federal' and 'unitary' systems of government. In the former case, sovereignty (i.e. the power to make decisions) is divided between two levels of government, each with independent powers that are usually laid down in a written constitution which is interpreted by the courts. In the United States, for example, education is in the hands of the individual state (i.e. subnational government), whilst defence and foreign affairs are federal responsibilities (i.e. national government). In Germany, the federal government has exclusive control over defence, foreign policy and environmental protection, while the Lander (states) control education and the police.

In contrast, in a unitary system ultimate authority rests with the central government and any powers given to subnational levels of government can be rescinded. Since central government is responsible for establishing the system of 'local' authorities, it is within the constitutional power of the centre to abolish these authorities by the ordinary statutory processes. Thus, in the United Kingdom, the seven Metropolitan County authorities (Greater London, Greater Manchester, Tyne and Wear, West Midlands, West Yorkshire, South Yorkshire, Merseyside) were established under the Local Government Act of 1972, and the London Government Act of 1963. These authorities were subsequently abolished by Parliament in 1986 and their responsibilities transferred to the metropolitan districts (or boroughs) or to new authorities created by central government.

Whatever form it takes, the spatial decentralisation of political power has important consequences for business activity and no analysis of a country's political system would be complete without a review of the organisation, role and responsibilities of the main agencies involved. This can be demonstrated by examining the system of local government in the United Kingdom – a key element of the country's system of institutionalised democracy and a major actor in the national as well as in the local economy.

As one form of local administration, local government has a number of distinctive features. For a start it involves self-government by the people of the locality as well as for them, with local authorities exercising considerable discretion in the ways they apply national laws within their areas. In addition, local decision-makers (councillors) are elected to oversee multi-purpose authorities, financed by revenue raised predominantly from local sources – although the proportion from central government has risen in recent years. In short, each local authority constitutes a miniature political and administrative system: each has the institutions and processes of government – including an electoral system, a legislative body (the council), appointed officials (local government officers), party activity, and conflict between individuals and groups within the local community over the allocation of resources and the enforcement of values.[5]

Figure 3.4 illustrates this parallel between the basic operation of government at central and local level. The electorate in each local constituency (e.g. district, county, metropolitan district) periodically choose between candidates who are mostly representing the same parties as those found at national level and the successful

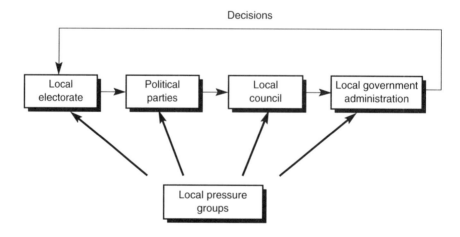

Fig. 3.4 The local government system

candidates in the election are elected to represent their constituency in the deliberating body (the council). Senior members of this body are chosen to serve on the various committees and subcommittees, with the leading party on the council having an in-built majority in the committee system, where most decisions are formally made prior to being sanctioned (or not) by the full council. For the most part, senior councillors are the political heads of the various local authority departments and agencies (e.g. housing, social services, education, and so on) that are responsible for providing those services within the local community which national laws require or, in some cases (e.g. sports centres), do not forbid. Much of this work is carried out by local officials who are appointed by the local authority to administer local services and to advise councillors on policy matters. As the local equivalent of civil servants, local government officers exercise considerable influence over the formulation as well as the implementation of local decisions. For this reason, they too tend to be targeted by local pressure groups which operate at all levels and stages of the political process in their attempts to influence local decision-making.

The present overall structure of local government in the United Kingdom is illustrated in Table 3.3, though this is currently under review and seems destined to change in the relatively near future. In essence, outside the metropolitan areas and Northern Ireland, a two-tier structure exists, with the 'counties' (or 'regions' in Scotland) being responsible for the provision of the larger services (e.g. education, social services, emergency services), whilst the districts (or boroughs or cities) have responsibility for a range of other services (such as housing, leisure, refuse collection and local planning). In contrast, in the metropolitan areas, the abolition of the metropolitan county councils has given rise to a one-tier structure, with all important services being provided by the 'districts' (or 'boroughs' in London) or by new joint boards under their control. Whilst in Northern Ireland most key services are provided, directly by UK central government agencies or by area boards, with the local district councils retaining few powers of any significance.

Table 3.3 The structure of UK local government, 1993

	Types of local authority	
England and Wales	*Scotland*	*N. Ireland*
Non-Metropolitan Areas County councils District councils	**Mainland Scotland** Regional councils District councils	Most important services are provided direct by UK central government agencies or through area boards.
Metropolitan areas Metropolitan district councils (plus joint boards)	**Western Isles, Orkney and Shetland** Island Councils	The district councils have limited powers (e.g. collecting rubbish and providing leisure facilities).
London London boroughs (plus City of London and joint boards)		

Recent pronouncements indicate that central government would like to see some reform of the current structure of local government. To this end, a Local Government Commission, headed by the former Director-General of the Confederation of British Industry (Sir John Banham) has been appointed to sample local opinion in the shire counties, as a prelude to recommending changes which could be implemented by the end of the 1990s. The Commission has been asked to assess whether a single tier authority 'would better reflect the identities and interests of local communities and secure effective and convenient local government' and to recommend what is the most appropriate structure of local government in *each* local area. Though the Commission's work is still far from complete, initial indications are that it favours a reduction in the number of local authorities and the return of larger, all-purpose authorities within a single-tier structure – an approach likely to meet fierce resistance from the threatened authorities and their representative organisations.[6]

SUPRANATIONAL GOVERNMENT

Decisions and law affecting business activity are increasingly being made at supranational as well as national and subnational levels. Nowhere is this more evident than in western Europe, where the influence of the European Community is profound. As a significant part of the political environment of the major world economies, the EC deserves special consideration, particularly since its decisions often have global as well as regional consequences – affecting not only firms within its Member States, but also businesses and governments trading with these states both directly and indirectly. In the following analysis, attention is focused on the political institutions of the Community and their relative importance in the process of decision-making.[7] The economic significance of the EC within the international marketplace is discussed in Chapter 13.

The European Parliament

The European Parliament is a directly elected body of 518 members (MEPs), with each Member State's representation being roughly equivalent to the size of its population.[8] The United Kingdom, for example, has 81 MEPs, elected at five-yearly intervals by UK citizens in special single-member constituencies in England, Scotland and Wales, using the traditional first-past-the-post voting system. In contrast, in Northern Ireland, as elsewhere in the Community, MEPs are elected using a form of proportional representation – a system which enhances the prospects of representation of smaller political parties from the different member states. Thus in the current European Parliament (1989–94), the elected MEPs represent nearly 80 different national political parties, with the majority sitting in one of the ten political groups in the House, so that most groups contain MEPs from several countries. Table 3.4 illustrates the number of MEPs supplied by each member state and their group membership by nationality as it stood in September 1991.

Table 3.4 Membership of the European Parliament by nationality and political group, 1991

Group	B	DK	G	Gr	S	F	IRL	I	L	N	P	UK	Total
Socialists	8	4	31	9	27	22	1	14	2	8	8	46	180
European People's Party	7	2	32	10	17	6	4	27	3	10	3	1	122
Liberal and Democratic Reformists	4	3	4	–	6	13	2	3	1	4	9	–	49
European Democrats	–	2	–	–	–	–	–	–	–	–	–	32	34
Greens	3	–	7	–	1	8	–	7	–	2	1	–	29
European Unitarian Left	–	1	–	1	4	–	–	22	–	–	–	–	28
European Democratic Alliance	–	–	–	1	2	13	6	–	–	–	–	–	22
European Right	1	–	3	–	–	10	–	–	–	–	–	–	14
Left Unity	–	–	–	3	–	7	–	–	–	–	3	–	14
Rainbow Group	1	4	1	–	2	1	1	3	–	–	–	1	14
Independents	–	–	3	–	1	1	–	5	–	1	–	1	12
Totals	24	16	81	24	60	81	16	81	6	25	24	81	518

Key:
B – Belgium	**IRL** – Ireland	
DK – Denmark	**I** – Italy	
G – Germany	**L** – Luxembourg	
Gr – Greece	**N** – Netherlands	
S – Spain	**P** – Portugal	
F – France	**UK** – United Kingdom	

Source: European Parliament UK office. Reproduced with permission.

The importance of the political groupings within the European Parliament is emphasised by the fact that MEPs sit in the chamber not by country but in party groupings, with the Socialists currently (1993) the largest single group within the Parliament. In order to decide its attitude to an issue or policy proposal coming before the Parliament or one of its committees, a group would normally meet for several days in the week before each session and the issue would be discussed and an agreed line would be decided. As in the case of national parliaments, the attitudes of the political groups have a significant impact on the discussions and decisions within the European Parliament, both in committee and when the House is in full session. Given the number of party groups, however, and the fact that no single group tends to have an absolute majority – unlike in some national parliaments – there is often a need for a group to try to build a coalition of support if it is to achieve its objectives in Parliament. Understandably – and perhaps inevitably – decisions by the European Parliament thus tend to involve compromise between individuals and groups, with the final outcome frequently being a course of action which is 'acceptable' to a majority.

In terms of its role and methods of operation, the European Parliament essentially mirrors national parliaments. Much of its detailed work is handled by specialist committees, meeting mostly in Brussels, which report on and offer recommendations to full sessions of the House which take place in Strasbourg. Membership of each committee is broadly representative of the strengths of the party groupings and the Chairmen and women of the permanent committees tend to be influential figures in their own right. In addition to carrying out detailed examination and amendment of draft laws, the committees discuss issues (e.g. women's rights, consumer protection, employment), question officials, hold public hearings at which experts and representatives of specialist organisations give evidence, and generally offer their opinion and advice on issues of concern to the Community. As in the case of national parliaments, detailed discussion in committee prior to debate and decision by the full house provides Parliament with an effective means of carrying out its duties and serves as a mechanism for scrutinising the work of both the Council and the Commission.

With regard to its functions, these predominantly fall into four main areas:

1 *Legislation* The Parliament's formal approval is required on most proposals before they can be adopted by the Council of Ministers.
2 *The budget* Along with the Council of Ministers, the Parliament acts as the Community's 'budgetary authority' and can reject the Council's draft budget and may modify expenditure proposals on 'non-compulsory' items.
3 *Supervision* The Parliament supervises the Commission, which it has the power to dismiss by a vote of censure and whose work it scrutinises using a variety of mechanisms.
4 *Initiative* This includes debates on important regional and international issues and demands for changes to existing policies and/or legislation.

In the legislative field, authority has traditionally rested with the Council of Ministers and the Commission, and the Parliament's role has largely been to sanction proposals put before it. Recent changes, however, have led to an increase in the Parliament's powers in this area. Following the introduction of the 'co-operation procedure' under the Single European Act (1987), the Parliament can now also give an opinion on the 'common position' adopted by the Council of Ministers on the Commission's proposals, particularly with regard to Single Market measures. The aim of this development is to allow the European Parliament to suggest amendments to a proposal after the Council has formed an opinion on it, but before it is formally adopted as Community law – a procedure which is felt to widen the Parliament's opportunities for political manoeuvring and thus to increase its influence on Community legislation.

MEPs have been given enhanced powers in an effort to appease critics who have suggested that the EC has lacked democratic accountability. In future, not only will they be able to veto membership of the Commission, but they will also have a greater say over legislation regarding the Single Market, health, education, the environment, consumer protection, transport, energy, cultural spending and technological research. In addition the European Parliament will have the power to ask the Commission to frame formal legislative proposals on an issue if a majority of MEPs agree action is required and will appoint an ombudsman to investigate complaints of maladministration in the implementation of Community laws.

The Council of Ministers

The Council of Ministers – the Community's ultimate decision-making body – comprises one minister from each of the 12 Member States, with participants on the Council varying according to the issue under discussion (e.g. agricultural issues are discussed by Ministers of Agriculture from each State). Meetings of the Council, which are mainly held in Brussels, are chaired by the minister from the country holding the Presidency, which rotates on a six-monthly basis (e.g. the UK held the Presidency of the Council in the second half of 1992). Along with the meetings of ministers are regular meetings of officials (Council Working Groups), together with the work of the Committee of Permanent Representatives of the Member States (COREPER) whose task is to co-ordinate the groundwork for Community decisions undertaken by the numerous meetings of senior officials. In addition, the Council is serviced by a general secretariat of about 2,000, also based in Brussels.

In essence, the role of the Council of Ministers is to make major policy decisions and to respond to legislative proposals put forward mainly by the Commission. In general, major Community decisions require unanimity in the Council, but increasingly many decisions are now being taken by a qualified majority vote (qmv) – with Germany, France, Italy and the United Kingdom having 10 votes each, Spain 8, Belgium, Greece, the Netherlands and Portugal 5 each, Denmark and Ireland 3 each, and Luxembourg 2.[9] For a measure to be adopted by 'qmv' 54 votes are needed (out of a total of 76).

Whilst the 'right of initiative' under the Treaties rests with the Commission, the ultimate power of decision essentially lies with the Council, which may adopt Commission proposals as drafted, amend them, reject them, or simply take no decision, having consulted the European Parliament and normally a number of other bodies (see below). If adopted, Council of Ministers' decisions have the force of law and are described as regulations, directives, decisions, or recommendations and opinions. Regulations apply directly to all Member States and do not have to be confirmed by national Parliaments to have binding legal effect. Directives, lay down compulsory objectives, but leave it to Member States to translate them into national legislation. Decisions are binding on those states, companies or individuals to whom they are addressed. Whilst recommendations and opinions have no binding force, but merely state the view of the institution which issues them.

The Council's power to pass a law – even if the European Parliament disagrees with it – has been reduced under the Maastricht Treaty. In future in specified policy areas, joint approval will be necessary and MEPs have an effective veto if the two sides cannot reach agreement following conciliation. Moreover Maastricht also provides for a new Committee of the Regions which will advise the Commission and the Council on issues concerning the European regions – a development which should help to ensure a stronger regional voice at European level. That said, it is still the case that the Council remains responsible for setting general policy within the Community and relies on the Commission to take decisions on the detailed application of Community legislation or to adapt legislative details to meet changing circumstances. To this extent – and given the Commission's other responsibilities – the ultimate influence over Community decisions is to say the very least open to question, as is often the case at national level.

The European Council

The work of the 'specialist' Councils within the Council of Ministers (e.g. Agriculture, Economics and Finance, Employment and Social Affairs) is co-ordinated by the General Affairs Council, comprising the Foreign Ministers of the twelve Member States. This Council is also responsible for preparing for the meetings of the European Council which occur two or three times each year. The European Council is attended by the Heads of Government of each Member State along with their Foreign Ministers and the President of the Commission, and its work invariably attracts substantial media coverage. Under the chairmanship of the country holding the Presidency, the European Council's role is to discuss important policy issues affecting the Community and to propose policy to the Council of Ministers. As the meeting at Maastricht in December 1991 indicates, these 'summits' of Heads of Governments can have a profound effect on the development of the Community and its institutions.

The European Commission

The Commission, which has its headquarters in Brussels and Luxembourg, is the Community's bureaucratic arm, comprising 17 Commissioners chosen by their respective governments (the 5 largest members send 2 Commissioners, the others send 1) and a staff of about 14,000 civil servants drawn from all Member States. Headed by a President – currently Jacques Delors – and organised into Directorates-General, each with a Commissioner responsible for its work, the European Commission's role is essentially that of initiator, supervisor and executive. More specifically its tasks are:

1 To act as guardian of the Treaties so as to ensure that Community rules and principles are respected.
2 To propose policies and legislation for the Council of Ministers to discuss and, if appropriate, adopt or amend.
3 To implement Community policies and supervise the day-to-day running of these policies, including managing the funds which account for most of the Community budget (e.g. FEOGA, ERDF, ECSC[10]).

In carrying out these duties, the Commissioners are required to act in the interest of the Community as a whole and may not receive instructions from any national government or from any other body (Article 157 of the Treaty of Rome). Moreover, whilst each Commissioner is responsible for formulating proposals within his or her area of responsibility, the final decision is taken on a collegiate basis and the work is subject to the supervision of the European Parliament. As mentioned above, Parliament is the only body which can force the Commission to resign collectively – a power it has never used; interestingly, it has no authority over individual Commissioners, although following Maastricht its endorsement will be needed when the President of the Commission and the other Commissioners are appointed.

Much of the undoubted power and influence of the Commission stems from its central involvement in the legislative process. Proposals for consideration by the Council and the Parliament are initially drafted by the Commission, usually following consultation with the Community's Economic and Social Committee (representing the interests of employers, trades unions, farmers, consumers, etc.) and other advisory bodies as appropriate. Moreover Community treaties specifically give the Commission the power to make regulations, issue directives, take decisions, make recommendations and deliver opinions, as well as to implement Community policies based on either Council decisions or Treaty provisions. Thus, whilst legislative power in the Community in general rests with the Council of Ministers, the Commission is also able to legislate in order to implement earlier Council regulations, particularly where technical or routine matters are concerned – a situation which has parallels in the operation of government at national level.

Further powers with regard to specific sectors of the Community (e.g. coal and steel) or particular aspects of Community work (e.g. the budget, international agreements) serve to enhance the Commission's influence and to confirm its position as the 'driving force' of the Community. Perhaps understandably, pressure groups seeking to influence the policy process within the European Community regard the Commission as an important institution to target, together with Parliament and the Council of Ministers. Recent and proposed changes in the relationship between these three institutions will undoubtedly have an effect not only on the legislative process, but also on the practice of lobbying within the Community context.

The European Court of Justice

The European Court of Justice, which sits in Luxembourg, comprises 13 judges who are appointed for a six-year period by consent of the 12 Member States and 6 advocates-general. The Court's role is:

1 To pass judgement, at the request of a national court, on the interpretation or validity of points of Community law.
2 To quash, at the request of a Community institution, government or individual, any measures adopted by the Commission, the Council or national governments which are judged to be incompatible with the Community's treaties.

The court can also be invited to offer an opinion, which then becomes binding, on agreements the Community proposes to undertake with third countries.

Three aspects of its work are particularly worthy of note:

1 Individuals as well as member states can bring cases to the Court and its judgements and interpretations apply to all (i.e. Community institutions, Member States, national courts and private citizens) and in future will be backed by a system of penalties for non-compliance.
2 Its rulings on matters of European law, which has primacy over national law, are final and its decisions are binding on member countries.
3 The Court has tended to follow the principle that Community Treaties should be interpreted with a degree of flexibility so as to take account of changing conditions and circumstances. This has permitted the Community to legislate in areas where there are no specific Treaty provisions, such as the fight against pollution.

Recent developments

Apart from its institutional changes the Maastricht Treaty was also significant for a number of other proposals which look likely to influence the future shape of the European Community.[11] Foremost amongst these was the establishment of the principle of 'subsidiarity' which effectively means that the Community should only take action in areas that do not fall within its competence, when member states cannot achieve the goals as well themselves. Additionally, the Treaty called for greater harmonisation of defence and foreign policy and of justice and home affairs – all of which are likely to prove controversial and difficult to implement at Community level. It also envisaged the establishment of a Conference of the Parliament which would bring together representatives of the European Parliament and national parliaments to discuss the development of the Community.

In follow-up discussions on the Treaty, the European Council agreed that in future Community legislation should be more limited, clearer and better explained and that Community institutions should be more open to the media ('transparency') and to a wider range of influences. It was also confirmed that negotiations would take place in the near future with a view to enlarging the EC, with Austria, Sweden, Finland and Norway likely to be the first of a number of countries gaining membership in the coming years.

A MODEL OF THE POLICY PROCESS

It is appropriate to conclude this examination of the political environment with a brief discussion of the process of governmental decision-making in democratic systems. Here, the basic model of the organisation in its environment introduced in Chapter 1 serves as a useful analytical tool (see Figure 3.5). Governments, like firms, are organisations which transform inputs into output and they do so in an environment largely the same as that which confronts other types of enterprise. Like other organisations, government is a user of resources, especially land, labour, capital, finance and expertise, but in addition all governments face political demands and supports when considering their policy options.

As indicated above, political demands – including those directly or indirectly impinging on business activity – become translated into action through a variety of mechanisms, including the electoral system, party activity, pressure group influence and political communication; hence a government is always keen to point out that electoral victory implies that it has a mandate for its policies. The supports of the political

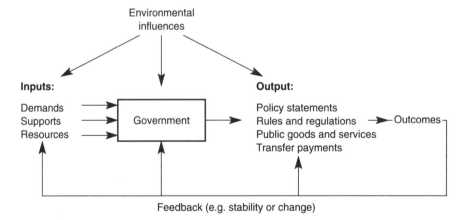

Fig. 3.5 Government and its environment

system are those customs, conventions, rules, assumptions and sentiments which provide a basis for the existence of the political community and its constituent parts and thus give legitimacy to the actions and existence of the incumbent government. In democratic systems, the belief in democratic principles, and the doctrines and practices emanating from that belief, is seen as central to the activities of government and its agencies.

The outputs of the political system vary considerably and range from public goods and services – provided predominantly from money raised through taxation – to rules and regulations (e.g. legislation, administrative procedures, directives) and transfer payments (i.e. where the government acts as a reallocator of resources, as in the case of the provision of state benefits). Taken together, the nature, range and extent of government output not only tend to make government the single biggest 'business' in a state, but they also influence the environment in which other businesses operate and increasingly in which other governments make decisions.

As far as governmental decision-making is concerned, this is clearly a highly complex process which in practice does not replicate the simple sequence of events suggested by the model. Certainly governments require 'means' (inputs) to achieve 'ends' (output), but the outputs of the political system normally only emerge after a complex, varied and ongoing process involving a wide range of individuals, groups and agencies. To add further confusion, those involved in the process tend to vary according to the decision under discussion as well as over time, making analysis fraught with difficulties. One possible solution may be to distinguish between the early development of a policy proposal ('initiation') and its subsequent 'formulation' and 'implementation', in the hope that a discernible 'policy community' can be identified at each stage. But even this approach involves a degree of guesswork and arbitrary decision, not least because of the difficulty of distinguishing precisely between the different stages of policy-making and of discerning the influence of individuals and groups at each phase of the process.

Notwithstanding these difficulties, it is important for students of business and for businesses themselves to have some understanding of the structure of decision-making and of the underlying values and beliefs which tend to shape governmental action, if they are to appreciate (and possibly 'influence') the political environment in which they exist. In short, studies of political systems, institutions and processes help to provide insight into how and why government decisions are made, who is important in shaping those decisions and how influence can be brought to bear on the decision-making process. As an increasing number of individuals and groups recognise, knowledge of this kind can prove a valuable organisational resource that on occasions is of no less significance than the other inputs into the productive process.

SYNOPSIS

Laws and policies which influence business activity are made by politicians and bureaucrats, operating at a variety of spatial levels. In the United Kingdom, the decisions of local and central government emanate from a complex process of discussion and negotiation involving a range of formal and informal institutions, including political parties and pressure groups, and frequently involving international and supranational bodies. This process is part of the democratic approach to decision-making and provides opportunities for individuals and groups to influence government thinking on both the formulation and implementation of policy and legislation. Students of business and managers need to have a broad understanding of this political environment in order to appreciate one of the key influences on a firm's operations.

CASE STUDY: THE UK CAR LOBBY

For much of the 1980s the UK car industry benefited from a booming economy, with both production and sales rising and confidence high, despite an influx of imported vehicles. By the end of the decade, however, the euphoria was rapidly beginning to evaporate as the world car market went into recession and the industry was faced with a large measure of over-capacity and the need to cut production and distribution costs.

To add to its worries, the UK motor industry was accused by consumers and their representative organisations of overpricing its vehicles and of excessive profiteering at the expense of the buyer. Equivalent vehicles bought on the Continent, for example, were said to be considerably cheaper than those sold in Britain and the critics pointed to market imperfections (e.g. the restrictive distribution system) as a primary cause of this situation. To a Conservative government committed to free enterprise, such criticisms could not be ignored and accordingly the government asked the Monopolies and Mergers Commission (MMC) to investigate the UK car market to see if any aspect of its operations were against the public interest (see Chapter 14).

Following a lengthy period of investigations – beginning in 1990 – the MMC started to fashion its report, which initially confirmed that the pre-tax prices of UK cars were often significantly higher than on the Continent. The leaking of this draft report to the press in 1991 brought an immediate response from the big car manufacturers, who challenged the Commission's findings and began an orchestrated campaign to persuade the public and government that the MMC had got its facts wrong. Undeterred, the MMC evidently wrote to the major car producers and importers informing them of a list of 20 measures it was considering recommending to overcome the effects of their monopoly over the distribution and sales of vehicles (see *The Independent*, 6 February 1992). These measures included the publication of the different discounts available to fleet and private buyers and of the prices at which UK consumers could purchase identical cars on the Continent, together with a relaxation of the restrictive system of car distribution.

The car lobby's response was to challenge the MMC's proposals, both by letter and through representation at further meetings of the Commission, where it eagerly pointed out the likely adverse consequences for jobs of any significant changes in the current operation of the UK car market. As a result of the outcry, the Secretary of State for Trade and Industry (Peter Lilley) ordered the MMC to delay publication of its report in order to give it more time to consider the industry's criticisms. When the report finally appeared in February 1992, the 20 measures for combating the effective monopoly of the large producers had been reduced to just five and the manufacturers were largely cleared of profiteering, despite the existence of some significant price differences between the UK and other European markets.

As far as UK motor manufacturing and retailing were concerned, the MMC accepted that two monopoly situations existed: a scale monopoly in favour of Ford which had a 25 per cent share of the market and a complex monopoly arising from the selective and exclusive distribution system used by most car suppliers. The Commission recommended, however, that the basic arrangements should remain intact and proposed that competition could be sharpened in a number of other ways, including a relaxation of the curbs imposed on dealers by manufacturers operating exclusive distribution deals and changes in the taxation of company cars to remove the distorting effects of this 'perk' on model prices and specifications.

Commenting on the Commission's recommendations, the consumer lobby called it a 'sell-out' that would benefit the industry at the expense of the consumer and would leave the British motorist at a significant price disadvantage. In contrast, the industry itself was more impressed by the findings, claiming that they indicated that buyers *were* getting a fair deal from a highly competitive marketplace and that differences in price levels were largely the result of comparatively high levels of government taxation.

NOTES AND REFERENCES

1   See, for example, Barker, A., *Quangos in Britain*, Macmillan, London, 1982.
2   Individual ministerial responsibility should not be confused with collective Cabinet responsibility, both of which apply to ministers of the Crown.
3   Senior civil servants who are in a position to influence policy are sometimes called 'mandarins'. This term only applies to a very small percentage of the civil service.
4   See, for example, *The Guardian*, 20 May 1993.
5   Smith, B., *Policy Making in British Government: An analysis of power and rationality*, Martin Robertson, London, 1976, p. 115.
6   See, for example, *The Guardian*, 11 May 1993 and 22 June 1993. Given recent reforms in the functions of local government, all-purpose authorities seem inevitable in some areas.
7   Numerous books exist on the EC (see Further Reading). Students can also gain information by contacting the Community's institutions directly, particularly through their national offices.
8   The number of MEPs is to increase in the future to take into account German reunification. Britain is to get six new members.
9   The use of 'qmv' was extended under the Maastricht Agreement.
10 European Agriculture Guarantee and Guidance Fund (FEOGA); European Regional Development Fund (ERDF); European Coal and Steel Community (ECSC).
11 The European Community has recently been renamed the European Union.

REVIEW AND DISCUSSION QUESTIONS

1   To what extent do you think a change of government in the United Kingdom would affect the business community?

2   Many top civil servants take directorships in large companies on retirement from government. Why should companies be keen to recruit retired bureaucrats?

3   How far is the proposed enlargement of the European Community likely to benefit UK businesses?

4   In what ways could a business organisation seek to influence central government decision-makers on issues in which it has an interest (e.g. taxes on company profits or the level of interest rates)?

ASSIGNMENTS

1   You are employed as a research assistant by the Confederation of British Industry (CBI). Recent by-election results have suggested that the Conservatives may lose the next general election. As part of its contingency planning, the CBI has asked for an analysis of Labour Party policy on the economy in general and on business in particular. Draft a report on these

topics, using contemporary sources of material (e.g. manifestos, policy statements, press articles).

2 Imagine you are employed as a political lobbyist, with a special interest in conservation issues. You have been approached by a local conservation group which is concerned about government plans to build a bypass round a village in its area. The government's proposals for the road would cause significant damage to a Site of Special Scientific Interest (SSSI) and the group is determined to oppose the plans. Your brief is to draft an 'action plan' for the group, indicating what forms of pressure group activity you would recommend, in what sequence and using which channels of potential influence.

FURTHER READING

Budd, S. A. and Jones, A., *The European Community: A guide to the maze*, 3rd edition, Kogan Page, 1989.
George, S., *Politics and Policy in the European Community*, 2nd edition, OUP, 1992.
Greenwood, J. and Wilson, D., *Public Administration in Britain Today*, 2nd edition, Unwin Hyman, 1989.
Kingdom, J., *Government and Politics in Britain*, Polity Press, 1991.
Preston, J. (ed.), *Cases in European Business*, Pitman, 1992.

CHAPTER 4

The Macroeconomic Environment

Ian Worthington

**Business organisations operate in an economic environment which shapes and is
shaped by their activities. In market-based economies this environment comprises
variables which are dynamic, interactive and mobile and which, in part, are affected by
government in pursuit of its various roles in the economy. As a vital component in the
macroeconomy, government exercises a significant degree of influence over the flow of
income and hence over the level and pattern of output by the public and private sectors.
Other key influences include a country's financial institutions and the international
economic organisations and groupings to which it belongs or subscribes.**

OBJECTIVES

1 To compare alternative economic systems and their underlying principles and to discuss the
   problems of transition from a centrally planned to a market-based economy.
2 To examine flows of income, output and expenditure in a market economy and to account
   for changes in the level and pattern of economic activity.
3 To analyse the role of government in the macroeconomy, including government
   macroeconomic policies and the objectives on which they are based.
4 To consider the role of financial institutions.
5 To survey the key international economic institutions and organisations which influence the
   business environment in open, market economies.

INTRODUCTION

In September 1992, following a period of sustained turbulence on the foreign
exchanges, the British government decided to withdraw sterling from the Exchange
Rate Mechanism (ERM) of the European Monetary System (EMS). As a result, the
value of the pound continued to fall against a number of currencies, particularly the
Deutschmark (DM) and large-scale speculation against sterling forced its value down to
a level well below its previously agreed 'floor' in the ERM. Freed from the constraints
of the ERM, the British government announced a series of cuts in interest rates in an
effort to boost the British economy, which at the time was in the midst of a substantial
recession. These cuts in interest rates – together with the more favourable exporting
conditions resulting from a weaker pound – were welcomed by most British businesses

who were struggling to find customers. At the same time, a number of influential commentators from both the academic and business world warned of the likelihood of increased inflation in the future as a result of dearer import prices and of the uncertainties caused by a free floating currency. Business leaders, in particular, called for a statement of government intentions and for a clear guide to future government economic policy with regard to inflation, recession and membership of the ERM.

What this simple example is designed to demonstrate is the intimate relationship between business activity and the wider economic context in which it takes place, and a glance at any quality newspaper will provide a range of similar illustrations of this interface between business and economics. What is important at this point is not to understand the complexities of exchange rate systems or their effect on businesses (these are discussed in Chapter 13), but to appreciate in broad terms the importance of the macroeconomic environment for business organisations and, in particular, the degree of compatibility between the preoccupations of the entrepreneur and those of the economist. To the economist, for example, a recession is generally marked by falling demand, rising unemployment, a slowing down in economic growth and a fall in investment. To the firm, it usually implies a loss of orders, a likely reduction in the workforce, a decline in output (or a growth in stocks) and a general reluctance to invest in capital equipment and/or new projects.

Much of the detailed discussion of the economic aspects of business can be found in Parts 3 and 4. In this chapter the focus is on the broader question of the economic structure and processes of a market-based economy and on the macroeconomic influences affecting and being affected by business activity in this type of economic system. As suggested in the previous chapter, an understanding of the overall economic context within which businesses operate and its core values and principles is central to any meaningful analysis of the business environment. This point is underlined by recent developments in the economies of eastern Europe, discussed later on in the chapter.

Three further points are worth highlighting at this juncture. First, business activity is not only shaped by the economic context in which it takes place, but helps to shape that context; consequently the success or otherwise of government economy policy depends to some degree on the reactions of both the firms and markets (e.g. the stock market) which are affected by government decisions. Secondly, economic influences operate at a variety of spatial levels – as illustrated by the plight of the pound – and governments can find that circumstances largely or totally beyond their control can affect businesses either favourably or adversely. Thirdly, the economic (and for that matter, political) influence of industry and commerce can be considerable and this ensures that business organisations – both individually and collectively – usually constitute one of the chief pressure groups in democratic states. This political and economic relationship between government and business is discussed more fully in Chapter 10.

ECONOMIC SYSTEMS

The concept of economic scarcity

Like 'politics', the term 'economic' tends to be used in a variety of ways and contexts to describe certain aspects of human behaviour, ranging from activities such as producing, distributing and consuming, to the idea of frugality in the use of a resource (e.g. being 'economical' with the truth). Modern definitions stress how such behaviour, and the institutions in which it takes place (e.g. households, firms, governments, banks), is concerned with the satisfaction of human needs and wants through the transformation of resources into goods and services which are consumed by society. These processes are said to take place under conditions of 'economic scarcity'.

The economist's idea of 'scarcity' centres around the relationship between a society's needs and wants and the resources available to satisfy them. In essence, economists argue that whereas needs and wants tend to be unlimited, the resources which can be used to meet those needs and wants are finite and accordingly no society at any time has the capacity to provide for all its actual or potential requirements. The assumption here is that both individual and collective needs and wants consistently outstrip the means available to satisfy them, as exemplified, for instance, by the inability of governments to provide instant health care, the best roads, education, defence, railways, and so on, at a time and place and of a quality convenient to the user. This being the case, 'choices' have to be made by both individuals and society concerning priorities in the use of resources, and every choice inevitably involves a 'sacrifice' (i.e. forgoing an alternative). Economists describe this sacrifice as the 'opportunity cost' or 'real cost' of the decision that is taken (e.g. every pound spent on the health service is a pound not spent on some other public service) and it is one which is faced by individuals, organisations (including firms), governments and society alike.

From a societal point of view the existence of economic scarcity poses three serious problems concerning the use of resources:

1 What to use the available resources for? That is, what goods and services should be produced (or not produced) with the resources (sometimes described as the 'guns v. butter' argument)?
2 How best to use those resources? For example, in what combinations, using what techniques and what methods?
3 How best to distribute the goods and services produced with them? That is, who gets what, how much and on what basis?

In practice, of course, these problems tend to be solved in a variety of ways, including barter (voluntary, bilateral exchange), price signals and the market, queueing and rationing, government instruction and corruption (e.g. resources allocated in exchange for personal favours), and examples of each of these solutions can be found in most, if not all, societies, at all times. Normally, however, one or other main approach to resource allocation tends to predominate and this allows analytical distinctions to be made between different types of economic system. One important distinction is between those economies which are centrally planned and those which operate predominantly through market forces, with prices forming the integrating mechanism. Understanding this distinction is fundamental to an examination of the way in which business is conducted and represents the foundation on which much of the subsequent analysis is built.

The centrally planned economy

In this type of economic system – associated with the post Second World War socialist economies of eastern Europe, China, Cuba and elsewhere – most of the key decisions on production are taken by a central planning authority, normally the state and its agencies. Under this arrangement, the state typically:

- owns and/or controls the main economic resources;
- establishes priorities in the use of those resources;
- sets output targets for businesses which are largely under state ownership and/or control;
- directs resources in an effort to achieve these predetermined targets; and
- seeks to co-ordinate production in such a way as to ensure consistency between output and input demands.

The fact that an economy is centrally planned does not necessarily imply that all economic decisions are taken at central level; in many cases decision-making may be devolved to subordinate agencies, including local committees and enterprises. Ultimately, however, these agencies are responsible to the centre and it is the latter which retains overall control of the economy and directs the use of scarce productive resources.

The problem of co-ordinating inputs and output in a modern planned economy is, of course, a daunting task and one which invariably involves an array of state planners and a central plan or blueprint normally covering a number of years (e.g. a five-year plan). Under such a plan, the state planners would establish annual output targets for each sector of the economy and for each enterprise within the sector and would identify the inputs of materials, labour and capital needed to achieve the set targets and would allocate resources accordingly. Given that the outputs of some industries (e.g. agricultural machinery) are the inputs of others (e.g. collective farms), it is not difficult to see how the overall effectiveness of the plan would depend in part on a high degree of co-operation and co-ordination between sectors and enterprises, as well as on good judgement, good decisions and a considerable element of good luck. The available evidence from planned economies suggests that none of these can be taken for granted and each is often in short supply.

Even in the most centralised of economies, state planning does not normally extend to telling individuals what they must buy in shops or how to use their labour, although an element of state direction at times may exist (e.g. conscription of the armed forces). Instead, it tends to condition *what* is available for purchase and the *prices* at which exchange takes place, and both of these are essentially the outcome of political choices, rather than a reflection of consumer demands. All too often consumers tend to be faced by queues and 'black markets' for some consumer products and overproduction of others, as state enterprises strive to meet targets frequently unrelated to the needs and wants of consumers. By the same token, businesses which make losses do not have to close down, as the state would normally make additional funds available to cover any difference between sales revenue and costs. This being the case, the emphasis at firm level tends to be more on meeting targets than on achieving efficiency in the use of resources and hence a considerable degree of duplication and wastage tends to occur.

In such an environment, the traditional entrepreneurial skills of efficient resource management, price-setting and risk-taking have little, if any, scope for development and managers behave essentially as technicians and bureaucrats, administering decisions largely made elsewhere. Firms, in effect, are mainly servants of the state and their activities are conditioned by social and political considerations, rather than by the needs of the market – although some market activity normally occurs in planned economies (especially in agriculture and a number of private services). Accordingly, businesses and their employees are not fully sensitised to the needs of the consumer and as a result quality and choice (where it exists) may suffer, particularly where incentives to improved efficiency and performance are negligible. Equally, the system tends to encourage bribery and corruption and the development of a substantial black market, with differences in income, status and political influence being an important determinant of individual consumption and of living standards.

The free-market economy

The free-market (or capitalist) economy stands in direct contrast to the centrally planned system. Whereas in the latter the state controls most economic decisions, in the former the key economic agencies are private individuals (sometimes called 'households') and firms who interact in free markets, through a system of prices, to determine the allocation of resources.

The key features of this type of economic system are as follows:

● Resources are in private ownership and the individuals owning them are free to use them as they wish.
● Firms, also in private ownership, are equally able to make decisions on production, free from state interference.
● No blueprint (or master plan) exists to direct production and consumption.
● Decisions on resource allocation are the result of a decentralised system of markets and prices, in which the decisions of millions of consumers and hundreds of thousands of firms are automatically co-ordinated.
● The consumer is sovereign i.e. dictates the pattern of supply and hence the pattern of resource allocation.

In short, the three problems of what to produce, how to produce and how to distribute are solved by market forces.

The diagram in Figure 4.1 illustrates the basic operation of a market economy. In essence individuals are owners of resources (e.g. labour) and consumers of products; firms are users of resources and producers of products. What products are produced – and hence how resources are used – depends on consumers, who indicate their demands by purchasing (i.e. paying the price) or not purchasing, and this acts as a signal to producers to acquire the resources necessary (i.e. pay the price) to meet the preferences of consumers. If consumer demands change, for whatever reason, this will cause an automatic reallocation of resources, as firms respond to the new market conditions. Equally, competition between producers seeking to gain or retain customers is said to guarantee that resources are used efficiently and to ensure that the most appropriate production methods (i.e. how to produce) are employed in the pursuit of profits.

The distribution of output is also determined by market forces, in this case operating

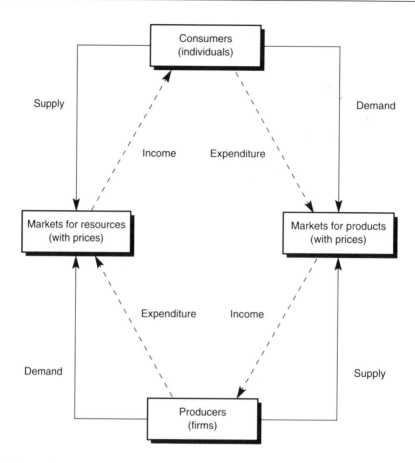

Fig. 4.1 The market economy

in the markets for productive services. Individuals supplying a resource (e.g. labour) receive an income (i.e. a price) from the firms using that resource and this allows them to purchase goods and services in the markets for products, which in turn provides an income for firms that can be spent on the purchase of further resources (see below). Should the demand for a particular type of productive resource increase – say, as a result of an increase in the demand for the product produced by that resource – the price paid to the provider of the resource will tend to rise and hence, other things being equal, allow more output to be purchased. Concomitantly, it is also likely to result in a shift of resources from uses which are relatively less lucrative to those which are relatively more rewarding.

This matching of supply and demand through prices in markets is described in detail in Chapter 11 and the analysis can also be applied to the market for foreign currencies (see Chapter 13). In practice, of course, no economy operates entirely in the manner suggested above; firms after all are influenced by costs and supply decisions as well as by demand and generally seek to shape that demand, as well as simply responding to it. Nor for that matter is a market-based economy devoid of government involvement in the process of resource allocation, as evidenced by the existence of a public sector responsible for substantial levels of consumption and output and for helping to shape the conditions under which the private sector operates. In short, any study of the market economy needs to incorporate the role of government and to examine, in particular, its influence on the activities of both firms and households. Such an analysis can be found below in the later sections of this chapter.

EASTERN EUROPE: ECONOMIES IN TRANSITION

The political and economic disintegration of eastern Europe in the late 1980s provides an excellent example of the difficulties faced by states moving from one form of economic system to another.

Prior to the collapse of the old order, the communist states of eastern Europe had systems of centralised state planning basically of the type described above, although some countries, especially Hungary, were experimenting with various forms of free enterprise. Growing dissatisfaction with the command system, and in particular with its failure to deliver living standards equivalent to those enjoyed by most citizens in the market economies of western Europe (see Table 4.1), gave rise to demands for reform, and these were translated into political action with the election of Mikhail Gorbachev to the post of Soviet leader in the mid-1980s. Gorbachev's programme of economic reconstruction (*perestroika*) signalled the start of a move towards a more market-based economic system and this was bolstered by his commitment to greater openness (*glasnost*) and democratic reform. By the late 1980s and early 1990s, the old Soviet empire had effectively ceased to exist and the newly independent states, almost without exception, had committed themselves to radical economic change of a kind unthinkable just a few years before.

Table 4.1 Comparative economic indicators, 1988

	Population (million)	GDP ($ billion)	GDP per Capita ($)
East Germany	17	156	9,360
Czechoslovakia	16	118	7,600
Hungary	11	69	6,500
Bulgaria	9	51	5,630
Poland	37	207	5,540
Romania	23	94	4,120
European Community	325	4,745	14,609
West Germany	61	1,202	19,575

Source: *The Amex Bank Review*, November 1989

For states anxious to move from an entrenched system of state planning to a market-based economic system, the obstacles have proved formidable and may yet help to sabotage the progress of economic (and political) reform. Amongst the problems faced by eastern European countries in the transitionary phase have been:

- The need to create a legal and commercial framework to support the change to a market economy (e.g. company laws, laws on property rights, competition, external trade, the development of an appropriate accounting system).
- The need to establish different forms of free enterprise and to develop financial institutions capable of providing risk and venture capital, at commercial rates of return.
- The need to develop truly competitive markets, free from state control and protection.
- The need to liberalise labour markets and to develop entrepreneurial skills in a workforce traditionally demotivated by the old bureaucratic system.
- The need to allow prices to move to levels determined by market forces, rather than by political decision.
- The need to achieve macroeconomic stability as markets become more open both internally and externally.
- The need to reduce the burden of international debt.
- The need to attract substantial overseas investment to assist in the rebuilding of the collapsed old socialist economies.

Meeting these requirements has not been made any easier by economic collapse and the perceived need on the part of some reformers to bring about rapid economic change whatever the consequences (e.g. the Shatalin Plan).

Current (1993) evidence suggests that, given these and other requirements, the process of systemic change is destined to be long and painful and will be subject to political as well as economic developments, many of which are as yet unpredictable. Central to this process will be the attitude of western countries towards such issues as debt relief, financial assistance, investment and other forms of help, and, perhaps understandably, the approach thus far has been relatively cautious – as exemplified by the British government's willingness to contribute relatively modest sums to a 'know-how' fund and to provide advice, but not to undertake a long-term financial commitment to support economic reform.

The reasons for this caution are not difficult to imagine, particularly given the uncertainty that comes from dealing with countries historically perceived to be adversaries. According to an analysis by the accountants Ernst & Young in 1992, a combination of factors – including differential levels of political risk, economic stability and credit worthiness – suggests that this uncertainty is at its greatest in countries such as Russia, the Ukraine and Albania and at its least in Hungary, Czechoslovakia and Poland, where reforms are often further down the road (see Table 4.2). Hungary's high notional score, for instance, is justified by its relative degree of political and economic stability and its favourable attitude to foreign investment, backed by a legal framework to encourage it. In contrast, in Albania – one of the most rigid of the old communist régimes – political and economic instability, limited business opportunities and a reluctance to change are seen as considerable obstacles to involvement on the part of western companies and governments.

With regard to western corporate involvement, this has taken a variety of forms including direct acquisition, joint ventures (which tend to carry tax advantages) and the development of local distribution networks, and much of it has been undertaken by multinational companies seeking to establish market share and to gain low-cost

Table 4.2 E. Europe: A comparative risk analysis

	Business opportunities	Political risk	Credit rating	Status of economy	Stability of local economy	Business infrastructure	Total
Hungary	2	1	2	3	2	2	12
Czechoslovakia	2	3	2	3	2	2	14
Poland	2	3	3	3	3	2	16
Baltic States	4	3	3	4	3	3	20
Bulgaria	4	3	4	4	3	3	21
Romania	4	4	4	4	4	3	23
Russia and Ukraine	1	4	5	5	4	4	23
Albania	5	4	4	5	5	4	27

Source: Adapted from *The Daily Telegraph*, 13 May 1992, copyright © The Telegraph plc, London, 1992.
Note: Countries are rated on a scale 1 to 5, where low scores are best and high scores worst.

production sites. Coca-Cola, Pepsico, Levi Strauss, Philip Morris, BAT, Mars, Unilever, Procter & Gamble and General Electric are just some of the organisations who have sought to take advantage of the growing demand for western consumer goods, and Hungary, Poland and Czechoslovakia have proved the most favourable locations for much of the investment.[1]

How far this interest in eastern Europe will continue in the future is open to question, particularly in view of recent political developments in the Balkans and in the former Soviet Union and because of the severe economic problems arising from the move to a market-based system (e.g. hyperinflation). Some observers believe that in the circumstances a policy of 'wait-and-see' is the best option for western companies looking for market expansion at a time of low growth in their traditional markets. Others argue that the risks involved are far outweighed by the potential benefits and that businesses willing to take a long-term view and commitment will come to dominate some of the fastest growing markets of the future, at the expense of competitors who are more cautious or conservative.[2]

POLITICO-ECONOMIC SYNTHESIS

The economic problem of resource allocation, described above, clearly has a political dimension, given its focus on the ownership, control and use of wealth-producing assets within society. This allows links to be made between a country's chosen economic system and its political régime. A useful way of representing possible relationships is illustrated in Figure 4.2. As suggested in Chapter 3, political systems can be characterised as ranging from democratic to authoritarian, depending on the degree of public involvement in decision-making processes. Similarly, economic systems can be seen to range from free-market to planned, according to the level of state intervention in the process of resource allocation. This two-dimensional model thus provides for four major combinations of politico-economic systems, ranging from democratic–free-market on the one hand (quandrant 1) to authoritarian–planned on the other (quadrant 3).

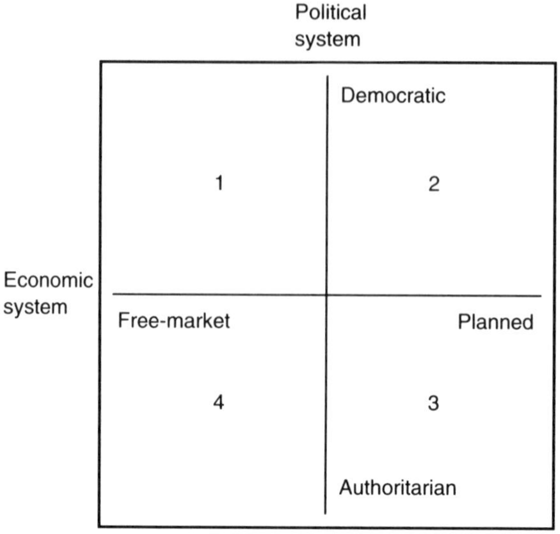

Fig. 4.2 Politico-economic systems

In applying this model to specific cases, it is clear that free-market approaches to resource allocation are predominantly associated with democratic states. Such a link is not surprising. Democracy, after all, includes the notion of individuals being able to express their preferences through the ballot box and having the opportunity to replace one government with another at periodic intervals. In free markets similar processes are at work, with individuals effectively 'voting' for goods and services through the price system and their expressed preferences being reflected in the pattern of resource allocation.

A link between authoritarian régimes and planned economic systems can equally be rationalised, in that government control over the political system is considerably facilitated if it also directs the economy through the ownership and/or control of the means of production, distribution and exchange. In effect, the relative absence of democratic mechanisms, such as free elections and choice between alternative forms of government, is echoed in the economic sphere by the inability of individuals to exercise any real influence over resource allocation. At the extreme, this could involve a government ban on any forms of free enterprise and total government control of the pattern of output and consumption in an economy which is devoid of effective consumer sovereignty.

In practice, of course, the picture is much more complicated than suggested by this simple dichotomy. Some authoritarian states, for instance, have predominantly capitalist economic systems (quadrant 4), whilst some democratic countries have a substantial degree of government intervention (i.e. moving them towards quadrant 2), either by choice or necessity (e.g. wartime). Added to this, even in states where the political or economic system appears to be the same, considerable differences can occur at an operational and/or institutional level and this gives each country a degree of uniqueness not adequately portrayed by the model. That said, it is still the case that the basic congruity between democracy and free-market systems represents a powerful and pervasive influence in the business environment of the world's principal democratic states. Pressures for economic reform – as in eastern Europe – accordingly tend to be accompanied by corresponding pressures for political change and these are often resisted by régimes not prepared to give up their political and economic powers and their elite status.

THE MACROECONOMY

Levels of analysis

As indicated above, economics is concerned with the study of how society deals with the problem of scarcity and the resultant problems of what to produce, how to produce and how to distribute. Within this broad framework the economist typically distinguishes between two types of analysis:

1 *Microeconomic analysis*, which is concerned with the study of economic decision-taking by both individuals and firms.
2 *Macroeconomic analysis*, which is concerned with interactions in the economy as a whole (i.e. with economic aggregates).

The microeconomic approach is exemplified by the analysis of markets and prices undertaken in Chapter 11 which shows, for example, how individual consumers in the market for beer might be affected by a price change. This analysis could be extended to an investigation of how the total market might respond to a movement in the price, or how a firm's (or market's) decisions on supply are affected by changes in wage rates or production techniques or some other factor. Note that in these examples, the focus of attention is on decision-taking by individuals and firms in a single industry, whilst interactions between this industry and the rest of the economy are ignored: in short, this is what economists call a 'partial analysis'.

In reality, of course, all sectors of the economy are interrelated to some degree. A pay award, for example, in the beer industry (or in a single firm) may set a new pay norm that workers in other industries take up and these pay increases may subsequently influence employment, production and consumer demand in the economy as a whole, which could also have repercussions on the demand for beer. Sometimes such repercussions may be relatively minor and so effectively can be ignored. In such situations the basic microeconomic approach remains valid.

In contrast, macroeconomics recognises the interdependent nature of markets and studies the interaction in the economy as a whole, dealing with such questions as the overall level of employment, the rate of inflation, the percentage growth of output in the economy and many other economy-wide aggregates – exemplified, for instance, by the analysis of international trade in Chapter 13 and by the macroeconomic model discussed below. It should be pointed out, however, that whilst the distinction between the micro and macro approaches remains useful for analytical purposes, in many instances the two become intertwined. Nigel Lawson's decision (in 1988) to cut the top rate of UK income tax from 60 per cent to 40 per cent was presented as a means of boosting the economy by providing incentives for entrepreneurs – clearly a macroeconomic proposition. However, to investigate the validity of the Chancellor's view, it is necessary to lean heavily on microeconomic analysis to see how lower taxation might influence, say, an individual's preference for work over leisure. Given that macroeconomic phenomena are the result of aggregating the behaviour of individual firms and consumers, this is obviously a common situation and one which is useful to bear in mind in any study of either the firm or the economy as a whole.

The 'flows' of economic activity

Economic activity can be portrayed as a flow of economic resources into firms (i.e. productive organisations), which are used to produce output for consumption, and a corresponding flow of payments from firms to the providers of those resources, who use them primarily to purchase the goods and services produced. These flows of resources, production, income and expenditure accordingly represent the fundamental activities of an economy at work. Figure 4.3 illustrates the flow of resources and of goods and services in the economy – what economists describe as 'real flows'.

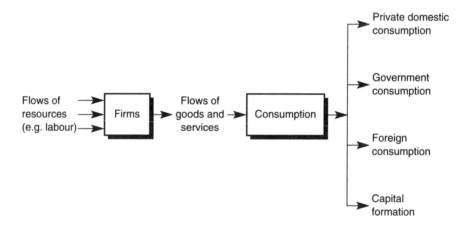

Fig. 4.3 'Real flows' in the economy

In effect, firms use economic resources to produce goods and services, which are consumed either by private individuals (private domestic consumption) or government (government consumption) or by overseas purchasers (foreign consumption) or by other firms (capital formation). This consumption gives rise to a flow of expenditures that represents an income for firms, which they use to purchase further resources in order to produce further output for consumption. This flow of income and expenditures is shown in Figure 4.4.

The interrelationship between income flows and real flows can be seen by combining the two diagrams, which for the sake of simplification assumes only two groups operate in the economy: firms as producers and users of resources, and private individuals as consumers and providers of those resources (see Figure 4.5). Real flows are shown by the arrows moving in an anti-clockwise direction; income flows by the arrows flowing in a clockwise direction.

Despite a degree of over-simplification, the model of the economy illustrated in Figure 4.5 is a useful analytical tool which highlights some vitally important aspects of

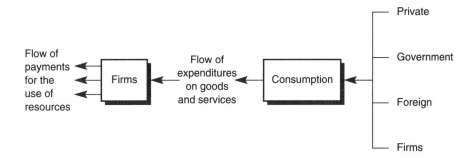

Fig. 4.4 Income flows in the economy

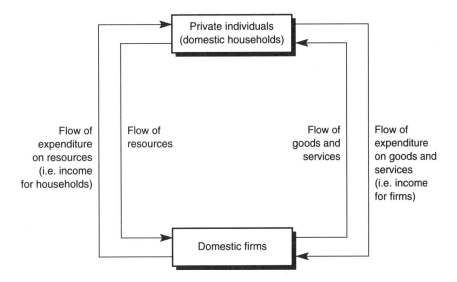

Fig. 4.5 A simplified model of real flows and income flows

economic activity which are of direct relevance to the study of business. The model shows, for example, that:

1 Income flows around the economy, passing from households to firms and back to households and on to firms, and so on, and that these income flows have corresponding real flows of resources, goods and services.

2 What constitutes an income to one group (e.g. firms) represents an expenditure to another (e.g. households), indicating that income generation in the economy is related to spending on consumption of goods and services and on resources (e.g. the use of labour).

3 The output of firms must be related to expenditure by households on goods and services, which in turn is related to the income the latter receive from supplying resources.

4 The use of resources (including the number of jobs created in the economy) must also be related to expenditure by households on consumption, given that resources are used to produce output for sale to households.

5 Levels of income, output, expenditure and employment in the economy are, in effect, interrelated.

From the point of view of firms, it is clear from the model that their fortunes are intimately connected with the spending decisions of households and any changes in the level of spending can have repercussions for business activity at the micro as well as the macro level. In the late 1980s, for instance, the British economy went into recession, largely as a result of a reduction in the level of consumption that was brought about by a combination of high interest rates, a growing burden of debt from previous bouts of consumer spending, and a decline in demand from some overseas markets also suffering from recession. Whilst many businesses managed to survive the recession, either by drawing from their reserves or slimming down their operations, large numbers of firms went out of business, as orders fell and costs began to exceed revenue. As a result, output in the economy fell, unemployment grew, investment by firms declined, and house prices fell to a point where some houseowners owed more on their mortgage than the value of their property (known as 'negative equity'). The combined effect of these outcomes was to further depress demand, as individuals became either unwilling or unable to increase spending and as firms continued to shed labour and to hold back on investment. By late 1992, few real signs of growth in the economy could be detected, unemployment stood at almost 3 million, and business confidence remained persistently low.

The gradual recovery of the British economy from mid-1993 – brought about by a return in consumer confidence in the wake of a cut in interest rates – further emphasises the key link between consumption and entrepreneurial activity highlighted in the model. Equally, it shows, as did the discussion on the recession, that a variety of factors can affect spending (e.g. government policy on interest rates) and that spending by households is only one type of consumption in the real economy. In order to gain a clearer view of how the economy works and why changes occur over time, it is necessary to refine the basic model by incorporating a number of other key variables influencing economic activity. These variables – which include savings, investment spending, government spending, taxation and overseas trade – are discussed below.

Changes in economic activity

The level of spending by consumers on goods and services produced by indigenous firms is influenced by a variety of factors. For a start, most households pay tax on income earned which has the effect of reducing the level of income available for consumption. Added to this, some consumers prefer to save (i.e. not spend) a proportion of their income or to spend it on imported products, both of which mean that the income of domestic firms is less than it would have been had the income been spent with them. Circumstances such as these represent what economists call a 'leakage' (or 'withdrawal') from the circular flow of income and help to explain why the revenue of businesses can fluctuate over time (see Figure 4.6).

At the same time as such 'leakages' are occurring, additional forms of spending in

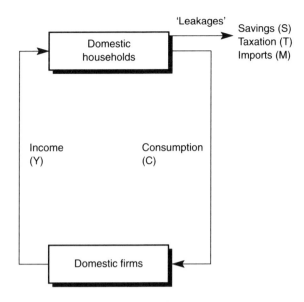

Fig. 4.6 The circular flow of income with 'leakages'

the economy are helping to boost the potential income of domestic firms. Savings by some consumers are often borrowed by firms to spend on investment in capital equipment or plant or premises (known as investment spending) and this generates income for firms producing capital goods. Similarly, governments use taxation to spend on the provision of public goods and services (public or government expenditure) and overseas buyers purchase products produced by indigenous firms (export spending). Together, these additional forms of spending represent an 'injection' of income into the circular flow (see Figure 4.7).

Whilst the revised model of the economy illustrated in Figure 4.7 is still highly simplified (e.g. consumers also borrow savings to spend on consumption or imports; firms also save and buy imports; governments also invest in capital projects), it demonstrates quite clearly that fluctuations in the level of economic activity are the result of changes in a number of variables, many of which are outside the control of firms or governments. Some of these changes are autonomous (i.e. spontaneous), as in the case of an increased demand for imports, whilst others may be deliberate or overt, as when the government decides to increase its own spending or to reduce taxation in order to stimulate demand. Equally, from time to time an economy may be subject to 'external shocks', such as the onset of recession amongst its principal trading partners or a significant price rise in a key commodity (e.g. the oil price rise in the 1970s), which can have an important effect on internal income flows. Taken together, these and other changes help to explain why demand for goods and services constantly fluctuates and why changes occur not only in an economy's capacity to produce output, but also in its structure and performance over time.

It is important to recognise that where changes in spending do occur, these invariably have consequences for the economy that go beyond the initial 'injection' or

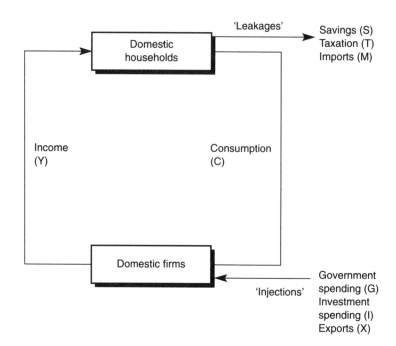

Fig. 4.7 The circular flow of income with 'injections' added

'withdrawal' of income. For example, a decision by government to increase spending on infrastructure would benefit the firms involved in the various projects and some of the additional income they receive would undoubtedly be spent on hiring labour. The additional workers employed would have more income to spend on consumption and this would boost the income for firms producing consumer goods, who in turn may hire more staff, generating further consumption and so on. In short, the initial increase in spending by government will have additional effects on income and spending in the economy, as the extra spending circulates from households to firms and back again. Economists refer to this as the 'multiplier effect' to emphasise the reverberative consequences of any increase or decrease in spending by consumers, firms, governments or overseas buyers.

Multiple increases in income and consumption can also give rise to an 'accelerator effect', which is the term used to describe a change in investment spending by firms as a result of a change in consumer spending. In the example above it is possible that the increase in consumption caused by the increase in government spending may persuade some firms to invest in more stock and capital equipment to meet increased consumer demands. Demand for capital goods will therefore rise, and this could cause further increases in the demand for industrial products (e.g. components, machinery) and also for consumer goods, as firms seek to increase their output to meet the changing market conditions. Should consumer spending fall, a reverse accelerator may occur and the same would apply to the multiplier as the reduction in consumption reverberates through the economy and causes further cuts in both consumption and investment. As Peter Donaldson suggests, everything in the economy affects everything else; the economy is dynamic, interactive and mobile and is far more complex than implied by the model used in the analysis above.[3]

GOVERNMENT AND THE MACROECONOMY: OBJECTIVES

Notwithstanding the complexities of the real economy, the link between business activity and spending is clear to see. This spending, as indicated above, comes from consumers, firms, governments and external sources and collectively can be said to represent total demand in the economy for goods and services. Economists frequently indicate this with the following notation:

Aggregate monetary demand =   Consumer spending + Investment spending + Government
spending + Export spending – Import spending

or

$$AMD = C + I + G + X - M$$

Within this equation, consumer spending (C) is regarded as by far the most important factor in determining the level of total demand.

Whilst economists might disagree about what are the most significant influences on the component elements of AMD,[4] it is widely accepted that governments have a crucial role to play in shaping demand, not only in their own sector but also on the market side of the economy. Government policies on spending and taxation or on interest rates clearly have both direct and indirect influences on the behaviour of individuals and firms, which can affect both the demand and supply side of the economy in a variety of ways. Underlying these policies are a number of key objectives which are pursued by government as a prerequisite to a healthy economy and which help to guide the choice of policy options. Understanding the broad choice of policies available to government, and the objectives associated with them, is of prime importance to students of the business environment.

Most governments appear to have a number of key economic objectives, the most important of which are normally the control of inflation, the pursuit of economic growth, a reduction in unemployment, the achievement of an acceptable balance of payments situation, controlling public (i.e. government) borrowing, and a relatively stable exchange rate.

Controlling inflation

Inflation is usually defined as an upward and persistent movement in the general level of prices over a given period of time; it can also be characterised as a fall in the value of money. For governments of all political complexions reducing such movements to a minimum is seen as a primary economic objective (e.g. in 1993 the UK government's stated target range for inflation was 1 per cent to 4 per cent).

Monitoring trends in periodic price movements tends to take a number of forms; in the UK these include:

1 The use of a Retail Price Index (RPI), which measures how an average family's spending on goods and services is affected by price changes.
2 An examination of the 'underlying rate of inflation', which excludes the effects of mortgage payments.
3 Measuring 'factory gate prices', to indicate likely future changes in consumer prices.
4 Comparing domestic inflation rates with those of the United Kingdom's chief overseas competitors, as an indication of the international competitiveness of UK firms.

In addition, changes in monetary aggregates, which measure the amount of money (and therefore potential spending power) in circulation in the economy, and movements of exchange rates (especially a depreciating currency – see Chapter 13) are also seen as a guide to possible future price increases, as their effects work through the economy.

Explanations as to why prices tend to rise over time vary considerably, but broadly speaking fall into two main categories. First, supply-siders tend to focus on rising production costs – particularly wages, energy and imported materials – as a major reason for inflation, with firms passing on increased costs to the consumer in the form of higher wholesale and/or retail prices. Secondly, demand-siders, in contrast, tend to emphasise the importance of excessive demand in the economy, brought about, for example, by tax cuts, cheaper borrowing or excessive government spending, which encourages firms to take advantage of the consumer's willingness to spend money by increasing their prices. Where indigenous firms are unable to satisfy all the additional demand, the tendency is for imports to increase. This may not only cause further price rises, particularly if imported goods are more expensive or if exchange rate movements become unfavourable, but it can also herald a deteriorating balance of payments situation and difficult trading conditions for domestic businesses.

Government concern with inflation – which crosses both party and state boundaries – reflects the fact that rising price levels can have serious consequences for the economy in general and for businesses in particular, especially if a country's domestic inflation rates are significantly higher than those of its main competitors. In markets where price is an important determinant of demand, rising prices may result in some businesses losing sales, and this can affect turnover and may ultimately affect employment if firms reduce their labour force in order to reduce their costs. Added to this, the uncertainty caused by a difficult trading environment may make some businesses unwilling to invest in new plant and equipment, particularly if interest rates are high and if inflation looks unlikely to fall for some time. Such a response, whilst understandable, is unlikely to improve a firm's future competitiveness or its ability to exploit any possible increases in demand as market conditions change.

Rising prices may also affect businesses by encouraging employees to seek higher wages in order to maintain or increase their living standards. Where firms agree to such wage increases, the temptation, of course, is to pass this on to the consumer in the form of a price rise, especially if demand looks unlikely to be affected to any great extent. Should this process occur generally in the economy, the result may be a wages/prices inflationary spiral, in which wage increases push up prices which push up wage increases which further push up prices and so on. From an international competitive point of view, such an occurrence, if allowed to continue unchecked, could be disastrous for both firms and the economy.

Economic growth

Growth is an objective shared by governments and organisations alike. For governments, the aim is usually to achieve steady and sustained levels of non-inflationary growth, preferably led by exports (i.e. export-led growth). Such growth is normally indicated by annual increases in real national income or gross domestic product (where 'real' = allowing for inflation, and 'gross domestic product (gdp)' = the economy's annual output of goods and services measured in monetary terms).[5] To compensate for changes in the size of the population, growth rates tend to be expressed in terms of real national income per capita (i.e. real gdp divided by population).

Exactly what constitutes desirable levels of growth is difficult to say, except in very broad terms. If given a choice, governments would basically prefer:

● steady levels of real growth (e.g. 3–4 per cent p.a.), rather than annual increases in output which vary widely over the business cycle;
● growth rates higher than those of one's chief competitors; and
● growth based on investment in technology and on increased export sales, rather than on excessive government spending or current consumption.

It is worth remembering that, when measured on a monthly or quarterly basis, increases in output can occur at a declining rate. In the United Kingdom, for example, a recession is officially said to exist if output is falling in three successive quarters, even if the output figures are still positive compared to twelve months previously.

From a business point of view, the fact that increases in output are related to increases in consumption suggests that economic growth is good for business prospects and hence for investment and employment, and by and large this is the case. The rising living standards normally associated with such growth may, however, encourage increased consumption of imported goods and services at the expense of indigenous producers, to a point where some domestic firms are forced out of business and the economy's manufacturing base becomes significantly reduced (often called 'deindustrialisation'[6]). Equally, if increased consumption is based largely on excessive state spending, the potential gains for businesses may be offset by the need to increase interest rates to fund that spending (where government borrowing is involved) and by the tendency of government demands for funding to 'crowd-out' the private sector's search for investment capital. In such cases, the short-term benefits from government-induced consumption may be more than offset by the medium and long-term problems for the economy which are likely to arise.

Where growth prospects for the economy look good, business confidence tends to increase, and this is often reflected in increased levels of investment and stock holding and ultimately in levels of employment. In Britain, for example, the monthly and quarterly surveys by the Confederation of British Industry (CBI) provide a good indication of how output, investment and stock levels change at different points of the business cycle and these are generally seen as a good indication of future business trends, as interpreted by entrepreneurs. Other indicators – including the state of the housing market and construction generally – help to provide a guide to the current and future state of the economy, including its prospects for growth in the short and medium term.

Reducing unemployment

In most democratic states the goal of 'full employment' is no longer part of the political agenda; instead government pronouncements on employment tend to focus on job creation and maintenance and on developing the skills appropriate to the demands of the late twentieth century. The consensus seems to be that in technologically advanced market-based economies some unemployment is inevitable and that the basic aim should be to reduce unemployment to a level which is both politically and socially acceptable.

As with growth and inflation, unemployment levels tend to be measured at regular intervals (e.g. monthly, quarterly, annually) and the figures are often adjusted to take into account seasonal influences (e.g. school-leavers entering the job market). In addition, the statistics usually provide information on trends in long-term unemployment, areas of skill shortage and on international comparisons, as well as sectoral changes within the economy. All of these indicators provide clues to the current state of the economy and to the prospects for businesses in the coming months and years, but need to be used with care. Unemployment, for example, tends to continue rising for a time even when a recession is over; equally, it is not uncommon for government definitions of unemployment to change or for international unemployment data to be based on different criteria.

The broader social and economic consequences of high levels of unemployment are well documented: it is a waste of resources, it puts pressure on the public services and on the Exchequer (e.g. by reducing tax yields and increasing public expenditure on welfare provision), and it is frequently linked with growing social and health problems. Its implication for businesses, however, tends to be less clear cut. On the one hand, a high level of unemployment implies a pool of labour available for firms seeking workers (though not necessarily with the right skills), generally at wage levels lower than when a shortage of labour occurs. On the other hand, it can also give rise to a fall in overall demand for goods and services which could exacerbate any existing deflationary forces in the economy, causing further unemployment and with it further reductions in demand. Where this occurs, economists tend to describe it as cyclical unemployment (i.e. caused by a general deficiency in demand) in order to differentiate it from unemployment caused by a deficiency in demand for the goods produced by a particular industry (structural unemployment) or by the introduction of new technology which replaces labour (technological unemployment).

A favourable balance of payments

A country's balance of payments is essentially the net balance of credits (earnings) and debits (payments) arising from its international trade over a given period of time (see Chapter 13). Where credits exceed debits a balance of payments surplus exists; the opposite is described as a deficit. Understandably governments tend to prefer either equilibrium in the balance of payments or surpluses, rather than deficits. However, it would be fair to say that for some governments, facing persistent balance of payments deficits, a sustained reduction in the size of the deficit may be regarded as signifying a 'favourable' balance of payments situation.

Like other economic indicators, the balance of payments statistics come in a variety of forms and at different levels of disaggregation, allowing useful comparisons to be made not only on a country's comparative trading performance, but also on the international competitiveness of particular industries and commodity groups or on the development or decline of specific external markets. Particular emphasis tends to be given to the balance of payments on current account, which measures imports and exports of goods and services and is thus seen as an indicator of the competitiveness of an economy's firms and industries. Sustained current account surpluses tend to suggest favourable trading conditions, which can help to boost growth, increase employment and investment and create a general feeling of confidence amongst the business community. They may also give rise to surpluses which domestic firms can use to finance overseas lending and investment, thus helping to generate higher levels of corporate foreign earnings in future years.

Whilst it does not follow that a sustained current account deficit is inevitably bad for the country concerned, it often implies structural problems in particular sectors of its economy or possibly an exchange rate which favours importers rather than exporters. Many observers believe, for instance, that the progressive decline of Britain's visible trading position after 1983 represents an indication of the growing uncompetitiveness of its firms, particularly those producing finished manufactured goods for consumer markets at home and abroad. By the same token, Japan's visible trade surplus of around $135 billion in 1992 was seen as a sign of the cut-throat competition of Japanese firms, particularly those involved in producing cars, electrical and electronic products, and photographic equipment.

Controlling public borrowing

Governments raise large amounts of revenue annually, mainly through taxation, and use this income to spend on a wide variety of public goods and services (see below). Where annual revenue exceeds government spending, a budget surplus occurs and the excess is often used to repay past debt (known in the United Kingdom as the 'public sector debt repayment' or PSDR). The accumulated debt of past and present governments represents a country's National Debt.

In practice, most governments face annual budget deficits rather than budget surpluses and hence have a 'public sector borrowing requirement' or PSBR (in the United Kingdom in 1993 this was estimated initially to be in excess of £50 billion). Whilst such deficits are not inevitably a problem, in the same way that a small personal overdraft is not necessarily critical for an individual, large scale and persistent deficits are generally seen as a sign of an economy facing current and future difficulties which require urgent government action. The overriding concern over high levels of public borrowing tends to be focused on:

1 Its impact on interest rates, given that higher interest rates tend to be needed to attract funds from private sector uses to public sector uses.
2 The impact of high interest rates on consumption and investment and hence on the prospects of businesses.
3 The danger of the public sector 'crowding out' the private sector's search for funds for investment.

4 The opportunity cost of debt interest, especially in terms of other forms of public spending.
5 The general lack of confidence in the markets about the government's ability to control the economy and the likely effect this might have on inflation, growth and the balance of payments.

The consensus seems to be that controlling public borrowing is best tackled by restraining the rate of growth of public spending rather than by increasing revenue through changes in taxation, since the latter could depress demand.

A stable exchange rate

A country's currency has two values: an internal value and an external value. Internally, its value is expressed in terms of the goods and services it can buy and hence it is affected by changes in domestic prices. Externally, its value is expressed as an 'exchange rate' which governs how much of another country's currency it can purchase (e.g. £1 = $1.50 or DM 2.35 or FF 9.60). Since foreign trade normally involves an exchange of currencies, fluctuations in the external value of a currency will influence the price of imports and exports and hence can affect the trading prospects for business, as well as a country's balance of payments and its rate of inflation (see Chapter 13).

On the whole, governments and businesses involved in international trade, tend to prefer exchange rates to remain relatively stable, because of the greater degree of certainty this brings to the trading environment; it also tends to make overseas investors more confident that their funds are likely to hold their value. To this extent, mechanisms which seek to fix exchange rates within predetermined levels, such as the Exchange Rate Mechanism (ERM), tend to have the support of the business community which prefers predictability to uncertainty where trading conditions are concerned.

GOVERNMENT AND THE MACROECONOMY: POLICIES

Governments throughout Europe and beyond play various key roles in their respective economies. These include the following functions:

- consumer of resources (e.g. employer, landowner);
- supplier of resources (e.g. infrastructure, information);
- consumer of goods and services (e.g. government spending);
- supplier of goods and services (e.g. nationalised industries);
- regulator of business activity (e.g. employment laws, consumer laws);
- regulator of the economy (e.g. fiscal and monetary policies); and
- redistributor of income and wealth (e.g. taxation system).

The extent of these roles and their impact on the economy in general and on business in particular, varies from country to country as well as over time.

Despite the economic significance of these roles, in most market-based economies democratically elected governments prefer levels and patterns of production and consumption to be determined largely by market forces, with a minimum of government interference. This approach is exemplified by the philosophical stance of the UK and US governments in the 1980s, that became colloquially known as 'Thatcherism' (UK) and 'Reaganomics' (US). At the same time, the recognition that market forces alone are unable to guarantee that an economy will automatically achieve the objectives established by governments has meant that state intervention – to curb inflation, encourage growth, reduce unemployment, correct a balance of payments or budgetary problem or restore currency stability – invariably occurs to some degree in all countries. In broad terms, this intervention usually takes three main forms, described as fiscal policy, monetary policy and direct controls. These policy instruments – or 'instrumental variables' – and their effects on the business community are discussed below.

Fiscal policy

As indicated above, each year governments raise and spend huge amounts of money. The UK government's accounts for 1991/2, for example, show that government spending was about £244 billion and was allocated in the manner illustrated in Figure 4.8. This spending was funded mainly from taxation and from borrowing, with the latter estimated at least £14 billion for the financial year (see Figure 4.9).

Fiscal policy involves the use of changes in government spending and taxation to influence the level and composition of aggregate demand in the economy and, given the amounts involved, this clearly has important implications for business. Elementary circular flow analysis suggests, for instance, that reductions in taxation and/or increases in government spending will inject additional income into the economy and will, via the multiplier effect, increase the demand for goods and services, with favourable consequences for business. Reductions in government spending and/or increases in taxation will have the opposite effect, depressing business prospects and probably discouraging investment and causing a rise in unemployment.

Apart from their overall impact on aggregate demand, fiscal changes can be used to achieve specific objectives, some of which will be of direct or indirect benefits to the business community. Reductions in taxes on company profits and/or increases in tax allowances for investment in capital equipment can be used to encourage business to increase investment spending, hence boosting the income of firms producing industrial products and causing some additional spending on consumption. Similarly, increased government spending targeted at firms involved in exporting, or at the creation of new business will encourage increased business activity and additionally may lead to more output and employment in the economy.

In considering the use of fiscal policy to achieve their objectives, governments tend to be faced with a large number of practical problems that generally limit their room for manoeuvre. Boosting the economy through increases in spending or reductions in taxation could cause inflationary pressures, as well as encouraging an inflow of imports and increasing the public sector deficit, none of which would be particularly welcomed by entrepreneurs or by the financial markets. By the same token, fiscal attempts to restrain demand in order to reduce inflation will generally depress the economy, causing a fall in output and employment and encouraging firms to abandon or defer investment projects until business prospects improve.

Added to this, it should not be forgotten that government decision-makers are

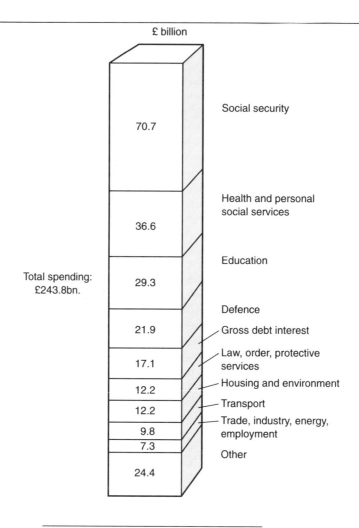

£ billion

Total spending:
£243.8bn.

Social security — 70.7

Health and personal social services — 36.6

Education — 29.3

Defence — 21.9

Gross debt interest — 17.1

Law, order, protective services — 12.2

Housing and environment — 12.2

Transport — 9.8

Trade, industry, energy, employment — 7.3

Other — 24.4

Note: Totals do not tally exactly because of rounding.

Figure 4.8   The allocation of UK government spending 1991/2
Source: Central Statistical Office. *The CSO Blue Book*, 1992 edition.

politicians who need to consider the political as well as the economic implications of their chosen courses of action. Thus whilst cuts in taxation may receive public approval, increases may not, and, if implemented, the latter may encourage higher wage demands. Similarly, the redistribution of government spending from one programme area to another is likely to give rise to widespread protests from those on the receiving end of any cuts; so much so that governments tend to be restricted for the most part to changes at the margin, rather than attempting a radical reallocation of resources.

Other factors too – including changes in economic thinking, external constraints on borrowing and international agreements – can also play their part in restraining the use of fiscal policy as an instrument of demand management, whatever a government's preferred course of action may be. Simple prescriptions to boost the economy through large-scale cuts in taxation or increases in government spending, often fail to take into account the political and economic realities of the situation faced by most governments.

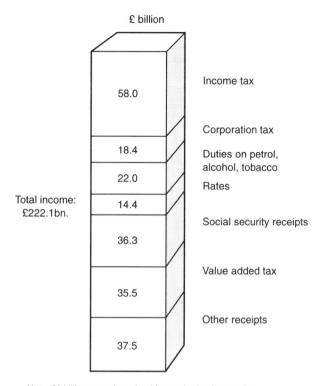

£ billion

Income tax

58.0

Corporation tax

18.4

Duties on petrol,
alcohol, tobacco

22.0

Rates

Total income:
£222.1bn.

14.4

Social security receipts

36.3

Value added tax

35.5

Other receipts

37.5

Note: £8 billion was also raised from privatisation receipts.
This counts as negative government spending.

Figure 4.9   Sources of government revenue 1991/2
Source: Central Statistical Office. *The CSO Blue Book*, 1992 edition.

Monetary policy

Monetary policy seeks to influence monetary variables such as the money supply or rates of interest in order to regulate the economy. Whilst the supply of money and interest rates (i.e. the cost of borrowing) are interrelated, it is convenient to consider them separately.

As far as changes in interest rates are concerned, these clearly have implications for business activity, as circular flow analysis demonstrates. Lower interest rates not only encourage firms to invest as the cost of borrowing falls, but they also encourage consumption as disposable incomes rise (predominantly through the mortgage effect) and as the cost of loans and overdrafts decreases. Such increased consumption tends to be an added spur to investment, particularly if inflation rates (and, therefore 'real' interest rates) are low and this can help to boost the economy in the short term, as well as improving the supply side in the longer term.[7]

Raising interest rates tends to have the opposite effect – causing a fall in consumption as mortgages and other prices rise, and deferring investment because of the additional cost of borrowing and the decline in business confidence as consumer spending falls. If interest rates remain persistently high, the encouragement given to savers and the discouragement given to borrowers and spenders may help to generate a recession, characterised by falling output, income, spending and employment and by increasing business failure.

Changes in the money stock (especially credit) affect the capacity of individuals and firms to borrow and, therefore, to spend. Increases in money supply are generally related to increases in spending and this tends to be good for business prospects, particularly if interest rates are falling as the money supply rises. Restrictions on monetary growth normally work in the opposite direction, especially if such restrictions help to generate increases in interest rates which feed through to both consumption and investment, both of which will tend to decline.

As in the case of fiscal policy, government is able to manipulate monetary variables in a variety of ways, including taking action in the money markets to change interest rates and controlling its own spending to influence monetary growth. Once again, however, circumstances tend to dictate how far and in what way government is free to operate. Attempting to boost the economy by allowing the money supply to grow substantially, for instance, threatens to cause inflationary pressures and to increase spending on imports, both of which run counter to government objectives and do little to assist domestic firms. Similarly, policies to boost consumption and investment through lower interest rates, whilst welcomed generally by industry, offer no guarantee that any additional spending will be on domestically produced goods and services, and also tend to make the financial markets nervous about government commitments to control inflation in the longer term.

This nervousness amongst market dealers reflects the fact that in modern market economies a government's policies on interest rates and monetary growth cannot be taken in isolation from those of its major trading partners and this operates as an important constraint on government action. The fact is that a reduction in interest rates to boost output and growth in an economy also tends to be reflected in the exchange rate, which usually falls as foreign exchange dealers move funds into those currencies which yield a better return and which also appear a safer investment if the market believes a government is abandoning its counterinflationary policy. As the UK government found in the early 1990s, persistently high rates of interest in Germany severely restricted its room for manoeuvre on interest rates for fear of the consequences for sterling if relative interest rates got too far out of line.

Direct controls

Fiscal and monetary policies currently represent the chief policy instruments used in modern market economies and hence they have been discussed in some detail. Governments, however, also use a number of other weapons from time to time in their attempts to achieve their macroeconomic objectives. Such weapons, which are designed essentially to achieve a specific objective – such as limiting imports or controlling wage increases – tend to be known as direct controls. Examples of such policies include:

- *Incomes policies*, which seek to control inflationary pressures by influencing the rate at which wages and salaries rise.
- *Import controls*, which attempt to improve a country's balance of payments situation, by reducing either the supply of, or the demand for, imported goods and services (see Chapter 13).

● *Regional and urban policies*, which are aimed at alleviating urban and regional problems, particularly differences in income, output, employment, and local and regional decline (see Chapter 10).

A brief discussion of some of these policy instruments is found at various points in the text below. Students wishing to study these in more detail are recommended to consult the books referred to at the end of this chapter.

THE ROLE OF FINANCIAL INSTITUTIONS

Interactions in the macroeconomy between governments, businesses and consumers take place within an institutional environment that includes a large number of financial intermediaries. These range from banks and building societies to pension funds, insurance companies, investment trusts and issuing houses, all of which provide a number of services of both direct and indirect benefit to businesses. As part of the financial system within a market-based economy, these institutions fulfil a vital role in channelling funds from those able and willing to lend, to those individuals and organisations who wish to borrow in order to consume or invest. It is appropriate to consider briefly this role of financial intermediation and the supervision exercised over the financial system by the central bank, before concluding the chapter with a review of important international economic institutions.

Elements of the financial system

A financial system tends to have three main elements:

1 *Lenders and borrowers*, who may be individuals, organisations or governments.
2 *Financial institutions*, of various kinds which act as intermediaries between lenders and borrowers and which manage their own asset portfolios in the interest of their shareholders and/or depositors.
3 *Financial markets*, in which lending and borrowing takes place through the transfer of money and/or other types of asset, including paper assets such as shares and stock.

Financial institutions, as indicated above, comprise a wide variety of organisations, many of which are public companies with shareholders. Markets include the markets for short-term funds of various types (usually termed 'money markets') and those for long-term finance for both the private and public sectors (usually called the 'capital market'). Stock exchanges normally lie at the centre of the latter, and constitute an important market for existing securities issued by both companies and government.

The vital role played by financial intermediaries in the operation of the financial system is illustrated in Figure 4.10 and reflects the various benefits which derive from using an intermediary rather than lending direct to a borrower (e.g. creating a large pool of savings; spreading risk; transferring short-term lending into longer-term borrowing; providing various types of funds transfer services). Lenders on the whole prefer low risk, high returns, flexibility and liquidity; whilst borrowers prefer to minimise the cost of borrowing and to use the funds in a way that is best suited to their

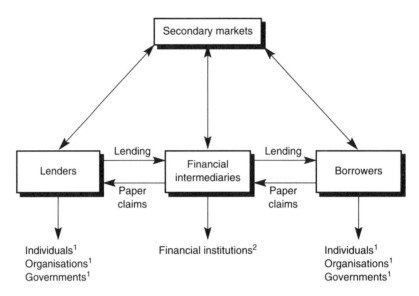

Notes: [1] both domestic and foreign;

[2] including retail and wholesale banks, building societies,
overseas banks, pension funds, and so on.

Figure 4.10 The role of financial intermediaries

needs. Companies, for example, may borrow to finance stock or work-in-progress or to meet short-term debts and such borrowing may need to be as flexible as possible. Alternatively, they may wish to borrow in order to replace plant and equipment or to buy new premises – borrowing which needs to be over a much longer term and which hopefully will yield a rate of return which makes the use of the funds and the cost of borrowing worthwhile.

The process of channelling funds from lenders to borrowers often gives rise to paper claims, which are generated either by the financial intermediary issuing a claim to the lender (e.g. when a bank borrows by issuing a certificate of deposit) or by the borrower issuing a claim to the financial intermediary (e.g. when government sells stock to a financial institution). These paper claims represent a liability to the issuer and an asset to the holder and can be traded on a secondary market (i.e. a market for existing securities), according to the needs of the individual or organisation holding the paper claim. At any point, financial intermediaries tend to hold a wide range of such assets (claims on borrowers), which they buy or sell ('manage') in order to yield a profit and/or improve their liquidity position. Decisions of this kind, taken on a daily basis, invariably affect the position of investors (e.g. shareholders) and customers (e.g. depositors) and can, under certain circumstances, have serious consequences for the financial intermediary and its stakeholders (e.g. the bad debts faced by western banks in the late 1980s and early 1990s).

Given the element of risk, it is perhaps not surprising that some financial institutions tend to be conservative in their attitude towards lending on funds deposited with them, especially in view of their responsibilities to their various stakeholders. UK retail banks, for instance, have a long-standing preference for financing industry's working capital rather than investment spending, and hence the latter has tended to be financed largely by internally generated funds (e.g. retained profits) or by share issues. In comparison, banks in Germany, France, the United States and Japan tend to be more ready to meet industry's medium- and longer-term needs and are often directly involved in regular discussions with their clients concerning corporate strategy, in contrast to the arm's length approach favoured by many of their UK counterparts.[8]

The role of the central bank

A critical element in a country's financial system is its central or state bank; in the United Kingdom, the Bank of England. Like most of its overseas counterparts, the Bank of England exercises overall supervision over the banking sector, and its activities have a significant influence in the financial markets (especially the foreign exchange market, the gilts market and the sterling money market). These activities include the following roles:

- banker to the government;
- banker to the clearing banks;
- manager of the country's foreign reserves;
- manager of the National Debt;
- manager of the issue of notes and coins;
- supervisor of the monetary sector; and
- implementer of the government's monetary policy.

In the last case, the Bank gives advice to government and, in particular, the Treasury, but ultimate responsibility lies with the elected representatives (most notably the Chancellor of the Exchequer) and the Bank currently remains an arm of government and an important part of the public sector.[9]

In contrast, in Germany the Deutsche Bundesbank is independent of government and has the primary task of protecting the value of the country's currency, together with the normal central banking functions of banker to the government, issuer of bank notes, controller of the money supply and lender of last resort. This independence gives the Bundesbank a critical role in the German economy and in the foreign exchange market, and its decisions have important implications for other economies in Europe and elsewhere, given the leading role of the Deutschmark in the currency markets. The reluctance of the Bundesbank to reduce German interest rates, for instance, in 1992–93 – in order to sustain the external value of the Deutschmark – reduced the ability of the UK government to lower its own interest rates, for fear that the pound would come under sustained pressure on the foreign exchanges. The UK government's desire to boost its ailing economy by a reduction in interest rates was tempered by the knowledge that such a move could cause a run on sterling, as currency dealers lost faith in the government's commitment to control inflation. As a result, interest rate decisions in Britain tended to be determined by exchange rate considerations and, to a large degree, by the actions of the Bundesbank, not by the needs of UK businesses, many of whom were calling for lower interest rates to help boost demand in the economy.

INTERNATIONAL ECONOMIC INSTITUTIONS AND ORGANISATIONS

The influence of the Bundesbank on UK economic policy – and hence on business prospects – serves to emphasise that external factors constrain the ability of governments to regulate their economy. It is appropriate to conclude this analysis of the macroeconomic context of business, therefore, with a brief review of a number of important international economic institutions and organisations which affect the trading environment. Foremost amongst these is the European Community which is examined at length in Chapters 3 and 13. In the discussions below attention is focused on the International Monetary Fund (IMF), the Organisation for Economic Cooperation and Development (OECD) and the General Agreement on Tariffs and Trade (GATT).

The International Monetary Fund (IMF)

The IMF came into being in 1946 following discussions at Bretton Woods which sought to agree a world financial order for the post Second World War period that would avoid the problems associated with the worldwide depression in the interwar years. In essence, the original role of the institution – which today incorporates most countries in the world – was to provide a pool of foreign currencies from its member states that would be used to smooth out trade imbalances between countries, thereby promoting a structured growth in world trade and encouraging exchange rate stability. In this way, the architects of the Fund believed that the danger of international protectionism would be reduced and that all countries would consequently benefit from the boost given to world trade and the greater stability of the international trading environment.

Whilst this role as international 'lender of last resort' still exists, the IMF's focus in recent years has tended to switch towards helping the developing economies with their mounting debt problems and in assisting eastern Europe with reconstruction, following the break-up of the Soviet empire.[10] To some extent its role as an international decision-making body has been diminished by the tendency of the world's leading economic countries to deal with global economic problems outside the IMF's institutional framework. The United States, Japan, Germany, France, Italy, Canada and Britain now meet regularly as the 'Group of Seven' (G7) leading industrial economies to discuss issues of mutual interest (e.g. GATT, the environment, eastern Europe). These world economic summits, as they are frequently called, have tended to supersede discussions in the IMF and as a result normally attract greater media attention.

The Organisation for Economic Cooperation and Development (OECD)

The OECD came into being in 1961, but its roots go back to 1948 when the Organisation for European Economic Cooperation (OEEC) was established to co-ordinate the distribution of Marshall Aid to the war-torn economies of western Europe. Today it comprises 24 members, drawn from the rich industrial countries and including the G7 nations, Australia, New Zealand and most other European states. Collectively, these countries account for less than 20 per cent of the world's population, but produce two-thirds of its output – hence the tendency of commentators to refer to the OECD as the 'rich man's club'?

In essence the OECD is the main forum in which the governments of the world's leading industrial economies meet to discuss economic matters, particularly questions concerned with promoting stable growth and freer trade and with supporting development in poorer non-member countries. Through its council and committees, and backed by an independent secretariat, the organisation is able to take decisions which set out an agreed view and/or course of action on important social and economic issues of common concern. Whilst it does not have the authority to impose ideas, its influence lies in its capacity for intellectual persuasion, particularly its ability through discussion to promote convergent thinking on international economic problems. To assist in the task, the OECD provides a wide variety of economic data on member countries, using standardised measures for national accounting, unemployment and purchasing – power parities. It is for this data – and especially its economic forecasts and surveys – that the organisation is perhaps best known.

The General Agreement on Tariffs and Trade (GATT)

The General Agreement on Tariffs and Trade was signed in 1947 by 23 industrialised countries; today there are over a hundred signatories to the agreement who collectively account for around 90 per cent of world trade.

Like the IMF and the International Bank for Reconstruction and Development (or World Bank) which were established at the same time, GATT was part of an attempt to reconstruct the international politico-economic environment in the post Second World War period. Central to this process was the perceived need to reduce tariff and other barriers to international trade and to eliminate discrimination in trade between nations. The GATT sought to achieve these objectives by establishing commercial policies based on non-discrimination and reciprocity. Non-discrimination required countries to treat their trading parties equally and to establish 'most favoured nation' (MFN) arrangements (i.e. trade barriers identical to those facing the most favoured nation). Reciprocity implied the development of procedures under the GATT which encouraged countries to swap trading concessions on a bilateral basis.

International discussions under the GATT have traditionally taken place in 'rounds' lasting over a number of years and have been concerned with the means of liberalising world trade through institutional arrangements and through the removal or reduction of trade barriers. As the number of countries involved in the accord has grown, these rounds of talks have increasingly focused on multilateral agreements on broad areas of trade policy, rather than on bilateral issues or problems of a specific nature. They have also incorporated discussions on topics often wholly or largely excluded from earlier negotiations, such as agricultural subsidies which have been allowed to exist over a long period of time under the terms of the General Agreement.

Indicative of this shift in emphasis is the current 'Uruguay Round' of talks which began in 1986 and which is still incomplete at the time of writing (seven years later). Areas under discussion during this round have included food and drink, intellectual property rights, textiles, services and farm subsidies, and a considerable degree of agreement has been reached in many of these areas. Agricultural exports and subsidies, however, have remained a critical stumbling block to an overall agreement and the United States and the EC have yet to settle their much publicised dispute over the level of agricultural support given to European farmers under the Common Agricultural Policy (CAP).[11]

In world trading terms, a GATT deal is seen as a key to world economic recovery in the 1990s. It is estimated that such a deal would boost world trade by about $200 billion per annum, with US, Japanese and EC businesses being the main recipients of the majority of the accruing benefits. Failure to complete such a deal – particularly if it were accompanied by increased protectionism – could have serious consequences for all countries and for the world trading system as a whole, and this is likely to focus the minds of negotiators seeking to settle the talks. Political and economic self-interest notwithstanding, few countries would wish to reverse a process of negotiations that has helped to reduce the average tariff on manufactured goods in the main industrialised countries from 40 per cent to under 5 per cent since the General Agreement came into being.

SYNOPSIS

Business and economics are inextricably linked. Economics is concerned with the problem of allocating scarce productive resources to alternative uses – a fundamental aspect of business activity. In market-based economies, this problem of resource allocation is largely solved through the operation of free markets, in which price is a vital ingredient. The existence of such markets tends to be associated primarily, though not exclusively, with democratic political régimes.

In all democratic states, government is a key component of the market economy and exercises considerable influence over the level and pattern of business activity – a point illustrated by the use of elementary circular flow analysis. A government's aims for the economy help to shape the policies it uses and these policies have both direct and indirect consequences for business organisations of all kinds.

In examining the economic context in which firms exist, due attention needs to be paid to the influence of a wide range of institutions and organisations, some of which operate at international level. Equally, as markets become more open and business becomes more global, the fortunes of firms in trading economies become increasingly connected and hence subject to fluctuations that go beyond the boundaries of any individual state.[12]

CASE STUDY: TOYOTA UK

Toyota's origins can be traced back to the early twentieth century when the inventor of Japan's first automatic loom, Sakidu Toyoda, established a spinning and weaving company. By the 1930s, using funds from selling patent rights to a British machine maker, the company had begun to invest in automotive technology research and soon produced its first prototype passenger vehicle. In August 1937, Kiichiro Toyoda, the son of the original owner, established the Toyota Motor Company, beginning mass production at its Koromo plant in 1938, just before the outbreak of the Second World War.

Despite experiencing considerable difficulties in the postwar period, Toyota recommenced production and began to build up a sales network to market its vehicles. In 1950, the company was split into two parts – production and sales – with the Toyota Motor Company the

---

manufacturing arm of the organisation. Using techniques, which have subsequently been emulated by other large companies (e.g. total quality control, just-in-time), Toyota began to increase its output and sales and was beginning to make significant inroads into overseas markets by the mid-1960s. By 1982, when the sales and manufacturing arms of the organisation merged to form the Toyota Motor Corporation, export sales of vehicles had exceeded domestic registrations and Toyota had grown into a large multinational corporation with a range of interests in various parts of the world.

For much of the early postwar period, Toyota focused its attention on the American market and established sales facilities in California in 1957, to be followed by a design base in 1973 and a joint production venture with General Motors in 1984. Less than two years later, the Corporation established its first wholly-owned production plant at Georgetown in Kentucky, from which the first of many US-built Toyota's emerged in 1988.

Toyota's development in postwar Europe proceeded along broadly similar lines, with the company establishing local sales and distribution networks, followed by design and production facilities. Initially, production took place under licence (e.g. in Portugal in 1968) or through joint ventures (e.g. with Volkswagen in 1989) and was restricted to commercial vehicles and fork-lift trucks. By the late 1980s, however, the company had signalled its intention of establishing a passenger vehicle manufacturing facility in Europe, as part of its programme of overseas market development. This plant was opened in mid-1992 at Burnaston near Derby and was followed by the opening of an engine plant at Deeside, North Wales, some months later.

Toyota's decision to establish production facilities in Europe is best understood against the political and economic realities of the period. Japan's postwar success in export markets had, by the 1980s, given rise to a huge Japanese balance of payments surplus that was bitterly resented by US and European governments and became the focus of attention in numerous meetings of the G7 countries. As part of this success, the Japanese car industry was under pressure from US and European car manufacturers and their governments to restrain exports, and this ultimately culminated in a system of agreed voluntary restraints (known as VERs) by Japanese car producers, for fear of more draconian measures. Since these restraints did not apply to vehicles produced by Japanese factories overseas ('transplants'), establishing a manufacturing presence outside Japan made sound commercial and political sense. This was particularly true in western Europe, where the EC's Common External Tariff made cars imported from Japan more expensive to consumers and hence relatively less competitive than locally produced vehicles.

The EC's decision to establish a 'single market' within the Community added a further impetus to the decision by Japanese car manufacturers (and others) to seek a European presence. The fact that the United Kingdom was a favoured location for Toyota – and for many other Japanese companies – is not difficult to explain. Apart from providing direct access to the largest single market for motor vehicles in the world, the United Kingdom had a substantial market in its own right and a developed vehicle manufacturing industry with a significant parts and component sector. Added to this, the favourable response given to direct foreign investment by United Kingdom national and local government – including the use of financial and other inducements – made the United Kingdom an attractive proposition and a location of minimal risk for investing multinational corporations.

As far as the choice of Burnaston was concerned, this seems to have been dictated by economic and commercial rather than political factors, although Derbyshire County Council actively lobbied the parent company and offered it a number of inducements to locate in the Midlands. Being centrally placed in Britain and close to the M1, Burnaston offered direct access to all parts of the country and a relatively quick route to the continent, via the ports and the Channel Tunnel. It also boasted a highly skilled local workforce, a developed infrastructure and a large site with room for further expansion.

There is no doubt that the £700 million Toyota development in Derbyshire will have a considerable impact on the local economy over a number of years. Apart from the jobs created in building and operating the car plant, further employment will be created directly among local component suppliers and indirectly amongst those involved in providing services and materials and from the extra spending resulting from the growth of jobs. As the company moves towards its target of producing 200,000 cars a year by 1997–98, these benefits are likely to increase and should help to breath life into a housing sector currently struggling to overcome the effects of a prolonged recession. How far these gains will be at the expense of the other car-producing areas of Britain remains to be seen, but economic analysis suggests they may prove significant.

NOTES AND REFERENCES

1   See, for example, *Creditanstalt/EIU Vienna 1992*, Eastern Investment Survey.
2   *Financial Times*, 2 March 1992.
3   Donaldson, P. and Farquhar, J., *Understanding the British Economy*, Penguin, 1988, p. 84.
4   See, for example, Griffiths, A. and Wall, S. (eds) *Applied Economics*, 5th edition, Longman, 1993, Chapter 11.
5   For a fuller discussion of the technology see: Artis M.J. (ed.), Prest and Coppock's *The UK Economy: A manual of applied economics*, 13th edition, Weidenfeld & Nicolson, 1992.
6   See, for example, Griffiths and Wall, *op. cit.* Chapter 1.
7   Real interest rates allow for inflation.
8   See, for example, Neale, A and Haslam, C., *Economics in a Business Context*, Chapman & Hall, 1991, p. 141.
9   There are increasing calls for the Bank of England to become independent of government, along the lines of the Deutsche Bundesbank.
10   The role of assisting reconstruction in eastern Europe is also undertaken by the European Bank for Reconstruction and Development (EBRD).
11   The GATT deadlock was said to be broken in early July, 1993, following a meeting of the G7 (see *The Guardian*, 8 July 1993). By early October 1993, however, a final agreement was still in doubt. By mid-December 1993 a compromise deal was agreed.
12   The prospect for further recovery in the UK economy, for example, is likely to be influenced adversely by the current recession amongst its chief trading partners, particularly Germany and France.

REVIEW AND DISCUSSION QUESTIONS

1   To what extent do you agree with the proposition that the market economy is the 'best' form of economic system? Do you have any reservations?

2   Explain how interest rates could be used to boost the economy. Why, then, do governments frequently hesitate to take such steps?

3   Using circular flow analysis, suggest why a large programme of capital expenditure by government (e.g. on new motorways, roads, railways) will benefit businesses. How could such a programme be financed?

4   Using contemporary source material, explain why a successful solution to the 'Uruguay Round' of the GATT talks is felt to be important for UK businesses.

ASSIGNMENTS

1   Imagine you work in the economic development unit of a local authority. Produce a draft report outlining the benefits to the local economy of encouraging direct inward investment. Indicate any disadvantages.

2 You are a trainee journalist on a regional or national newspaper. As part of your first big assignment, you have been asked to provide information on the 'privatisation' of eastern European economies. Using journals and newspapers, provide a scrapbook of information indicating the different ways in which western companies have sought to exploit business opportunities in eastern Europe.

FURTHER READING

Donaldson, P. and Farquhar, J., *Understanding the British Economy*, Penguin, 1988.
Griffiths, A. and Wall, S., (eds), *Applied Economics*, 5th edition, Longman, 1993.
Neale, A. and Haslam, C., *Economics in a Business Context*, Chapman & Hall, 1991.

CHAPTER 5

People, technology and natural resources

Chris Britton

Businesses carry out a variety of activities, but their main activity is to produce goods and services to be sold on the market. In the production process inputs are turned into outputs. The inputs into the production process are people, technology and natural resources.

OBJECTIVES

1   To be aware of the importance of people, technology and natural resources to business.
2   To understand what determines the quantity and quality of labour in the economy.
3   To recognise the effect of technological change on business.
4   To understand the main issues affecting natural resources.

INTRODUCTION

The main aim of business is to produce goods and services that people want. This production cannot take place without people, technology and natural resources. In economics these three are called the factors of production and are categorised under the headings of labour, capital and land. This chapter will consider each of these in turn. Resources can be renewable or non-renewable. Renewable resources would include labour, water, fishing stocks, soil, air and solar power even though many of these might not be renewable for a long period of time. Non-renewable resources would be most minerals including oil, iron ore and coal, agricultural land, forests and electricity (in so far as most electricity is derived from minerals).

PEOPLE

People are important in the economy as both producers and consumers of goods and services. For most products that are produced people are the most important input into the production process. Therefore the quantity and quality of the people available in an economy will have a considerable impact upon the economy's ability to produce.

The quantity of people available for work depends upon a variety of factors:

- the size of the total population;
- the age structure of the population;
- the working population;
- the length of the working week; and
- the wage level.

As well as the quantity of labour, productivity will be affected by its quality. This in turn depends upon:

- education and training;
- working conditions;
- welfare services (e.g. national insurance schemes which cover sickness pay, NHS which maintains the health of workers; also many firms provide their own welfare services like private pension plans, and so on);
- motivation; and
- the quality of the other factors of production.

Most of these factors will be considered in some detail in the next sections of this chapter.

The population of the UK

The UK population was estimated to be 57.5 million in 1991 and forecast to be 61.2 million in 2031.[1] This makes it the third largest country by population in western Europe after West Germany and Italy. Figure 5.1 shows population size for selected years in the United Kingdom since 1851. Population size and the growth of population depends on many things, but the main determinants are the birth rate, the death rate and the net migration rate.

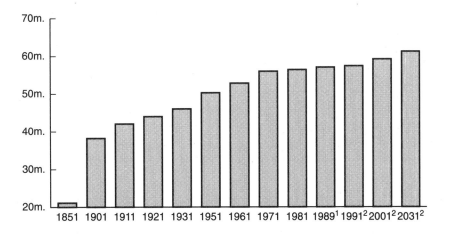

Note: [1] estimated figure; [2] projected figures.

Fig. 5.1 Population of the United Kingdom (000,000s)

The birth rate

The birth rate is the number of live births per thousand of the population in a given year. In 1990 the birth rate in the United Kingdom was 14, which was slightly higher than the EC average of 13. Table 5.1 shows the UK birth rates for selected time periods since the turn of the century.

Table 5.1 Birth rates in the UK
(number of births per 1,000 population)

Year	Number
1900–02	28.6
1910–12	24.6
1920–22	23.1
1930–32	16.3
1940–42	15.0
1950–52	16.0
1960–62	17.9
1970–72	15.8
1980–82	13.0
1989–[1]	13.6

Note: [1]Provisional.
Source: *Annual Abstract of Statistics*, 1992.

The picture is one of steady decline in the birth rate since 1900. There are many reasons for this:

- There has been a trend towards smaller families as people become better off and as health improves and the death rate falls. This is evident from comparisons of birth rates between the developed and less developed countries. In less developed countries, where mortality is higher, family size also tends to be higher as insurance against loss of children.
- Availability of contraception. This has had a dramatic effect on the birth rate as people now have much greater control over family size than previously.
- Changes in attitudes towards family size and marriage and the role of women in society. Smaller families ensure a higher standard of living. There seems to be a trend away from having children within marriage. In the United Kingdom and France nearly five out of ten children are now born outside of marriage. In Denmark the proportion is even higher. There has also been a change in the attitude towards women and work; a higher proportion of women work now than ever before and it is much more acceptable in society.

Although the trend since the beginning of the century is downward, Table 5.1 shows that the trend is not smooth. There are variations in the birth rate which will be considered further in the section on the age structure of the population.

The death rate

This is the number of deaths per thousand of a population in a given year. Over the last 100 years there has been a dramatic fall in the death rate in the United Kingdom, although over the past 20 years it has been fairly stable. It stood at 11 per thousand population in 1990, exactly the same as the EC average. In 1993 the life expectancy of a man in the United Kingdom was 72 years and for a woman was 80 years. The death rate is forecast to decline further and the average life expectancy is therefore forecast to rise. The death rate has fallen because of the following factors:

- increased medical knowledge;
- more health care;
- better food, housing and clothing;
- better educated population;
- better working conditions;
- better sanitation conditions; and
- a decline in infant mortality due to better antenatal and postnatal care. (In 1990 the number of infant mortalities per thousand live births in the United Kingdom was 8, substantially below the EC average of 11.)

If the birth rate is greater than the death rate there is a process of natural population growth.

Migration

People leave (or emigrate from) a country and others enter (or immigrate into) a country. The balance between these will be the level of net migration. If more are entering than leaving there will be net immigration and population size will be increasing. If more are leaving than entering there will be net emigration and population size will be falling. In the United Kingdom the level of net migration has been small and insignificant in recent years, sometimes positive and sometimes negative. The Single European Market may impact upon this as it makes movement around Europe freer. It is also likely that as time passes businesses will become increasingly centralised in Brussels.

Population change

The total population in a country changes as a result of changes in the birth rate, death rate and the level of migration. The death rate is now fairly stable, but expected to continue to fall gradually into the future. The birth rate is slightly more variable and dependent on external factors but again has stabilised, as too has migration. This means that the UK population is now fairly stable. The forecast growth rate in population up to 2025 is 4.2 per cent.

The age distribution of the population of the UK

The most important factors which have influenced the age structure of the population are the decline in the death rate, which has resulted in a greater number of old people in the population, and changes in the birth rate. As Table 5.1 and Figure 5.2 show there have been quite marked changes in birth rates, which have affected the age structure of the population. There was a sharp decline in the number of births during

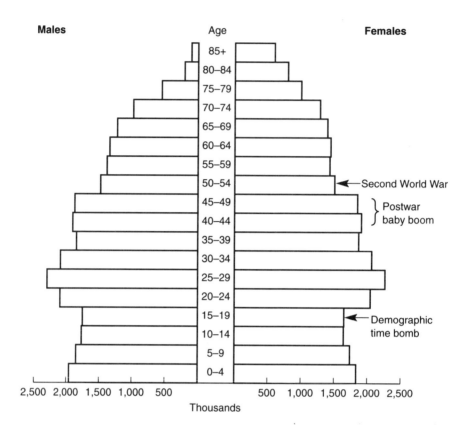

Fig. 5.2 The age structure of the UK population, 1992

the Second World War and immediately afterwards a postwar baby boom. These two changes are shown by the low numbers of fifty-year-olds and the relatively high number of forty-five-year-olds. The postwar baby boom in turn lead to a further baby boom in the 1960s, as the females of the first boom reached child-bearing age. This is shown by the large numbers of the population in the thirty-year age group. Since the 1960s there has been a fairly rapid decline in the birth rate, and this has been referred to as the 'demographic time bomb', because of the possible problems of labour shortage that it might create. Again the diagram shows the low numbers of teenagers born in the 1970s who will shortly enter the labour force.

Because of the falling birth rate and falling death rate the population in the United Kingdom is 'ageing', and thus the average age is increasing. This has a number of implications for the economy. First, there will be changes in the patterns of demand for goods and services. It has long been recognised that patterns of demand differ between age groups and this will have implications for production of goods and services. Secondly, as pensioners do not work, the burden on those in work will be increased to pay for the support services like health care and pensions which are financed out of taxation. Thirdly, there will be an impact upon the mobility of the labour force as older people are less mobile than younger people.

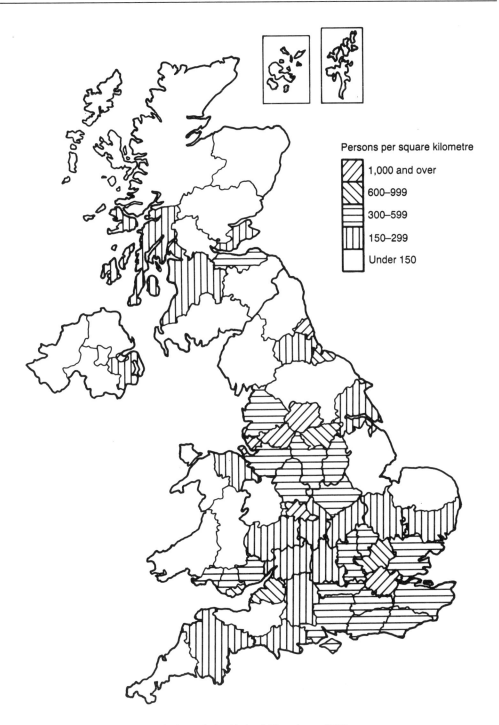

Fig. 5.3 Location of the population of the United Kingdom, 1989
Source: Office of Population Censuses and Surveys; General Register Offices for Scotland and Northern Ireland

The sex distribution of the population

There are more women than men in the UK population. The 1981 census records 26.8 million men and 28.3 million women. There are more men in the younger age groups than women because there are a greater number of male births. And there are more women in the older age groups because the death rate amongst women is now lower. The sex distribution of the population has important implications for the make up of the working population because of the differing activity rates of the sexes.

The location of the population

The majority of the population lives in the South and the Midlands and there is a concentration of the older age groups around the South coast (see Figure 5.3). The majority of people in the United Kingdom live in cities and towns rather than the country.

The working population

The working population is the number of people who are eligible and available to work and offer themselves up as such. The size of the working population will be determined by the age at which people can enter employment, which in the United Kingdom is 16 years, and the age at which they leave employment. In the United Kingdom the retirement age still stands at 60 years for women and 65 years for men. Those included in the definition of the working population will be:

- those working in paid employment, even if they are over retirement age;
- part-time workers;
- those registered as unemployed;
- members of the armed forces; and
- the self-employed.

The working population in 1989 was 28.5 million, which is about 49 per cent of the total population. The importance of the working population is twofold: it produces the goods and services needed in the economy; and through the payment of taxes it supports the dependent population (i.e. the very old and the very young).

An important determinant of the size of the working population is the participation

Table 5.2 Economic activity by sex and marital status (%) 1991 of persons of working age (16 to 59/64 years)

	All	Men	Women All	Married	Unmarried
Economically active	80	88	71	71	71
In employment	73	80	66	67	64
Unemployed	7	8	5	4	7
Economically inactive	20	12	29	29	29

Source: *Employment Gazette*, September 1992. Crown Copyright.

rate (i.e. the proportion of the population who actually work).

Table 5.2 shows that the participation rate for women was 71 per cent in 1991, somewhat lower than the male figure of 88 per cent. The figures have however been converging over the years. In 1979 only 63 per cent of women were economically active, while the corresponding figure for men was 91 per cent. Activity rates were the same for married and unmarried women.

The trend has been for increased participation rates for women over time as families have become smaller and because of the changing role of women in society as a whole, labour saving devices in the home and government legislation to promote equal pay and treatment. Also important in this process are the changes in industrial structure which have led to more part-time service jobs (see Chapter 9). Figure 5.4 shows how

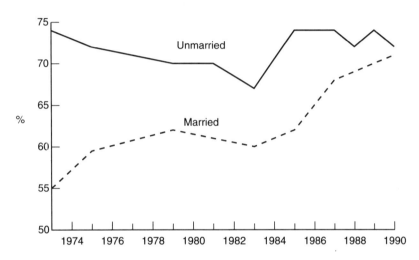

Fig. 5.4 Participation rates of married and unmarried women (percentage of 16- to 59-year-olds), 1973–1990
Source: Smyth, M. and Browne, F. *General Household Survey, 1990*, London HMSO (1992)

participation rates for women have changed in selected years.

The participation rates for both married and unmarried women have moved in a cyclical way, both dipping during the recession of the early 1980s. The general trend, however, is quite different. The participation rate of unmarried women has hardly changed at all over the period (74 per cent to 72 per cent), despite some slight deviation from the trend. The participation rates for married women has increased dramatically over the period, from 55 per cent in 1973 to 71 per cent in 1990.

Table 5.3 gives some comparisons with other EC countries. The United Kingdom has the second highest activity rates for both men and women after Denmark in the EC. There are marked differences in the activity rates for women across the EC, but in every country they were lower than the male activity rate.

The length of the working week

The average length of time for which people work is also a significant determinant of the quantity of labour that is available in an economy. Generally, the shorter the

Table 5.3 Economic activity rates[1] by sex 1990 (%) in selected EC countries

	Males	*Females*	*All*
UK	75.6	53.2	64.0
EC average	70.0	42.7	55.9
Belgium	62.0	37.1	49.1
Denmark	75.8	61.9	68.7
France	67.1	47.5	56.8
Germany (Fed. Rep.)	72.9	45.9	58.7
Italy	66.8	35.5	50.5

Note: [1]The civilian labour force aged 16 years and over as a percentage of the population aged 16 and over.
Source: *Social Trends*, 23, 1993

working week, the less labour that is available. There has been, over the last 100 years, a gradual reduction in the length of the working week, 40 hours is now the norm, and a gradual increase in the number of holidays that people take. More recent developments in the area of job sharing and increased flexibility will also impact upon the quantity of labour available.

Wages

It is clear that wages will affect how much people are willing to work and therefore the overall supply of labour in the economy. The analysis here will use the basic tools of demand and supply described in Chapter 11. It is advisable to review that chapter before proceeding. The market for labour can be likened to the market for any other commodity, in that there will be a demand for and a supply of labour. The demand for labour will come from the firm which wishes to produce goods and services that can be sold in the market. The demand for labour is a 'derived demand' as its demand is derived from the demand that exists for what it produces. The demand curve can be assumed to be a normal downward-sloping demand curve which indicates that – everything else being equal – as the wage rate goes up the demand for labour goes down.[2] The supply of labour comes from people. It is equally likely that the total supply curve has the normal upward slope, indicating that as the wage rate increases the supply of labour increases. It is argued that as the wage rate increases past a certain level people would prefer to substitute leisure for wages. The individual supply curve will therefore bend backwards at that wage rate. The total supply curve, however, will be upward sloping indicating that those not working will be encouraged to offer their services and that those already working might be encouraged to work overtime.

Assuming for the time being that the labour market is a totally free market, the wage rate and the amount of labour being used will be determined by the forces of demand and supply, as in Figure 5.5. The equilibrium wage rate is £W and the equilibrium quantity of labour is L. If there is a change in the level of demand or supply, there will be a corresponding change in the wages and quantity of labour.

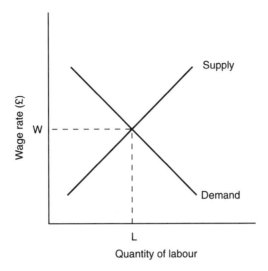

Fig. 5.5 The market for labour

Trade unions and wages

There are four different types of trade union:

1 *Craft unions* They represent one particular craft or skill, like the Boilermakers Union, which was formed in 1834 and was the longest-lived craft union in the TUC when it merged with the GMB in 1982. These were the earliest type of union.
2 *Industrial unions* They have members doing different jobs but in the same industry. Industrial unions are more common in other countries but some UK unions come close to this type; for example, the National Union of Miners.
3 *General unions* They contain members doing different jobs in different industries, like the Transport and General Workers Union.
4 *White collar unions* They represent the non-manual workers like teachers, social workers, and so forth. An example is NALGO.

One of the main aims for all types of union has been to counteract and protect their members from the power of the employer. As far as wages are concerned, this has been achieved through collective bargaining. Over the years a situation has been reached where hardly any wage contracts are negotiated individually, but are collectively negotiated by trade unions and employers. Although there does seem to be a trend away from collective bargaining, coinciding with the anti-trade union legislation of the 1980s and decline in the membership and power of the trade unions, the majority of wage increases are still negotiated by trade unions.

It is argued that the activities of trade unions through collective bargaining have served to increase the wage rate above its equilibrium level and thus cause unemployment. Figure 5.6 demonstrates this effect. Assume that the market clearing wage rate is £W and the quantity of labour being used is L. Assume now that a trade union enters the market that has the power to enforce a wage increase to £W₁. At this

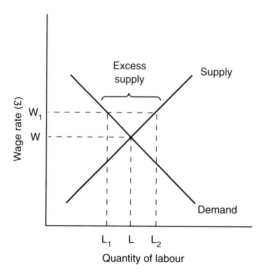

Fig. 5.6   The effect of trade unions on the labour market

wage rate the market does not clear, the demand for labour is L_1 while the supply of labour is L_2. There is therefore excess supply of labour or unemployment. In this way trade unions are blamed for keeping wages at too high a level so that the market cannot clear.

   Although this argument seems plausible enough, it is not quite as simple as it seems. There are other market imperfections which prevent the market from operating as smoothly as suggested and which contribute towards creating unemployment. There are some industries which have only one or two employers who can exercise a great deal of power over the market but from the opposite side to trade unions. There are also other factors which prevent people moving easily and smoothly between jobs. People cannot easily change jobs because they are both geographically and occupationally immobile.

Immobility of labour

People are geographically immobile for a variety of reasons:

● The cost of moving. It is an expensive business to move to another part of the country, particularly to areas where housing costs are high, like London.
● There may be shortages of housing in certain areas, or it may be difficult or even impossible to sell a house in other areas.
● There will be many social ties in the form of family and friends that people may be reluctant to leave.
● For people with children, schooling will be important. For example, parents are reluctant to relocate when their children are working for GCSE or 'A' level examinations.

People are also immobile occupationally for the following reasons:

- Some jobs require some natural ability that an individual might not possess (e.g. entertainers, footballers, and so on).
- Training is required by many occupations (e.g. doctors, engineers). Without this training an individual could not do the job and the length of training might be a deterrent.
- To enter some occupations (like starting up your own business), a certain amount of capital is required. In some cases the amount of capital needed will be very high (dry cleaning for example where the machines are expensive to purchase), and for many this might prove to be a barrier to mobility.

In order to help people to be more mobile so that the labour market works more smoothly, the government over the years has evolved a variety of policies. Job centres and the like attempt to overcome the lack of knowledge of jobs that are available. Training schemes are offered so that people can retrain, and relocation allowances can be paid to alleviate the cost of moving. Government policy in this area is considered more fully in Chapter 14.

These are some of the factors that determine the number of people who are available in an economy for producing goods and services. But it is not just the quantity of labour but also its quality that is important. The quality of the workforce is determined by many factors already mentioned, but most importantly by the level of education and training of the workforce.

The level of education and training of the workforce

An educated workforce is necessary for an advanced industrial nation, both in terms of general qualifications and specific job-related training. The United Kingdom does not fare well in either of these areas compared with other countries. Table 5.4 shows the situation with regard to school qualifications, and although there has been an improvement over the period shown, it is still true that in 1988 more than 40 per cent of school leavers in the United Kingdom left school with no formal qualifications.

Government policies through the 1960s were designed to increase the proportion of those staying on at school after the statutory minimum leaving age. And although the staying-on rate at school has improved in the United Kingdom it still remains low internationally. More recently the thrust of policy has been towards vocational courses for the over-16s. There have been many initiatives in this area in recent years. Table 5.5 gives a summary of a few of the more recent ones.

Table 5.4 % leaving school with different educational qualifications

Qualifications	1977/78	1980/81	1983/84	1987/88
One or more 'A' levels	16.8	17.8	18.9	20.6
One or more GCSE	35.2	35.7	37.0	38.5
No qualifications	48.0	46.6	44.1	41.0

Source: *Annual Abstract of Statistics*, 1992

Table 5.5 Examples of vocational courses for over-16s

Year	Scheme	Description
1983	Youth Training Scheme	Provided work-related training for 16- and 17-year-olds, both on and off the job. Largely introduced to fill the gap left by the demise of the traditional apprenticeships.
1985	Certificate of Pre-vocational Education	Full time vocational courses for over-16s containing an element of work experience.
1992	National Vocational Qualifications (NVQs)	A comprehensive system of vocational qualifications at four levels of achievement.

As far as higher education is concerned it is difficult to make international comparisons because of the differences between countries. For example, an average degree in the United Kingdom takes 4 years to complete while in the United States the average is 7 years. Despite these difficulties comparisons have been made by looking at the number of students who enrol on a course of higher education and the number who complete such a course, as a percentage of a standardised age group.[3] In such comparisons the United Kingdom does well against other European countries. However, a large proportion of UK students are enrolled on sub-degree-level courses. The spending on higher education as a percentage of GDP is lower in the United Kingdom than most other European countries.

As well as school and higher education, job-related training is important in improving the quality of the workforce. Training at work can be of two types: on the job training and off the job training. There has been the development of a competence-based approach to training, which partly stems from the introduction of NVQs. The system is designed to be easily understood and to provide workers with the skills that are needed by industry. It is designed to unify what is a very diverse system of qualifications existing in the United Kingdom at present.

The number of apprenticeships fell rapidly at the beginning of the 1980s and has not really recovered. The numbers have remained relatively stable throughout the whole of the 1980s as Table 5.6 shows.

Table 5.6   Number of apprenticeships in UK (thousands)

Year	Number
1984	332
1985	357
1986	318
1987	314
1988	329
1989	367
1990	352
1991	330

Source: *Employment Gazette*, August 1992. Crown Copyright.

Table 5.7 Numbers of employees receiving job-related training in the four weeks before the Labour Force Survey in selected years %

	1984	1986	1988	1989	1990	1991
All	9.2	10.8	13.3	14.5	15.4	14.9
Men	9.7	11.5	13.4	14.4	15.3	14.8
Women	8.5	9.9	13.1	14.5	15.6	15.0

Source: *Labour Force Survey* (various)

The number of women receiving training (both on the job training and off the job training) has increased over the period relative to men, and there has been a gradual increase for both sexes over the time period (see Table 5.7). These averages hide significant differences between industries, with, for example, the service sector having a much higher level of training than agriculture, forestry and fishing. Also, those in professional occupations were much more likely to have had some training in the four weeks preceding the annual survey. It is also true that the vast majority of those receiving training already held some other qualification. Those without any previous training were highly unlikely to be receiving training.

Occupational structure of the population

There will be changes in the occupational structure of the population over time. These will be caused by changes in industrial structure and technological change. There are

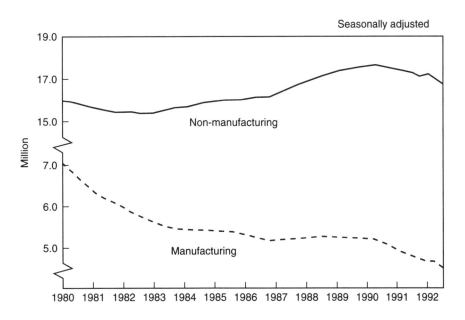

Fig. 5.7 Manufacturing and non-manufacturing employees in United Kingdom
Source: *Employment Gazette.* Crown Copyright

more women in the workforce now because there has been an increase in demand for the types of goods that have been produced by women. There has also been an increase in the availability and quality of labour saving devices in the home which has released women into the workforce. There has been a decrease in the average family size so that if women leave the workforce to look after their children they now do so for a shorter period of time. There has also been a change in attitude towards women working.

Figure 5.7 shows quite clearly that there has been an increase in the number of non-manufacturing jobs at the same time as a fall in the number of manufacturing jobs. From Figure 5.8 much information can be gleaned about the structure of occupations in the United Kingdom. First, there is a higher percentage of men than women in the professional/managerial occupations for both of the years. For both sexes the percentages in professional/managerial occupations have increased between 1971 and 1991. There are more men working in skilled, semi-skilled and manual occupations than women. However, the proportions have moved in opposite directions over the period, with the percentage of women in such occupations rising and the percentage of men falling. Women are clearly concentrated in clerical/selling-type occupations.

Another trend evident throughout the 1980s is the increasing use of part-time

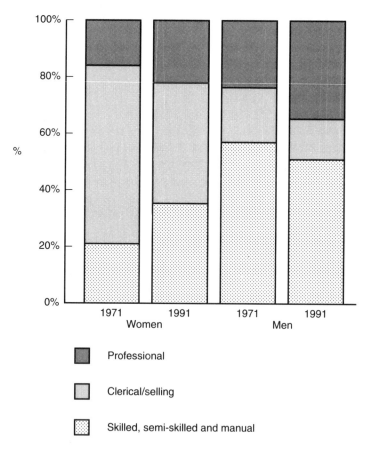

Fig. 5.8 Occupational structure of the UK workforce, 1971 and 1991
Source: *Annual Abstract of Statistics*, 1992

employment and a decrease in full-time employment. Much of this is in response to the changing industrial structure, as full-time manufacturing jobs have disappeared and part-time service jobs have replaced them. There has also been an increase in the 'flexible workforce' (temporary workers), as firms attempt to minimise the impact of recession during the 1980s and 1990s.

TECHNOLOGY

Technology is defined as 'the sum of knowledge of the means and methods of producing goods and services' (*Penguin Dictionary of Economics*). It is increasingly science based, encompassing things like chemistry, physics and electronics and refers to the organisation of production as well as the actual techniques of production itself. Technological change leads to the introduction of new products, changes in the methods and organisation of production, changes in the quality of resources and products, new ways of distributing the product, and new ways of storing and disseminating information. Technology has a very big impact upon the world of business in all of these areas and has an important effect on the level and type of investment that takes place in an economy and therefore the rate of economic growth.

Technological change

There have been massive changes in technology in the past ten years. This section will consider a few of these and assess their impact upon business and the economy.

Information technology

Developments in information technology have had the effect of transforming existing business activities as well as creating entirely new ones, involving the collection, handling, analysis and transmission of information. It is estimated that by the year 2000 two-thirds of the workforce in the United States will be working in information. There has been a massive increase in the demand for information, and, on the supply side, continued advances in the miniaturisation of components. These will continue even when the capabilities of the silicon chip have been exhausted, with the development of superconductors and optronics. There are also the advances in the computing area such as the development of new languages and artificial intelligence.

Advances in information technology have many impacts upon business. They are creating new products and making old products more profitable to produce through things like computer-aided design (CAD). The effects they are having on the different functions carried out by businesses can easily be seen:

● *Administration* The administration of businesses has been revolutionised by the introduction of information technology. Most businesses have computer systems and records have been computerised and filing has become unnecessary. Communication has been eased by the introduction of electronic mail fax machines and E mail. Between 1988 and 1994 it is forecast that the number of users of electronic message handling facilities in the EC will rise by 775 per cent.

- *Production* The use of CAD will shorten the design and planning phase of the product and shorten the life cycle of the product. Japan applied this very early on in the field of consumer electronics and many of the products are withdrawn from sale and redesigned within a very short period of time.
- *Storage and distribution* The computerisation of stock control has had implications for the storage requirements of firms. It has made implementation of the just-in-time method of stock control possible. This is easily seen in the case of supermarkets where the use of bar-codes on products makes it possible to carry out a stock check of a whole supermarket in a matter of hours. The shelves can then be loaded up as the stock check continues. Similarly, the use of bar-codes with Electronic Point of Sale (EPOS) makes stock control simpler.
- *Electronic Funds Transfer at Point of Sale (EFTPOS)* This system has also had a revolutionary effect in the area of retailing. Most shops now accept credit cards or Switch cards where funds are immediately transferred from bank accounts to the supermarkets.

Other technological developments

- *New materials* There are two main developments in this area: the development of materials in the high-tech industries like technical ceramics and the upgrading of materials used in lower-range products like coated sheet metal.
- *Biotechnology* Biotechnology is expected to have wide-ranging effects on many fields. The development of new products like computers that can imitate the activity of the brain can shorten the development process for certain products by speeding up existing processes.
- *Energy* The kind of developments that can take place in this field are the use of superconductors to transport electricity and research which might make solar energy a viable source of energy.

These are the new emerging industries which are creating new products and making old products more profitable to produce. It has been estimated that the output of these emerging industries are 20 per cent for consumption within the industries themselves, 20 per cent for final consumption and 60 per cent for consumption in the traditional industries.

Technology and investment

The second input into the production process after people is capital. In economics, capital has a special meaning; it refers to all man-made resources which are used in production. Capital is usually divided into working capital and fixed capital. Working capital consists of the stocks of raw materials and components used in producing things. Fixed capital consists of buildings, plant and machinery. The main difference between the two is that fixed capital gives a flow of services over a long period of time, while working capital needs to be replaced on a regular basis. Because of its nature, working capital is much more mobile than fixed capital (i.e. it can be used for other purposes much more easily). Capital is a 'stock' of goods used in the production process, a stock which is continually being used and therefore needing to be replaced. This stock provides a flow of services for the production process.

Capital includes a wide diversity of items, ranging from factory premises to machinery to raw materials in stock to transport vehicles to partly finished goods. As well as these, there is also what is often called 'social capital', which refers to capital that is owned by the community such as schools and hospitals. There is also spending on the infrastructure, which is important to all businesses rather than being linked to one particular business. The main components of this are transport, energy, water and information. The transportation system is obviously very important to a developed economy. Road, rail, air, and water are used to transport goods, services and raw materials. The capital stock in transport was £70.4 billion in 1990, and the value of road vehicles, rolling stock, ships and aircraft in use was £1,367 million (both in 1985 prices). The same is true for energy and water; both are used by industry in great quantities, and a good infrastructure in these is essential. The information distribution system is also part of the infrastructure and would include telephone systems and the post.

Table 5.8 shows the capital stock of the United Kingdom in 1981 and 1990 by industry. The level of capital stock increased over the period by 23.8 per cent, but there are marked differences between industries ranging from a growth of 103.2 per cent in banking, financial and business services to a fall of −14 per cent in transport.

The increase in the stock of capital over time is called investment. Investment will serve to increase the productive potential of the firm and the economy. Investment usually refers to the purchase of new assets, as the purchase of second-hand assets merely represents a change in ownership and therefore does not represent a change in productive potential. Investment is important for the firm as it is a mechanism for growth; it is an integral part of the innovation process and can have disastrous results for a firm if an investment goes wrong. Generally the higher the level of investment in a country the higher will be the level of economic growth.[4]

Table 5.8 Gross capital stock in 1981 and 1990 in the UK by industry at 1985 replacement cost (£ billion)

Industry	1981	1990	% change
Agriculture, forestry and fishing	29.3	30.1	+2.7
Extraction of mineral oil and natural gas	26.6	36.8	+38.3
All other energy and water supply	143.6	150.7	+4.9
Manufacturing	255.2	281.8	+10.4
Construction	15.6	16.8	+7.7
Distribution, hotels and catering, repairs	75.8	115.6	+52.5
Transport	81.9	70.4	−14.0
Communication	38.0	51.9	+36.6
Banking, finance, insurance, business services and leasing	75.7	153.8	+103.2
Other services	202.3	266.6	+31.8
Dwellings	459.7	563.3	+22.5
Total	1,403.6	1,737.6	+23.8

Source: *Annual Abstract of Statistics*, 1992

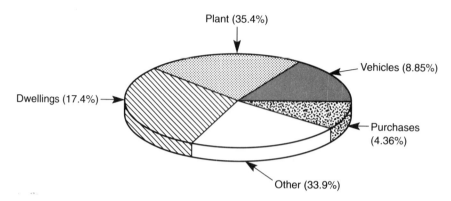

Fig. 5.9 Categories of investment in the United Kingdom in 1991
Source: *Economic Trends*, 1992

Total or gross investment can be broken down into replacement investment which is investment to replace obsolete or worn out machines and new investment which is any investment over and above this. In the United Kingdom in 1990, gross investment was £106,028 million, replacement investment was £61,126 million and net investment was £44,902 million. This figure includes investment by firms, individuals (in dwellings mainly) and governments (see Figure 5.9). It can be seen that the level of investment is affected by the state of the economy. There was a fall in the level of investment in the early 1980s and again in 1991, both of these as a result of the recession in the economy (see Figure 5.10). The level of investment in 1991 represented 19 per cent of GDP.

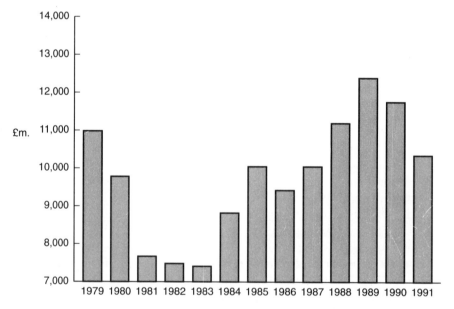

Fig. 5.10 Gross fixed investment in UK manufacturing industry (1985 prices), 1979–1991
Source: *Economic Trends*, 1993

There is an important relationship between investment and technological change which runs in both directions. Investment can form the basis for improvements in technology while improved technology which brings about new ways of producing goods will lead to greater investment. For private firms the main determinants of the level of investment will be the rate of technological change and the scope for extra profit as a result of these changes.

Innovation and technology

There are two types of innovation that can occur as a result of technological change: product innovation and process innovation. Product innovation is the development of new products, like the microprocessor, which will have far reaching effects on business. New products impact upon the industrial structure of a country, as new industries grow and old industries disappear. This in turn will lead to changes in the occupational structure of the workforce, as we have seen. It has even had the effect of reducing the benefits large firms derive from economies of scale in cases where the technological change can be exploited by small firms as well as it can by large firms. Another example of product innovation which has affected the level of competition in the market is the development of quartz watches, which allowed Japan to enter the market and compete with Switzerland. Process innovation, on the other hand, refers to changes that take place in the production process, like the introduction of assembly-line production in the manufacture of cars. The two types of innovation are related, as the above examples show. The microprocessor (product innovation), which is a new product, has lead to massive changes in the way that production and offices operate (process innovation).

Not all innovation is technological in nature; for example, changes in fashion in clothing are not technological. Innovative activity is important for all industry whether manufacturing or non-manufacturing. In some industries (e.g. pharmaceuticals, computers), innovation is essential if firms wish to remain competitive.

Research and development

Most, but not all, of the technological changes that have occurred have occurred through the process of research and development. 'Research' can be theoretical or applied, and 'development' refers to the using of the research in the production process. Most research and development carried out by private companies is directed towards applied research and development. It is designed to develop new products and production processes which will render production more profitable. It is also aimed at improving existing products and processes. Most basic theoretical research carried out in the United Kingdom is financed from public sources and is undertaken in places like the universities.

Table 5.9 shows that the level of research and development expenditure in the UK in 1990 was £8,082.4 million, which represents about 2 per cent of GDP. The increase over the previous year was 8 per cent but if the effect of inflation is removed there was a 1 per cent fall in the level of R and D expenditure between 1989 and 1990. From the table it can be seen that there are wide differences in the expenditure between

Table 5.9 Spending on R & D (£ million) in 1990 (current prices)

Product group	£m	%
All product groups	8,082.4	100
All products of manufacturing industry	6,929.3	86
Chemicals industries	1,923.1	24
Mechanical engineering	232.9	3
Electronics	2,327.3	29
Other electrical engineering	148.1	2
Aerospace	1,212.2	15
Motor vehicles	501.3	6
Other manufactured products	584.3	7
Non-manufactured products	1,153.1	14

Source: *Annual Abstract of Statistics*, 1992

industries, with manufacturing involved in a great deal more research and development spending than non-manufacturing. Even within the broad category of manufacturing there are wide differences, with chemicals and electronics accounting for more than half of the expenditure. Table 5.10 shows the sources from which R & D is financed. As can be seen the majority of R & D is financed by companies themselves, the percentage not really changing by very much over the period. If R & D is split into civil and defence spending, it is clear that the government finances the majority of defence R & D, as would be expected.

The United Kingdom fares badly in international comparisons of R & D spending. OECD figures show that in 1991 R & D spending as a percentage of GDP was 2.8 per cent in the United States, 2.6 per cent in Germany, 2.8 per cent in Japan and 2.2 per cent in the United Kingdom. The UK figure is only slightly above the EC average of 2 per cent. Of this spending, a higher percentage is financed by the government in the United Kingdom than in other countries, which means that out of a lower percentage expenditure on R & D in the United Kingdom, less of it is financed by private industry.

The spending on research and development can be protected by firms applying for patents whereby other firms have to pay to see the information and wait a specified period of time before the idea can be used. Patents have the effect of reducing the possibility and scope of technology transfer. If the number of patents granted is used as

Table 5.10 Sources of funds for R & D within industry in the UK 1985, 1989 and 1990 (current prices)

	1985	*1989*	*1990*
Total (£m)	5,121.6	7,649.8	8,024.4
Government funds (%)	23	17	17
Overseas funds (%)	11	13	15
Mainly own funds (%)	66	69	68

Source: *Annual Abstract of Statistics*, 1993

a measure of the level of R & D, the United Kingdom again fares badly. The Cabinet office reported that between 1963 and 1988, the number of US patents granted to inventors in the United Kingdom had not changed, but the number had more than doubled for Germany and increased tenfold for Japan.

Limits to technological change

Technological change has many effects on the economy and the environment and if uncontrolled can lead to problems, like high levels of unemployment or the exhaustion of natural resources. One area of concern is energy. The world's stock of energy is finite and we are still heavily dependent upon fuel which was formed millions of years ago. The development of nuclear power again represents a finite source of energy, and also carries with it other problems like the disposal of nuclear waste and the possibility of accidents. For these and other reasons the scale of technological change needs to be controlled.

It is also the case that technological change can lead to high levels of unemployment in industries that are in decline. This type of unemployment often takes on a regional bias as the older traditional industries tend to be located in particular parts of the country. Technological unemployment is in some respects inevitable as in a changing world it would be expected that new industries would emerge and old industries die. The problem can be tackled by the government and industry through retraining, but what is also needed is a new and more flexible view of work where less time is spent working and more on leisure. Technological change can also give rise to the opposite problem of skill shortage in new industries, where particular skills are required.

NATURAL RESOURCES

In economics, natural resources are put under the heading of land as a factor of production. It would include all natural resources like the soil, minerals, oil, forests, fish, water, the sun, and so on.

Although the area of land in a country is fixed, land as a factor of production is not completely fixed in supply as more land can be made available through land reclamation schemes and better irrigation. The productivity of agricultural land can be increased by the use of fertilisers. It is true, however, that our natural resources are in finite supply. And often their true extent is not known with certainty, as Table 5.11 shows for oil and natural gas. The wide range of total recoverable reserves is based on 'best guesses'.

It is in the area of natural resources that the distinction between renewable and non-renewable resources is most important. Natural resources can be either. Land can often be used for more than one purpose – for example, agricultural land can be used one year to grow one crop and another the next – but oil, once it is used up, cannot be used again. And even though land can be used for more than one purpose it is still immobile both geographically and between different uses. Land can be used for agriculture or industry, but using it for one purpose makes it more difficult to use it for another. If a factory is built on a piece of land, it would be both expensive and time

Table 5.11 Oil and gas reserves in UK in 1991

UK Continental shelf	Oil (m.t.)	Gas (bn.ft)^3
Fields already discovered		
Proven reserves	2,020	1,345
Probable reserves	675	695
Possible reserves	730	570
Estimates in potential future discoveries	540–3,395	260–1,252
Total recoverable reserves	2,560–6,820	1,605–3,862

Source: *Social Trends*, 1993

consuming to clear the land for farming. Figure 5.11 shows the usage of land in the United Kingdom in 1991.

Increased knowledge of the effects of depletion of natural resources has lead to increased environmental awareness amongst the population. There has been an increased interest in conservation and recycling and the search for alternative forms of energy. The United Kingdom is not well endowed with high grade minerals, the main natural resource is energy. There is a good deposit of coal and the discovery of North Sea oil and gas has made the United Kingdom self-sufficient in energy supplies.

The OECD predicts that the energy requirements of western Europe will increase by 13 per cent until the year 2000. The proportion of this being met from oil will fall from 43 per cent to 40 per cent, the deficiency being taken up by natural gas. There is not expected to be any growth in nuclear power over the next decade, although this may change in the long term as the non-renewable energy sources are used up. There is a demand for alternative sources of energy. The alternatives of hydro, wind, and solar energy sources will also grow in importance. In the United Kingdom the government has tried to promote the search for renewable energy sources through projects like the Non-Fossil Fuel Obligation which requires regional electricity boards to obtain a

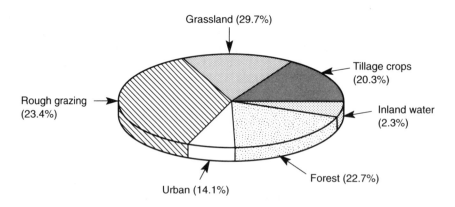

Fig. 5.11 Usage of land in the United Kingdom, 1991
Source: *Annual Abstract of Statistics*, 1992

certain percentage of their electricity from clean sources. It also funds experimental work in the search for new sources of energy. More is said about energy in the case study at the end of this chapter.

The location of industry

There are many factors which affect the location of industry in a country. These include ready access to the following utilities:

- Energy sources.
- Raw materials.
- Markets.
- A supply of labour.
- Transport system.
- Cheap land space.
- External economies of scale. These are benefits which accrue to firms producing the same good when they locate near to one another. The local infrastructure becomes geared up to the particular needs of the industry. For example, specialised labour will be available, local colleges will offer specialised courses, local bank managers will become expert in the financial needs of the industry, and so on.

The relative importance of these factors will vary depending upon the industry under consideration and over time.

Some industries are 'tied' to a particular location because of what they produce and what they need to produce the goods. For instance, a firm involved in the extraction of a particular mineral is obviously tied to the location of that mineral. The location of heavy industry in the United Kingdom follows the pattern established during the Industrial Revolution, when the main source of energy was coal. There was a choice between locating near to the coal field or having to transport coal, which would have been expensive and difficult. Once a pattern of location is established it is perpetuated through a 'multiplier' process. The coal mines themselves create jobs, other industries locate nearby for ease of access to coal, which creates more jobs. These workers demand other goods and services, which means that other related industries set up in the location and so more jobs are created. This led to a concentration of industry and also population around the coal fields during and after the Industrial Revolution.

Two changes occurred to change this pattern of location: first, the decline of the old traditional industries; and secondly, the decline in the importance of coal as an energy source and the establishment of the national grid which provided electricity as a readily available source of energy. As a result, industry has moved away from the old traditional industrial areas and the multiplier process described above is set in motion in the opposite direction. Jobs are lost in the traditional industries, the coal industry, and the other industries which grew up to meet the demands of those workers. Hence the old industrial areas become depressed.

Over the years many industries have become less tied to specific locations, because of the nature of the goods they produce and the low bulk of raw materials and parts (e.g. transistors), which makes them cheap to transport. The role of raw materials in the choice of location of industry is much less important than it was. More important now are the markets for the firm's products. If raw materials are not bulky but the finished products are, the obvious location is near to the market.

Footloose industries are industries that could produce anywhere and are not tied to any particular location by anything. In the United Kingdom they seem to have chosen to locate in the South East. Such industries will look at costs in deciding where to locate. Wages will vary across the country and between countries, as too will other manufacturing costs.

Another major impact upon the location of industry has been government policy over the years. The decline of the old industrial areas as new products and markets have come into existence has lead to problems of structural unemployment in those areas. Much of government regional policy has been directed towards this problem since the depression of the 1930s.

SYNOPSIS

This chapter looked at the three main inputs into the production process: people, technology and natural resources. It considered each in turn and examined their importance to business and the main factors which determine both the quality and the quantity of these factors of production.

People are important in two ways: they are the producers of goods and services and also the consumers of goods and services. The quantity of human resources available in an economy depends upon things like total population size, participation rates, length of working week and wages. The quality depends upon such things as the level of health care, education and training.

One of the main features of the last fifty years has been the massive changes in technology that have had an enormous impact upon business, resulting in new products and markets and new methods of production and distribution.

As far as natural resources are concerned, the traditional view was that they were fixed in supply and therefore did not receive much consideration. However, with increased environmental awareness there is growing concern that this is not the case and that many of our natural resources are non-renewable and therefore need to be conserved.

Each of the three inputs into the production process has been considered separately but they are interlinked and difficult to separate in reality. It has already been said that the productivity of people will be affected by the technology at their disposal, and this is also true of natural resources. All of the three inputs are 'stocks', from which a stream of resources flow to firms. These flows are crucial to business, as without them production could not take place. Both the quantities and qualities of our stocks of these resources are important, as too is the replacement of the stocks that are being used.

CASE STUDY: ELECTRICITY

The total world demand for energy has increased around ten times over in the last 100 years. Within this period there has been a change in the relative importance of the different sources of energy. For example, although the worldwide consumption of coal has increased it has lost its place as the most important source of energy to oil. More recently natural gas has increased in importance. In the United Kingdom the picture is similar although there are differences in the usage of different sources of energy between countries.

Table 5.12 shows that coal is a much less important source of energy now than it was 40 years ago. There are many reasons for this including changes in relative prices, changes in tastes away from coal, the growth of road transport at the expense of the railways, and the change from steam to diesel trains. The use of both oil and natural gas has increased rapidly mainly due to the discovery of North Sea oil and gas in the United Kingdom.

Table 5.12 Primary energy usage in the UK (heat supplied basis) % of total

	1950	1970	1984	1990
Solid fuel	78.6	30.7	11.4	11.6
Gas	5.9	10.7	32.3	31.7
Oil	12.2	47.2	42.1	41.9
Electricity	3.3	11.4	14.2	14.7

Source: *Annual Abstract of Statistics*

Electricity generation is regarded as being a natural monopoly and as such is under the control of a single supplier in most countries, often the state. This, however, has changed in recent years with the drive towards privatisation, although the monopolistic nature of the industry is still recognised by the need for some form of independent regulation. Before consideration is given to the structure of the industry in the United Kingdom some general points need to be made about the nature of the product and its market.

Demand characteristics

In the United Kingdom the demand for energy has increased by 30 per cent since 1950 and the demand for electricity as a primary fuel within this has increased by a massive 506 per cent. Electricity is used by all sectors of the economy, as Table 5.13 shows. The domestic sector is the largest in terms of number of customers but the industrial sector uses more electricity. The table also shows the differentials in price charged to the different users.

Table 5.13 Sales of electricity in Great Britain 1988

	Number of customers (%)	Sales gigawatt-hour (%)	Selling price per therm (p)
Domestic	90.6	35.0	5.77
Farms	0.9	1.5	5.28
Public lighting	0.02	1.0	4.57
Railways	–	1.1	4.14
Commercial	7.5	25.0	5.04
Industrial	0.9	36.7	3.69

Source: *Digest of UK Energy Statistics.* Reproduced with permission of HMSO.

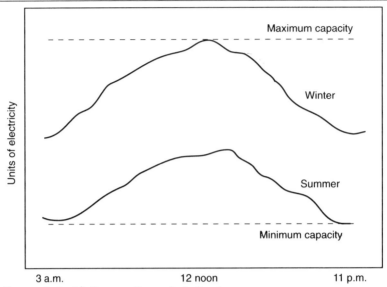

Fig. 5.12 Usage of electricity over the period of a day

Within the upward trend in the level of demand, there is a cyclical pattern; demand rises and falls with the state of the economy. There is also a shorter-term cycle which has nothing to do with the state of the economy. The nature of electricity makes it a special type of good as it cannot be stored; demand must be met immediately. The level of demand will depend upon the time of day, the time of year, the weather, and so forth (see Figure 5.12). There will be a maximum demand and a minimum demand, and the electricity supplier will need to decide on what capacity to produce in the knowledge that the ability to always meet maximum demand would be expensive and wasteful, and the ability to only meet minimum levels of demand would result in unfulfilled demand and interruptions in supply.

Supply factors

The production of electricity depends on the heating up of water to drive the steam turbines which produce electricity. This can be done in a variety of ways. The water can be heated by coal, oil, gas or nuclear power. Or alternatively the turbines can be turned by other means like water (hydroelectricity) or wind. The relative costs of these sources of electricity are as shown in Table 5.14. The main fuel used to generate electricity in the United Kingdom is coal as Figure 5.13 indicates.

Table 5.14 Relative costs of electricity sources

	Capital costs	Operating costs
Most expensive	Gas	Hydro
	Oil	Nuclear
	Coal	Coal
	Nuclear	Oil
Least expensive	Hydro	Gas

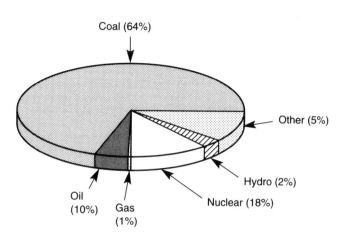

Coal (64%)

Other (5%)

Hydro (2%)

Oil
(10%)

Gas
(1%)

Nuclear (18%)

Fig. 5.13 Fuel used in the generation of electricity in the United Kingdom, 1990 (%)
Source: *Annual Abstract of Statistics*, 1992

The Central Electricity Generating Board (the only electricity generator in the United Kingdom prior to 1990) used to meet the basic level of demand for electricity through the use of coal and nuclear power and the surges in demand through the use of oil and gas. This was largely to do with the costs of production. As the costs of production change so too will the pattern. For example, with the oil crisis of the 1970s and the resulting increase in the price of oil, coal became more important in the generation of electricity while oil became less important. More recently there has been a change towards gas as a direct result of the privatisation of electricity (see below).

Economies of scale are very important in the electricity industry. It is this that makes the industry a natural monopoly as it would be wasteful to have competition in either the generation of electricity or the distribution of electricity by having two national grids running side by side. Despite this, competition has been introduced into the market through privatisation.

Privatisation of electricity in England

Prior to privatisation there was one nationalised electricity generator in the United Kingdom called the Central Electricity Generating Board (CEGB). There were 12 regional boards who bought electricity from the CEGB and distributed it to their localities. The regional boards also ran the local Electricity showrooms and carried out repairs and service.

With privatisation, the CEGB has been split up into two generating companies – Powergen and National Power. There are 12 regional distribution companies who together own the national grid. There is competition between Powergen and National Power in the generation of electricity and the regional companies are also allowed to build their own capacity. Thus competition in the market is increased. Nuclear power posed a problem as it was to be kept in public ownership because of the safety considerations and because the government wanted to keep nuclear power competitive, and its relative expense might have prevented this happening in the free market. The new structure of the industry is shown in Figure 5.14.

However, privatisation has changed the balance between the different sources of electricity. As already mentioned the CEGB met the basic level of demand for electricity with coal and nuclear power and the excess demand with gas and oil. With privatisation this started to change as the regional companies decided to build their own capacity to produce electricity. This would diversify their source of supply so that they did not have to buy electricity from Powergen or

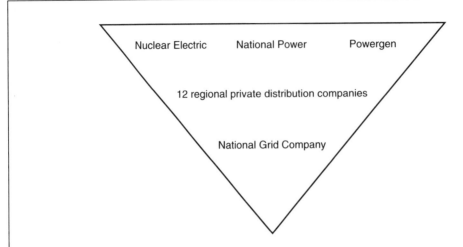

Fig. 5.14 Structure of the privatised electricity industry in England

National Power. Eleven out of the twelve distribution companies have already started to build their own capacity. The choice for this new capacity is gas, based mainly on cost terms – British Gas initially supplied gas at their preferential industrial rates – and because the level of risk involved is low.

The 'dash for gas' by the regional boards directly contributed to the crisis in the coal mining industry in late 1992. The resulting fall in the demand for coal added to the stock piles of coal that already existed, and this led to the announcement that 31 pits were to be closed with the loss of 30,000 jobs. As a result of public opinion the government was forced to rethink its strategy and to look again at its policy towards energy.

NOTES AND REFERENCES

1 *Annual Abstract of Statistics*, CSO, 1992.
2 For further reading on this area see Begg, D., Fischer, S., and Dornbusch, R., *Economics*, McGraw-Hill, 1991.
3 Williams, G., 'British higher education in the world league', *Oxford Review of Economic Policy*, 8(2), 1992.
4 The relationship between investment and the rate of growth is difficult to prove, but there does seem to be high correlation between the level of investment in a country and its associated level of economic growth. It should be remembered, however, that high correlation does not prove that one thing causes another.

REVIEW AND DISCUSSION QUESTIONS

1 The demand for electricity has special characteristics. What are the effects of these characteristics on the electricity industry?

2 Why are industries such as electricity 'natural monopolies'? What other examples are there of natural monopolies?

3 Think of one technological advance that has recently been made. What have been the effects of that change on the economy, business and the consumer?

4 In what ways can the general and specific skills of the British workforce be improved?

ASSIGNMENTS

1 You work in the economic development unit of your local council. The unit is compiling a bid to central government in order to win some resources to improve the basic infrastructure in the locality. Your job is to identify the economic problems which exist in your local town and explain why an increase in resources would overcome the problems. Write a briefing paper to the management committee of the unit on your results.

2 You have been asked to give a brief talk on the 'Social Chapter' of the Maastricht Treaty to a local trade union branch. They are especially interested in the effects the proposals will have on their working conditions. (Information on the Social Chapter will be available in most local libraries.)

FURTHER READING

Donaldson, P., *Understanding the British Economy*, Penguin, 1988.
Jones, T. T. and Cockerill T. A. J., *Structure and Performance of Industries*, Philip Allan, 1984.
Joshi, H. (ed.), *The Changing Population of Britain*, Blackwell, 1989.
Census 1991: National Report, Great Britain, Office of Population Census and Surveys, HMSO, 1993.

CHAPTER 6

The legal environment

Diane Belfitt

Businesses, like individuals, exist and carry on their activities within a framework of law which derives from custom and practice, the judicial decisions of the courts and from statutes enacted by governments. This legal environment not only constrains and regulates a firm's operations, but also provides an enabling mechanism through which it is able to pursue its objectives, particularly the achievement of profits through entrepreneurial activity. Like the political and economic environment with which it is intertwined, the legal environment of business is a key influence on the business organisation and an important area of study for students of business. This can be demonstrated by an examination of a number of the fundamental areas in which the law impinges on the operations of an enterprise.

OBJECTIVES

1 To gain a broad understanding of the idea of 'law' and the sources from which laws are derived.
2 To examine the court system, including the role of the European Court of Justice.
3 To discuss the basic features of the laws of contract and agency.
4 To analyse the reason for statutory intervention to protect the consumer and some of the principal pieces of legislation in this field.

INTRODUCTION

It is almost universally accepted that for a society to exist and function in an ordered way a set of rules is required to regulate human behaviour. Irrespective of whether these rules are laid down in custom or practice or in statute, they constitute a means of regulating and controlling the activities of individuals and groups and of enforcing minimum standards of conduct – even though they may be ignored or flouted on occasions. This framework of rules and the institutions through which they are formulated and enforced represent what is normally understood as the 'law', which invariably evolves over time in response to changing social, economic and political circumstances (e.g. the influence of pressure groups). As one of the constraining (and enabling) influences on business organisations, this legal environment is an important area of study for students of business, hence the tendency for courses in business-related subjects to have specialist modules or units on different aspects of business law (e.g. contract, agency, property, and so on).

The aim of this chapter is not to examine business law in detail or to provide a definitive insight into particular areas of the law as it relates to business organisations. Rather it is to raise the reader's awareness of the legal context within which businesses function and to comment briefly on those aspects of law which regularly impinge on a firm's operations. Students wishing to examine business law in more detail should consult the many specialist texts which have been written in this field, a sample of which is to be found at the end of this chapter.

CLASSIFICATION OF LAW

Laws relating to both individuals and organisations can be classified in a number of ways: international and national, public and private, criminal and civil. In practice there are no hard and fast rules to classification and some categories may overlap (e.g. where a person's behaviour is deemed to infringe different areas of law). Nevertheless, distinguishing laws in these terms serves as an aid to explanation and commentary, as well as helping to explain differences in liabilities and in legal remedies (e.g. a child under the age of ten cannot be held criminally liable).

Public and private law

Put simply, public law is the law which concerns the state, whether in international agreements or disputes or in the relationship between the state and the individual. Thus public law consists of international treaties and conventions, constitutional law, administrative law and criminal law. In contrast, private law is law governing the relationships between individuals and comprises laws in respect of contract, tort, property, trusts and the family.

Criminal law

Criminal laws relate to a legal wrong (criminal offence) – a breach of a public duty, punishable by the state on behalf of society. Decisions on whether or not to bring a prosecution in a particular instance are taken by the Crown Prosecution Service (in England and Wales) and the matter may or may not involve trial by jury, according to the seriousness of the alleged offence and the plea of the defendant(s). In some cases, the consent of both magistrates and defendants is required for a case to remain in the magistrates' court. Moreover whilst the criminal process may also arise from a private prosecution, these are rare and, in such cases, the Attorney-General (the government's senior law officer) has the right to intervene if he or she sees fit.

Tort

A tort is a civil wrong other than a breach of contract or a breach of trust and is a duty fixed by law on all persons (e.g. road users have a duty in law not to act negligently). The law of tort, therefore, is concerned with those situations where the conduct of one party threatens or causes harm to the interests of another party and the aim of the law is to compensate for this harm. The most common torts are negligence, nuisance, defamation and trespass.

Trusts

A trust is generally defined as an 'equitable obligation imposing on one or more persons a duty of dealing with property, over which they have control, for the benefit of other persons who may enforce the obligation'. This property may be in the form of money or stocks and shares or in other types of asset particularly land, where trusts have become a very common way of permitting persons who are forbidden to own legal estates in land to enjoy the equitable benefits of ownership. Partnerships, for example, cannot hold property as legal owners, so often several partners will act as trustees for all the partners (as a partnership has no separate corporate identity it cannot own property – see Chapter 7). Similarly, minors may not hold legal estates, so their interests must be protected by a trust, administered by an individual or an institution.

SOURCES OF LAW

Laws invariably derive from a number of sources including custom, judicial precedent, legislation, and international and supranational bodies (e.g. the EC). All of these so-called legal sources of the law can be illustrated by reference to English law which applies in England and Wales. Where laws made by Parliament are to apply only to Scotland or Northern Ireland the legislation will state this. Similarly, any act which is to apply to all four home countries will contain a statement to this effect.

Custom

Early societies developed particular forms of behaviour (or 'customs') which came to be accepted as social norms to be followed by the members of the community to which they applied. Many of these customary rules ultimately became incorporated into a body of legal principles known as the common law. Today customs would be regarded as usage recognised by law, whether by judicial precedent (case law) or through statutory intervention and hence they are largely of historical interest. Occasionally, however, they are recognised by the courts as being of local significance and may be enforced accordingly as exceptions to the general law (e.g. concerning land usage).

Judicial precedent

Much of English law is derived from judicial precdent (previous decisions of the courts). The present system of binding precedent, however, is of fairly recent origin, dating from the latter part of the nineteenth century when advances in recording legal judgements and a reorganisation of the court structure facilitated its general acceptance.

In essence, judicial precedent is based on the rule that the previous decisions of a higher court must be followed by the lower courts – hence the significance of the court structure. In any judgement will be found a number of reasons, arguments, explanations and cases cited and these must all be considered carefully by judges to determine whether there are material differences in the case before the court and the earlier decision. To reach a decision, the court must find what is termed the *ratio* (or *rationes* in the plural) *decidendi* of the previous case. Put very simply, the *ratio* of a case is the essential step in the legal reasoning which led the court to make that particular decision. Anything which cannot be regarded as a ratio is termed *obiter dicta* or 'things said by the way'. The whole of a dissenting judgment in a case is regarded as *obiter. Obiter dicta* are not binding but may be regarded as persuasive arguments if the facts of the case permit.

Clearly there are times when, perhaps because of the position of a court in the hierarchy, decisions are not to be regarded as binding precedent. However, if the judgement has been delivered by a jurisdiction which has a common law system (e.g. Canada, Australia) or, most importantly, by the Judicial Committee of the Privy Council, then those decisions will be regarded as being of persuasive precedent, and may be used to help the court reach its own decision.

Legislation

A substantial proportion of current law – including laws governing the operations of business organisations – derives from legislation or statute, enacted by the Queen (or King) in Parliament. As Chapter 3 indicated, the initiative in this sphere lies effectively with the government of the day which can virtually guarantee a bill will become law, if it has a working majority in the House of Commons.

Apart from a limited number of bills proposed by backbench MPs (private members' bills), the vast majority of legislation emanates from government and takes the form of Acts of Parliament or delegated legislation. Acts of Parliament are those bills which have formally been enacted by Parliament and have received the Royal Assent and, except where overriden by EC law, they represent the supreme law of the land. In addition to creating new laws (e.g. to protect the consumer), statutes may also be used to change or repeal existing laws. In some instances they may be designed to draw together all existing law (a consolidating Act) or to codify it or to grant authority to individuals or institutions to make regulations for specific purposes (an enabling Act). Under the Consumer Credit Act 1974, for instance, the Secretary of State for Trade and Industry is permitted to make regulations governing the form and content of credit agreements under delegated authority from Parliament.

As its name suggests, delegated legislation is law made by a body or person to which Parliament has given limited powers of law-making – as illustrated by the example above. More often than not, authority will be delegated to a Minister of the Crown, but it may also be conferred on local authorities or other public undertakings, either through the use of a statutory instrument or some other means of delegation. Since Parliament remains sovereign, such legislation is required to receive parliamentary approval and scrutiny, but time tends to prevent anything other than a cursory glance at a limited proportion of the legislation of this kind. It does, however, remain subject to judicial control, in so far as the body granted authority may be challenged in the courts for exceeding its powers (*ultra vires*).

In addition to these two principal forms of domestic legislation, developments in the law also emanate from Britain's membership of the European Community. Under the Community's main treaties – or those parts to which the British government has agreed – Community legislation becomes part of the law and takes precedence over domestic legislation, although the latter may sometimes be required to implement it. Accordingly law which is inconsistent with Community law is repealed by implication and British citizens, like their counterparts elsewhere in the EC, become subject to the relevant Community laws (unless an 'opt-out' has been negotiated).

Whereas the provision of the main treaties represent primary legislation, the regulations, directives and decisions emanating from the Community's institutions are secondary (or subordinate) legislation, made under the authority conferred by the Treaty of Rome (1957) and by subsequent acts (e.g. the Single European Act 1987, the Maastricht Act 1992). As Chapter 3 indicated, regulations are of general application throughout the Member States and confer individual rights and duties which must be recognised by the national courts. Their purpose is to achieve uniformity throughout the Community, as in the requirement for heavy goods vehicles to fit tachographs to control drivers' hours.

Directives by contrast are not directly applicable; they are addressed to Member States and not individuals, although a directive may create rights enforceable by an individual citizen. The aim of Community directives is to seek harmonisation or approximation between national laws rather than to achieve uniformity; hence the method of implementation is left to the discretion of the individual state, usually within a given time limit (e.g. the Companies Act of 1981 implemented the Community's fourth directive on company accounts by allowing small and medium-sized companies to reduce the amount of information provided to the Registrar of Companies).

Decisions, too, are binding, but only on the member state, organisation or individual to whom they are addressed and not on the population generally. In practice Community decisions become effective from the date stated in the decision, which is generally the date of notification, and they are enforceable in national courts if they impose financial obligations.

THE LEGAL SYSTEM: THE COURTS

A country's legal system can be said to have two main functions: to provide an enabling mechanism within which individuals and organisations can exist and operate (e.g. companies are constituted by law) and to provide a means of resolving conflicts and of dealing with those who infringe the accepted standards of behaviour. These functions are carried out by a variety of institutions including the government and the courts and a detailed analysis of the legal system within a state would require consideration of the interrelationship between politics and law. Since the political system has been examined in Chapter 3, the focus here is on the courts as a central element of a country's legal system, with responsibility for interpreting the law and administering justice in democratic societies. It is worth remembering, however, that political and governmental activity take place within a framework of law and that framework is itself a product of the political process at a variety of spatial levels.

The English legal system

Under the English legal system, a useful distinction can be made between courts on the basis of their status. The superior courts are the House of Lords, the Court of Appeal and the High Court; these are the courts to which cases are reported. Inferior courts, in contrast, have limited jurisdiction and are subject to the supervisory jurisdiction of the High Court. The current hierarchy of courts is illustrated in Figure 6.1. For domestic purposes (i.e. not concerning EC legislation), the highest court is the House of Lords which is the final court of appeal for both civil and criminal cases. Decisions reached by the Law Lords are binding on all other courts, though not necessarily on their Lordships themselves.

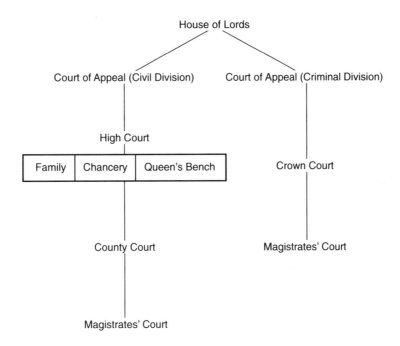

Fig. 6.1 The hierarchy of courts

Like the House of Lords, the Court of Appeal has only appellate jurisdiction. In the case of the Civil Division of the court, its decisions bind all inferior courts and it is bound by its own previous decisions and by those of the House of Lords. The Criminal Division similarly is bound by the decisions of the Law Lords, but not by the Court of Appeal's Civil Division; nor is it bound by its own previous decisions where these were against a defendant, as exemplified in a number of celebrated cases in recent years.

The High Court is divided into three separate divisions, Chancery, Queen's Bench and Family, and has virtually unlimited original jurisdiction in civil matters, many of which are of direct relevance to business organisations. The Family court deals with such things as adoption, wardship and contested divorce cases, whilst the Chancery court deals with cases concerning trusts, property and taxation. Claims in contract and tort are the responsibility of the Queen's Bench division, which has two specialist courts to deal with commercial matters and with ships and aircraft. It also exercises the criminal jurisdiction of the High Court – the latter being entirely appellate in instances referred to it by the magistrates' courts or the Crown Court.

In criminal cases the Crown Court has exclusive original jurisdiction to try all indictable offences and can hear appeals against summary conviction or sentence from magistrates' courts. Broadly speaking, the latter largely deal with less serious offences (especially motoring offences), where trial by judge and jury is not required – a right currently under discussion following the publication of the Runciman Report (1993). Whereas magistrates' courts have both criminal and civil jurisdiction – with the emphasis towards the former – the jurisdiction of the county courts is entirely civil and derived solely from statute. Amongst the issues they deal with are conflicts between landlords and tenants and disputes involving small claims (e.g. concerning consumer matters) where a system of arbitration provides for a relatively inexpensive and quick method of resolving problems.

In disputes with a supranational dimension – involving EC member states, institutions, organisations, companies or individuals – ultimate jurisdiction rests with the European Court of Justice. Under Article 164 of the Treaty of Rome, the court is required to ensure that in the application and interpretation of the Treaty the law is observed. As indicated elsewhere, in carrying out this function, the court has adopted a relatively flexible approach in order to take account of changing circumstances (see Chapter 3). Few would dispute that its judgments have had, and will continue to have, a considerable influence on the development of Community law.

As a final comment, it is perhaps worth stating that whilst conflict remains an enduring feature of daily life, many disputes are settled without recourse to the courts, often through direct negotiation between the parties concerned (e.g. Richard Branson's attempts to reach a negotiated settlement with British Airways over its alleged 'dirty tricks' campaign). Moreover even where negotiations fail or where one party declines to negotiate, a dispute will not necessarily result in court action, but may be dealt with in other ways. Disputes over employment contracts, for example, tend to be dealt with by a specialist tribunal, set up by statute to exercise specific functions of a quasi-legal nature. Similarly, complaints concerning maladministration by public (and increasingly private) bodies are generally dealt with by a system of 'ombudsmen', covering areas as diverse as social security benefits, local authority services, banking and insurance.

BUSINESS ORGANISATIONS AND THE LAW

Business organisations have been described as transformers of inputs into output in the sense that they acquire and use resources to produce goods or services for consumption. As Table 6.1 illustrates, all aspects of this transformation process are influenced by the law.

It is important to emphasise from the outset that the law not only constrains business activity (e.g. by establishing minimum standards of health and safety at work which are enforceable by law), but it also assists it (e.g. by providing a means by which a business unit can have an independent existence from its members), and in doing so

Table 6.1 Law and the business organisation

Business activity	Examples of legal influences
Establishing the organisation	Company laws; partnerships; business names
Acquiring resources	Planning laws, property laws, contract, agency
Business operations	Employment laws, health and safety laws, contract, agency
Selling output for consumption	Consumer laws, contract, agency

helps an enterprise to achieve its commercial and other objectives. In short, the legal environment within which businesses operate is an enabling as well as a regulatory environment and one which provides a considerable degree of certainty and stability to the conduct of business both within and between democratic states.

Given the extensive influence of the law on business organisations, it is clearly impossible to examine all aspects of the legal context within which firms function. Accordingly, in the analysis below attention is focused primarily on contract law, agency, and some of the more important statutes enacted to protect the interests of the consumer, since these are areas fundamental to business operations. Laws relating to the establishment of an enterprise and to the operation of markets are discussed in Chapters 7 and 14 respectively.

CONTRACT LAW: THE ESSENTIALS

All businesses enter into contracts, whether with suppliers or employees or financiers or customers, and these contracts will be important – and possibly crucial – to the firm's operations. Such contracts are essentially agreements (oral or written) between two or more persons which are legally enforceable, providing they comprise a number of essential elements. These elements are: offer, acceptance, consideration, intention to create legal relations and capacity.

Offer

An offer is a declaration by which the offeror intends to be legally bound by the terms stated in the offer if it is accepted by the offeree (e.g. to supply component parts at a particular price within a specified time period). This declaration may be made orally or in writing or by conduct between the parties and must be clear and unambiguous. Furthermore it should not be confused with an 'invitation to treat', which is essentially an invitation to make an offer, as is generally the case with advertisements, tenders, auctions and goods on display.

Termination of an offer can happen in several ways. Clearly an offer is ended when it is accepted but, that apart, an offer may be revoked at any time up to acceptance. It is of no consequence, legally, that an offer may be kept open for a certain time. It is only when some consideration is paid for 'buying the option' that the time factor is important and this 'buying the option' would generally be a separate contract in any case. If an offer is for a certain length of time, then later acceptance is ineffective, and even where there is no specified time limit, the courts will imply a reasonable time. Thus, in *Ramsgate Victoria Hotel* v *Montefiore* (1866), shares in the hotel were offered for sale. After several months the offer was 'accepted' but the court held that too much time had passed, bearing in mind that the purpose of the shares offer was to raise money.

Another way for an offer to come to an end is by the failure of a condition. Although a genuine offer is always held to be firm and certain, sometimes it may be conditional and not absolute. Thus, should A wish to buy a model car from B, B may agree but impose conditions on the deal, such as stating that A must collect at a specific time on a certain day at a particular place and must pay in cash. This is known as a 'condition precedent' and failure to complete the conditions will nullify the agreement. There is another type of condition, called a 'condition subsequent' where there is a perfectly good contract which runs until something happens. For instance, a garage may have a good contract with an oil company to buy petrol at £x per 1,000 litres until the price of oil at Rotterdam reaches $x per barrel. It is only when oil reaches the stipulated price that the contract ends.

Acceptance

Just as an offer must be firm and certain, the acceptance of an offer by the person(s) to whom it was made must be unequivocal and must not contain any alterations or additions. Accordingly any attempt to alter the terms of an offer is regarded as a counter-offer and thus a rejection of the original offer, leaving the original offeror free to accept or decline as he or she chooses.

Whilst acceptance of an offer normally occurs either in writing or verbally, it may also be implied by conduct. In the case of *Brogden* v *Metropolitan Railways* Co. (1877) Mr Brogden had supplied the company for many years without formalities. It was then decided to regularise the position and a draft agreement was sent to him. He inserted a new term, marked the draft 'approved' and returned it to the company where it was placed in a drawer and forgotten about, although both parties traded with each other on the terms of the draft for more than two years. Following a dispute, Mr Brogden claimed there was no contract. The House of Lords decided differently saying that a contract had been created by conduct.

Inferring the acceptance of an offer by conduct is quite different from assuming that silence on the part of the offeree constitutes acceptance: silence cannot be construed as an acceptance. Equally, whilst the offeror may prescribe the method of acceptance (although this is regarded as permissive rather than directory), the offeree may not prescribe a method by which he or she will make acceptance. For instance, an offer may be made by telex, thus implying that a fast response is required; therefore a reply accepting the offer which is sent by second-class mail may well be treated as nugatory.

There are some rules about acceptance which are important. Postal acceptance, for example, is a good method of communication and one which is universally used by businesses; but to be valid for contractual purposes a communication must be properly addressed and stamped and then placed into the hands of the duly authorised person (i.e. the post box or over the counter). An acceptance sent to a home address may be nullified if there has been no indication that this is acceptable. Similarly, acceptance of the offer must be effectively received by the offeror where modern, instantaneous methods of communication are used. Thus if a telephone call is muffled by extraneous sound, then the acceptance must be repeated so that the offeror hears it clearly.

Consideration

Together, offer and acceptance constitute the basis of an 'agreement' or meeting of minds, provided the parties are clear as to what they are agreeing about (i.e. a consensus *ad idem* exists). Central to this agreement will be a 'consideration' which has been defined as some right, interest, profit or benefit accruing to one party or some forbearance, detriment, loss or responsibility given, suffered or undertaken by the other. In commercial contracts, the consideration normally takes the form of a cash payment in return for the goods or services provided (i.e. the 'price' in a contract of sale). In contracts involving barter, however, which are sometimes used in international trade, goods are often exchanged for goods or for some other form of non-pecuniary consideration (e.g. information or advice).

Intention to create legal relations

Not every agreement is intended to create a legally binding relationship. For example, most domestic agreements – such as the division of household chores – would not constitute a contract recognised in law. In commercial agreements, however, it is generally accepted that both parties intend to make a legally binding contract and therefore it is unnecessary to include terms to this effect. Should such a presumption be challenged, the burden of proof rests with the person who disputes the presumption.

Capacity

A contract may be valid, voidable or void and one of the factors which determines this is the contractual capacity of the respective parties to the agreement. Normally speaking, an adult may make a contract with another adult which, if entered into freely and without any defects, and which is not contrary to public policy, is binding upon them both (i.e. valid). However, the law provides protection for certain categories of persons deemed not to have full contractual capacity (e.g. minors, drunks and the mentally disordered); hence the practice by firms of excluding people under the age of 18 from offers of goods to be supplied on credit.

Concentrating on minors – those below voting age – the law prescribes that they can only be bound by contracts for 'necessaries' (e.g. food, clothing, lodging) and contracts of employment that are advantageous or beneficial, as in the case of a job which contains an element of training or education. In most other instances, contracts with minors are void or voidable and as such will either be unenforceable or capable of being repudiated by the minor.

In the case of business, legal capacity depends on the firm's legal status. Unincorporated bodies (e.g. sole traders, partnerships) do not have a distinct legal personality and hence the party to the agreement is liable for their part of the bargain. Limited companies, by contrast, have a separate legal identity from their members and hence contractual capacity rests with the company, within the limits laid down in the objects clause of its Memorandum of Association (see Chapter 7).

Other factors

To be enforceable at law a contract must be legal (i.e. not forbidden by law or contrary to public policy). Similarly, the agreement must have been reached voluntarily and result in a genuine meeting of minds. Consequently, contracts involving mistakes of fact, misrepresentation of the facts, or undue influence or duress may be void or voidable, depending on the circumstances. In insurance contracts, for instance, the insured is required to disclose all material facts to the insurer (e.g. health record, driving record), otherwise a policy may be invalidated. In this context a 'material fact' is one which would affect the mind of a prudent insurer, even though the materiality may not be appreciated by the insured.

AGENCY

As business activity has become more specialised and complex, firms have increasingly turned to outside individuals to carry out specialist functions such as freight forwarding, overseas representation, insurance broking and commercial letting. These individuals (known as agents) are authorised by the individual or organisation hiring them (known as the principal) to act on their behalf, thus creating an agency relationship. As in other areas of commercial activity, special rules of law have evolved to regulate the behaviour of the parties involved in such a relationship.

In essence, the function of an agent is to act on behalf of a principal so as to effect a contract between the principal and a third party. The agent may be a 'servant' of the principal (i.e. under their control as in the case of a sales representative) or an 'independent contractor' (i.e. their own master as in the case of an estate agent) and will be operating with the consent of the principal whether by contract or implication. Having established a contractual relationship between the principal and the third party, the agent generally leaves the picture and usually has no rights and duties under the contract thus made.

With regard to an agent's specific obligations under an agency agreement, these are normally expressly stated under the terms of the agreement, although some may also be implied. The common law of agency prescribes, however, that agents:

- *Obey the lawful instruction of the principal*, otherwise they may be in breach of contract.
- *Exercise due care and skill*, in order to produce a deal which is to the principal's best advantage.
- *Act personally*, rather than delegate, unless expressly or implicitly authorised to do so.
- *Act in good faith*, thus avoiding conflicts of interest or undisclosed profits and bribes.
- *Keep proper accounts*, which separate the principal's funds from those which belong personally to the agent.

Moreover, in so far as an agent is acting under the principal's authority, the principal is bound to the third party only by acts which are within the agent's authority to make. Consequently *ultra vires* acts only affect the principal if he or she adopts them by ratification and the agent may be liable for the breach of the implied warranty of authority to the third party.

LAW AND THE CONSUMER

Economic theory tends to suggest that laws to protect the consumer are unnecessary. If individuals are behaving rationally when consuming goods and services, they would arrange their consumption to maximise their satisfaction (or 'utility') in the words of the economist. Products which because of poor quality or some other factor reduced a consumer's utility would be rejected in favour of those which proved a better alternative and this would act as an incentive to producers (and retailers) to provide the best products. In effect, market forces would ensure that the interest of the consumer was safeguarded as suppliers in a competitive market arranged their production to meet the needs and wants of rational consumers.

The 'ideal' view of how markets work is not always borne out in practice. Apart from the fact that consumers do not always act rationally, they often do not have access to information which might influence their choice of products; in some cases they do not even have a choice of products (e.g. where a monopoly exists). Also, given the relative resources of producers and consumers, the balance of power in the trading relationship tends to favour producers who can influence consumer choices using a range of persuasive techniques, including advertising.

Taken together, these and other factors call into question the assumption that the consumer is 'sovereign' and hence the extent to which individuals have inherent protection in the marketplace from powerful (and, in some cases, unscrupulous) suppliers. It is in this context that the law is seen to be an important counterbalance in a contractual relationship where the consumer is, or may be, at a disadvantage, and this can be said to provide the basis of legal intervention in this area.

Existing laws to protect consumers are both civil and criminal and the relevant rights, duties and liabilities have been created or imposed by common law (especially contract and tort) or by statute. Significantly, as the examples below illustrate, a large element of current consumer law has resulted from statutory intervention, much of it in the last twenty-five years. These laws – covering areas as diverse as trade descriptions, the sale of goods and services, and consumer credit and product liability – indicate a growing willingness on the part of governments to respond to the complaints of consumers and their representative organisations and to use legislation to regulate the relationship between business organisations and their customers. As suggested elsewhere, such intervention could reasonably be construed as a political response to some of the socially unacceptable characteristics of a capitalist economy.[1]

Trade Descriptions Act 1968

The main aim of the Trade Descriptions Act is to protect consumers from traders who deliberately misdescribe goods or give a false description of services in the process of trade. Under the Act – which imposes an obligation on local authorities to enforce its provisions – a trader can be convicted of a criminal offence in three main areas:

1 Making a false trade description of goods.
2 Making a false statement of price.
3 Making a false trade description of services.

The penalty for such offences can be a fine on summary conviction and/or imprisonment following conviction on indictment.

With regard to goods, the Act applies both to goods which have been sold and those which are offered for sale and to which a false description, or one which is misleading to a material degree, has been applied. It can also apply to advertisements which are 'economical with the truth', such as claims regarding a second-hand car for sale by a local dealer. Similarly, with services it is an offence to make false or misleading statements as to the services offered to consumers and it is possible for an offence to be committed even if the intention to mislead is not deliberate.

In the case of price, the Act outlaws certain false or misleading indications as to the price of goods, such as claims that prices have been reduced from previously higher levels. For this claim to be within the law, a trader needs to show that the goods have been on sale at the higher price for a period of 28 consecutive days during the preceding six months. If not, this must be made quite clear to the consumer when a price reduction is indicated.

The Consumer Credit Act 1974

The Consumer Credit Act, which became fully operational in May 1985, controls transactions between the credit industry and private individuals (including sole traders and business partnerships) up to a limit of £15,000. Under the legislation consumer credit agreement is defined as a personal credit providing the debtor with credit up to the accepted limit. This credit may be in the form of a cash loan or some other type of financial accommodation (e.g. through the use of a credit card). The Act also covers hire purchase agreements (i.e. a contract of hire which gives the hirer the option to purchase the goods), conditional sale agreements for the sale of goods or land, and credit sale agreements, where the property passes to the buyer when the sale is effected.

The main aim of this consumer protection measure is to safeguard the public from trading malpractices where some form of credit is involved. To this end the Act provides, amongst other things, for a system of licensing controlled by the Director General of Fair Trading (see Chapter 14) who must be satisfied that the person seeking a licence is a fit person and the name under which he or she intends to be licensed is neither misleading nor undesirable. Providing credit or acting as a credit broker without a licence is a criminal offence, as is supplying a minor with any document inviting them to borrow money or obtain goods on credit, unless there are mitigating circumstances.

A further protection for the consumer comes from the requirements that the debtor be made fully aware of the nature and cost of the agreement and his or her rights and liabilities under it. The Act stipulates that prior to the contract being made the debtor must be supplied with certain information, including the full price of the credit agreement (i.e. the cost of the credit plus the capital sum), the annual rate of the total charge for credit expressed as a percentage (i.e. the annual percentage rate), and the amounts of payments due and to whom they are payable. In addition, the debtor must be informed of all the other terms of the agreement and of their right to cancel if this is applicable. In the case of the latter, this applies to credit agreements drawn up off business premises and is designed to protect individuals from high-pressure doorstep sellers who offer credit as an incentive to purchase.

Sale of Goods Act 1979

Under both the Fair Trading Act 1973 and the Unfair Contract Terms Act 1977 consumers are essentially seen as individuals who purchase goods or services for their own personal use from other individuals or organisations selling them in the course of business. A computer sold, for example, to a student is a consumer sale, whilst the same machine sold to a secretarial agency is not, since it has been acquired for business purposes. This legal definition of a consumer is important in the context of laws designed specifically to provide consumer protection, as in the case of the Sale of Goods Act which governs those agreements whereby a seller agrees to transfer ownership in goods to a consumer in return for a monetary consideration, known as the 'price'. Where such an agreement or contract is deemed to exist the legislation provides consumers with rights in respect of items which are faulty or which do not correspond with the description given to them, by identifying a number of implied conditions to the sale. In the case of contracts for the supply of services (e.g. repair work) or which involve an exchange of goods (i.e. involving no monetary exchange), almost identical rights are provided under the Supply of Goods and Services Act 1982.

The three main implied conditions of the 1979 Act are relatively well known. Under section 13, goods which are sold by description must match the description given to them and it is of no significance that the goods are selected by the purchaser. This description may be on the article itself or on the packaging or provided in some other way, and will include the price and possibly other information (e.g. washing instructions) which the consumer believes to be true. A shirt described as 100 per cent cotton, for instance, must be just that, otherwise it fails to match the description given to it and the consumer is entitled to a return of the price for breach of an implied condition of the contract.

The second condition relates to the quality of the goods provided. Under section 14 of the Act goods have to be of 'merchantable quality', except where any defects are drawn specifically to the attention of the purchaser before the contract is made or where the buyer has examined the goods before contracting and the examination ought to have revealed such defects. Precisely what constitutes 'merchantable quality' is a matter of some controversy, but the general expectation is that a product should be fit for the purpose or purposes for which it is normally bought, bearing in mind questions of age, price, and any other relevant factors (e.g. brand name). A new top-of-the-range car should have no significant defects on purchase, whereas a high-mileage second-hand car sold for a few hundred pounds could not reasonably evoke such expectations in the mind of the consumer. Thus, whilst the implied condition of merchantability applies to sale goods and second-hand goods as well as to full-price purchases of new goods, it needs to be judged in light of the contract description and all the circumstances of a particular case, including the consumer's expectations.

The third implied condition also derives from section 14 of the legislation, namely that goods are fit for a particular purpose i.e. capable of performing the tasks indicated by the seller. Accordingly, if the seller, on request from the purchaser, confirms that goods are suitable for a particular purpose and this proves not to be the case, this would represent a breach of section 14(3). Equally, if the product is unsuitable for its normal purposes, then section 14(2) would also be breached and the consumer would be entitled on a refund of the price.

It is worth noting that 'merchantability' and 'fitness for a purpose' are closely related and that a breach of one will often include a breach of the other. By the same token, failure in a claim for a breach of section 14(2) is likely to mean that a claim for a breach of section 14(3) will also fail. Moreover, if, on request, a seller disclaims any knowledge of a product's suitability for a particular purpose and the consumer is willing to take a chance, any subsequent unsuitability cannot be regarded as a breach of section 14(3). The same applies if the buyer's reliance on the skill or judgement of the seller is deemed 'unreasonable'.

Whereas in business contracts the implied terms in sections 13 to 15 of the 1979 Act can be excluded – subject to the test of 'reasonableness' – in consumer contracts they cannot. Clauses or statements which purport to limit or exclude liability are void under the Unfair Contract Terms Act 1977 and it is a criminal offence to attempt to exclude these implied conditions (e.g. a 'no money refunded' notice), even though this still occurs on a relatively frequent basis. Thus, where a reference is made on a product or its container or in a related document to a consumer's rights under sections 13 to 15, there must be a clear and accessible notice informing consumers that their statutory rights are not affected when returning an item deemed unsatisfactory. The aim is to ensure that buyers are made fully aware of their legal rights and are not taken advantage of by unscrupulous traders who seek to deny them the protection afforded by the law.

As a final comment, it is important to note that where services are concerned, equivalent rights are afforded consumers under the Supply of Goods and Services Act 1982. Under section 13 of the Act, moreover, there is an implied condition that a supplier acting in the course of business must carry out the service with reasonable care and skill and within a reasonable time, where a specific deadline is not stated in the contract. Reasonable care and skill tends to be seen as that which might be expected of an ordinary competent person performing the particular task, though this will, of course, depend on the particular circumstances of the case and the nature of the trade or profession. As in the case of the Sale of Goods Act, any attempt to deprive the consumer of any of the implied conditions represents a breach of the Unfair Contract Terms Act 1977 and may constitute a criminal offence, usually resulting in a fine on conviction.

The Consumer Protection Act 1987

The Consumer Protection Act 1987 came into force in March 1988 as a result of the government's obligation to implement EC directive 85/374 which concerned product liability. In essence the Act provides for a remedy in damages for anyone who suffers personal injury or damage to property as a result of a defective product by imposing a 'strict' liability on the producers of defective goods (including substances, growing crops, ships, aircraft and vehicles). Naturally, the onus is on the plaintiff to prove that any loss was caused by the claimed defect and a claim can be made by anyone, whether damage to property, personal injury or death has occurred. In the case of the latter, for example, a relative or friend could pursue an action and, if American experience is anything to go by, could be awarded very substantial damages if liability can be proven. As far as property is concerned, damage must be to private rather than commercial goods and property and must exceed £275 for claims to be considered.

Whilst the Act is intended to place liability on the producers of defective goods, this liability also extends to anyone putting a name or distinguishing mark on a product which holds that person out as being the producer (e.g. own brand labels). Similarly, importers of products from outside the EC are also liable for any defects in imported goods, as may be firms involved in supplying components or parts of the process of manufacture of a product. To prevent a firm escaping its liability by a supplier claiming it is unable to identify its own suppliers, the legislation provides a remedy: any supplier unable or unwilling to identify the importing firm or previous supplier becomes liable itself for damages under the Act.

Firms seeking to avoid liability for any claim have a number of defences under section 4 of the Act. Specifically these are:

- That the defendant did not supply the product in question.
- That the product was not manufactured or supplied in the course of business (e.g. goods sold in a school bazaar).
- That the defect did not exist at the time the product was distributed.
- That where a product has a number of components, the defect is a defect of the finished product or due to compliance with any instructions issued by the manufacturer of the finished product.
- That the defect is attributable to the requirement to comply with existing laws.
- That the state of scientific and technical knowledge at the time the product was supplied was not sufficiently advanced for the defect to be recognised.

Of these, the last – the so-called development risks defence – is the most contentious, given that it applies largely to products such as new drugs and new technology where the implications of their usage may not be apparent for some years. As recent cases have shown, manufacturers faced with damages from claimants who appear to have suffered from the use of certain products often decide to settle out of court without accepting liability for their actions.

CODES OF PRACTICE

Alongside the protection provided by the law, consumers may be afforded a further measure of security when the organisation they are dealing with belongs to a trade association which is operating under a code of practice (e.g. the Association of British Travel Agents). In essence, codes of practice represent an attempt by trade associations to impose a measure of self-discipline on the behaviour of their members by establishing the standards of service customers should expect to receive and by encouraging acceptable business practices. In addition, such codes of conduct invariably identify how customer complaints should be handled and many offer low-cost or no-cost arbitration schemes to help settle disputes outside the more formal legal process.

Whilst codes of practice do not in themselves have the force of law, they are normally seen as a useful mechanism for regulating the relationship between business organisations and their customers and accordingly they have the support of the Office of Fair Trading which often advises trade associations on their content. Businesses, too, usually find them useful, particularly if through the establishment of a system of self-regulation they are able to avoid the introduction of restrictions imposed by the law.

SYNOPSIS

All business activities, from the establishment of the organisation through to the sale of the product to the customer, are influenced by the law. This legal environment within which businesses exist and operate evolves over time and is a key influence on firms of all sizes and in all sectors, as illustrated by an examination of some of the main laws governing the relationship between a business and its customers. The majority of consumer laws are of relatively recent origin and derive from the attempts by successive governments to provide individuals with a measure of protection against a minority of firms which behave in ways deemed to be unacceptable. Concomitantly, they also provide reputable organisations with a framework within which to carry out their business and, as such, act as an incentive to entrepreneurial activity in market-based economies.

CASE STUDY: LEGAL ASPECTS OF BANKING

Many aspects of the relationship between individuals and business organisations are conditioned by the law. This can be demonstrated by an examination of an everyday activity – banking. Rather than concentrating on a specific example, the following analysis discusses the essentials of the contractual relationship between one form of business organisation (a bank) and its customers, and illustrates that both parties to the agreement have both rights and duties imposed by law.

Banking

The bank–customer relationship is essentially a contractual one with the bank being the debtor and the customer the creditor, at least until the customer acquires a loan facility or overdraft. The relationship is not *per se* a fiduciary one (*Foley* v *Hill* (1848)).

Although all the basic elements of a valid contract must be present, the terms are regarded slightly differently with the distinction between condition and warranty being less prominent. However, the relationship does have some implied terms and conditions unique to banking. For example, the bank is under a duty of secrecy as far as a customer's account is concerned (*Joachimson* v *Swiss Bank Corporation* (1921)) although the duty has been modified by *Tournier* v *National Provincial and Union Bank of England Ltd* (1924). Disclosure is now justified in the following circumstances:

- Where required by law.
- Where there is a public duty.
- Where the interests of the bank require it.
- Where the customer expressly or impliedly permits it.

Occasionally, the court will order a bank to disclose certain information about a customer's account but may restrict the use of the information so obtained.

Most banks have their own standard form contracts which, not unnaturally, contain the terms and conditions which the particular bank finds most acceptable and, in the main, these forms are perfectly proper and create no problems either for the bank or the potential customer. Although it usually does not have any great practical significance *when* the contractual relationship begins, it could be important if the bank collects a cheque on behalf of a potential customer. The protection afforded to banks by section 4 of the Cheques Act 1957 cannot be invoked unless the bank collects on behalf of a customer, and if the relationship has not yet been established, the offeror is not yet a customer. Section 4 provides that there is no liability to a true owner of a cheque where the customer has defective title or no title just because the bank has received payment of the cheque. The bank must not act negligently but, because a cheque is not endorsed or is endorsed irregularly that is not evidence of negligence. In all other cases, however, the bank must show that it took reasonable care over the transaction. Reasonable care is the standard to be expected of an ordinary, competent bank, the criterion being based on current banking practice.

Although in strict law, references are not essential – the bank may already have prior knowledge of the customer, either personally, or through a person the bank considers to be of good standing – the bank must have acted as any reasonable bank would act. Sometimes, good banking practice and the law may be in direct conflict. The Sex Discrimination Act 1975, as amended, makes it unlawful to discriminate against a person solely on the ground of gender; thus questions put to a potential customer who is female regarding marital status and the employment of a spouse should not be asked unless similar questions are asked of male customers. Case law suggests that failure to ask such pertinent questions of this nature where the customer is a married woman might be regarded as not acting reasonably. Many banks appear to evade the problem by not asking such questions of any potential customer; how far the courts would agree that this is reasonable is uncertain.

Any loan facility or overdraft for less than £15,000 falls under the Consumer Credit Act 1974 although the Banking Act 1979, s. 38(1) obliges the Director of Fair Trading to exempt banks from all the paperwork required at least as far as overdrafts are concerned. Periodic statements of account required by s. 78 (4) may be dispensed with where there is more than one party to an overdraft to the extent that all such parties need not receive such account (s. 185).

Guarantees

Often, when a customer requires a loan facility, even for a fairly short time, a bank may require some form of security for it. Should the customer not possess such security then a guarantor may be required. This means that should the customer default on the loan the guarantor will have to pay the money: if the guarantor has pledged property as the security they stand to lose it. A guarantee must be evidenced by some form of memorandum in writing and is unenforceable if it is not. If a bank is not specifically requested for information about the way in which the borrower's account has been run it need not volunteer the information but, if it does volunteer information, it must be full and frank. Any questions the guarantor asks must be answered clearly and with certainty. The guarantor is entitled to receive information about the indebtedness at any time but is not entitled to inspect, or have details of, the customer's account unless, of course, the customer has agreed to this.

Rights and duties of the bank

A bank has the right to charge its customers reasonable fees for the services it provides. It may charge interest on any loans and, where an account has been permitted an overdraft facility, it may make a repayment on demand call. It is also entitled to be indemnified by a customer for all expenses and liabilities incurred by acting on the customer's behalf. A bank may not exercise a lien over articles left in a safety deposit box for any monies owed the bank (a lien is a right to keep possession of someone else's property in lieu of payment; once payment is made the lien is at an end). A bank also has the right to do with as it pleases any and all monies deposited by a customer just as long as cheques are honoured: such cheques, of course, must be valid ones and the bank has the further right to expect a customer to exercise reasonable care in drawing cheques. One right which banks have of which many customers are apparently unaware, is the right to 'set off' accounts. This means that where a customer has more than one account, the bank is permitted and entitled, in the absence of any contrary instruction by the customer, to make a transfer of money from an account in credit to cover any shortfall in an account in debit.

A bank is bound to abide by any express, lawful instruction of a customer, to pay a standing order, for instance. This duty does not arise if there are insufficient funds to meet it. A bank also has the duty to honour properly drawn cheques (on an account in credit or with overdraft facilities); a properly drawn cheque is one which is not 'stale' (most banks regard cheques which have been in circulation for 6 months or longer as being stale) or overdue. An overdue cheque is one which has been in circulation for an unreasonable length of time. Unreasonable will be interpreted according to the facts and circumstances in each case. If a customer has countermanded ('stopped') a cheque, then a bank must not pay out on it but the countermanding must be done in the proper manner in writing and is not effective unless and until it comes to the attention of the bank (*Curtice* v *London City and Midland Bank Ltd* (1908)). A countermand cannot be made for a cheque made against a cheque guarantee card.

A bank may not make payments from an account where there is a legal bar such as an injunction or a garnishee order. Furthermore if a customer dies or becomes bankrupt or becomes incapable of handling his or her own affairs a bank may not make payments: the bank must know of these things. This is because, in each of the three instances, another party acquires the right to run the account: the Trustee in bankruptcy, the executors/administrators of an estate, or an authorised person for the mentally incapacitated customer. As mentioned earlier, a bank may not disclose information about a customer's account except in certain, defined situations but all banks have a duty to inform the appropriate authorities where it is suspected that the monies in an account result from drugs or terrorist activities. Clearly, this may prove to be a rather delicate situation. The Drugs Trafficking Offences Act 1986 requires a bank to inspect the deposits into an account and make the necessary enquiries if large, regular and unexplained amounts are paid in – the Act makes it a criminal offence to hold or invest such monies.

Banks must fulfil the normal banking requirements of collecting cheques and other instruments and crediting them to the customer's account whilst exercising proper skill and care. The duty of skill and care may, of course, go beyond the mere running of an account. If a bank acts as an investment adviser, for example, the duty arises (*Woods* v *Martins Bank Ltd* (1959)). Finally, a bank has the right to close an account, even one kept in credit, if it so desires. This sometimes happens when, for instance, the account is used for just one transaction per month. The bank must give the account holder reasonable notice of the intention to close so that the customer may make alternative arrangements. Where the account is a loan account, a breach of the terms of the agreement must be made before the account may be closed. There is no difficulty about closing a debit account since an overdraft is normally payable on demand.

Rights and duties of a customer

Although a bank must keep accurate records of the transactions on the account of a customer, customers do not have a duty to check the statements which are issued and even if the customer does check them that does not prevent a later claim of inaccuracy (*Tai Hing Cotton Mill Ltd* v *Liu Chong Hing Bank Ltd* (1985)) (a Privy Council decision). Naturally, given all the duties of the bank as far as the running of the account is concerned, the customer is under certain duties: to ensure that cheques are properly drawn; to countermand in the proper manner; to keep sufficient funds in the account to meet any standing orders and direct debits as well as any issued cheques.

Over-debit and over-credit of an account

If a bank over-debits an account the money must be reimbursed as soon as the error is found and, if cheques have been dishonoured as a result of the over-debit, the bank must compensate the customer for the injury to credit and reputation – there is no reason why the customer should not also require the bank to write to each recipient of an unpaid cheque stating the position. Such over-debiting may, on occasion, lead to the issuance of a writ for defamation.

Where an account has been over-credited, the bank may not be able to recoup the excess payment if the customer can satisfy three conditions (*United Overseas Bank* v *Jiwani* (1979)):

1 The state of the account must have been misrepresented to the customer by the bank.
2 The customer must have been misled by the misrepresentation (i.e. believed it).
3 The customer must have relied on the misrepresentation to such an extent, changing his or her position in such a way, that it would be inequitable to order him or her to repay.

NOTES AND REFERENCES

1 Beardshaw, J. and Palfreman, D., *The Organisation in its Environment*, 4th edition, Pitman, 1990, p 308.

REVIEW AND DISCUSSION QUESTIONS

1 Why are laws to protect the consumer felt to be necessary? What other means do consumers have of protecting their interest in the marketplace?

2 To what extent does the supranational structure of European Community law infringe the principle of the supremacy of Parliament?

3 Do you think that tobacco companies should be made retrospectively liable for the safety of their product? Justify your answer.

4 Examine the case for and against increased government control over business practices.

ASSIGNMENTS

1 You are a trading standards officer in a local authority trading standards department. You have been asked to talk to a group of school sixth-form students on the Sale of Goods Act 1979. Prepare suitable overhead transparencies outlining the following:
   (a) The main provisions of the 1979 Act.
   (b) The customer's rights in the event of a breach of the implied conditions.
   (c) The sources of help and advice available to an individual with a consumer problem.

2 Imagine you work for a Citizens Advice Bureau. A large part of your work involves offering advice to individuals with consumer problems. Design a simple leaflet indicating some of the principal pieces of legislation in the field of consumer protection and their main provisions. Your leaflet should also give guidance as to further specialist sources of help and advice.

FURTHER READING

Atiyah, P., *The Sale of Goods*, 8th edition, Pitman, 1990.

Bradgate, J. R. and Savage, N., *Commercial Law*, Butterworths, 1991.

Davies, F. R., *Contract: Concise college texts*, 6th edition, Sweet & Maxwell, 1991.

PART 3

Firms

CHAPTER 7

Legal structures

Ian Worthington

Market-based economies comprise a rich diversity of business organisations, ranging from the very simple enterprise owned and operated by one person, to the huge multinational corporation with production and distribution facilities spread across the globe. Whatever the nature of these organisations or their scale of operation, their existence is invariably subject to legal definition and this will have consequences for the functioning of the organisation. Viewing the business as a legal structure provides an insight into some of the important influences on business operations in both the private and public sectors.

OBJECTIVES

1 To examine the legal structure of UK business organisations in both the private and public sectors.
2 To compare UK business organisations with those in other parts of Europe.
3 To consider the implications of a firm's legal structure for its operations.
4 To discuss franchising, licensing and joint ventures.

INTRODUCTION

Business organisations can be classified in a variety of ways, including:

- size (e.g. small, medium, large);
- type of industry (e.g. primary, secondary, tertiary);
- sector (e.g. private sector, public sector); and
- legal status (e.g. sole trader, partnership, and so on).

These classifications help to distinguish one type of organisation from another and to focus attention on the implications of such differences for an individual enterprise. In the discussion below, business organisations are examined as legal structures and the consequences of variations in legal status are discussed in some detail. Subsequent chapters in this section investigate alternative structural perspectives in order to highlight how these too have an important bearing on the environment in which businesses operate.

PRIVATE SECTOR ORGANISATIONS

The sole trader

Many individuals aspire to owning and running their own business – being their own boss, making their own decisions. For those who decide to turn their dream into a reality, becoming a sole trader (or sole proprietor) offers the simplest and easiest method of trading.

As the name suggests, a sole trader is a business owned by one individual who is self-employed and who may, in some cases, employ other people either on a full-time or part-time basis. Normally using personal funds to start the business, the sole trader decides on the type of goods or services to be produced, where the business is to be located, what capital is required, what staff (if any) to employ, what the target market should be and a host of other aspects concerned with the establishment and running of the enterprise. Where the business proves a success, all profits accrue to the owner and it is common for sole traders to reinvest a considerable proportion of these in the business and/or use them to reduce past borrowings. Should losses occur, these too are the responsibility of the sole trader who has unlimited personal liability for the debts of the business.

Despite this substantial disadvantage, sole proprietorship tends to be the most popular form of business organisation numerically. In the United Kingdom, for example, it is estimated that about 80 per cent of all businesses are sole traders and in some sectors – notably personal services, retailing, building – they tend to be the dominant form of business enterprise. Part of the reason for this numerical dominance is the relative ease with which an individual can establish a business of this type. Apart from minor restrictions concerning the use of a business name – if the name of the proprietor is not used – few other legal formalities are required to set up the enterprise, other than the need to register for Value Added Tax if turnover exceeds a certain sum (£45,000 in 1993) and/or to fulfil any special requirements laid down by the local authority prior to trading (e.g. some businesses require licences). Once established, of course, the sole trader, like other forms of business, will be subject to a variety of legal requirements (e.g. contract law, consumer law, employment law) – though not the requirement to file information about the business in a public place. For some, this ability to keep the affairs of the enterprise away from public scrutiny provides a further incentive to establishing this form of business organisation – some of which may operate wholly or partly in the 'black economy' (i.e. beyond the gaze of the tax authorities).

A further impetus towards sole ownership comes from the ability of the individual to exercise a considerable degree of control over their own destiny. Business decisions – including the day-to-day operations of the enterprise as well as long-term plans – are in the hands of the owner and many individuals evidently relish the risks and potential rewards associated with entrepreneurial activity, preferring these to the relative 'safety' of employment in another organisation. For others less fortunate, the 'push' of unemployment rather than the 'pull' of the marketplace tends to be more of a deciding factor and one which clearly accounts for some of the growth in the number of small businesses in the United Kingdom in the 1980s.

Ambitions and commitment alone, however, are not necessarily sufficient to guarantee the survival and success of the enterprise and the high mortality rate amongst businesses of this kind, particularly during a recession, is well known and well documented. Part of the problem may stem from developments largely outside the control of the enterprise – including bad debts, increased competition, higher interest rates, falling demand – and factors such as these affect businesses of all types and all sizes, not just sole traders. Other difficulties, such as lack of funds for expansion, poor marketing, lack of research of the marketplace and insufficient management skills are to some extent self-induced and emanate, at least in part, from the decision to become a sole proprietor rather than some other form of business organisation. Where such constraints exist, the sole trader may be tempted to look to others to share the burdens and the risks by establishing a partnership or co-operative or limited company or by seeking a different approach to the business venture, such as through 'franchising'. These alternative forms of business organisation are discussed in detail below.

The partnership

The Partnership Act 1890 defines a partnership as 'the relation which subsists between persons carrying on a business in common with a view to profit'. Like the sole trader, this form of business organisation does not have its own distinct legal personality and hence the owners – the partners – have unlimited personal liability both jointly and severally. This means that in the case of debts or bankruptcy of the partnership, each partner is liable in full for the whole debt and each in turn may be sued or their assets seized until the debt is satisfied. Alternatively, all the partners may be joined into the action to recover debts, unless by dint of the Limited Partnership Act 1907, a partner (or partners) has limited liability. Since it tends to be much easier to achieve the same ends by establishing a limited company, limited partnerships are not common; nor can all partners in a partnership have limited liability. Hence in the discussion below, attention is focused on the partnership as an unincorporated association, operating in a market where its liability is effectively unlimited.

In essence, a partnership comes into being when two or more people establish a business which they own, finance and run jointly for personal gain, irrespective of the degree of formality involved in the relationship. Such a business can range from a husband and wife running a local shop as joint owners, to a very large firm of accountants or solicitors, with in excess of a hundred partners in offices in various locations. Under the law, most partnerships are limited to 20 or less, but some types of business, particularly in the professions, may have a dispensation from this rule (Companies Act 1985, s. 716). This same Act requires businesses which are not exempt from the rule and which have more than 20 partners to register as a company.

Whilst it is not necessary for a partnership to have a formal written agreement, most partnerships tend to be formally enacted in a Deed of Partnership or Articles since this makes it much easier to reduce uncertainty and to ascertain intentions when there is a written document to consult. Where this is not done, the Partnership Act 1890 lays down a minimum code which governs the relationship between partners and which provides, amongst other things, for all partners to share equally in the capital and profits of the business and to contribute equally towards its losses.

In practice, of course, where a Deed or Articles exist, these will invariably reflect differences in the relative status and contribution of individual partners. Senior partners, for example, will often have contributed more financially to the partnership and not unnaturally will expect to receive a higher proportion of the profits. Other arrangements – including membership, action on dissolution of the partnership, management responsibilities and rights, and the basis for allocating salaries – will be outlined in the partnership agreement and as such will provide the legal framework within which the enterprise exists and its co-owners operate.

Unlike the sole trader, where management responsibilities devolve on a single individual, partnerships permit the sharing of responsibilities and tasks and it is common in a partnership for individuals to specialise to some degree in particular aspects of the organisation's work – as in the case of a legal or medical or veterinary practice. Added to this, the fact that more than one person is involved in the ownership of the business tends to increase the amount of finance available to the organisation, thus permitting expansion to take place without the owners losing control of the enterprise. These two factors alone tend to make a partnership an attractive proposition for some would-be entrepreneurs; whilst for others the rules of their professional body – which often prohibits its members from forming a company – effectively provide for the establishment of this type of organisation.

On the downside, the sharing of decisions and responsibilities may represent a problem, particularly where partners are unable to agree over the direction the partnership should take or the amount to be reinvested in the business; unless such matters are clearly specified in a formal agreement. A more intractable problem is the existence of unlimited personal liability – a factor which may inhibit some individuals from considering this form of organisation, particularly given that the actions of any one partner are invariably binding on the other members of the business. To overcome this problem, many individuals, especially in manufacturing and trading, look to the limited company as the type of organisation which can combine the benefits of joint-ownership and limited personal liability – a situation not necessarily always borne out in practice. It is to this type of business organisation which the discussion now turns.

Limited companies

In law a company is a corporate association having a legal identity in its own right (i.e. it is distinct from the people who own it, unlike in the case of a sole trader or partnership). This means that all property and other assets owned by the company belong to the company and not to its members (owners). By the same token, the personal assets of its members (the shareholders) do not normally belong to the business, such that in the event of insolvency an individual's liability is limited to the amount invested in the business, including any amount remaining unpaid on the shares for which they have subscribed.[1] One exception to this would be where a company's owners have given a personal guarantee to cover any loans they have obtained from a bank or other institution – a requirement for many small, private limited companies. Another occurs where a company is limited by guarantee rather than by shares, with its members' liability being limited to the amount they have undertaken to contribute to the assets in the event of the company being wound up. Companies of this type are normally non-profit making organisations – such as professional, research or trade associations – and are much less common than companies limited by shares. Hence in the discussion below, attention is focused on the latter as the dominant form of business organisation in the corporate sector of business.[2]

Companies are essentially business organisations consisting of two or more individuals who have agreed to embark on a business venture and who have decided to seek corporate status rather than to form a partnership. Such status could derive from an Act of Parliament or a Royal Charter, but is almost always nowadays achieved through 'registration', the terms of which are laid down in the various Companies' Acts. Under the legislation – the most recent of which date from 1985 and 1989 – individuals seeking to form a company are required to file numerous documents, including a Memorandum of Association and Articles of Association, with the Registrar of Companies. If satisfied, the Registrar will issue a Certificate of Incorporation, bringing the company into existence as a legal entity. As an alternative, the participants could buy a ready-formed company 'off-the-shelf', by approaching a company registration agent who specialises in company formations. In the United Kingdom, advertisements for ready-made companies appear regularly in magazines such as *Exchange and Mart* and *Dalton's Weekly*.

Under British Law a distinction is made between public and private companies. Public limited companies (PLCs) – not to be confused with public corporations which are state-owned businesses (see below) – are those limited companies which satisfy the conditions for being a 'PLC'. These conditions require the company to have:

- a minimum of two shareholders;
- at least two directors;
- a minimum (at present) of £50,000 of authorised and allotted share capital;
- the right to offer its shares (and debentures) for sale to the general public;
- a certificate from the Registrar of Companies verifying that the share capital requirements have been met; and
- a memorandum which states it is to be a public company.

A company which meets these conditions must include the title 'public limited company' or 'PLC' in its name and is required to make full accounts available for public inspection. Any company unable or unwilling to meet these conditions is therefore, in the eyes of the law, a 'private limited company', normally signified by the term 'Limited' or 'Ltd'.

Like the public limited company, the private company must have a minimum of two shareholders, but its shares cannot be offered to the public at large, although it can offer them to individuals through its business contacts. This restriction on the sale of shares, and hence on its ability to raise considerable sums of money on the open market, normally ensures that most private companies are either small or medium-sized, and are often family businesses operating in a relatively restricted market; although there are some notable exceptions to this general rule (e.g. Clarks Shoes, Virgin). In contrast, public companies – many of which began life as private companies prior to 'going public' – often have many thousands, even millions, of owners (shareholders) and normally operate on a national or international scale, producing products as diverse as computers, petro-chemicals, cars and banking services. Despite being outnumbered numerically by their private counterparts, public companies dwarf private companies in terms of their capital and other assets, and their collective influence on output, investment, employment and consumption in the economy is immense.

Both public and private companies act through their directors. These are individuals chosen by a company's shareholders to manage its affairs and to make the important decisions concerning the direction the company should take (e.g. investment, market development, mergers, and so on). The appointment and powers of directors are outlined in the Articles of Association (the 'internal rules' of the organisation) and so long as the directors do not exceed their powers, the shareholders do not normally have the right to intervene in the day-to-day management of the company. Where a director exceeds his or her authority or fails to indicate clearly that they are acting as an agent for the company, they become personally liable for any contracts they make. Equally directors become personally liable if they continue to trade when the company is insolvent and they may be dismissed by a court if it considers that an individual is unfit to be a director in view of their past record (Company Directors Disqualification Act 1985).

It is usual for a board of directors to have both a chairperson and a managing director, although many companies chose to appoint one person to both roles. The chairperson, who is elected by the other members of the board, is usually chosen because of their knowledge and experience of the business and their skill both internally in chairing board meetings and externally in representing the best interest of the organisation. As the public face of the company, the chairperson has an important role to play in establishing and maintaining a good public image and hence many large public companies like to appoint well-known public figures to this important position (e.g. ex-Cabinet ministers). In this case knowledge of the business is less important than the other attributes the individual might possess, most notably public visibility and familiarity, together with a network of contacts in government and in the business world.

The managing director, or chief executive, fulfils a pivotal role in the organisation, by forming the link between the board and the management team of senior executives. Central to this role is the need not only to interpret board decisions but to ensure that they are put into effect by establishing an appropriate structure of delegated responsibility and effective systems of reporting and control. This close contact with the day-to-day operations of the company places the appointed individual in a position of considerable authority and they will invariably be able to make important decisions without reference to the full board. This authority is enhanced where the managing director is also the person chairing the board of directors and/or is responsible for recommending individuals to serve as executive directors (i.e. those with functional responsibilities such as production, marketing, finance).

Like the managing director, most, if not all, executive directors will be full-time executives of the company, responsible for running a division or functional area within the framework laid down at board level. In contrast, other directors will have a non-executive role and are usually part-time appointees, chosen for a variety of reasons including their knowledge, skills, contacts, influence, independence or previous experience. Sometimes, a company might be required to appoint such a director at the wishes of a third party, such as a merchant bank which has agreed to fund a large capital injection and wishes to have representation on the board. In this case, the individual tends to act in an advisory capacity – particularly on matters of finance – and helps to provide the financing institution with a means of ensuring that any board decisions are in its interests.

Recent public concern about the considerable power wielded by a company's directors – as highlighted by the Maxwell case – has given rise to demands for greater accountability to the shareholders and culminated in the establishment of a committee of enquiry under the chairmanship of Sir Adrian Cadbury. In its report, published in May 1992, the Cadbury Committee called for a non-statutory code of practice which it wanted applied to all listed public companies. Amongst its recommendations – which were seen as a guide to best practice in corporate governance – the Committee called for:

1 A greater role for non-executive directors, the majority of whom should be free and independent of any business or financial connection with the company.
2 Regular board meetings to retain full and effective control over the company and to monitor the executive management.
3 A clearly accepted division of responsibilities at the head of the company to ensure that no individual has unfettered powers of decision – including a strong independent element on the board.
4 A restriction of three years on executive directors' service contracts without shareholders' approval.
5 Full disclosure of directors' total emoluments.
6 The establishment of an audit committee and a remuneration committee of the board, dominated by non-executives.
7 An undertaking from the directors in the annual report that the business is a going concern, with supporting assumptions or qualifications as necessary.

Whilst the Committee stopped short of suggesting legislation, it called for all public companies to abide by the code of practice and to provide an explanation for those areas of the code they had failed to comply with. Widespread non-compliance, it suggested, would probably give rise to legislation and external regulation, in order to deal with some of the underlying problems of the current system of corporate management which the report had identified.

Co-operatives

Consumer co-operative societies

Consumer societies are basically 'self-help' organisations which have their roots in the anti-capitalist sentiment which arose in mid-nineteenth-century Britain and which gave rise to a consumer co-operative movement dedicated to the provision of cheap, unadulterated food for its members and a share in its profits. Today this movement boasts a multibillion pound turnover, a membership numbered in millions and an empire which includes 3,000 food stores, numerous factories and farms, dairies, travel agencies, opticians, funeral parlours, a bank and an insurance business. Taken together, these activities ensure that the 'Co-op' remains a powerful force in British retailing in the late twentieth century.

Although the co-operative societies, like companies, are registered and incorporated bodies – in this case under the Industrial and Provident Societies Act – they are quite distinct trading organisations. These societies belong to their members (i.e. invariably customers who have purchased a share in the society) and each member has one vote at the society's annual meeting which elects a committee (or board) to take responsibility for running the organisation. This committee appoints managers and staff to run its various stores and offices and any profits from its activities are supposed to benefit the members. Originally this took the form of a cash dividend paid to members in relation to their purchases, but this has largely disappeared, having been replaced either by trading stamps or by investment in areas felt to benefit the consumer (e.g. lower prices, higher-quality products, modern shops, and so on) and/or the local community (e.g. charitable donations, sponsorship).

The societies differ in other ways from standard companies. For a start, shares are not quoted on the Stock Exchange and members are restricted in the number of shares they can purchase and in the method of disposal. Not having access to cheap sources of capital on the stock market, co-operatives rely heavily on retained surpluses and on loan finance, and the latter places a heavy burden on the societies when interest rates are high. The movement's democratic principles also impinge on its operations and this has been a bone of contention in recent years as members have complained about their increasing remoteness from decision-making centres. Some societies have responded by encouraging the development of locally elected committees, to act in an advisory or consultative capacity to the society's board of directors and it looks likely that others will be forced to consider similar means of increasing member participation, which still remains very limited.

The movement's historical links with the British Labour Party are also worth noting and a number of parliamentary candidates are normally sponsored at general elections. These links, however, have tended to become slightly looser in recent years, although the movement still contributes to Labour Party funds and continues to lobby politicians both at national and local level. It is also active in seeking to influence public opinion and, in this, claims to be responding to customer demands for greater social and corporate responsibility. Amongst its initiatives are the establishment of a customer's charter (by the Co-operative Bank) and the decision to review both its investments and the individuals and organisations it does business with, to ascertain that they are acceptable from an ethical point of view.

Workers' co-operatives

In Britain, workers' co-operatives are found in a wide range of industries including manufacturing, building and construction, engineering, catering and retailing. They are particularly prevalent in printing, clothing and in wholefoods, and some have been in existence for over a century. The majority, however, are of fairly recent origin, having been part of the growth in the number of small firms which occurred in the 1980s.

As the name suggests, a workers' co-operative is a business in which the ownership and control of the assets are in the hands of the people working in it, having agreed to establish the enterprise and to share the risk for mutual benefit. Rather than form a standard partnership, the individuals involved normally register the business as a friendly society under the Industrial and Provident Societies Acts 1965–78, or seek incorporation as a private limited company under the Companies Act 1985. In the case of the former, seven members are required to form a co-operative, whilst the latter only requires two. In practice, a minimum of three or four members tends to be the norm and some co-operatives may have several hundred participants, frequently people who have been made redundant by their employers and who are keen to keep the business going.

The central principles of the movement – democracy, open membership, social responsibility, mutual co-operation and trust – help to differentiate the co-operative from other forms of business organisation and govern both the formation and operation of this type of enterprise. Every employee may be a member of the organisation and every member owns one share in the business, with every share carrying an equal voting right. Any surpluses are shared by democratic agreement and this is normally done on an equitable basis, reflecting, for example, the amount of time and effort an individual puts into the business. Other decisions, too, are taken jointly by the members and the emphasis tends to be on the quality of goods or services provided and on creating a favourable working environment, rather than on the pursuit of profits – although the latter cannot be ignored if the organisation is to survive. In short, the co-operative tends to focus on people and on the relationship between them, stressing the co-operative and communal traditions associated with its origins, rather than the more conflictual and competitive aspects inherent in other forms of industrial organisation.

Despite these apparent attractions, workers' co-operatives have never been as popular in Britain as in other parts of the world (e.g. France, Italy, Israel), although a substantial increase occurred in the number of co-operatives in the 1980s, largely as a result of growing unemployment, overt support across the political spectrum and the establishment of a system to encourage and promote the co-operative ideal (e.g. Co-operative Development Agencies).[3] More recently, however, their fortunes have tended to decline, as employee shareholding and profit schemes (ESOPs) have grown in popularity. It seems unlikely that workers' co-operatives will ever form the basis of a strong third sector in the British economy, between the profit-oriented firms in the private sector and the nationalised and municipal undertakings in the public sector.

PUBLIC SECTOR BUSINESS ORGANISATIONS

Public sector organisations come in a variety of forms. These include:

- central government departments (e.g. Department of Trade and Industry);
- local authorities (e.g. Lancashire County Council);
- regional bodies (e.g. regional health authorities);
- quangos (e.g. the Arts Council);
- central government trading organisations (e.g. HMSO); and
- public corporations and nationalised industries (e.g. British Coal).

Some of these were discussed in Chapter 3, which examined the political environment and numerous other references to the influence of government on business activity can be found throughout the book, most notably in Chapters 4, 8, 10, 12, 13 and 14. In the discussion below, attention is focused on those public sector organisations which most closely approximate businesses in the private sector, namely, public corporations and municipal enterprises. An examination of the transfer of many of these public sector bodies to the private sector – usually termed 'privatisation' – is contained in Chapter 14.

Public corporations

Private sector business organisations are owned by private individuals and groups who have chosen to invest in some form of business enterprise, usually with a view to personal gain. In contrast, in the public sector the state owns assets in various forms, which it uses to provide a range of goods and services felt to be of benefit to its citizens, even if this provision incurs the state in a 'loss'. Many of these services are provided directly through government departments (e.g. social security benefits) or through bodies operating under delegated authority from central government (e.g. local authorities, health authorities). Others are the responsibility of state-owned industrial and commercial undertakings, specially created for a variety of reasons and often taking the form of a 'public corporation'. These state corporations are an important part of the public sector of the economy and still contribute significantly to national output, employment and investment. Their numbers, however, have declined substantially following the wide-scale 'privatisation' of state industries which occurred in the 1980s and this process looks set to continue into the 1990s with the government's plans to sell off British Rail and British Coal amongst others.

Public corporations are statutory bodies, incorporated (predominantly) by special Act of Parliament and, like companies, have a separate legal identity from the individuals who own them and run them. Under the statute setting up the corporation, reference is made to the powers, duties and responsibilities of the organisation and to its relationship with the government department which oversees its operations. These operations currently range from providing a variety of national and international postal services (the Post Office), to the provision of entertainment (the BBC), an energy source (British Coal) and a national rail network (British Rail). Where such provision involves the organisation in a considerable degree of direct contact with its customers from whom it derives most of its revenue, the corporation tends to be called a 'nationalised industry'. In reality, of course, the public corporation is the legal form through which the industry is both owned and run and every corporation is to some degree unique in structure as well as in functions.

As organisations largely financed as well as owned by the state, public corporations are required to be publicly accountable and hence they invariably operate under the purview of a 'sponsoring' government department, the head of which (the Secretary of State) appoints a board of management to run the organisation. This board tends to exercise a considerable degree of autonomy in day-to-day decisions and operates largely free from political interference on most matters of a routine nature. The organisation's strategic objectives, however, and important questions concerning reorganisation or investment, would have to be agreed with the sponsoring department, as would the corporation's performance targets and its external financing limits.

The link between the corporation and its supervising ministry provides the means through which Parliament can oversee the work of the organisation and permits ordinary Members of Parliament to seek information and explanation through question time, through debates and through the select committee system. Additionally, under the Competition Act 1980, nationalised industries can be subject to investigation by the Monopolies and Mergers Commission (MMC), and this too presents opportunities for further parliamentary discussion and debate, as well as for government action.

A further opportunity for public scrutiny comes from the establishment of industry-specific Consumers' or Consultative Councils, which consider complaints from customers and advise both the board and the department concerned of public attitudes to the organisation's performance and to other aspects of its operations (e.g. pricing). In a number of cases, including British Rail, pressure on government from consumers and from other sources has resulted in the establishment of a 'Customers' Charter', under which the organisation agrees to provide a predetermined level of service or to give information and/or compensation where standards are not achieved. Developments of this kind are already spreading to other parts of the public sector and in future may be used as a means by which governments decide on the allocation of funds to public bodies, as well as providing a vehicle for monitoring organisational achievement.

It is interesting to note that mechanisms for public accountability and state regulation have been retained to some degree even where public utilities have been 'privatised' (i.e. turned into public limited companies). Industries such as gas, electricity, water and telecommunications are watched over by newly created regulatory bodies which are designed to protect the interests of consumers, particularly with regard to pricing and the standard of service provided. Ofgas, for example, which regulates British Gas, monitors gas supply charges to ensure that they reasonably reflect input costs and these charges can be altered by the 'regulator' if they are seen to be excessive. Similarly, in the case of non-gas services, such as maintenance, the legislation privatising the industry only allows prices to be raised to a maximum of the current rate of inflation less 2 per cent, to ensure that the organisation is not able to take full advantage of its monopoly power.

An additional source of government influence comes from its ownership of a 'golden share' in a privatised state industry which effectively gives the government a veto in certain vital areas of decision-making. This notional shareholding – which is written into the privatisation legislation – tends to last for a number of years and can be used to protect a newly privatised business from a hostile take-over, particularly by foreign companies or individuals. Ultimately, however, the expectation is that this veto power will be relinquished and the organisation concerned will become subject to the full effects of the market – a point exemplified by the government's decision to allow Ford to take over Jaguar in 1990, having originally blocked a number of previous take-over bids.

The existence of a 'golden share' should not be equated with the decision by government to retain (or purchase) a significant proportion of issued shares in a privatised (or already private) business organisation, whether as an investment and/or future source of revenue, or as a means of exerting influence in a particular industry or sector. Nor should it be confused with government schemes to attract private funds into existing state enterprises, by allowing them to achieve notional company status in order to overcome Treasury restrictions on borrowing imposed on public bodies. In the latter case, which often involves a limited share issue, government still retains full control of the organisation by owning all (or the vast majority) of the shares – as in the case of Rover prior to its sale to British Aerospace. Should the government wish to attract additional funds into the organisation or ultimately to privatise it, it can do so relatively easily by selling all or a proportion of its holding to private investors.

Municipal enterprises

Local authorities have a long history of involvement in business activity. In part this is a function of their role as central providers of public services (e.g. education, housing, roads, social services) and of their increasing involvement in supporting local economic development initiatives (see Chapter 10). But their activities have also traditionally involved the provision of a range of marketable goods and services, not required by law but provided voluntarily by a local authority and often in direct competition with the private sector (e.g. theatres, leisure services, museums). Usually such provision has taken place under the aegis of a local authority department which appoints staff who are answerable to the council and to its committees through the department's chief officer and its elected head. Increasingly, though, local authorities are turning to other organisational arrangements – including the establishment of companies and trusts – in order to separate some of these activities from the rest of their responsibilities and to create a means through which private investment in the enterprise can occur.

One example of such a development can be seen in the case of local authority controlled airports which are normally the responsibility of a number of local authorities who run them through a joint board, representing the interests of the participating district councils (e.g. Manchester Airport). Since the Airports Act 1986, local authorities with airports have been required to create a limited company in which their joint assets are vested and which appoints a board of directors to run the enterprise. Like other limited companies, the organisation can, if appropriate, seek private capital and must publish annual accounts, including a profit and loss statement. It can also be 'privatised' relatively easily if the local authorities involved decide to relinquish ownership (e.g. East Midlands Airport).

Such developments, which have parallels in other parts of the public sector, can be seen to have at least four benefits:

1 They provide a degree of autonomy from local authority control that is seen to be beneficial in a competitive trading environment.
2 They give access to market funds by the establishment of a legal structure that is not fully subject to central government restrictions on local authority borrowing.
3 They help local authority organisations to compete more effectively under Compulsory Competitive Tendering (CCT), by removing or reducing charges for departmental overheads that are applied under the normal arrangements.
4 They provide a vehicle for further private investment and for ultimate privatisation of the service.

Given these benefits and the current fashion for privatisation, there is little doubt that they will become an increasing feature of municipal enterprise in the foreseeable future.

BUSINESS ORGANISATIONS IN MAINLAND EUROPE

Sole traders, partnerships, co-operatives and limited companies are to be found throughout Europe and beyond, and in many cases their legal structure is similar to that of their British counterparts. Where differences occur, these are often a reflection of historical and cultural factors which find expression in custom and practice as well as in law. Examples of some of these differences are contained in the discussion below, which focuses on France, Germany, Denmark and Portugal.

France

Numerically, the French economy is dominated by very small businesses (i.e. less than ten employees), the majority of which are sole traders. As in Britain, these are owner-managed-and-operated enterprises, with a husband and wife often assuming joint responsibility for the business. Formal requirements in this type of organisation tend to be few, although individuals as well as companies engaging in a commercial business are required to register before trading officially begins. Since this process is relatively simple and there are no minimum capital requirements nor significant reporting obligations, sole tradershipstend to be preferred by the vast majority of individuals seeking to start a business and they are particularly prevalent in the service sector. They carry, however, unlimited personal liability for the owner, whose personal assets are at risk in the event of business failure.

Most of the remaining French business organisations are limited companies, many of which are Petites et Moyennes Enterprises (PMEs) – small and medium enterprises – employing between 10 and 500 employees. These companies come in a variety of legal forms, but two in particular predominate: the Société à Responsabilité Limitée (SARL) and the Société Anonyme (SA).

The SARL tends to be the form preferred by smaller companies, whose owners wish to retain close control of the organisation; hence many of them are family businesses – an important feature of the private sector in France. This type of enterprise can be established (currently) with a minimum capital of FF 50,000, cannot issue shares to the general public, has restrictions on the transfer of shares and is run by individuals appointed by the shareholders – usually the shareholders themselves and/or relatives. In practice, these various restrictions help to ensure that the owner-managers remain dominant in the organisation and the appointed head of the company will invariably be the most important decision-maker. Concomitantly, they help to provide the organisation with a defence against hostile take-over, particularly by overseas companies looking for a French subsidiary in order to avoid the special rules which apply to branches and agencies (e.g. a foreign parent company has unlimited liability for the debts of its branch or agency, since these do not have a separate legal identity).

The SA is the legal form normally chosen by larger companies seeking access to substantial amounts of capital. In the case of a privately owned company, the minimum capital requirement is currently FF 250,000; if publicly owned the minimum is FF 1.5 million. Where capital assets are substantial, this tends to ensure that financial institutions are large shareholders in SAs and many of them have interests in a wide range of enterprises which they often manage through a holding company (see below).

One advantage of this arrangement is that it provides the financial institution with a means of managing its investments and of exerting influence over companies in which it has a large minority stake. Another is that it provides a means of defending French companies from hostile take-overs and hence small and medium enterprises often seek backing from holding companies to help fend off foreign predators.

As in Britain, the legal basis of the SA provides for a clear distinction between the roles of the owners (the shareholders) and the salaried employees, and it is the former who appoint the company's board of directors. In smaller companies, the chairperson and managing director is often the same person and many smaller French companies continue to have extremely strong central control, often by the head of the owning family. In larger companies, the two roles are normally separated, with the managing director assuming responsibility for the day-to-day operations of the enterprise and forming the link between the board and the company's senior executives and managers, some of whom may have considerable delegated authority.

It is worth noting that in companies with more than 50 employees, there is a legal requirement to have elected work councils and workers' delegates have the right to attend board meetings as observers and to be consulted on matters affecting working conditions. In companies with more than ten employees, workers have the right to elect representatives to look after their interests and regular meetings have to take place between management and workers, over and above the obligation of employers to negotiate annually on pay and conditions. Despite these arrangements and the legal right for unions to organise on a company's premises, trade unions membership – outside state-run companies – remains low and hence union influence tends to be limited. Recent steps to encourage local agreements on pay and conditions seem destined to reduce this influence even further – a situation which has parallels in Britain.

Germany

All major forms of business organisation are to be found in Germany, but it is the limited company which is of particular interest. Some of these are of relatively recent origin, having formerly been East German state-owned enterprises which have undergone 'privatisation' following the reunification of the country.

In numerical terms it is the private limited company (Gessellschaft mit beschränkter Haftung – GmbH) which predominates and which is the form chosen by most foreign companies seeking to establish an enterprise in Germany. As in Britain, this type of organisation has to be registered with the authorities and its founding members must prepare Articles of Association for signature by a public notary. The Articles include information on the purpose of the business, the amount of capital subscribed, the members' subscriptions and obligations and the company's name and registered address. Once the registration process is complete – usually a matter of a few days – the personal liability of the members becomes limited to the amount invested in the business. Currently, the minimum amount of subscribed share capital required for registration is DM 50,000, half of which must be paid up by the company itself.

A large numbers of GmbHs are owned and run by German families, with the banks often playing an influential role as guarantors of part of the initial capital and as primary sources of loan finance. As in France, this pattern of ownership makes hostile take-overs less likely, as well as ensuring that the management of the enterprise remains in the hands of the owners. Significantly, the management of a proposed GmbH is subject to quality control, being required to prove that they are qualified for the task prior to trading. This requirement stands in stark contrast to arrangements in Britain, where no such guarantees are needed, other than those implicit in a bank's decisions to help finance a proposed venture on the basis of a business plan.

The procedures for establishing other types of business organisation are similar to those of the GmbH, although in the case of the public limited company (Aktiengessellschaft – AG), the current minimum amount of capital required at start-up is DM 100,000 in negotiable share certificates. Unlike British companies, the AG usually consists of two boards of directors, one of which (the supervisory board) decides on longer-term strategy, whilst the other (the managing board) concentrates on more immediate policy issues, often of an operational kind. Normally half the members of the supervisory board (Aufsichtrat) are elected by shareholders, while the other half are employees elected by the workforce, and it is the responsibility of the board to protect the interests of employees as well as shareholders.

Such worker representation at senior levels is an important element of the German system of business organisation and even in smaller enterprises workers have the right to establish works councils and to be consulted on social and personnel issues and on strategic decisions. Equally, all employees have a constitutional right to belong to a trade union – most of which are organised by industry rather than by craft or occupation, as is largely the case in the United Kingdom. Consequently, German companies typically negotiate with only one union; usually in an atmosphere which stresses consensus and an identity of social and economic interests, rather than conflict and confrontation.

Corporate finance is another area in which German experience differs from that in the United Kingdom, although the situation has changed to some degree in recent years. In Britain a substantial amount of company finance is raised through the stock market and this is also the case in the United States and Japan (see Table 7.1). In Germany (and for that matter in France, Italy and Spain), the banks and a number of other special credit institutions play a dominant role, with bank loans far outstripping joint-stock financing as a source of long-term capital. Traditionally, German banks

Table 7.1 Stock Market capitalisation (29/12/89)

Country	Billion ECU	% of GDP
United Kingdom	557	74.1
West Germany	236	21.8
France	182	21.1
Spain	62	18.1
Italy	95	12.1
Japan	2,632	102.3
United States	1,968	34.8

Source: F. Somers (ed.), *European Economies: A Comparative Study,* Pitman Publishing, 1991

have been willing to take a longer-term view of their investment, even at the expense of short-term profits and dividends and this has benefited German companies seeking to expand their operations. In return, the banks have tended to exert a considerable amount of influence in the boardrooms of many German companies, usually by providing a substantial number of members of a company's supervisory board, including the chairperson.

Denmark

Denmark, like France, is a country whose economy is dominated by small businesses, many of which are sole traders. As in other countries, there are very few regulations governing the establishment of this type of enterprise, other than the need to register for VAT if turnover exceeds a predetermined limit and to meet taxation and social security requirements. In keeping with practice throughout Europe and beyond, sole traders have unlimited personal liability and this imposes a considerable burden on the organisation's owner and family, who often run the business jointly. The same conditions also apply in the case of Danish partnerships – whether formal or informal – with the joint owners having full and unlimited liability for all debts accruing to the organisation.

Limited companies in Denmark also reflect practice elsewhere, being required to register under the Companies Act and having a legal existence separate from the owners and employees. Three types of limited liability company can be distinguished:

1 The Anpartselskaber (ApS), which is a private joint-stock company, often run by a family and owned and controlled by a handful of individuals, one of whom may simultaneously occupy the roles of main owner, chairperson and managing director. Many of these companies began life as sole traders, but for reasons of taxation and liability have registered as an ApS.
2 The Aktieselskaber (A/S), which is a quoted or (more regularly) unquoted public limited company, subject essentially to the same regulations as the ApS, but having a much larger minimum capital requirement on registration. A large number of A/S are still small businesses, run by family members who wish to retain control of the enterprise as an increase in assets occurs.
3 The AMBA is a special kind of limited company – in essence a tax-free co-operative with its own regulations. Many of these companies have grown over the years through merger and acquisition and some of them belong to larger Danish companies and employ a substantial number of workers. They tend to be concentrated in farm-related products, but can also be found in the service sector, especially wholesaling and retailing.

Portugal

A brief look at Portuguese business organisations reveals a range of legal structures which includes sole traders, joint ventures, complementary groups, unlimited companies, limited partnerships, and public and private limited companies. In the case of the latter, capital requirements tend to be an important distinguishing feature. The Public Limited Company or Corporation (Sociedade Anonima – SA) currently requires a minimum capital of 5 million escudos, at least five shareholders (unless the state owns more than 50 per cent) and shares with a fixed par value of at least Esc 1,000. Requirements for private companies (Sociedade Por Quotas or Limitada – LDA) are similar to those in other countries, with a minimum capital requirement of Esc 400,000, at least two shareholders, a minimum shareholding of Esc 20,000 and no public subscription for shares. Under Portuguese law, however, shareholders in the Limitada are liable not only to the extent of their own paid-up capital, but also for the capital of any shareholder who may default.

THE PUBLIC SECTOR IN MAINLAND EUROPE

Given the number of countries involved, it is impossible to survey the whole of the public sector in the rest of Europe. Students with an interest in this area are encouraged to read further and to consult the various specialist sources of information covering the countries they wish to investigate. A number of general points, however, are worthy of note:

1 Public sector business organisations can be found in all countries and invariably exist because of the decision by the state to establish a particular organisation under state ownership and control, or to nationalise an existing private business (or industry).
2 In some countries (e.g. France, Greece, Portugal) the state plays an important role in business and controls some key sectors of the economy.
3 State involvement in business often includes significant shareholdings in a number of large enterprises, not only by the national government but also by regional and/or local government (e.g. in Germany).
4 State intervention often occurs in organisations or industries which can be deemed 'problematic' (e.g. in Greece).
5 Privatisation of state-owned enterprises has occurred throughout Europe and in other parts of the world. In the former East Germany, for example, most of the state-owned companies are currently being transferred to private ownership, by turning them initially into trusts which will become the vehicle for privatisation and/or joint ventures. Similarly in Portugal, the wholesale nationalisation of the economy after the 1974 Revolution has been reversed and the government is committed to a phased programme of privatisation, involving employees and small investors as well as large national and international organisations.

This latter point serves to re-emphasise that the business environment is subject to change over time and the fashions of today may tomorrow become things of the past. This fluctuating environment is as applicable to the public sector as it is to the private sector of the economy.

LEGAL STRUCTURE: SOME IMPLICATIONS

For businesses in the private sector, the choice of legal structure has important implications. Amongst the factors which the aspiring entrepreneur has to take into account when deciding what form of business enterprise to establish are:

● the degree of personal liability;
● the willingness to share decision-making powers and risks;
● the costs of establishing the business;
● the legal requirements concerning the provision of public information;
● the taxation position;
● commercial needs, including access to capital; and
● business continuity.

For some, retaining personal control will be the main requirement, even at the risk of facing unlimited personal liability and reducing the opportunities for expansion. For others, the desire to limit personal liability and to provide increased capital for growth will dictate that the owner seeks corporate status, even if this necessitates sharing decision-making powers and may ultimately result in a loss of ownership and/or control of the enterprise.

This link between an organisation's legal structure and its subsequent operations can be illustrated by examining three important facets of organisational life: the organisation's objectives, its sources of finance, and its stakeholders. As the analysis below illustrates, in each of these areas significant differences occur between alternative forms of business organisation, both *within* the private sector and *between* the state and non-state sectors of the economy. In some cases, these differences can be attributed directly to the restraints (or opportunities) faced by an organisation as a result of its legal status, suggesting that the legal basis of the enterprise conditions its operations. In other cases operational considerations tend to dictate the organisation's legal form, indicating that these are as much a cause of its legal status as a result of it – a point well illustrated by the workers' co-operative and the public corporation.

Organisational objectives

All business organisations pursue a range of objectives and these may vary to some degree over time. New private sector businesses, for example, are likely to be concerned initially with survival and with establishing a position in the marketplace, with profitability and growth seen as less important in the short term. In contrast, most well-established businesses will tend to regard profits and growth as key objectives and may see them as a means towards further ends, including market domination, maximising sales revenue and/or minimising operating costs.

Organisational objectives are also conditioned by the firm's legal structure. In sole traders, partnerships and some limited companies, control of the enterprise rests in the hands of the entrepreneur(s) and hence organisational goals will tend to coincide with the personal goals of the owner(s), whatever the point in the organisation's life cycle. In public companies, however – where ownership tends to be separated from control – the goals of the owners (shareholders) may not always correspond with those of the directors and senior managers who run the organisation, particularly when the latter are pursuing personal goals to enhance their own organisational position, status and/or rewards.

It is worth noting that the possibility of goal conflict also occurs where an individual company becomes a subsidiary of another organisation, whether by agreement or as a result of a take-over battle. This parent–subsidiary relationship may take the form of a holding company which is specially created to purchase a majority (sometimes all) of the shares in other companies, some of which may operate as holding companies themselves. Thus, whilst the individual subsidiaries may retain their legal and commercial identities and may operate as individual units, they will tend to be controlled by a central organisation which may exercise a considerable degree of influence over the objectives to be pursued by each of its subsidiaries. It is not inconceivable, for example, that some parts of the group may be required to make a loss on paper, particularly when there are tax advantages to be gained by the group as a whole from doing so.

Workers' co-operatives and public corporations provide further evidence of the relationship between an organisation's legal status and its primary objectives. In the case of the former, the establishment of the enterprise invariably reflects a desire on the part of its members to create an organisation which emphasises social goals (e.g. democracy, co-operation, job creation, mutual trust) rather than the pursuit of profits – hence the choice of the 'co-operative' form. Similarly in the case of the public corporation, a decision by government to establish an entity which operates in the interests of the public at large (or 'national interest') favours the creation of a state-owned-and-controlled organisation, with goals laid down by politicians and generally couched in social and financial terms (e.g. return on assets, reinvestment, job creation) rather than in terms of profit maximisation.

This apparent dichotomy between the profit motive of the private sector and the broader socio-economic goals of public bodies has, however, become less clear cut over the last decade, as an increasing number of state-owned organisations have been 'prepared' for privatisation. Equally, in other parts of the public sector – including the health service and local government – increasing stress is being laid on 'value for money' and on operating within budgets – concepts which are familiar to businesses in the private sector. Whilst it is not inconceivable that a change in government would reverse this trend, current evidence suggests that a shift in cultural attitudes has occurred and public bodies can no longer rely on unfettered government support for their activities. If this is the case, further convergence is likely to occur between state and privately owned bodies, with the former moving towards the latter rather than vice versa.

Finance

Business organisations finance their activities in a variety of ways and from a range of sources. Methods include reinvesting profits, borrowing, trade credit, and issuing shares and debentures. Sources include the banks and other financial institutions, individual investors and governments, as well as contributions from the organisation's original owners.

Whilst it is beyond the scope of this book to discuss business finance in detail, it is appropriate to make a number of general observations about the topic in the context of the business environment:

1 All organisations tend to fund their activities from both internal (e.g. owner's capital, reinvested profits) and external sources (e.g. bank borrowing, sale of shares).

2 Financing may be short-term, medium-term or longer-term, and the methods and sources of funding chosen will reflect the time period concerned (e.g. bank borrowing on overdraft tends to be short-term and generally needed for immediate use).

3 Funds raised from external sources inevitably involve the organisation in certain obligations (e.g. repayment of loans with interests, personal guarantees, paying dividends) and these will act as a constraint on the organisation at some future date.

4 The relationship between owner's capital and borrowed funds – usually described as an organisation's 'gearing' – can influence a firm's activities and prospects in a variety of ways (e.g. high-geared firms with a large element of borrowed funds will be adversely affected if interest rates are high).

5 Generally speaking, as organisations become larger many more external sources and methods of funding become available and utilising these can have implications for the structure, ownership and conduct of the organisation.

This latter point is perhaps best illustrated by comparing sole traders and partnerships with limited companies. In the case of the former, as unincorporated entities neither the sole trader nor partnership can issue shares (or debentures) and hence their access to large amounts of external capital is restricted by law. Companies have no such restrictions – other than those which help to differentiate a private company from a public one – and consequently they are able to raise larger amounts by inviting individuals (and organisations) to subscribe for shares. Where a company is publicly quoted on the stock market, the amounts raised in this way can be very large indeed and the resultant organisation may have millions of owners who change on a regular basis as shares are traded on the second-hand market.

Organisations which decide to acquire corporate status in order to raise funds for expansion (or for some other purposes) become owned by their shareholders, who may be the original owners or may be individual and institutional investors holding equity predominantly as an investment and with little, if any, long-term commitment to the organisation they own. As indicated above, in the latter case, a separation tends to occur between the roles of owner (shareholder) and controller (director) and this can lead to the possibility of conflicting aims and objectives or differences in opinion over priorities within the enterprise – a problem discussed in more detail below under 'Stakeholders'.

A further illustration of the relationship between an organisation's legal structure and its ability to raise finance is provided by the public corporation. In this case, as a public body accountable to Parliament and the public via government, the public corporation is required to operate within a financial context largely controlled by government and normally conditioned by the government's overall fiscal policy, including its attitude to the size of the Public Sector Borrowing Requirement (PSBR). One aspect of this context in Britain has been the establishment of external financing limits (EFLs) for each nationalised industry, arrived at by negotiation between government and the board running the public corporation, and used as a means of restraining monetary growth and hence the size of the PSBR. Unfortunately this has also tended to prevent the more financially sound corporations, such as British Telecom before privatisation, from borrowing externally on a scale necessary to develop their business – a restriction which tends to disappear when the corporation becomes a fully fledged public company, either through privatisation or some other means.

Stakeholders

All organisations have stakeholders; these are individuals and/or groups who are affected by or affect the performance of the organisation in which they have an interest. Typically they would include employees, managers, creditors, suppliers, shareholders (if appropriate) and society at large. As Table 7.2 illustrates, an organisation's stakeholders have a variety of interests which range from the pursuit of private gain to the more nebulous idea of achieving public benefit. Sometimes these interests will clash as, for example, when managers seek to improve the organisation's cash flow by refusing to pay suppliers' bills on time. On other occasions, the interests of different stakeholders may coincide, as when managers plan for growth in the organisation and in doing so provide greater job security for employees and enhanced dividends for investors.

Table 7.2 Organisational stakeholders and their interests

Types of stakeholder	Possible principal interests
Employees	Wage levels; working conditions; job security; personal development
Managers	Job security; status; personal power; organisational profitability; growth of the organisation
Shareholders	Market value of the investment; dividends; security of investment; liquidity of investment
Creditors	Security of loan; interest on loan; liquidity of investment
Suppliers	Security of contract; regular payment; growth of organisation; market development
Society	Safe products; environmental sensitivity; equal opportunities; avoidance of discrimination

The legal structure of an organisation has an impact not only on the type of stakeholders involved but also to a large degree on how their interests are represented. In sole traders, partnerships and smaller private companies, the coincidence of ownership and control limits the number of potential clashes of interest, given that objectives are set by and decisions taken by the firm's owner-manager(s). In larger companies, and, in particular, public limited companies, the division between ownership and control means that the controllers have the responsibility of representing the interests of the organisation's shareholders and creditors and, as suggested above, their priorities and goals may not always correspond.

A similar situation occurs in public sector organisations, where the interest of taxpayers (or ratepayers) is represented by both government and by those individuals chosen by government to run the organisation. In this case, it is worth recalling that the broader strategic objectives of the enterprise and the big decisions concerning policy, finance and investment tend to be taken by politicians, operating with advice from their officials (e.g. civil servants, local government officers) and within the context of the government's overall economic and social policies. The organisation's board of management and its senior executives and managers are mainly responsible for the day-to-day operations of the business, although the board and the person chairing it would normally play a key role in shaping overall objectives and decisions, through regular discussions with government and its officials.

One important way in which public sector organisations differ from their private sector counterparts is in the sanctions available to particular groups of stakeholders who feel that the organisation is not representing their best interest. Shareholders, for example, in a company could withdraw financial support for a firm whose directors consistently disregard their interests or take decisions which threaten the security and/or value of their investment, and the possibility of such a reaction normally guarantees that the board pays due attention to the needs of this important groups of stakeholders. The taxpayer and ratepayer have no equivalent sanction and in the short term must rely heavily on government and its agencies or, if possible, their power as consumers to represent their interest *vis-à-vis* the organisation. Longer term, of course, the public has the sanction of the ballot box, although it seems highly unlikely that the performance of state enterprises would be a key factor in determining the outcome of general or local elections.

The relative absence of market sanctions facing state-owned organisations has meant that the public has had to rely on a range of formal institutions (e.g. parliamentary scrutiny committees, consumer consultative bodies, the audit authorities) and on the media to protect its interest in areas such as funding, pricing and quality of service provided. As these organisations are returned to the private sector, the expectation is that the sanctions imposed by the free market will once again operate and shareholders in privatised utilities will be protected like any other group of shareholders in a privately owned enterprise. To what extent this will occur in practice, of course, is open to question, whilst the newly privatised public corporations face little, if any, competition. Government, it seems, prefers to hedge its bets on this question, at least in the short term – hence the establishment of 'regulators' with powers of investigation into performance and some degree of control over pricing.

FRANCHISING, LICENSING AND JOINT VENTURES

To complete this review of the legal structure of business organisations, it is useful to consider three developments which have a legal aspect: franchising, licensing and joint ventures. All three may be seen as a means of carrying out a business venture in a way which reduces some of the risks normally faced by the entrepreneur.

Franchising

Franchising, which has grown significantly in the last ten years, is an arrangement where one party (the franchiser) sells the right to another party (the franchisee) to market its product or service. In terms of their legal status the parties involved could be any of the forms described above, but in practice it is usually the case that the franchiser is a company whilst the franchisee tends to be a sole trader or partnership. Both parties in law have a separate legal identity, but the nature of the contract between them makes their relationship interdependent and this has important implications for the operation of the franchise.

Franchise arrangements come in a variety of forms. Probably the best known is the 'business format franchise' (or 'trade name franchise') under which the franchiser agrees to allow the franchisee to sell the product or service with the help of a franchise package which contains all the elements needed to set up and run a business at a profit. These would typically include the brand name, any associated supplies, promotional material and other forms of support and assistance. In return the franchisee usually pays an initial sum or fee for the use of the service and its various elements, remits royalties based on sales and/or profits, agrees to make a contribution for consultancy, training and promotion, and undertakes to maintain standards. Wimpy, Kentucky Fried Chicken, Burger King, Prontaprint and Dynorod are examples of this type of franchise.

Other forms include manufacturer/retailer franchises (e.g. car dealers), manufacturer/ wholesaler franchises (e.g. Coca-Cola, Pepsi) and wholesaler/retailer franchises (e.g. Spar and Mace) and it is estimated by the industry's trade body – the British Franchise Association – that in retailing alone franchising accounts for over 20 per cent of sales in the United Kingdom. One indication of its growing significance is the spread of franchising into further and higher education, with universities and other colleges of higher education franchising some of their courses to local further education colleges, who in turn may franchise some of their courses to schools and/or sixth-form colleges. Another indicator is the decision by many clearing banks and firms of accountants to establish franchise sections to help and advise individuals who want to open a franchise or who have already done so and are seeking further guidance.

Undoubtedly the mutual benefits to be derived from a franchise arrangement help to explain its popularity as a way of doing business in both domestic and external markets and it has proved an attractive vehicle for some companies seeking rapid overseas expansion, without undertaking substantial direct investments – although this is sometimes necessary to support the operation (e.g. McDonald's had to invest in a plant to make hamburger buns in the United Kingdom). Equally, many would-be entrepreneurs find the security of a franchise more attractive than other methods of starting a business, especially as there is some evidence to suggest that franchises have better survival rates than the more conventional forms of independent enterprise (e.g. sole traders).

Current indications are that this popularity will continue in the 1990s, although it is more likely that greater selectivity of potential franchisees will occur as the franchise industry becomes more mature and attempts to gain an increased degree of public respectability. Franchisees, too, are likely to become more particular about the businesses they agree to deal with, as they endeavour to join the enterprise culture. It is, after all, the franchisee who has to bear the financial risk of the business in return for a share in the profits; the franchiser has a reputation to think about.

Licensing

Licensing is another form of non-equity agreement under which a firm in one country (the licensor) authorises a firm in another country (the licensee) to use its intellectual property (e.g. patents, copyrights, trade names, know-how) in return for certain considerations, usually royalty payments. Licences may be granted to individuals, independent companies, subsidiaries of a multinational company or to government agencies and the rights granted may be exclusive or non-exclusive.

Companies invariably enter into licensing agreements to gain certain advantages. These might include:

- Reducing competition by sharing technology.
- Seeking overseas profits without direct foreign investment.
- Protecting an asset from potential 'pirates'.
- Avoiding restrictions on foreign investment or imports imposed by other countries.
- Recouping some research and development costs.
- Gaining a share of an overseas market.

Needless to say, most organisations granting licences tend to be based in the advanced industrial economies and are frequently multinationals who regard their trademarks and technologies as an integral part of their asset base. One problem of transferring the use of such assets to another firm is that the owner loses a degree of control over the asset, including the quality of production, and this may affect the product's image and sales elsewhere. Another is the possibility of the licensee dominating the market after the agreement ends, even to the extent of excluding the licensor from the marketplace by aggressive competition or the development of an alternative product.

Joint ventures

The term 'joint venture' tends to be used in two ways: to describe a contractual agreement involving two or more parties; or to describe a jointly owned and independently incorporated business venture involving more than one organisation. It is the latter usage which is mainly applied here.

Joint ventures – which are popular with international companies – can take a variety of legal forms and almost every conceivable type of partnership may exist, ranging from two companies joining together in the same domestic market (e.g. Sainsbury's and British Home Stores set up the Savacentre chain), to joint private/public sector ventures between participants from different countries. Sometimes numerous organisations may be involved and these may be based on one country or in several. Where this occurs the term 'consortium' is often used, as in the case of TransManche Link (TML), the international joint venture to construct the Channel Tunnel.

As with licensing and franchising, joint ventures have increased in popularity in the last twenty-five to thirty years and have been one of the ways in which international companies have sought to develop an overseas market, particularly in the face of import restrictions, or heavy research and development costs. Multinational car companies have been active in this field – as evidenced by the links between General Motors and Toyota, Leyland and Honda, Ford and Mazda – and these arrangements look likely to continue with the development of the Single European Market and the changes in eastern Europe described above. For western companies wishing to exploit the gradual 'privatisation' of the former planned economies of eastern Europe, joint ventures with indigenous producers are likely to prove a safer bet than direct inward investment, particularly given the degree of economic and political uncertainty. They are also likely to prove more politically acceptable in states seeking to establish their own economic independence and identity after almost fifty years of regional domination.

SYNOPSIS

Market-based economies throughout Europe and beyond have a range of business organisations with broadly similar legal structures. These legal structures help to determine not only the ownership and control of the enterprise, but also other aspects of its operations, including its objectives, its access to finance and its external relationships and obligations. Viewing businesses as legal entities provides a useful insight into a number of the external influences which impinge upon their daily existence and highlights some of the consequences faced by organisations which transfer from public (i.e. state) to private ownership. It also sheds light on other important developments in entrepreneurial activity, including franchising, licensing and joint ventures.

CASE STUDY: THE ENTREPRENEURIAL SPIRIT

Business studies textbooks teach us that new businesses invariably come into existence to satisfy the needs and ambitions of their owners. Once established, it is assumed that an enterprise will begin to grow and that the owner(s) will sanction this and take steps to bring it about. As the two case studies below illustrate, these assumptions may be correct or not, according to specific circumstances. Arguing from the particular to the general needs to be approached with caution in business, as in any other field of study.

T & S Stores

Like many medium- to large-sized businesses, T & S Stores started from relatively modest origins and was the brainchild of one individual, Kevin Threlfall, a Wolverhampton entrepreneur.

A barrow boy by background, Threlfall received his early business training working from the age of 12 on his parents' pitch in West Midlands markets. Despatched to public school, Threlfall soon found this market background was treated contemptuously by his fellow pupils and this made him determined to prove his worth in the business world. On leaving school he began providing pet-foods in bulk, before selling out his business and founding the Lo Cost food chain in 1972. This was subsequently bought for £1.5 million by Oriel Foods, later owned by the Argyll Group.

Threlfall's T & S Stores grew from the Wolverhampton market stalls and quickly expanded into retail outlets, with their emphasis on discount tobacco and convenience shopping. Using day-glo starbursts offering low-priced cigarettes, Threlfall cleverly attracted customers into his stores where they were tempted by the use of colourful confectionery gondolas and other techniques into impulse purchases of products carrying high margins. By keeping costs to a minimum, Threlfall was able to turn his company into a highly profitable enterprise with a stock market capitalisation of almost £140 million by 1991 and a chain of almost 600 stores.

In 1989, T & S acquired the Dillons and Preedy chains from Next for £54 million and subsequently purchased 22 stores from Johnson News Group for £4.25 million in February 1991, thus helping to increase the organisation's interest in convenience stores which Threlfall believed would be the company's main area of future growth. Trading from outlets larger than most of the T & S shops and offering an extended range of grocery and frozen-food lines, Threlfall's convenience stores have generally achieved higher gross margins than the core tobacco shops and helped to contribute to the company's strong net cash position in the early 1990s. Despite these developments, Threlfall has maintained close contacts with what is happening on the ground and has attempted to maintain a degree of individual customer attention in a field of retailing which is rapidly changing. How long this can continue remains to be seen.

Dave Noble (Windsurfing)

Unlike Kevin Threlfall, Dave Noble came from a non-business background and had no ambitions as a child to seek a career in industry or commerce. Following 'A' levels at the local grammar school in Woking, Noble went to Aberyswyth University where he obtained a degree in philosophy, before continuing his studies at postgraduate level. After a brief spell doing research, he left university and worked on building sites, subsequently returning to study for a postgraduate certificate of education, a move which was to take him into teaching in Loughborough.

With the start of a family, Noble gave up his full-time teaching post to look after the children, continuing as a supply teacher as and when circumstances allowed. As a keen windsurfer, with an established reputation in the sport, he decided to use some of his time at home to make his own boards, buying the necessary fittings from suppliers to the trade. As requests from friends for similar equipment began to grow, Noble found himself dealing with suppliers on a larger scale and spending an increasing amount of his time making and equipping windsurfing boards. Before he had fully realised what was happening, Noble found himself in business as a sole trader, operating in the leisure industry, a growing sector in the UK economy.

With an initial injection of his own capital, supported by a weekly income from the government's Enterprise Allowance Scheme, Noble established his own venture in late 1986/early 1987, operating from home in Shepshed in Leicestershire. Despite only limited expenditure on advertising, the business began to grow quickly, allowing the venture to become totally self-financing. Before long, it became obvious that new premises would be needed and so in 1989 the Noble family (now five in total) moved to a Georgian house in the village of Wymeswold on the Leicestershire/Nottinghamshire border. Apart from providing adequate space for a growing family, the new house had numerous outbuildings suitable for making and selling equipment and for storing supplies and material. It was also sufficiently close to Shepshed to allow Noble to keep his existing customer and supplier bases which were fundamental to the success of the business.

Noble's initial enthusiasm at working from his village home – in a manner reminiscent of a traditional cottage industry – was soon to be dampened following complaints from neighbours who objected to the traffic from customers seeking boards and other equipment. Consequently, the business was forced to relocate to the nearby Wymeswold Airfield Industrial Estate, where Noble acquired two units from which to operate. Like other units on the estate, Noble's premises were relatively basic, but provided sufficient space for production, storage and sales and had more than adequate parking for customers and suppliers. Being in a rural location, with no houses in the immediate vicinity, complaints concerning disturbance ceased to be a problem for the business.

Despite the successive moves, Noble's business continued to grow, even in the recession years in the early 1990s. Part of this growth was manifestly attributable to the increased demand for leisure products and the decision to add mountain bikes and ski equipment to the range of items on offer was clearly beneficial, although by no means part of a deliberate strategy of diversification. The most significant factor in the firm's success, however, and one which resulted in the need to hire additional staff to meet the increased demand, appears to have been Noble's deliberate policy of keeping customers and suppliers happy. By paying all his bills on time, Noble was able to strike good bargains with suppliers and to pass savings on to the customer in the form of highly competitive prices which other traders could not meet. In addition, Noble and his staff did their best to meet their customers' needs individually, even if it meant working extra hours and incurring some additional expense.

By 1993 Dave Noble (Windsurfing) had become a formidable operator in the marketplace, with a dominant share of the market in the East Midlands and a loyal and extensive customer base. Despite his success, Noble still remains self-effacing and determined to keep his business from growing any further for fear that he will lose his close contact with customers and suppliers. In this at least, Dave Noble and Kevin Threlfall are at one.

NOTES AND REFERENCES

1 Liability may be extended where a company continues trading after insolvency.
2 It is also possible to have unlimited companies.
3 A similar growth occurred in the number of 'community businesses' in Scotland during this period. Though not strictly 'co-operatives', they are also part of the so-called third sector of business.

REVIEW AND DISCUSSION QUESTIONS

1 Numerically, the sole proprietorship is the most popular form of business organisation throughout Europe. How would you account for this?

2 To what extent is corporate status an asset to a business organisation? Does it have any disadvantages?

3 Examine the implications of 'privatising' a public sector business organisation.

4 Discuss how the legal status of a business affects its objectives, its methods of finance and its stakeholders.

5 How would you explain the rise in the popularity of franchising in recent years?

ASSIGNMENTS

1 You have recently been made redundant and decide to set up your own small business, possibly with a friend. Assuming that you have £25,000 to invest in your new venture, draft a business plan which is to be presented to your bank manager in the hope of gaining financial support. Your plan should include a clear rationale for the legal form you wish your business to take, your chosen product(s) or service(s), evidence of market research, an indication of anticipated competition and supporting financial information.

2 You work in a local authority business advice centre. One of your clients wishes to start a business in some aspect of catering. Advise your client on the advantages and disadvantages of the various legal forms the proposed enterprise could take.

FURTHER READING

Beardshaw, J., and Palfreman, D., *The Organisation in its Environment*, 4th edition, Pitman, 1990.
Burns, P. and Dewhurst, J. (eds), *Small Business in Europe*, Macmillan, 1986.
Callaghan, P.M., Ellison, J.R.M., Harrison, T. and Watkin, J.S., *The Business Environment*, Edward Arnold, 1989.
Palmer, A. and Worthington, I., *The Business and Marketing Environment*, McGraw-Hill, 1992.

CHAPTER 8

Size structure of firms

Chris Britton

Businesses range in size from the single proprietor at one extreme to the large multi-national at the other which employs thousands of people over several countries. The structure of these businesses will be very different and the problems they face will vary as a result of the differences in size. The size structure of business will depend on many factors which range from choice (the sole proprietor may choose to remain small) to external factors which are beyond the control of the firm.

OBJECTIVES

1 To be aware of the size structure of UK industry.
2 To understand the reasons why organisations grow in size.
3 To understand the way in which organisations grow and the methods of finance.
4 To recognise the limitations to growth.
5 To survey the level of merger activity in the United Kingdom and the European Community.
6 To be aware of the role and importance of the small-firm sector.
7 To be aware of the role and importance of the multinationals.

INTRODUCTION

There has been an increase in the level of industrial concentration in the United Kingdom over the last 100 years. In 1909 the largest hundred companies produced 16 per cent of manufacturing output; by 1990 this had risen to around 30 per cent. Such an increase in the size of business organisation gives rise to worries about the concentration of power in the hands of a few producers and abuses of this power. If the companies are multinationals, they may be beyond even the control of national governments. More recently the trend towards greater concentration has been reversed, and there seems to be a movement towards employment in smaller units. This chapter will look at the size structure of British industry and the reasons for such a structure, with some international comparisons. It will consider the role of small and large firms in the economy. It will also examine the reasons for growth, the ways in which organisations grow, the financing of growth and the limits to growth. It will also consider the relatively more recent trend towards co-operation in production rather than competition through activities like joint ventures and networking.

THE SIZE STRUCTURE OF UK INDUSTRY

When looking at the size of firms it is important to define the terms used in official data. The firm, or 'enterprise', is the organisation as a whole, and it might be comprised of several units or 'establishments'. Small firms like the corner shop will mostly be enterprises with only one establishment. Large firms like Sainsburys will have many establishments as they have branches in most towns.

There are many different ways to measure the size of firms. Common measures used are turnover, the value of output, the capital employed or the level of employment. Such measurement is beset by problems, not least the difficulty of defining the small firm as will be seen later in this chapter. The three measures mentioned above might give conflicting pictures, as an industry which is becoming increasingly mechanised will probably have rising levels of average capital employed and output but falling average levels of employment. Table 8.1 shows the 'top ten' companies in the United Kingdom using two of these measures and it illustrates the point that different measures of the size of a firm will give different rankings.

Table 8.1 The ten largest companies in the UK 1990

Ranking by turnover £m		Ranking by employment	
1	British Petroleum	1	British Telecom
2	BAT Industries	2	Post Office
3	ICI	3	BAT Industries
4	British Telecom	4	Unilever
5	Grand Metropolitan	5	Grand Metropolitan
6	British Aerospace	6	GEC Ltd
7	British Gas	7	British Railways
8	BTR	8	ICI
9	Hanson	9	BET
10	J. Sainsbury	10	Electricity Council

Source: *The Financial Times*, 11 January 1991

Some of these names will be familiar to the reader while others are less so, BAT Industries for example is a large tobacco company which has diversified into many other areas.

The most common measure of size used is the level of employment. Table 8.2 shows the size structure of units in manufacturing industry by the number of employees in the United Kingdom in 1991. The table shows that smaller firms predominate in terms of numbers, with 94 per cent of firms employing less than 100 employees. In terms of employment, however, these firms account for only 35 per cent of the total level of employment in manufacturing. At the other end of the scale establishments with over 1,000 employees account for only 0.3 per cent of the total number but 17 per cent of total employment. The pattern of size structure varies across industries and over time. In the last 20 years there seems to have been an increase in the importance of small firms and a decline in the importance of large firms in their contribution to employment. In 1980 establishments with less than 200 employees accounted for 31.9

Table 8.2 Size structure of UK manufacturing industry by employment 1991

Employment size group	Number of units	Per cent of total	Employment (000s)	Per cent of total
1–9	105,125	67.2	307.3	6.5
10–19	15,952	10.2	244.9	5.2
20–49	18,003	11.5	554.8	11.7
50–99	7,883	5.0	547.7	11.6
100–199	4,855	3.1	674.7	14.2
200–499	3,318	2.1	1,010.2	21.3
500–999	905	0.6	613.1	12.9
1,000 and over	408	0.3	806.3	17.0

Source: *Annual Abstract of Statistics*, 1992

per cent of total employment in manufacturing and establishments with more than 1,000 employees accounted for 36.8 per cent. The comparable figures from Table 8.2 are 48.8 per cent and 17 per cent. More will be said about this trend later, but it reflects the growth of the service sector (which tends to have smaller units) and the process of decentralisation of production and increased subcontracting.

Although many parts of the service sector are heavily dominated by small firms, as in personal services and business services, there are parts which have experienced a trend towards increased size, such as retailing (see case study in Chapter 12), wholesaling and financial services.

Many of the large companies listed in Table 8.1 operate in more than one country and are therefore multinationals. Multinational corporations strictly defined are enterprises operating in a number of countries and having production or service facilities outside the country of their origin[1]. Multinationals pose particular problems for governments and economies because of their size. They are considered more fully later in this chapter.

ORGANISATIONAL GROWTH

The reasons for organisational growth

Firms grow in size for many reasons; growth could be an explicit objective of management or could be necessary for the successful operation of the firm:

- Growth could be a managerial objective if growth brings benefits to management such as greater security and higher remuneration (see Chapter 7 for a fuller discussion of this).
- It could be that the market in which the business operates is expanding and growth is necessary to maintain market share. This is especially the case as markets become more international.
- Growth enables the organisation to reap the benefits of economies of scale (see Chapter 12).
- Growth enables firms to diversify into other markets, which means that risk can be spread further.

- Industries which are capital intensive will of necessity be comprised of large firms.
- In the area of product development it is possible that the necessary research and development could only be carried out by large companies.
- Growth could be pursued as a defensive strategy, as a reaction to the activities of competitors.

Table 8.3 shows the results of a survey carried out by the European Commission in 1991 on the motivation for mergers that had taken place in 1990/91, and gives some indication of the reasons for growth.

Table 8.3 Main motives for mergers in 1990/91 in Europe

Motive	Mergers (% of replies)
Strengthening market position	35
Expansion	20
Diversification	2
Research and development	–
Co-operation	1
Synergy	10
Other	6
Not specified	26

Source: *21st EC Competition Policy Report*, 1991. Reproduced with permission of the Commission of the European Communities.

The fact that strengthening market position, expansion and synergy represent the main motives for 65 per cent of firms could indicate preparation for the Single European Market. It is interesting that the motives of diversification and research and development are not very important.

In industrial economics firm size is seen as a function of growth. It is suggested that although there is no limit on the size of a firm there are limits on the rate of expansion. Growth rates are seen to depend on different things by different theorists, including the availability of finance, the level of consumer demand and the limitations of management. These theories, however, are primarily concerned with large firms and their development. Small firms are seen as potentially large firms that failed to grow for some reason or other. One interesting theory of growth is the stages model, where the firm is seen as passing through various stages in its development from small sole proprietor/partnership through the decision to expand into a large organisation. This again is a 'grow or fail' theory which does not apply well to industries which are dominated by successful small firms as will be seen later in the chapter.

METHODS OF GROWTH

Firms grow in size internally as part of normal business operation or externally through take-over and merger.

Internal growth

Growth is a natural process for many firms that start small, capture a segment of the market and then continue to expand either by producing more of the same goods or by extending its product lines. The advantages of internal growth over external growth is that the company grows within the existing structure of management; there are none of the problems of bringing together two different management systems. There might also be economies of scale from building bigger plant that might not be available when companies merge and plant size does not change. Set against these, internal growth has certain disadvantages and this is why most of the growth in the size of organisations has occurred through external growth.

External growth

Growth by acquisition is called external growth and occurs through take-over or merger. A merger is the voluntary coming together of two companies with the agreement of the management of both companies, the result of which is the creation of a new legal identity. A take-over is where one company makes an offer to the shareholders of another. If the management of the threatened company resist it is called a hostile take-over, but if the price offered to shareholders is high enough they will accept. Take-over bids can be and have been successfully fought off by the management of the second firm. A holding company is a new company that is formed to acquire assets in other companies. The acquired companies retain their independent identities but are directed by the holding company.

External growth can be seen to have a number of advantages:

1 It is fast, so that productive capacity can be increased very quickly.
2 The acquiring firm has access to an established management team and system.
3 If the shares of the acquiring company have sufficiently high values relative to the acquired firm, there might be no need for additional cash to be raised.
4 The purchase of existing assets could be cheaper than building new productive capacity.

But set against these is the fact that the process might not be an easy one; it is a difficult job to merge two companies smoothly and successfully and there are likely to be many teething problems. Recent research by Coopers & Lybrand found that top executives regarded half of the take-overs in which they had been involved as failures. The main reasons for failure were lack of planning and managerial problems.

Although the definitions of merger and take-over are clear enough, it is often difficult to tell them apart in practice and they are usually put together in official publications under the heading of acquisitions. In order to understand fully the motivation for mergers and take-overs it is important to recognise that there are different types of mergers.

Horizontal mergers

A horizontal merger is where a combination between firms at the same stage in a production process takes place; for example, between two car manufacturers or between two brewers. The vast majority of mergers that take place are of this type and many of our largest companies have been formed through horizontal merger. A recent example of a horizontal merger is the take-over of Devenish, the west country pub chain by Greenalls. This has created one of the largest pub chains in the United Kingdom with in excess of 2,000 outlets. The motives for this type of merger are:

● *To benefit from economies of scale* Horizontal mergers allow the merged firms a greater level of specialisation and the benefits of other economies of scale (see Chapter 12).
● *Greater market share* When firms come together there will be a reduction in competition in the market and the resulting firm will have a much larger share of the market.
● *Rationalisation of output* If the level of demand for a good is shrinking, merger between the producers could be necessary in order to rationalise output.
● *Reaction to competitors* In markets where mergers are taking place, companies may feel that they have to do the same in order to maintain their market position.

Vertical mergers

This involves merger between firms at different stages of the same production process. It is vertical since it runs along the production process from extraction of raw materials to distribution. An example would be a merger between a car manufacturer and a metal-pressing company. Vertical integration can take place 'backwards' towards the beginning of the production process or 'forwards' towards the end of it and it can occur for several reasons:

1 In the case of backwards integration, to control the supplies of raw materials with respect to their quantity and quality. This brings greater security to the acquiring firm.
2 To restrict supplies of the raw materials to competitors.
3 In the case of forwards integration, to control the quality of the outlets for the finished product. Manufacturers finance the majority of advertising and they might well feel that a forwards merger would enable them to ensure that the good was being sold in the most appropriate setting.
4 In both cases, economies of scale are possible if different parts of the production process are brought together.
5 Again, vertical mergers can be carried out as a reaction to the activities of competitors.

Conglomerate mergers

These mergers are neither vertical nor horizontal but involve a merger between firms involved in producing different goods. An example would be the recent acquisition of the Yves Saint Laurent label by a subsidiary of the Elf Aquitaine oil company. The main motivation for this type of merger is diversification. It reduces the risk involved in producing for only one market and allows the firm to spread risk further. It can also provide the firm with another option if the original market declines in size.

As far as the economy is concerned, the main gains of mergers are in increased efficiency resulting from economies of scale and also the increased scope for research and development. A common view is that merger and take-over activity serves the purpose of rationalising business. The weak businesses go and the strong survive. Even when a take-over is carried out for the purpose of asset stripping this will be the case.

FINANCE FOR GROWTH

Internal sources

As part of its operation the firm will generate income in the form of profit. Part of this profit will be distributed in the form of dividends to shareholders, the rest can be used for reinvestment and to finance growth. Although this is seen as a relatively easy and cheap source of finance, it does carry an opportunity cost and therefore should be judged on its rate of return like any other source of finance. Table 8.4 shows that internal funds were the largest single source of finance for industry in 1990.

Table 8.4 Sources of funds for industry 1990 £ million

Source	£m
Internal funds	33,838
Banks and other short-term borrowing	19,911
Loans and mortgages	9,120
Ordinary shares	1,880
Debentures and preference shares	6,367
Other capital issues	7,485
Other overseas investment	11,233
Other	1,444
Total	91,278

Source: *Financial Statistics*, January 1993

External sources

As the size and availability of retained earnings will be limited, most firms will also have to seek other sources of finance for expansion. There are many external sources of finance and a typical firm's capital structure will be comprised of a combination of these. These sources are as follows.

Banks

Banks provide short- and medium-term finance to companies in the form of loans or overdrafts. The relative cost of these depends upon how the firm wishes to use the funds. Loans carry a lower rate of interest but the interest is paid on the whole amount, while the interest on overdrafts is only paid on the amount drawn. British banks have been criticised by many for failing to provide longer-term finance for business, as banks do in other countries.

Capital market

The capital market is the place where stocks and shares are traded and is therefore a key provider of long-term finance to firms. The main institution in the capital market is the Stock Exchange. The capital market is made up of two parts: the primary part which involves the buying and selling of new stocks and shares; and the secondary part which involves the buying and selling of existing stocks and shares. It is therefore the primary part of the market that is the source of finance for firms. The secondary part of the market is, however, also important in this process as individuals and organisations are more likely to buy stocks and shares with the knowledge that there is a ready market on which they can be traded at a later date.

The main institutions that buy stocks and shares are the insurance companies, pension funds, investment trusts, unit trusts and other large financial institutions such as building societies.

A new issue of shares takes place when an existing company needs extra finance or when a company becomes a public limited company.

Types of stocks and shares

1 *Preference shares* These are shares in a company which carry a fixed dividend. Holders have preference over other shareholders in the payment of dividends and on the liquidation of the firm. Preference shares usually carry no voting rights, and so holders have little influence over how the company is run.
2 *Ordinary shares* Ordinary shares are called the 'equity' of the company. They do not usually carry a fixed dividend, the company declares a dividend depending upon its performance in that year. This means that in good years ordinary shareholders could receive high dividends, while in bad years possibly none at all. Ordinary shares are therefore more risky than preference shares, and in recognition of this they usually carry voting rights, so that holders can exercise some influence over how the company is run.
3 *Debentures* Debentures or loan stock are bonds which are given in exchange for a loan to the company. The company agrees to repay the borrowed amount at some date in the future and to make annual payments of interest in the meantime. Interest on debentures is paid before payment of any dividends and the interest is allowable against tax. A debenture holder is a *creditor* of the company, a shareholder is an *owner* of the company.

New issue of shares

A company will go to an issuing house or merchant bank who will advise it on the type and number of shares to issue, the price at which they should be offered and other matters. They will often carry out the issue of shares on behalf of the firm. A new issue of shares is not a big source of finance for growth as it is fairly expensive; retained earnings are more convenient and cheaper. Also the amount of information that is required from companies which issue shares to the general public can act as a disincentive.

Money market

The money markets provide short-term finance for companies, often as short as overnight.

Government and other institutions

The government is a source of finance for firms. Through its regional policy it gives tax allowances, loans, grants and training allowances to firms in certain parts of the country (see Chapter 10). It has many schemes for helping business, particularly small businesses. This will be covered more fully later in this chapter.

Other sources

These include trade credit and hire purchase (i.e. receiving assets now and paying later). This is only a small source of finance for companies. As Table 8.4 shows industry draws a fairly high proportion of its funding from overseas. This includes finance from many different sources including individuals, governments, financial institutions overseas, and companies.

Firms will typically go for a mixture of different types of finance. The exact combination will depend upon many factors including their relative costs, their availability and the desired capital structure of the firm. A firm's desired capital structure will largely depend upon the type of market in which it operates. The different types of finance are classified under the two headings of debt and equity. Debt refers to all types of capital on which payments have to made each year regardless of how the firm has performed, this would include loans and preference shares. Equity refers to ordinary shares where the payment of a dividend depends upon the performance of the firm. As a source of finance, debt is generally cheaper but it is also more risky since in bad years the firm will have to meet the interest payments. The ratio of debt to equity is called the gearing of the company. Debt is not well suited to firms in industries where profits fluctuate and such firms will have lower gearing than those in more stable markets.

Limits to growth

Several factors tend to act as a limit to organisational growth:

- To finance growth, excessive borrowing might have taken place and the firm may have trouble meeting debt repayments; therefore there is increased risk of bankruptcy.
- A serious constraint to growth might be the abilities of management. As organisations grow in size they may experience diseconomies of scale, which are mainly to do with managerial problems, like communication and control.
- If the size of the market for the product is stagnant or declining it may be both unnecessary and impossible for the firm to grow.
- Government policies, too, can have an important impact on growth. Every government has policies on competition which seek to limit anti-competitive practices and which normally regulate merger activity (see Chapter 14).

Merger activity in the United Kingdom

Figure 8.1 shows the level of merger activity in terms of number of companies acquired and the value of the merger. It can be seen that there was a sharp rise in merger activity in the mid-1980s and a downturn in 1990. The cyclical pattern implies that the level of mergers is in some way related to the state of the economy. The rise in the mid-1980s was partly due to an improvement in the state of the economy and partly to the liberalisation of the financial markets which made finance for take-over bids more freely available. The fall in 1990 again is due partly to the recession and partly to the problems that some companies subsequently experienced by overstretching themselves in the mid-1980s.

There are also differences between industrial sectors as Figures 8.2 and 8.3 show. The number and value of mergers in the secondary sector is much greater than the tertiary sector which in turn is much greater than the primary sector.

Merger activity in Europe

There was a decrease in merger activity in 1990/91 in Europe after three years of very high increases. The number of financial operations was 1,009 in 1990/91, a decrease of

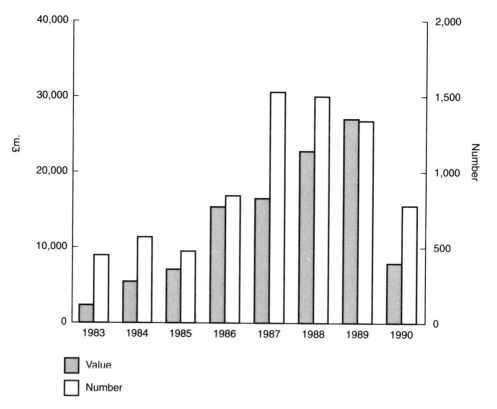

Fig. 8.1 UK merger activity by number and value, 1983–1990
Source: *Business Monitor PA1003*

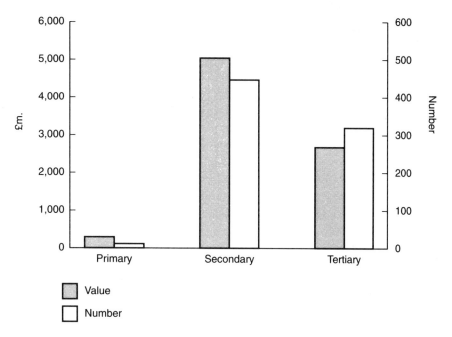

Fig. 8.2 Merger activity in the UK by sector, 1990
Source: *Business Monitor PA 1003.*

27 per cent on the previous year. 'Financial operations' includes mergers, acquisition of majority holdings and joint ventures. Of these, mergers and acquisitions of majority holdings accounted for 60 per cent of the total. Three-quarters of these operations were in the industrial sector. Table 8.5 gives some examples of different sectors and shows the variation in activity. Despite the fall in the number of operations the level of merger activity remains high.

International operations were more numerous than operations involving firms from the same Member State. This is in stark contrast to only a few years ago when wholly national operations out-numbered international ones (Figure 8.4).

Table 8.5 Merger activity in the EC 1990/91

Sector	Activity within Member States			EC			International		
	(a)	(b)	(c)	(a)	(b)	(c)	(a)	(b)	(c)
Industrial	186	60	33	170	55	49	99	31	45
Distributive	28	10	5	8	3	3	2	1	1
Banking	51	28	7	13	21	7	11	8	2
Insurance	15	10	5	7	12	6	6	8	3

Note: (a) mergers; (b) acquisition of majority holdings; (c) joint ventures.
Source: *21st EC Competition Policy Report.* Reproduced with permission of the Commission of the European Communities.

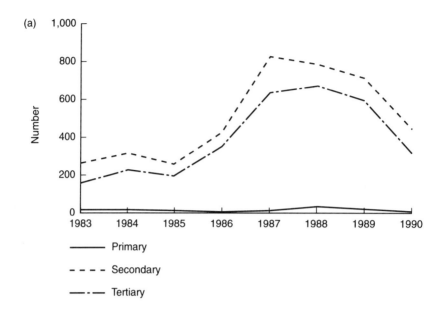

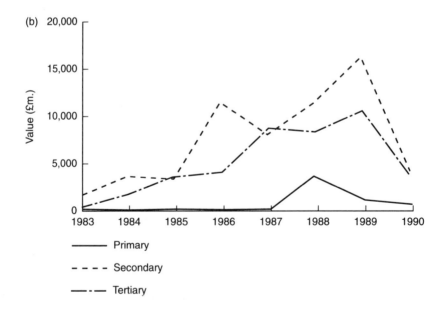

Fig. 8.3 Merger activity in the UK by sector: (a) by number, and (b) by value, 1983–90
Source: *Business Monitor PA1003*

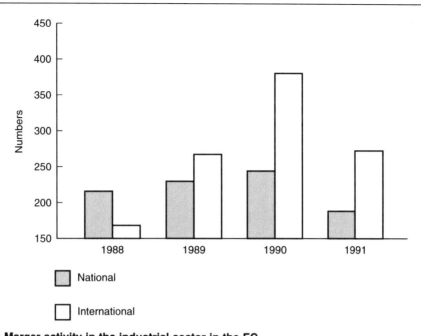

National

International

Fig. 8.4 Merger activity in the industrial sector in the EC
Source: *21st EC Competition Policy Report.* Reproduced with permission of the Commission of the European
Communities.

Table 8.6 shows the number of financial operations in selected EC countries over a
five-year period, and shows that activity is concentrated in France and West Germany
(a half of all operations). The level of activity decreased by more than 50 per cent over
1989/90 mainly because of the recession.

Table 8.6 Number of financial operations in selected EC countries

Year	Acquired/acquiring firms					
	Total (all EC members)	Belgium	Germany	France	Italy	United Kingdom
1986/87	303	3	69	63	35	90
1987/88	383	11	51	122	40	106
1988/89	492	18	90	112	49	111
1989/90	622	21	124	101	73	108
1990/91	455	9	111	115	51	82

Source: *21st EC Competition Policy Report.* Reproduced with permission of the Commission of
the European Communities.

Table 8.7 is a matrix which shows where activity takes place. It can be seen that in
France and Germany the United Kingdom is the most important foreign acquirer, while
in the United Kingdom this rank is held by the United States. As far as the acquiring
firm is concerned France, Germany and the United Kingdom accounted for 60 per cent
of all take-overs.

It is also significant to note that joint ventures (see Table 8.8) are increasing in

Table 8.7 Financial operations by country for 1990/91

Acquiring firm	Acquired firm				
	Belgium	Germany	France	Italy	United Kingdom
Belgium	1	1	2	2	1
Germany	–	60	8	6	7
France	3	10	55	8	5
Italy	–	–	4	18	3
United Kingdom	2	13	15	4	39
United States	2	10	9	6	11
Japan	–	1	5	1	5

Source: *21st EC Competition Policy Report*. Reproduced with permission of the Commission of the European Communities.

Table 8.8 Joint ventures in Europe (numbers)

	National	EC	International
1987/88	45	31	35
1988/89	56	36	37
1989/90	43	55	60
1990/91	33	49	44

Source: *21st EC Competition Policy Report*. Reproduced with permission of the Commission of the European Communities.

importance as a way of entering foreign markets. The ratio of foreign joint ventures to national joint ventures is 3 : 1.

SMALL FIRMS

There are serious problems in the analysis of the small-firm sector including the lack of data over a long period of time and the problem of defining exactly what is a small firm. The Bolton Report,[2] published in 1971, was the report of a committee set up to look into the role of small firms in the UK economy. It used various definitions for statistical purposes depending upon the industry being considered, on the grounds that what is small in one industry might be large in another. Table 8.9 shows the size distribution of firms based on their turnover for a selection of industries for 1990.

It is clear from this table that the definition of 'big' will vary with the industry. In the Bolton Report the definition used for small firms in manufacturing was 'less than 200 employees', while in construction it was 'less than 25 employees'. In some industries turnover limits were chosen whilst in others a mixture of employment and turnover was used. Although this is confusing and makes comparison between industries and countries difficult, it was accepted that there could not be a single definition which would apply to all sectors. No matter how small firms are defined, they will suffer from similar problems which are very different from those faced by larger companies.

Table 8.9 Size of companies by turnover across different industries 1990

Industry	Turnover size		
	Up to £250,000	£250,000 – £500,000	Over £500,000
Agriculture, forestry and fishing	89	7	4
Mining and quarrying and public utilities	45	12	43
Manufacturing	64	13	23
Construction	81	8	11
Wholesaling	52	14	34
Retailing	83	10	7
Financial services	80	8	12
Business services	81	7	12

Source: *Business Monitor PA1003*

Trends in the small firm sector

Figure 8.5 shows the share of small establishments in total manufacturing employment from 1935 to 1990. The definition used is less than 200 employees. The establishment is the reporting unit. It can be seen that the small-firm sector was in decline up to the late 1960s and early 1970s, after which its importance has increased.

Table 8.2 showed that for manufacturing industries small firms are very important in terms of the numbers of companies, accounting for 97 per cent of total firms according

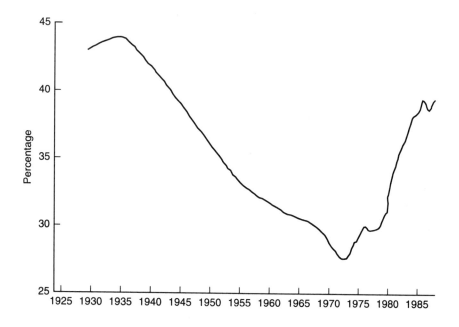

Figure 8.5 : Share of small establishments in total manufacturing employment 1930–1990
Source: J. Stanworth and C. Gray (eds), *Bolton 20 years On: The Small Firm in the 1990s*, Chapman, 1991, table 1.1.

to the Bolton Report definition. Even though they were less important in terms of employment they still accounted for nearly 50 per cent of total employment. This tends to understate their importance because it does not include the service sector, many parts of which are heavily dominated by small firms due to the nature of the production process. Although there is a great deal of information available from official sources on the manufacturing sector, the same scope of information is not available for the service sector, so accurate information is difficult to obtain.

Evidence suggests that the increased importance given to the small-firm sector in the United Kingdom also applies to other countries,[3] though the growth rates have generally been faster. EC figures put the growth rate in the numbers of small firms between 1983 and 1986 as 14.6 per cent in the United Kingdom, 6–7 per cent in West Germany and France, and 3 per cent in Italy. The contribution of the small-firm sector to GDP varies between countries and is low in the United Kingdom, as Table 8.10 shows.

Table 8.10 Share of SMEs* in non-primary private sector GDP, selected countries, mid-1980s

Country	Year	%
Japan	1982	60
USA	1982	50
W. Germany	1986	46
UK	1986	32

Source: J. Stanworth and C. Gray (eds), *Bolton 20 years On: The Small Firm in the 1990s*, Chapman, 1991 table 1.8.
*Small and medium-sized enterprises

Reasons for the growth in the small-firm sector

There has clearly been a resurgence in the importance of the small-firm sector which appears to have been more pronounced in the United Kingdom than other countries. Why? Some causal factors are as follows:

1 *The changing pattern of industry* In Chapter 12 it is clear that there has been a change in the industrial structure of the United Kingdom away from manufacturing and towards services. Since many services are dominated by small firms, there will be a corresponding change in average firm size. However, this does not provide the full explanation as there has been a growth in the share of small firms even in the manufacturing sector. And it does not explain the international differences since there have been similar changes in industrial structure in other countries too.

2 *Flexible specialisation and the growth of subcontracting* A debate which started in the late 1980s centres round the idea of the 'flexible firm'.[4] As a result of the recession of the early 1980s there was a drive by firms to reduce their costs in order to remain competitive. One way of reducing overhead costs was to move to a flexible firm structure whereby the firm's activities are divided into core and peripheral activities. The core activities which are central to the activities of the firm

would be kept 'in-house' and carried out by full-time permanent workers. The peripheral activities would be carried out by temporary workers or would be subcontracted. The firm has then reduced its overheads and can react to peaks in demand by increasing the amount of temporary labour it uses or increasing the amount of subcontracting. This might also have had the effect of increasing the relative importance of the small-firm sector.

3 *Government policy* After the Bolton Report there was a much greater interest in the role of the small firm in the regeneration of the economy and in the provision of jobs. But most of the initiatives designed to help the small firm came after the start of the resurgence of the small-firm sector in early 1970s.

4 *The growth in self-employment* A large part of the growth in the small-firm sector has been due to the growth in the number of self-employed. The self-employed accounted for 7 per cent of the workforce in 1978 and 11.7 per cent in 1990 (see Table 8.11). This represents a 73 per cent increase in the number of those self-employed over this period.

The level of self-employment is likely to be related to the level of unemployment, so that as unemployment rose over the 1970s and 1980s there was an increase in the level of self-employment. This goes a long way to explaining the international differences as the growth in self-employment in the United Kingdom has far outstripped that in other countries. Again, however, it does not provide the full explanation as business births were growing in the late 1960s when unemployment was falling.

5 *Technological change* Changes in technology, particularly information technology and the miniaturisation of components has made it possible for small firms to benefit to a similar extent to large firms. This has had the effect of reducing the importance of economies of scale and enabling small firms to compete more effectively with large ones.

Table 8.11 Percentage of workforce self-employed 1978–1990

Year	Self-employed (%)
1978	7.0
1979	6.9
1980	7.3
1981	7.7
1982	8.0
1983	8.1
1984	8.9
1985	9.2
1986	9.3
1987	10.0
1988	10.4
1989	11.2
1990	11.7

Source: *Annual Abstract of Statistics*, 1992

6 *Competitive forces* As far as the international differences are concerned, the Bolton Report found that industry in the United Kingdom was biased towards large size in comparison with other countries. So what may have happened as a result of competitive forces is that the balance of industry in the United Kingdom has moved towards the norm of other countries.

The role of the small-firm sector

The growing importance of the small-firm sector implies that small firms do have a valuable role in the economy apart from being a mere provider of employment. The areas in which the small firm has advantages over large firms are where there are:

1 *Clearly defined small markets* In such markets it is not worthwhile large firms entering since there are no economies of scale and no scope for mass production.
2 *Specialist, quality, non-standardised products* Again it would not be worth a large firm entering such a market as the benefits of large-scale production cannot be reaped.
3 *Geographically localised markets* For example, the small corner shop.
4 *Development of new ideas* It is often argued that the small firm is the 'seedbed' of ideas and that because of greater motivation and commitment on the part of the owner of the small firm, it is very conducive to invention and innovation.

Aid to the small firm sector

The thinking on small firms has changed over time. Initially they were viewed favourably, but after the Second World War the dominant thinking was that large-scale production could take advantage of large economies of scale and that costs would be lower and production more efficient. It was not until more recently that the interest in the small-firm sector has increased again. The main reasons for the renewed interest has been the results of empirical studies which have shown that the role of the small firm is greater than previously thought in areas such as innovation, the balance of payments and employment.

The basic argument for the provision of aid to the small-firm sector is that they are at a disadvantage with respect to large businesses in areas such as raising capital, research and development and risk-bearing. It is also accepted that they have a valuable role to play in the economy. In the 1980s, for example, small firms were seen as a mechanism for reducing the very high levels of unemployment.

Government policy

In the early 1980s, government policy was aimed at encouraging start-ups; more recently the emphasis has changed to encouragement for firms to grow. There are many schemes which provide aid to business and they undergo frequent revision. The main government department that provides aid is the Department of Trade and Industry, which through its Enterprise Initiative gives regional aid, business consultancy, assistance to exports and aid for research and technology transfer. The Department of the Environment has the prime responsibility for urban regeneration through the Urban

Development Corporations in large cities, and City Action teams in some smaller cities like Leicester (see Chapter 10). The Department of Employment has responsibility for training and other labour market measures.

There has been a shift away from centralised aid to more localised provision through the TECs. There has also been an emphasis on the partnership between the public and private sectors in the provision of that aid (Chapter 10).

Networking between firms

A more recent trend in industry which is well documented is towards co-operation rather than competition.[5] This co-operation can take many forms: for example, subcontracting, networking (both formal and informal) and joint ventures. Such co-operation can be (and is) used by large as well as small- and medium-sized enterprises. For large companies it is a way to grow and diversify without risk. For smaller firms it allows them to stay small but at the same time to benefit from some of the advantages of large-scale production like specialisation.

Subcontracting

There has been an increase in the amount of subcontracting, where firms do not carry out the whole of the production process themselves but subcontract some of their activities to other firms. This represents a rejection of vertical integration and it is related to the notion of the flexible firm mentioned earlier. Subcontracting goes some way to explaining the phenomenal growth rate in 'business services' that occurred in the 1980s. It is increasingly common for businesses to subcontract specialist work in areas such as human resource management to outside consultancies. 'Partnering' between companies and consultancies is becoming more common where the consultancy is retained on a semi-permanent basis to give advice on a whole range of human resource matters from recruitment to planning for succession. This will obviously boost the small firm sector.

Networking

This refers to the relationships that exist between organisations and the people within those organisations. These relationships can be of different types, both formal and informal, and there is increasing recognition of the importance of these relationships, especially to small firms (e.g. they may be based on the exchange of goods and services, like the relationship between a firm and its supplier or client). Subcontracting is an example of this kind of network but there are other links not based on exchange, like the relationship between a firm and the bank manager or other advisors. There are also informal links between the entrepreneur and family and friends, and between entrepreneurs in different organisations. There might also be co-operative links between firms. This can be seen in the market for executive recruitment where there has been a growth in the links between consultancies particularly for international work. The creation of the Single European Market and the increased internationalisation of business left the smaller consultancies in a weak position relative to the large international recruitment firms like MSL, who have branches in most European countries. The smaller consultancies have reacted by forming networks. There are basically two types of network:

1 Where firms are members of a network but where the network has a different name from the individual firms and the firms operate under their own name (i.e. the network has an identity of its own). The members are independent firms that co-operate in carrying out their business. There are 16 such groups in Europe including EMA partners and International Search Associates.
2 Where firms are part of a network of independent firms but where the network does not have a separate identity and the firms operate under their own names. There are ten such groups in Europe.

The firm is seen as existing within a spider's web of relationships as Figure 8.6 shows. It is possible for two firms to be linked in a variety of ways; in one market they may be competitors, in the next co-operators, customers in another and suppliers in another.

Networking has taken on greater significance because of changes that are taking place in the economy, which include the reversal of the trend towards higher industrial concentration, the adoption of Japanese methods of production, the decline of 'mass markets', and technological change that requires greater specialisation than previously. All of these changes favour the formation of networks.

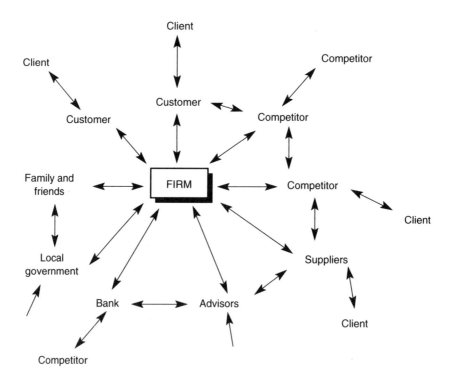

Fig. 8.6 A typical network

Joint ventures

As Chapter 7 indicated, companies that wish to diversify into new areas may well do so by entering into a joint venture with another company in that field. Joint ventures benefit both parties as both companies have diversified with the benefit of the experience of the other company and the level of risk is minimised. Joint ventures are also a good way for firms to enter other countries' markets as seen earlier. Again there are examples in the area of executive recruitment. The International Search Group, for instance, was set up as a joint venture between five companies in France, United Kingdom, Austria, Germany and Italy in order to offer a European service to its customers.

Consortia

In some industries co-operative behaviour has come about for particular reasons. In process plant contracting, for example, the projects are often too large for single firms and so they form consortia in order to bid for the contract. The consortia will include contractors, suppliers and bankers who together will have the expertise and the resources to carry out the project.

MULTINATIONALS

At the opposite end of the scale from the very small business are companies which have the capability to produce goods or services in more than one country but where control usually resides in a central location. For example, ICI, a UK-based multinational, has its headquarters in the United Kingdom but has more than 300 subsidiaries around the world operating in many different markets. Multinationals are often well-known household names, as the examples below illustrate:

- UK multinationals – BP, ICI.
- European multinationals – Nestlé, Volkswagen.
- USA multinationals – General Motors, IBM.

These multinationals are huge organisations and their market values often exceed the GNP of many of the countries in which they operate. They are estimated to account for a quarter of the world's output.

The growth in the multinationals is due to relaxation of exchange controls making it easier to move money between countries, and the improvements in communication which make it possible to run a worldwide business from one country.

The operation of multinationals

Multinationals can diversify operations across different countries. This brings them great benefits:

1 Multinationals can locate their activities in the countries which are best suited. For example, production planning can be carried out in the parent country, the production itself can be carried out in one of the newly industrialised countries

where labour is relatively cheap and marketing can be done in the parent country where such activities are well developed. This relocation of production may go some way to explaining the decline in the manufacturing sector in the developed nations.

2 A multinational can cross-subsidise its operations. Profits from one market can be used to support operations in another one. The cross-subsidisation could take the form of price cutting, increasing productive capacity or heavy advertising campaigns.

3 The risk involved in production is spread, not just over different markets but also different countries.

4 Multinationals can avoid tax by negotiating special tax arrangements in one of their host countries (tax holidays) or through careful use of transfer pricing. Transfer prices are the prices at which internal transactions take place. These can be altered so that high profits are shown in countries where the tax rate is lower. In 1993 Nissan was found to have done just this; by inflating the cost of importing cars from Japan to the United Kingdom, its profits appeared smaller and the burden of corporation tax was reduced.

The very size of multinationals gives rise to concern as their operations can have a substantial impact on the economy. For example, the activities of multinationals will affect the balance of payments of countries. If a subsidiary is started in one country there will be an inflow of capital to that country. Once it is up and running, however, there will be outflows of dividends and profits which will affect the invisible balance. Also there will be flows of goods within the company and therefore between countries, in the form of semi-finished goods and raw materials. These movements will affect the exchange rate as well as the balance of payments and it is likely that the effects will be greater for developing countries than for developed countries.

Added to this, multinationals take their decisions in terms of their overall operations rather than with any consideration of their effects on the host economy. There is therefore a loss of economic sovereignty for national governments. The main problem with multinationals is the lack of control that can be exerted by national governments. There is also the possibility of exploitation of less developed countries and it is debatable whether such footloose industries form a viable basis for economic development. Against this is the fact that without the presence of multinationals, output in host countries would be lower.

SYNOPSIS

This chapter has looked at the size structure of industry in the United Kingdom and Europe as a whole. It examined the motives for and the methods of growth, as well as the sources of finance for such growth. The role of the small firm was considered, as too was the role of the multinational. Although many industries are dominated by huge companies, the trend seems to be moving away from growth towards a process of disintegration for a variety of reasons. As a result of this trend there has been an upsurge in the small-firm sector, and an increase in the level of co-operative behaviour between firms.

CASE STUDY: EXECUTIVE SEARCH AND SELECTION

As this chapter has shown, the size of firms within an industry depends upon many factors. The nature of the product and the production process are important in explaining why many service industries are dominated by small firms. Services have the following characteristics which differentiate them from goods and this has implications for the structure of the industry concerned:

- *Intangibility* Services are intangible while goods are tangible. This means that it is impossible to sample a service before it is purchased.
- *Inseparability* There is often no separation between the consumption and production of services. Goods are produced, sold and then consumed. Services are sold, then production and consumption begin simultaneously.
- *Heterogeneity* Given the nature of services, they are difficult to standardise; often each unit of a service sold is different. This stems from the central role that the buyer plays in service production.
- *Perishability* Services are perishable, they are destroyed in the process of consumption and cannot be stored.
- *Irreversibility* Many services are irreversible in that once consumed they cannot be returned nor can faults be rectified.

These characteristics have an important impact upon the shape of the industry and the firms that constitute the industry. This case study looks at two such service industries, executive search and selection.

Executive search and selection

Executive search and selection agencies are two parts of the executive recruitment market. Search is the recruitment of candidates through direct and personal contact by a specialist recruitment consultancy acting as an intermediary between employer and potential candidate(s) ('head-hunting'). Selection is the identification and short-listing of a small number of potential candidates through recruitment advertising.

The executive search and selection industries have both grown rapidly over the last 50 years. Search has developed to the point where it is the most common recruitment method for board-room appointments. There are two possible explanations for this growth: first, that the level of executive recruitment itself has increased and search and selection have maintained the same percentage of a growing market; or secondly, that search and selection consultants have increased their share of the market. The evidence suggests that both of these has happened: the market has grown and companies are making increasing use of recruitment consultants.

The typical firm in both industries is small. In search the average number of consultants per firm is 4.6 and the most common firm size is 2 consultants. In selection the average number of consultants is 6.2 and the most common firm size is 3 consultants. There are many reasons for this and some of these reasons apply equally to other services and are related to the service characteristics mentioned above. Some, however, are specific to executive search and selection:

- There is a large personal element in the service provided which means that the production process will be labour intensive. The only scope for technological change is through the computerisation of records and processes. This is likely to be true for many services and means that there is no scope for mass production and the typical firm size will remain small.
- The perishable nature of services means that stocks cannot be kept, and given that the demand for services will fluctuate firms with large numbers of consultants will have to bear the cost of excess capacity when demand is low. There is therefore a tendency towards small size.

- The higher the number of consultants the greater the possibility of one or more leaving and starting a new consultancy in competition with the original, and taking their contacts with them. This is a fairly common method of entry for new firms into these industries. For this reason, firms rarely have more than nine consultants.

- Executive search is unique in that the greater the number of client companies, the smaller the pool of candidates. Most search firms will not approach someone they have placed for at least two years. Therefore the more people they place, the more restricted will be the number of candidates.

- It could be that there is little scope for economies of scale; there are many firms with only one consultant surviving and performing well in both industries. Although the size of the firms in the industries is small, greater specialisation in the task can take place than in a personnel department. Many consultancies specialise by function or industry, which may lead to reduced search times due to the consultants' easier access to candidates and data banks and better understanding of the industry. There is also the effect of repetition on the skills of the producer. There is some evidence in both industries of economies of scale. The average number of assignments carried out in search for 1987 was 7.9 per consultant. The biggest fourteen firms averaged 12.5 assignments per consultant, while the rest averaged 7.1 assignments per consultant per annum. The same picture emerges in selection where the overall average is 10.8 per consultant per annum; for the larger firms the average is 29 and for the smaller firms the average falls to 8.2.

- Despite the fact that there may well be some scope for economies of scale in the industries, it is clear from the numbers of assignments involved that the minimum efficient scale of production is small. Firms can enter the industry and carry out a relatively small number of assignments and survive.

- Low barriers to entry and exit make the industries easy to enter and leave. Because of the characteristics of services it is difficult for the quality of the service being provided to be ascertained. To overcome this lack of information, many service industries (accounting and law for example) have strong regulatory bodies which can enforce certain behaviour patterns upon the firms in the industry. This, however, is not the case for executive search and selection. There is no regulatory body, there are no pre-entry educational requirements and there are no legal limitations to entry, apart from the acquisition of a licence under the 1973 Employment Agencies Act which can be obtained fairly easily for a small sum. Once a firm has entered there is little formal control over its operating methods; so legal barriers to entry are not high in search and selection. The capital required to set up in business is low, since all that is needed is a licence, a telephone, stationery, secretarial support and an office. The method of payment for assignments – which usually involves a part payment at the beginning of the assignment – reduces the 'break-in' period as loans can be quickly paid off. Consultancies become profitable after only a few assignments.

- The service characteristics of inseparability of production and consumption often places a geographical limit on markets that can be served, and this will impact upon firm size. Many services involve 'direct sales' with no intermediaries, and so firms are likely to locate near to the demand for their services or near to where the decision is taken to use that service. For example, if the decision is taken at a high level in an organisation it is likely that the location of head offices will be an important factor in the location of services. Executive search and selection are an extension of the management division of labour since they are the externalisation of previous internal personnel functions. Hence, if the location of search and selection consultancies is close to its demand, and the decisions to use recruitment consultants are located in head offices, then the location of these head offices plays a crucial part in the location of search and selection. This partly explains the geographical concentration of executive search and selection consultants in London and the South East (77.5 per cent of executive search and selection consultants are located in this area).

● The inseparability of production and consumption in services means that the concept of vertical integration loses meaning when applied to services. Most services involve direct production, so the whole production process takes place when the service is performed. The existence of many business and other services represents a process of disintegration, as firms are increasingly shedding their peripheral functions and buying in these functions from external sources. Search and selection are good examples of this process as recruitment and other personnel functions are increasingly being contracted out. Indeed a recent phenomenon within the industry is further disintegration as researchers are setting up their own firms and consultants are buying their services. There is no obvious reason why horizontal mergers should not take place in service industries. The motivation for and incidence of horizontal mergers will vary between the very different services which exist. As far as services with large personal inputs are concerned, there will be limited scope for economies of scale, and so this reason for merger is removed. Similarly services which are geographically localised are less likely to be horizontally integrated.

● The particular nature of service production makes diversification into other areas more difficult than in other types of production. The obvious directions for diversification are into products either produced with common technology or through the development of existing technology and into products that can be marketed through similar channels. Search and selection consultancies diversify by offering other services to management. The development of search and selection itself has partly been through a process of diversification as large accountancy firms have moved into the area of management consultancy, including recruitment.

Conclusion

Executive search and selection (like many other services) are characterised by firms of small size.

For service industries where the dominant size of firm is small, the traditional theories on growth of firms, which see development as a 'grow or fail' process, are often not very helpful. They are clearly not true when small firms not only survive but are successful. A more fruitful approach is to look at the constraints that might prevent the growth of firms in search and selection. The internal constraints are the personal nature of the production process which means that consultants can only handle a fairly small number of assignments per year. There is some evidence that an increase in support staff does increase the output of consultants but not by a significant amount – the range remains narrow. Another internal constraint might be a lack of individuals with the right skills. The skills required in a consultant are good interpersonal and communication skills, possibly some experience of recruitment work and, more importantly, contacts. An external constraint is that the service can be carried out by clients, which might well limit the extent of the market. Also, and unique to search, is the fact that consultants will not normally approach an individual they have placed for at least two years. Therefore as the number of consultants rise in a firm the possible pool of candidates shrinks. The bigger the consultancy, the higher is the probability that one or more consultants would leave to set up in competition against the original consultancy, taking all of their contacts with them. There have been examples of consultants doing this but taking with them researchers as well, leaving the original consultancy in a very weak position.

All of these factors serve to limit the growth of the firm and ensure that the typical search and selection consultancy is small. If there is little scope for economies of scale, the minimum efficient scale of production will be small.

NOTES AND REFERENCES

1   *Penguin Dictionary of Economics.*
2   *The Bolton Committee Report*, HMSO, 1971.
3   Stanworth, J. and Gray, C., *Bolton 20 Years On: The small firm in the 1990s*, Chapman, 1991.
4   Atkinson, J., 'Flexibility, uncertainty and manpower management', report no. 89, Institute of Manpower Studies, 1984.
5   Pyke, F., 'Co-operative practices among small and medium-sized establishments', *Work, Employment and Society*, 2, (3), September 1988.

REVIEW AND DISCUSSION QUESTIONS

1   Why are there no large firms in the executive search and selection industries?

2   How might these industries be affected by recession?

3   What advantages does networking bring to small firms and the economy as a whole?

4   How has the balance between large and small firms in manufacturing changed in the last ten years? Do you expect these trends to continue?

ASSIGNMENTS

1   You are an information officer at your local business advice centre and you have been given the job of designing and writing a leaflet aimed at the proprietors of small firms, outlining the government aid that is available to small businesses. Your brief is to keep the leaflet short and readable but with maximum information. (Information on government aid will be available at your local library or business advice centre.)

2   As part of 'Business Week' you have been asked to give a short talk to local sixth-formers doing Business Studies 'A' level on the size structure of UK industry. Prepare your talk by choosing two industries, describing and giving reasons for the typical size structure of the firms in those industries.

FURTHER READING

Griffiths, A. and Wall S., *Applied Economics: An introductory course*, 5th edition, Longman, 1993.
Stanworth, J. and Gray C., *Bolton 20 Years On: The small firm in the 1990s*, Chapman, 1991.

CHAPTER 9

Industrial structure

Chris Britton

Within any economy, there will be a whole range of industries that produce a variety of products for a variety of users. The particular combination of industries within a country is called the industrial structure of that country. There will be international differences in industrial structures, because of differences in the many factors that affect the determination of industrial structure.

OBJECTIVES

1 To understand what industrial structure is and how it is measured.
2 To examine the industrial structure of the United Kingdom and the European Community as a whole.
3 To identify the reasons for particular industrial structures and the factors which influence industrial structure.
4 To identify how and why the industrial structure of the United Kingdom and the European Community has changed over time.

INTRODUCTION

A country can produce many different and diverse types of goods and services ranging from the production of cars to the delivery of legal services to farming. The mix of these and the combination of industries that exist to produce them is called the industrial structure of a country. There are likely to be large differences in industrial structure between countries for many reasons. This chapter will look at the industrial structure of the European Community as a trading bloc and the United Kingdom in particular. There is a need for the industrial structure of a country to be measured in some way so that changes over time can be identified and international comparisons made. This chapter will look at the definitions of industries, the problems with such definitions and the official classification of industry used by the government in the United Kingdom. It will also identify the changes in industrial structure and the causes of these changes.

INDUSTRIAL STRUCTURE

The process of production

In Chapter 5 the three factors of production – labour, land and capital – were considered. Textbooks often add a fourth factor of production to this list, called 'entrepreneurship'. Entrepreneurship is the process of bringing together the other factors in order to produce goods and services. A firm produces goods and services because they are demanded and because a profit can be earned by selling them. Figure 9.1 shows a much simplified profit and loss account for a car manufacturer.

Revenues	£m.	Expenditures	£m.
Sales of cars	30.0	Raw materials	7.5
		Wages and salaries	10.0
		Overheads (rent, rates, lighting, etc.)	2.5
			20.0
		Profit	10.0
	30.0		30.0

Fig. 9.1 A simplified profit and loss account

The items on the expenditure side represent the payments to the factors of production. Wages are payments to labour, raw materials and an element of overheads would be the payment to capital, and the payment for land would be included in overheads. The payment to the entrepreneur is in the form of profit. What has happened in this process is that the factors of production have been combined to make finished cars and in the process value has been added to the initial value of the raw materials.

The car manufacturer can be thought of as being in the centre of a process of production which links together raw materials at one end with the consumers at the other end. The raw materials are extracted, processed and then the finished goods are sold. In economic terminology, the extraction of raw materials is called *primary* production, the manufacture of cars is called *secondary* production and the distribution of the finished cars is called *tertiary* production (see Figure 9.2). Although this simple path from primary production through to tertiary production is the case for many industries, it is likely to be much more complicated in practice.

The discussion at present is confined to a single firm, but it can be moved to the industry level. The industries that deal with natural resources like farming and mining comprise the primary sector. Industries which process these natural resources comprise the secondary sector, which will include manufacturing, construction and energy suppliers. The service industries make up the tertiary sector. There are great difficulties involved in such a classification of industry, as will be seen later, but consideration will now be given to the official classification of industry in the United Kingdom.

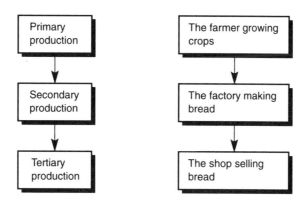

Fig. 9.2 A simplified production process

The Standard Industrial Classification

The Standard Industrial Classification (SIC) of economic activity is the official classification of industries in the United Kingdom into different sectors. It was first introduced in 1948 and has been updated and changed on occasions to take account of the development of new products and industries for producing those products. The last change took place in 1980, mainly in order to bring the United Kingdom classification in line with the activity classification used by the Statistical Office of the European Communities (Eurostat) which is called Nomenclature générale des activités économiques dans les Communautés européennes (NACE).

The 1980 SIC is shown in Table 9.1.

Table 9.1 SIC (1980)

Division	Industry
0	Agriculture, forestry and fishing
1	Energy and water supply industries
2	Extraction of minerals and ores other than fuels; manufacture of metals, mineral products and chemicals
3	Metal goods, engineering and vehicles industries
4	Other manufacturing industries
5	Construction
6	Distribution, hotels and catering; repairs
7	Transport and communication
8	Banking, finance, insurance, business services and leasing
9	Other services

The 1980 classification has 10 *divisions* (denoted by a single digit). Each of these is divided into *classes* (two digits), which in turn are divided into *groups* (three digits) and *activity headings* (four digits). In total there are 10 divisions, 60 classes, 222 groups and 334 activity headings. Table 9.2 gives an example of these.

Table 9.2 Division 4 of SIC(1980)

Division 4	Other manufacturing industries
Class 43	Textiles
Group 431	Woollen and worsted industry
Group 438	Carpets and other textile floor covering

The term 'production industries' refers to divisions 1 to 4 of the above classification, the term 'manufacturing industries' refers to divisions 2 to 4. The SIC does not comply exactly with the broad classification of industry used in the last section. The primary sector of the economy is found in divisions 0 and parts of divisions 1 and 2; the secondary sector in parts of divisions 1 and 2 and all of divisions 3 to 5. The tertiary sector would be divisions 6 to 9.

The SIC is changed periodically to reflect changes taking place in industry, but this SIC has been used since 1980 as the basis for all officially collected data on industry. In 1990 the EC approved a new statistical classification of economic activities in the EC (NACE Rev. 1). This means that the United Kingdom had to introduce a new SIC in 1992. The standardisation of industrial classification across Europe will make interstate comparisons easier. The SIC(92) which will replace SIC(80) is based on NACE Rev. 1, the only deviation being the addition of a fifth digit to further subdivide classes where it seemed necessary.

The SIC(92) has 17 sections instead of the 10 divisions of SIC(80); each of these sections is denoted by a letter from A to Q. The sections are divided into subsections which are denoted by the addition of another letter. The subsections are then broken down into two digit divisions and again into groups (3 digits), into classes (4 digits) and into subclasses (5 digits). An example of this is given in Table 9.3.

Table 9.3 SIC (92)

Section D	Manufacturing
Subsection DA	Manufacture of food products, beverages and tobacco
Division 15	Manufacture of food products and beverages
Group 15.1	Production, processing and preservation of meat and meat products
Class 15.13	Production of meat and poultry meat products
Subclass 15.13/1	Bacon and ham production

There are 17 sections, 14 subsections, 60 divisions, 222 groups, 503 classes and 142 subclasses. The SIC(92) follows the NACE Rev. 1 exactly, except for the use of subclasses which have been used for some industries in the United Kingdom.

The structure of the new SIC is given in an appendix to this chapter. It shows that not all of the sections are subdivided into subsections, some are broken down straight into divisions. Also some sections are subdivided more than others, the obvious example is section D where there are 14 subsections and 23 divisions. The level of detail depends upon the diversity of production included within the section.

Differences between SIC(92) and SIC(80)

First, there is the obvious change in the numbering system, but there are also some changes in the order in which industries appear. For example, electricity, gas and water have moved further down the list to appear after manufacturing in the SIC(92). There is also now a much more detailed breakdown of the service sector; the old division 9 has been broken up into eight different sections. This illustrates the increased acceptance of the importance of the service sector in the economy. There have also been changes in the classification within sections. Table 9.4 gives a comparison of the two Standard Industrial Classifications.

Table 9.4 A comparison of SIC(92) and SIC(80)

SIC(92)		SIC(80)
A	Agriculture, hunting and forestry	0
B	Fishing	0
C	Mining and quarrying	1 and 2
D	Manufacturing	1, 2, 3 and 4
E	Electricity, gas and water supply	1
F	Construction	5
G	Wholesale and retail trade; repair of motor vehicles, motor cycles and personal household goods	6
H	Hotels and restaurants	6
I	Transport, storage and communication	7 and 9
J	Financial intermediation	8
K	Real estate, renting and business activities	8 and 9
L	Public administration and defence; compulsory social security	9
M	Education	9
N	Health and social work	9
O	Other community, social and personal service activities	9
P	Private households with employed persons	9
Q	Extra-territorial organisations and bodies	9

Problems in classifying industries

The classification of industry is problematic. Firms could be grouped together according to similarities in what they produce but some firms produce a range of goods for quite different markets. Firms could be grouped together according to what they 'do', so that if their production processes are similar they could be considered as part of the same industry. The service industries are particularly problematic as they have traditionally been defined by the function they perform, but developments in technology have led to these functions overlapping and therefore becoming more difficult to distinguish: for example, publishing and printing. All of this leads to industries that are seemingly very diverse being grouped together in the SIC. Although the SIC does not succeed in overcoming all of these problems, it does provide an accepted classification of industry which can be used for many purposes. The information collected provides a basis for comparing the structure of industry within a country over time and between countries.

Measuring industrial structure

The structure of industry in a country is not static, it changes over time for a variety of reasons. For example:

- The development of new products means that new industries come into existence (e.g. the inventions and innovations in the field of electronic games).
- New patterns of demand means that some industries will be declining while others become increasingly important (see case study for example).
- Changes in society will be reflected in industrial structure. For example, according to the Census, in 1851 22 per cent of the workforce in the United Kingdom was engaged in agriculture, forestry and fishing while in 1989 the figure was 1.3 per cent. This obviously reflects the movement away from an agriculturally based society to an industrial society.

Industrial structure is usually measured by the level of employment or output of the various sectors of the economy, and changes in industrial structure over time can be observed by looking at the changes in the employment and output levels in different industries. These will usually (but not always) paint the same picture; a sector in decline will have falling employment and output.

Industrial structure in the EC

Figure 9.3 shows the industrial structure of the EC as a whole as measured by employment in 1979 and 1988. During the 1980s there was a 20 per cent fall in the level of employment in agriculture, a 14 per cent fall in the level of manufacturing employment and a 15 per cent rise in the employment in the service sector. At the end of the 1980s, 8 per cent of the working population of the EC was employed in agriculture, 32 per cent in industry and 60 per cent in services. So there has been a gradual trend away from employment in the primary and industrial sectors in the EC as a whole and a gradual rise in employment in the service sector. Figure 9.4 indicates the changes in the relative sizes of the three sectors over the period 1980 to 1988.

The trends displayed in the EC are evident in other advanced industrial economies. Table 9.5 shows that whilst there are some differences in industrial structure between countries, the tertiary sector in all cases is predominant in employment terms. Within the EC, the United Kingdom has a much smaller agricultural sector than other EC countries and the EC average whilst West Germany has the largest manufacturing sector. Japan has a larger manufacturing sector than the EC average and the USA, and a smaller tertiary sector.

Industrial structure can also be gauged by looking at output figures. Figure 9.5 shows the relative sizes of the three broad sectors of the EC economy by output for 1970 and 1988. It can be seen that the trend is the same as for employment levels.

Fig. 9.3 Percentage shares in employment of the three main sectors in the European Community, 1979 and 1988
Source: *Panorama of EC Industry*, 1990

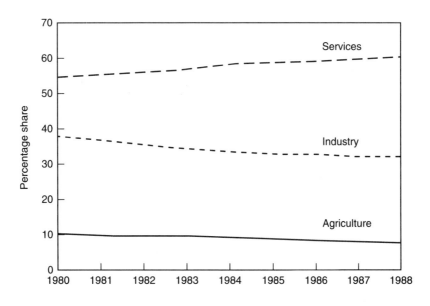

Fig. 9.4 Employment by sector in the European Community as a whole, 1980–1988
Source: *Panorama of EC Industry*, 1990

Table 9.5 Percentage employed in different sectors of selected countries (1986)

	Agriculture	Manufacturing	Services
United Kingdom	2.5	31.6	65.8
Spain	15.6	32.4	52.1
Italy	10.9	35.1	56.0
West Germany	5.3	40.9	53.8
France	7.6	32.1	60.4
EC average	8.0	32.0	60.0
Japan	8.5	34.5	57.1
United States	3.1	27.7	69.3

Source: *International Labour Statistics* 1989, ed. R. Bean, published by Routledge

Between 1970 and 1988, the share of agriculture in output has fallen from 5 per cent to 4 per cent, and industry from 32 per cent to 28 per cent, while the share of services has risen from 63 per cent to 68 per cent. In the United States the fall in the share of industry over the same period was more dramatic, declining by 9 per cent to stand at 28 per cent in 1988. In Japan the fall in the share of industry was 3 per cent, to stand at 41 per cent in 1988. Japan has a much larger industrial sector in terms of output than EC countries or the United States.

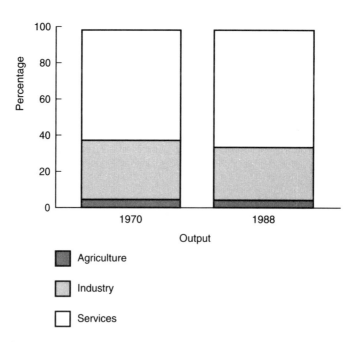

Fig. 9.5 Percentage shares in output of the three main sectors in the European Community, 1970 and 1988
Source: *Panorama of EC Industry*, 1990

For both employment and output the figures tell the same story (see Table 9.6): the primary and secondary sectors of the main industrial countries have declined in importance, while the tertiary sectors have increased in importance. The reasons for these changes will be considered later in this chapter.

The broad averages hide differences between the industries in each sector. Industries which grew faster than the average during the 1980s include communication services, office and EDP equipment, insurance, chemicals, wholesaling, retailing and electrical engineering. Some industries exhibited negative growth, these included metallic and non-metallic minerals, metal production, agricultural and industrial machinery, textiles and footwear and other manufactured goods (especially furniture). Generally speaking the industries which exhibited the fastest growth rates were the export-related goods and services.

Table 9.6 The ranking of major EC sectors by employment and output

NACE code		Rank by	
		Output	Employment
64	Retail trade	1	1
41	Food and drink (except tobacco)	2	5
25	Chemicals	3	7
35	Motor vehicles	4	8
34	Electrical engineering	5	3
50	Building and civil engineering	6	2
32	Mechanical engineering	7	4
31	Metal manufacturing	8	6
22	Production and processing of metals	9	12
43	Textile industry	10	9

Source: *Panorama of EC Industry*, 1990

In the EC there are three main reasons for the restructuring of manufacturing that has taken place over the past ten years: first, deregulation, which has lead to greater internal competition; secondly, greater competition both internally and externally from third-party countries, especially the less developed, low-wage countries; and thirdly, the creation of the Single European Market and the resulting increases in competition brought about by the elimination of barriers to trade. There are a great variety of ways in which companies have reacted to these changes but the *Panorama of EC Industry* identifies several 'typical' responses, some of which will have contradictory effects. These include:

● Increased investment for the prime purpose of increasing productivity. This has led to an increase in the level of unemployment in the EC as machinery has replaced the relatively expensive labour in the production process.
● A tendency towards greater concentration in industry both vertically and horizontally through merger and acquisition, in order to benefit from economies of scale and to be in a position to benefit from the increased competition.
● Greater specialisation in production. Many companies in quite diverse industries

(window frames, chemicals, clothing and textiles) have decided to reduce product lines and concentrate on particular market segments.

● Greater flexibility in the production process. This has been achieved by greater automation in production processes, the externalisation of certain activities, subcontracting, and increased use of part-time and temporary workers.

Industrial structure in the UK

The United Kingdom does not fare well in international comparisons, the trend is the same as in the EC but the decline in the manufacturing sector has been more pronounced in the United Kingdom and the jobs lost in manufacturing have not been offset by jobs created in the service sector. It is also true that while there has been a relative decline in the output of manufacturing in all countries, it is only in the case of the United Kingdom that there has been an absolute decline.

Figure 9.6 shows a graph of employment in manufacturing in four countries over the period 1969 to 1988. It is clear from this graph that the decline in employment in manufacturing has been much greater in the United Kingdom than the others. The United Kingdom started from a much higher base in 1969 and in 1988 had the lowest level of employment in manufacturing.

Table 9.7 gives an indication of the change in industrial structure in the United

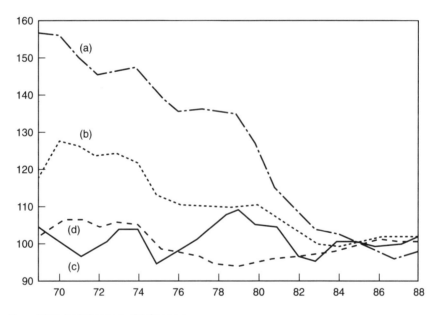

Key: (a) United Kingdom   (b) Germany

(c) United States   (d) Japan

Note: Index of employment in manufacturing: 1985 = 100.

Fig. 9.6 Index of employment in manufacturing industry in selected countries
Source: *Year Book of Labour Statistics*, 1993, copyright 1993, International Labour Organisation, Geneva.

Kingdom between 1969 and 1989. It shows the total numbers employed in various industries for 1969 and 1989. It is important to realise that when comparing two different years the figures will be affected by the state of the economy in each of those years, but nevertheless the comparison will give an indication of changes in the relative importance of the three sectors of the economy. The change in the Standard Industrial Classification that occurred during this period would have had a minimal effect on the figures and has been corrected as far as possible.

Table 9.7 Total numbers in employment in the United Kingdom in mid-June 1969 and 1989 (000s)

Sectors	1969	1989
Agriculture, forestry and fishing	492	280
Mining and quarrying	437	260
Total primary	929	540
Manufacturing	8,355	4,971
Construction	1,459	1,036
Gas, electricity and water	406	361
Total secondary	10,220	6,368
Transport and communication	1,561	1,342
Distributive trades	2,711	3,412
Financial, business, professional and scientific services	3,742	2,642
Catering, hotels, etc.	710	1,105
Miscellaneous services	1,284	
National government services	598	6,823
Local government services	867	
Total tertiary	11,473	15,324
Total employment	22,619	22,232

Source: *Annual Abstract of Statistics*, 1979 and 1990

There has been a slight fall in the level of total employment during this period but a substantial change in the pattern of employment between the different industries. The level of employment has fallen in the primary sector from 929,000 in 1969 to 540,000 in 1989. There has been a similar change in the level of employment in the secondary sector, which fell from 10.2 million to 6.4 million during the period. These falls were partly offset by the increase in the level of employment in the tertiary sector. The trend is clearly seen in Table 9.8, which shows the percentage share of total employment in the United Kingdom in the three broad sectors of the economy over a period of time.

It is clear from Table 9.8 and Figure 9.7 that there has been a shift in the pattern of employment which indicates a change in the structure of industry in the United Kingdom. The relative importance of the primary sector has declined over the period 1969 to 1990, accounting for 3.6 per cent of employment in 1969 and 2.5 per cent in 1989. The increase experienced at the beginning of the 1980s was due to North Sea oil. This fall is a continuation of a much longer trend of decline in the primary sector. There has also been a dramatic fall in the relative importance of the secondary sector in providing employment, which fell from 46.8 per cent to 28.1 per cent of employment

**Table 9.8 % share of total employment of primary,
secondary and tertiary sectors of the UK economy**

Year	Sector		
	Primary	Secondary	Tertiary
1969	3.6	46.8	49.3
1973	3.6	42.1	54.3
1979	3.1	38.2	58.7
1984	3.8	31.1	65.1
1985	3.6	30.5	65.8
1986	3.3	29.9	66.3
1987	3.0	29.5	67.6
1988	2.7	29.0	68.3
1989	2.4	28.5	68.9
1990	2.5	28.1	69.1

Source: *Annual Abstract of Statistics* (various years)

during the period. Again this table shows that the relative importance of the service sector has increased.

Before consideration is given to the reasons for these changes, the other key indicator of changes in industrial structure will be considered, the level of output. These figures show a similar pattern to those on employment. There has been a fall in the relative importance of the secondary sector and an increase in the importance of the tertiary sector. There was an increase in the importance of the oil and natural gas industries in the late 1970s and early 1980s because of the production of North Sea oil and gas; this

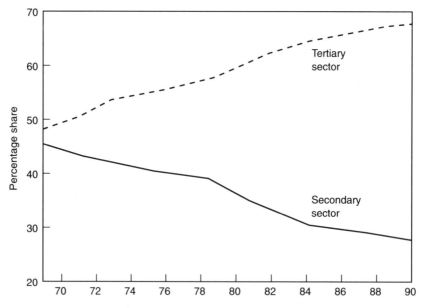

Fig. 9.7 Percentage share of total employment of the secondary and tertiary sectors of the UK economy
Source: *Annual Abstract of Statistics* (various years)

Table 9.9 Output by industry 1983 to 1990 (% of total GDP)

Industry	1983	1984	1985	1986	1987	1988	1989	1990
Agriculture, forestry and fishing	2.0	2.2	1.8	1.8	1.7	1.5	1.5	1.4
Energy and water supply	11.0	10.2	10.2	7.0	6.6	5.4	4.9	4.8
Manufacturing	22.8	22.9	22.8	22.6	22.4	22.4	21.8	21.2
Construction	5.8	5.8	5.6	5.9	6.3	6.8	7.0	7.2
Services	58.5	58.9	59.7	62.3	63.0	64.0	64.8	65.4

Source: *Annual Abstract of Statistics*, 1992

trend, however, has now been reversed. The broad classification used in Table 9.9 hides the fact that there are differences within the sectors, where some industries grow while others decline in importance. An example of this is shown in Table 9.10 for the broad heading of energy and water supply industries.

Table 9.10 Growth rate in output between 1985 and 1990 in selected industries

Energy and water supply	Growth rate (%)
Coal and coke	− 2.7
Extraction of mineral oil and natural gas	−26.6
Mineral oil processing	11.1
Other energy and water supply	16.0
Total energy and water supply	−11.2

Source: *Annual Abstract of Statistics*, 1992

It can be seen that the overall growth rate in the energy and water supply industries was −11.2 per cent between 1985 and 1990, but that within the sector there were marked differences, with mineral oil processing and other energy and water supply industries exhibiting positive growth rates while the others contracted in size. The extraction of mineral oil and natural gas industries have a growth rate of −26.6 per cent. This is just one example but there are also differences between the different industries within the manufacturing sector, with some industries growing and some declining in importance.

The changes in relative sizes of the different sectors of the economy in the United Kingdom are the same as in other countries. It is only in the United Kingdom that there have been periods of absolute decline in the output of manufacturing industries as Figure 9.8 shows. This decline in manufacturing is regarded by many as relatively unimportant; it is seen as a natural process of change which started with the Industrial Revolution and the movement from the land. To some extent this natural growth argument is supported by Table 9.5. Spain, which is the least developed of those in the table has the highest level of employment in the agricultural sector, nearly double the EC average. The United Kingdom is the only member of the EC shown to have a level of employment in the industrial sector lower than the EC average.

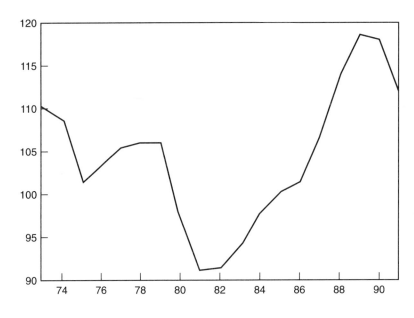

Note: 1985 = 100

Fig. 9.8 Output of manufacturing industry in the United Kingdom, 1973–1991
Source: *Annual Abstract of Statistics*

This change in industrial structure is a trend which is evident in other countries. It might also be the case that some of the growth in the service sector is illusory. For example, if firms are externalising services that they once carried out themselves, there is actually not an increase in the amount of work done but a change in where it is done. It is not surprising that employment levels in manufacturing should fall, given the expansion of services and increases in productivity. What is more disturbing is that the absolute value of output in manufacturing has fallen and whilst similar patterns can be observed in other countries, the United Kingdom does not fare very well in international comparisons.

Causes of changes in industrial structure

There are several explanations put forward for the changes that take place in industrial structure. Broadly speaking these can be classified into demand and supply factors.

Demand factors

Changing patterns of demand will cause changes in the structure of industry. Demand will change as a result of changes in tastes and fashions, changes in the structure of the population, and changes in the levels of income. As income increases there is normally an increase in total spending on goods and services but there will be differences between different types of goods. There will be relatively large increases in expenditure on goods which have high income elasticities of demand[1] and relatively small increases or even falls in demand for other goods. Goods with low income elasticities are

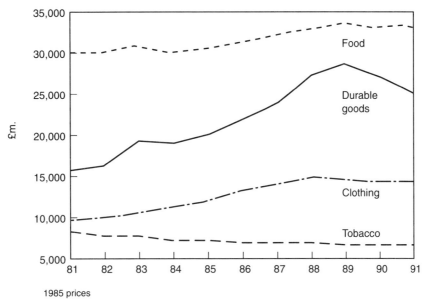

Fig. 9.9 Expenditure on selected goods in the United Kingdom, 1981–1991 (1985 prices)
Source: *Economic Trends*, 1993

necessities like food, fuel, clothing and footwear. Luxury items have high income elasticities of demand; these would include things like durable goods, alcohol and services like tourism and leisure activities. Naturally what constitutes a necessity and luxury would change over the years. Figures 9.9 and 9.10 show the trend in expenditure on selected goods and services over a period of time in the United Kingdom.

Figure 9.9 shows that the expenditure on food and clothing has remained fairly constant over time as expected. The expenditure on durable goods is much more affected by movements in the trade cycle and the level of income. Expenditure grew over the 1980s but fell back again during the recession of the late 1980s and early 1990s. The expenditure on tobacco fell steadily over the 1980s, probably as a result of increased health awareness. Figure 9.10 reinforces the findings above that services are like durables in that their demand is closely linked to the level of income. The pattern of expenditure is very similar to that for durables. It should also be remembered that suppliers have an impact upon the level of demand for products as they can manipulate demand through advertising and other forms of promotion.

The differential effects of rising income on demand for goods and services would in part explain the growth in the size of the service sector over the years. The change in industrial structure can then be seen as a natural process of change. During the Industrial Revolution there was a movement from agriculture to industry, in the same way as there is now a movement from manufacturing towards services. Changes in demand, however, cannot explain all of this change. Growth in the service sector does not necessarily mean that there should be a decline in the size of the manufacturing sector when there are high levels of unemployment in the economy. Labour can be drawn from the unemployed rather than from manufacturing industry. During the time period under consideration there have been periods of high unemployment. It is also the

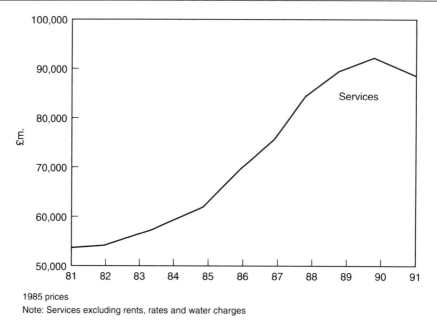

1985 prices
Note: Services excluding rents, rates and water charges

Fig. 9.10 Expenditure on services in the United Kingdom, 1981–1991 (1985 prices)
Source: *Economic Trends*, 1993

case that the import of manufactured goods has not fallen, so it is not that demand has fallen for those goods but that we are buying them from abroad.

Supply factors

Changes in industrial structure can also be triggered by changes in supply conditions. The oil crisis of the 1970s is a good example of this. As a result of the massive increase in oil prices, there was a concerted campaign to reduce the consumption of oil and a search for other forms of energy. Technological change gives rise to new products and/or new processes of production. Different industries will vary in the scope for technological change and for increases in productivity (this is considered more fully later in this chapter).

Demand and supply forces are interlinked so it is often difficult to separate their effects as new products will generate new demands or could be developed to meet new demand.

Added to these internal factors is the fact that the United Kingdom is part of an international economy and competition from abroad will have an impact on the structure of industry through both demand and supply factors.

Deindustrialisation

The decline in the importance of manufacturing has been termed 'deindustrialisation' by many economists. The following causes are put forward for deindustrialisation.

'Crowding out'

The argument here is that the growth in the size of the public sector has been at the expense of the private sector. The resources that could have been used to expand the private sector have instead been used in the public sector, so that the public sector has 'crowded out' the private sector. This was a popular argument used in the 1980s to call for reductions in public spending. With higher levels of unemployment the argument loses its validity because it is not just a matter of using resources in the private or public sector – they are lying idle. As a result the 'crowding out' argument is less popular now. It is also argued that the higher rates of interest which might accompany higher spending on the public sector discourages private spending. Again there is little concrete evidence that lower investment results from higher rates of interest. It could be that investment falls because of lower returns on that investment, and the returns on capital employed have been lower in the United Kingdom than other countries.

International competition

Because of competition from both the developed world and the developing world where wage rates are lower than the UK rates, the United Kingdom has lost markets. At home much demand for goods and services is met by imports. Internationally the United Kingdom has lost markets too, as the level of our exports has fallen. There is evidence of this from the UK balance of payments. For example, in the mid-1980s the United Kingdom started to import more manufactured goods than it exported for the first time since the Industrial Revolution, and there was a widening deficit on the balance of payments in manufactured goods. High exchange rates have not helped the situation and have contributed to the decline. It is argued that the United Kingdom competes badly in both price and quality.

Specialisation

The United Kingdom tends to specialise in sectors which do not have great export potential; its percentage shares in sectors like electrical equipment, computers, transport equipment are less than the EC averages. The energy sector is of great importance to the United Kingdom economy.

Research and development

In the United Kingdom the proportion of spending on research and development has not changed very much over the last 20 years. This is not the case for other countries. It is also true that in the United Kingdom a much greater percentage of R & D is financed by government rather than private industry (see Chapter 5).

The educational system

The educational system in the United Kingdom is said to be biased towards the arts and pure sciences rather than applied scientific, engineering and business-type subjects. In the United Kingdom, 30 per cent of engineers have a professional qualification, while in

Germany the figure is 70 per cent. Five per cent of UK retail workers have received training similar to an apprenticeship, in Germany the corresponding figure is 75 per cent. As far as international trade is concerned the United Kingdom also lags behind other European countries in its language training.

Level and type of investment

The level of investment in the United Kingdom is low. This means that the stock of capital may be too low and that it will be relatively 'old' (see Chapter 5).

Non-price factors

These factors include quality, design, and after sales service. The United Kingdom is late compared to other countries to take up total quality management. These techniques were started in the west but then taken up and honed by the Japanese and are now being used worldwide. Quality management schemes can only be successful if other conditions are right, like a well-trained and qualified and highly motivated workforce.

Skills shortages in manufacturing

Despite high unemployment, there are still skill shortages in certain areas. In 1990 a Department of Employment survey found that 22 per cent of firms interviewed had tried hard to fill vacancies and that 46 per cent had experienced some difficulties in the previous year. The areas where skills are shortest are engineering and information technology (IT).

The financial system

It is often argued that the UK banks are less supportive of business than in other countries. In the United Kingdom, banks tend to offer only short-term to medium-term finance for industry; the only long-term finance would be in the form of mortgages. In other countries banks are large providers of long-term finance to industry through the purchase of stocks and shares.

Lack of qualified managers

It is argued that manufacturing has not recruited the best qualified candidates for management, although management training can overcome this to some extent.

North Sea oil

The existence of North Sea oil has had a mixed effect on the United Kingdom. On one hand it has led to an inflow of cash which has helped the balance of payments, but it has also served to keep the exchange rate of the pound higher than it would have been in its absence. A higher exchange rate has the effect of making United Kingdom goods more expensive abroad and foreign goods cheaper in the United Kingdom. Thus there is a corresponding deterioration in the balance of payments. The high exchange rate makes the United Kingdom less competitive in international markets, and as the biggest part of what we export is industrial goods, this sector will be most affected.

Government policy

During the 1980s the United Kingdom government repeated the argument that the decline in manufacturing was not important. It was seen as the working of the market mechanism, and would be replaced by services. The government therefore took a relaxed view of the decline. In the early 1980s the adherence to a strict monetarist policy of high interest rates and cut-backs in government expenditure all contributed to the decline in manufacturing.

Productivity

The productivity of labour can be measured by the output per person employed, although there are problems with this as labour productivity will also depend upon the amount and productivity of the capital employed. Given the problems of measuring the efficiency with which capital is used, this problem will be ignored for the time being. Table 9.11 shows output per person employed in the whole economy and in manufacturing for selected years.

Table 9.11 Labour productivity in the UK

Year	Output per person employed in	
	Whole economy	Manufacturing industries
1964	67.2	54.9
1973	85.7	76.8
1981	89.2	79.2
1982	92.6	84.5
1983	96.7	91.8
1984	97.4	97.0
1985	100.0	100.0
1986	103.5	103.5
1987	106.3	109.8
1988	107.2	116.2
1989	106.9	120.8
1990	107.3	121.7
1991	108.0	121.6

Source: National Institute of Economic and Social Research, *Economic Review*, November 1992, no. 142

These figures show that for the whole economy, productivity grew by around 28 per cent in the 1960s, 18 per cent in the 1970s and 20 per cent in the 1980s.

Productivity growth in the 1980s compares favourably with other countries as Table 9.12 shows. However, despite the gains made in productivity in the 1980s in the United Kingdom, the performance relative to other countries before this was such that the United Kingdom had a great deal of catching up to do. It has been estimated that even with the fast growth in productivity in the 1980s the United Kingdom was between 22

Table 9.12 Productivity growth in selected countries as measured by gross product per worker (1980–1991)

	Growth (%)
United States	8.5
Japan	37.4
France	24.5
West Germany	16.3
United Kingdom	31.1

Source: National Institute of Economic and Social Research, *Economic Review*, November 1992, no. 142

per cent and 40 per cent behind West Germany in terms of productivity in 1987.[2]

Many reasons have been put forward for the relatively low productivity levels in the United Kingdom, including the educational system, the activities of trade unions, low levels of investment, and low research and development spending. Some of these have already been considered.

With regard to the increases in productivity during the 1980s, this has been attributed to various causes:

1 That the recession of the early 1980s had the effect of putting out of business all the companies which had low productivity levels so that there was a once-and-for-all increase in productivity.
2 That changes in the relations between management and trade unions reduced the ability of trade unions to hamper productivity through strategies like closed-shop arrangements, restrictive practices or restricting the installation of labour-saving devices.
3 That the loss of capital stock during the 1980/81 recession lead to the replacement of old obsolete machinery with new machinery which embodied new technology. This had the effect of increasing the level of labour productivity.

On balance the evidence seems to point to more efficient use of factor inputs as the source of increased productivity, rather than a fundamental change in underlying factors like investment in capital, human capital or research and development.[3] Anecdotal evidence from companies that have branches in the United Kingdom and other countries supports the belief that there are still differences between the productivities of British and other workers.

Low productivity has implications for international competitiveness. It can be offset by lower wages in order to stop costs from rising which might be passed on in the form of higher prices, and although United Kingdom wages are relatively low compared to many of its competitors, they are not low enough to offset the low productivity levels completely. Alternatively the exchange rate could fall so that prices remain competitive internationally, and although this has happened since the United Kingdom left the ERM, for long periods during the 1970s and 1980s our exchange rate was high, and hence our international competitiveness was adversely affected.

Labour productivity is not the only important factor as far as international competitiveness is concerned, the productivity of capital is also important. It seems that in the UK, the level of capital productivity is also rather low.

SYNOPSIS

Industrial structure refers to the relative sizes of the different industries in the economy. Firms are grouped together into industries and industries are grouped together into sectors in some way, although this is often difficult to do. The government has an official Standard Industrial Classification which has recently been changed to bring it in line with the EC classification.

The size of industries and sectors of the economy is measured by looking at the level of employment or the level of output. In the United Kingdom the primary sector is small and declining, although there was an increase in its importance in the 1980s due to the discovery and extraction of North Sea oil and gas. The secondary sector has also been declining in importance both in terms of employment and output. The biggest sector of the economy at present is the tertiary sector. This pattern is similar to what is happening in other industrialised countries, although the detail varies slightly between countries. The industrial structure of a country and the way it changes depends upon many factors, most of which have been considered in this chapter.

CASE STUDY: PROCESS PLANT CONTRACTING

To illustrate the way in which industrial structure changes, this case study will look at a relatively young industry – process plant contracting. Process plant contracting is the building of plant for the process industries (i.e. chemicals, metals, food and drink, and cement). Process plant contracting only came into existence in its present form in the 1940s in response to changes taking place in the process industries themselves and has undergone periods of growth and restructuring since then to arrive at its present state.

Process plant contracting

Process plant contractors build plant for the process industries, and to this end the contractor carries out a number of tasks as part of a contract: design of the plant, supply of parts and equipment, supervision of the construction, and organisation of the finance of the project. This means that the process plant contractor will have dealings with clients, suppliers, manufacturers, consulting engineers, financiers, and so on.

The process plant contracting industry is comprised of about 100 firms mainly based in the United States, western Europe and Japan. Many of the companies are parts of groups which operate in diversified areas. The size of the firms varies from around 3,000 employees to over 10,000 employees. The market is an international one and each firm in the industry carries out a high proportion of its work for exports. The industry therefore makes a significant contribution to the balance of payments. Since the 1970s the international process plant industry has become increasingly dominated by a small group of large firms.

The industry is a relatively new one, and although there were a few process plant contractors in existence before the Second World War, the industry began to develop in its present form only after the war. Prior to 1945 the process industries tended to design and build their own plant. This changed first in America in response to certain changes that occurred in the process industries themselves, particularly chemicals and oil refining. These changes led to an increased demand for capacity and an increase in the complexity of that plant. As the process industries were unable to meet this demand, specialist organisations developed – the process plant contractors. Once these firms had developed in the United States, they quickly began to operate internationally. The industries in different countries grew up in quite different ways. It has already been said that the American industry grew as a result of changes that took place in the chemicals and oil refining industries. In the United Kingdom many of the process plant contractors operated in the field of gas processing until they followed the US pattern and became process plant contractors. In Japan the process plant contractors have their origins in shipbuilding and engineering. More recently there has been some competition from countries like South Korea who are developing their own industries.

Since the Second World War the process plant contracting industry has grown rapidly, although the growth rate is cyclical. The demand for process plant contracting is a 'derived demand' since it derives from the demand that exists for the produce of the plant. The demand from different industries will depend upon the conditions in that industry (e.g. the size of plant that is needed, the design problems and the speed of technological change). These will obviously vary a great deal between industries. The demand will be affected by the trade cycle, and as with other forms of capital expenditure the cycles will tend to be exaggerated by an 'accelerator' effect. A simple example will illustrate. Assume that the level of demand for a product rises, that means that more capital investment is needed in machinery that will produce that good. It is likely that the cost of the plant and machinery needed to produce more of the good will be in excess of the value of the goods it produces. Therefore an initial increase in demand of say 10 per cent could lead to a much greater increase in the level of investment. The initial change has been 'accelerated'.

To minimise the problems caused by such patterns of demand, firms in the industry have diversified into other areas and have operated on a truly international scale. This, and a buoyant level of demand, means that the industry continued to grow up to a peak in 1981. Since then world recession and over-capacity have led to a fall in investment in process plant. The drive towards larger size in order to take advantage of the huge economies of scale that are present in the processing industries has meant that the projects are larger but that there are fewer of them. The demand for the services of process plant contracting has fallen by around 50 per cent since the early 1980s and there has been a corresponding fall in the level of employment in the industry.

It is likely that when the market does recover the projects will not be the large-scale projects that were seen in the 1960s and 1970s but smaller projects. There is over-capacity in many of the process industries worldwide so that any new demand is likely to come from the developing world. All of this means that the process plant contractors need to look to new directions for the future. There will be opportunities in the new technologies like biotechnology and the new environmental industries like the production of lead-free petrol.

Conclusion

This case study shows how industries develop and change over time. Although there are some differences in the way in which the industry developed in different countries, process plant contracting is an industry that came into existence because of changes taking place in the process industries themselves which meant that they were unable to continue to build their own plant. The main problem faced by the industry is that the demand for its output is a derived demand and so dependent on the demand for the output of the process industries. Added to this, the cyclical movements in demand are exaggerated because of the large-scale nature of the investments involved. For a long period of time the industry faced buoyant and growing demand and the industry grew at a rapid rate. As the firms in the process industries became larger in the quest for economies of scale, the number of contracts became larger but fewer, and as a result the process plant contracting industry become more international and more concentrated in the hands of a few large companies. The world recession of the 1980s and the resulting overcapacity in the process industries has led to a massive restructuring of the industry and the search for new areas for diversification.

NOTES AND REFERENCES

1 See Chapter 11.
2 O'Mahony, M., 'Productivity levels in British and German manufacturing industry', *National Institute Economic Review*, February 1992.
3 Crafts N., 'Reversing relative economic decline? The 1980s in historical perspective', *Oxford Review of Economic Policy*, 7, (3), 1991.

REVIEW AND DISCUSSION QUESTIONS

1 What are the implications of the fluctuating level of demand in the process plant contracting industry? What could firms do to protect themselves against these fluctuations?

2 On what basis could you judge whether manufacturing was more important to an economy than services?

3 What would be the effect on the industrial structure of a country of the discovery of large supplies of oil?

4 What is the difference between an industry and a market?

ASSIGNMENTS

1 You are the research assistant for an MP who is to participate in a debate on the importance of the manufacturing sector to the economy. She has asked you to produce a list of the arguments that are likely to be used by both sides in the debate: that is, reasons why the decline does matter and the set of counter-arguments. Provide a suitable list.

2 You work for the economic development unit of your local council and have been asked to do a presentation to a visiting Bulgarian delegation on the differences in industrial structures between their country and the United Kingdom. Using the figures in this chapter for the UK and the following for Bulgaria:

	Employment share, 1991 (%)
Agriculture	16
Industry	72
Services	13

Produce the overhead slides for your presentation, and a short commentary on the differences, the reasons for those differences and the changes they should expect as development continues.

FURTHER READING

Donaldson, P., *Understanding the British Economy*, Penguin, 1988.
Jones, T. T. and Cockerill, T. A. J., *Structure and Performance of Industries*, Philip Allan, 1984.
SIC(92), HMSO, 1992.

APPENDIX: The Standard Industrial Classification (SIC), 1992

Division	Industry
Section A	Agriculture, hunting and forestry
Section B	Fishing
Section C	Mining and quarrying
Subsection CA	Mining and quarrying of energy producing materials
Subsection CB	Mining and quarrying except energy producing materials
Section D	Manufacturing
Subsection DA	Manufacture of food products; Beverages and tobacco
Subsection DB	Manufacture of textiles and textile products
Subsection DC	Manufacture of leather and leather products
Subsection DD	Manufacture of wood and wood products
Subsection DE	Manufacture of pulp, paper and paper products; Publishing and printing
Subsection DF	Manufacture of coke, refined petroleum products and nuclear fuel
Subsection DG	Manufacture of chemicals, chemical products and man-made fibres
Subsection DH	Manufacture of rubber and plastic products
Subsection DI	Manufacture of other non-metallic mineral products
Subsection DJ	Manufacture of basic metals and fabricated metal products
Subsection DK	Manufacture of machinery and equipment not elsewhere classified
Subsection DL	Manufacture of electrical and optical equipment
Subsection DM	Manufacture of transport equipment
Subsection DN	Manufacturing not elsewhere classified
Section E	Electricity, gas and water supply
Section F	Construction
Section G	Wholesale and retail trade; repair of motor vehicles, motor-cycles and personal and household goods
Section H	Hotels and restaurants
Section I	Transport, storage and communication
Section J	Financial intermediation
Section K	Real estate, renting and business activities
Section L	Public administration and defence; compulsory social security
Section M	Education
Section N	Health and social work

Division	*Industry*
Section O	Other community, social and personal service activities
Section P	Private households with employed persons
Section Q	Extra-territorial organisations and bodies

CHAPTER 10

Government and business

Ian Worthington

In any society multiple interactions exist between government and business and these occur at a variety of spatial levels and in a wide range of contexts. One such interaction stems from the government's attempts to alleviate the problems of regional and/or local economic decay and decline and these tend to be the focus of governmental policies at local, regional, national and even supranational level. Whilst such measures are formulated and administered by governmental agencies, business organisations in market economies often exercise considerable influence on government decisions. This influence can be enhanced if the views of the business community are expressed through powerful and persuasive representative organisations.

OBJECTIVES

1 To consider the rationale for government involvement in the economy.
2 To investigate the nature and scope of United Kingdom government regional policy.
3 To survey government policy initiatives at sub-regional level, including the role of local government in economic development.
4 To examine the notion of corporate community involvement.
5 To provide examples of spatial policies elsewhere in Europe.
6 To consider the role of business as influence on government.

INTRODUCTION

All democratic market-based economies accept the need for government involvement in the day-to-day workings of the economy. The critical question, therefore, is not whether a role for government should exist, but *what* that role should be and *where* the boundaries should be drawn between private and public (i.e. collective) action. Governments of a 'socialist' persuasion normally favour a substantial role for the state as both producer and regulator, whereas non-socialists administrations tend to prefer limited state influence that is directed towards improving the operation of the free market. Either way, the actions of the state in the economy can be influential at both the macro and the micro level and this has important implications for the conduct of business in the non-state sector.

In examining the role of government in the macroeconomy, Chapter 4 emphasised how changes in fiscal and monetary policy could be used to influence aggregrate levels of income, output and employment in the economy and how attempts to regulate the overall level of economic activity were related to a government's macroeconomic policy objectives. By way of contrast, in this and a number of subsequent chapters (especially Chapter 14) the focus is on the ways in which government actions impinge upon the operations of firms and markets and the rationale underlying the decisions by the state to intervene at micro level. Such interventions may take place at the request of the business community or despite its opposition, but it is rare for them to occur without business expressing an opinion which it expects government to take into consideration. This role of business as an important influence on government policy is examined in the concluding section of this chapter.

GOVERNMENT AND BUSINESS: AN OVERVIEW

In considering reasons for government intervention in the economy, economists have traditionally pointed to the problem of 'market failure'. This is the notion that if left entirely to their own devices, markets can operate in a way which is not always economically or socially desirable. To this extent interventionist policies can be portrayed as an attempt by governments of all political complexions to deal with the problems inherent in the operation of free markets.

The key areas of 'market failure' are well known. Primary concerns include:

1 The unwillingness of markets to produce goods and services which are either unprofitable or which it is not practical to provide through private means (i.e. 'public goods' such as defence, social services, and so on).
2 The likely under-provision of certain goods and services felt to be of general benefit to the community (i.e. 'merit goods' such as education, libraries, and so on).
3 The failure to take into account the external costs and benefits of production or consumption (i.e. 'externalities' such as pollution, congestion, and so on).
4 The danger of monopoly power if businesses can be freely bought and sold.
5 The under-utilisation of economic resources (e.g. unemployment resulting from demand deficiency, new technology, or structural or frictional problems).
6 The tendency for output to be determined and distributed on the ability to pay rather than on the basis of need or equity.

Government responses to these problems have normally taken a number of forms including public ownership, legislation, and administrative or fiscal regulation, and examples of all these approaches can be found to a greater or lesser extent in all countries. In recent years, however, under the influence of economists of the 'new right', governments have begun to take steps to disengage the state from some of its activities (e.g. public ownership) and have increasingly turned to market solutions to problems emanating primarily from the operation of the market system itself (e.g. schemes to charge for the use of roads which are heavily congested).

Whilst all forms of government intervention in the economy invariably have direct or indirect consequences for businesses, it is possible to distinguish certain policies which are designed specifically to influence the industrial and commercial environment –

sometimes described as 'industrial policies'. In the United Kingdom and elsewhere, these have typically included:

- attempts at direct industrial intervention (e.g. the establishment of the National Enterprise Board);
- privatisation policies;
- policies relating to competition and monopoly control; and
- policies designed to influence industrial location and to encourage economic regeneration at different spatial levels.

Though it cannot be claimed that such measures amount to a single and coherent policy for business, nevertheless they indicate that successive governments accept they have an important role to play in shaping the environment in which private businesses function. Competition and privatisation policy – discussed in detail in Chapter 14 – tend to focus on the operation of markets and on the benefits which derive from private provision under a competitive market structure. Government spatial policies – the subject matter of this chapter – are mainly concerned with addressing the problems of regional disparities in income, employment and output, and the associated problem of localised economic decline as businesses fail or decide to relocate their premises.

REGIONAL POLICY

Regions

A region is a geographical area which possesses certain characteristics (e.g. political, economic, physical) which give it a measure of unity that allows boundaries to be drawn round it, thus differentiating it from surrounding areas. In the United Kingdom the standard planning regions are the North, North West, Yorkshire/Humberside, East Midlands, West Midlands, South West, East Anglia, South East, Wales, Scotland and Northern Ireland. Each of these is further divided into sub-regions based on administrative counties and on designated metropolitan areas. These planning regions and sub-regions form the units of classification for a wide range of official government statistics (see Chapter 16).

The basis of regional policy

Many countries have a recognisable 'regional policy' of one kind or another. Such policies are generally designed to identify and demarcate those geographical areas which are experiencing substantial economic and/or social problems and which are felt to require government assistance. Using a range of socio-economic indicators – including unemployment levels, occupational structure activity rates, population density, and so forth – governments tend to distinguish those regions which depart significantly from the 'national average' and designate these regions 'assisted areas'. These areas then become the focus of government assistance and tend to be given priority in the provision of financial aid for capital investment projects and for measures designed to increase employment and growth. Such aid generally comes in a variety of forms and may include assistance from international or supranational sources, as in the case of EC regional policy (see below).

UK regional policy

The origins of UK regional policy can be traced back to the 1930s when the government first began to provide help to a number of depressed areas in the form of low-interest loans, subsidised rents and the establishment of government trading estates. The main elements of the present system, however, date from November 1984 and comprise three types of 'assisted area' eligible for regional assistance. These are:

1 Development areas (DAs)
2 Intermediate areas (IAs)
3 Northern Ireland – which receives special regional help owing to the particular problems it is experiencing in attracting investment in industrial and commercial projects.

The areas qualifying for government assistance have recently been revised, with the new arrangements coming into effect on 1 August 1993.

As Figure 10.1 indicates, the majority of 'assisted areas' are in the north and the west and largely correspond with the older industrial conurbations (e.g. Manchester, Liverpool, South Wales, Glasgow). The recent changes, however, indicate that increasing recognition is being given by government to the problems being experienced in other parts of the country, particlarly the South East and East Anglia, and these are reflected in the decision to add some new 'travel-to-work areas' to the revised assisted areas map, whilst phasing out others.

Current policy provides for two major forms of regional grant assistance which are co-ordinated under the government's 'Enterprise Initiative' – the Department of Trade and Industry's (DTI) package of advice, guidance and practical help for United Kingdom businesses. These are Regional Selective Assistance and Regional Enterprise Grants.

1 *Regional Selective Assistance* (RSA) A discretionary form of assistance available to businesses of all sizes which reside in or are planning to set up in Development and Intermediate Areas. Designed to help with investment projects in manufacturing and some service sectors that might not otherwise go ahead, RSA provides for:
   (a) project grants related to capital expenditure or job creation; and/or
   (b) loans from Europe (through the Steel Community) and exchange risk cover on loans made in foreign currencies.
   To be eligible for assistance, businesses must demonstrate that a proposed project is viable, creates or safeguards employment, makes a contribution to both the regional and the national economy and needs assistance to proceed in its present form. The expectation is that firms will find most of the finance from their own or other private sector sources and hence grants are negotiated as the minimum necessary to ensure a project proceeds.
2 *Regional Enterprise Grants* A scheme specially designed to help small firms to get started, modernise, expand or diversify. Under this scheme, two types of discretionary assistance are currently available for viable projects:
   (a) Regional Investment Grants for manufacturing and some service sectors under which the government pays 15 per cent of the costs of fixed assets (to a maximum of £15,000 in 1993) for firms in Development Areas with less than 25 employees who can demonstrate a need for assistance. Grants are also available in the Intermediate Areas in Derbyshire, South Yorkshire, Plymouth and Fife

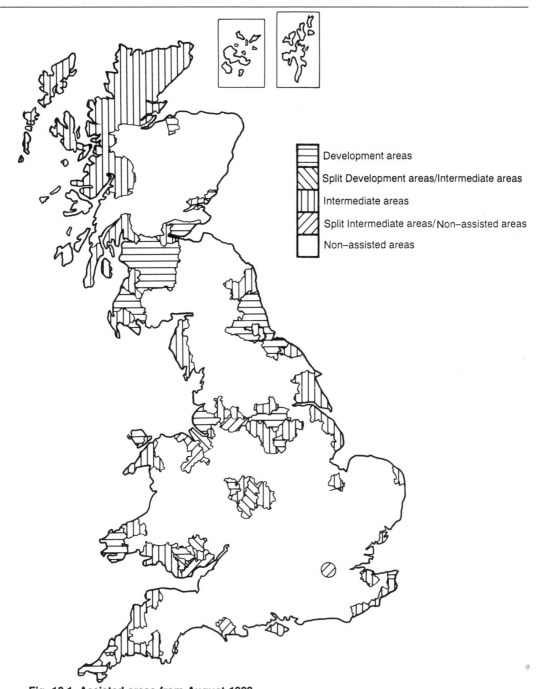

Fig. 10.1 Assisted areas from August 1993

Source: Department of Trade and Industry. Reproduced with permission of HMSO. Crown copyright.

under a number of European programmes (e.g. the European Community Programme for Shipbuilding – called RENAVAL).

(b) Regional Innovation Grants under which the government will pay 50 per cent of the costs of development and introduction of new or improved processes (to a maximum of £25,000 in 1993). To be eligible a firm must have less than 50 employees and the project must take place in a Development, Intermediate, Task Force, City Challenge or European Commission Objective 2 areas or in certain Scottish Inner Urban Areas eligible for assistance.

Firms in assisted areas and Urban Programme areas (see below) can also approach the DTI for help with the arrangement and costs of consultancy projects in fields such as design, marketing, quality, business planning, manufacturing, and services systems, and the government will pay two-thirds of the costs as long as a firm has fewer than 500 employees. In addition, through membership of the European Community, United Kingdom businesses have access to EC funds, particularly from the European Regional Development Fund (ERDF) which was established in 1975. Using money from the EC budget, which it allocates to Member States mainly on a quota basis, the ERDF provides finance for regional support with the expectation that funds will be used to supplement a government's existing package of regional aid. Understandably most of these funds tend to go to the EC's poorer regions in Southern Europe, although the United Kingdom has also benefited from such funding, particularly in the declining industrial areas.

Despite the use of such policy instruments, it is evident that the extent of regional assistance has been significantly reduced since 1979, both in terms of the amount of resources committed to the programme and the areas receiving assistance. Moreover aid has increasingly been targeted at small and medium-sized enterprises and has been progressively extended to include service as well as manufacturing industries. In part these changes represent a desire by successive Conservative governments to control public expenditure and to reduce the influence of the state in the working of the market economy by withdrawing from some areas of public support for industry. At the same time, government attempts to encourage 'enterprise' and to attract more private sector funding into business development has given rise to a number of new forms of government intervention aimed specifically at urban or inner city areas. This spatially selective approach to business creation and expansion has become known as 'urban policy'.

UK URBAN POLICY

The urban 'problem'

The progressive decline and decay of urban areas – with its associated unemployment amongst the low paid, unskilled and ethnic members of the population – first came to prominence in the 1960s and gave rise to an Urban Programme aimed predominantly at funding capital projects and education schemes in deprived inner-city locations. Implicit in this programme was the view that the urban 'problem' was largely one of physical decline coupled with failings on the part of individuals which could be corrected by selected government intervention, designed to improve the prospects and environment faced by local citizens. This largely 'pathological' perspective was ultimately exposed by both academic research and community projects undertaken in the 1970s, with the result that government came to see the problem as one of economic and social change and its impact on the local environment. This 'structuralist' view suggested that policy should be directed towards economic development through partnership between the centre, the localities and the private sector, with the emphasis on schemes to overcome structural weaknesses. Riots in several large UK cities in the 1980s served to emphasise that the problem was particularly acute in those inner-city core areas that had suffered a significant loss of industry and population over a number of years.

The focus of policy implementation

Whereas regional policy is managed centrally through a single government department, urban policy has traditionally operated through a variety of agencies including local authorities, voluntary organisations, quangos and a number of independent bodies set up by central Government. The relative importance of these agencies in implementing government policy has changed significantly over time.

The initial focus of policy implementation under the urban programme was the local authorities who acted as a channel for central government funds into projects designed to regenerate economic activity (e.g. by providing premises), to improve the physical environment (e.g. by clearing land or renovating buildings) and to meet social needs (e.g. by providing community facilities for deprived groups). This role was further enhanced by the Inner Urban Areas Act 1978 which conferred wide powers on certain designated local authorities to assist industry wherever a need was felt to exist and where government help was seen to be appropriate. Central to the government's strategy was its attempt to regenerate inner-city areas through capital investment and through environmental improvement, some of which was to be funded from the private sector. To encourage private sector investment, local authorities in the designated areas were allowed to declare industrial and commercial improvement areas and to give financial assistance to companies which located in such areas.

With the election of the Conservative government in 1979, a number of new initiatives were introduced which indicated a move towards an even more spatially selective policy for urban areas. These initiatives – which included Enterprise Zones, Urban Development Corporations, freeports and City Action Teams (see below) – frequently by-passed local authorities or reduced their powers over the allocation of resources and/or land use, and were seen by many commentators as a vote of no confidence in local government's ability to stimulate urban regeneration. At the heart of the new approach lay an attempt by central government to turn inner-city areas into investment opportunities for the private sector by clearing dereliction and improving infrastructure. The basic idea, as the *Financial Times* (30 October 1990) pointed out, was to reduce downside risk to a level where private investors would see enough potential to develop in cities rather than take softer profits elsewhere.

In March 1988 the government launched its 'Action for Cities' initiative which covered a range of programmes administered by different government departments that were designed to promote industrial and commercial investment and hence create employment in the inner-city areas. Programmes under this initiative are co-ordinated by a special unit located at the Department of the Environment and local co-ordination occurs through City Action Teams. Ultimately, responsibility for urban policy programmes is to be vested in the Urban Regeneration Agency scheduled to start work at the end of 1993.

URBAN POLICY INSTRUMENTS

The Urban Programme

The Urban Programme, which is designed to help combat the economic, social and environmental problems of urban areas, has traditionally been the main mechanism for allocating funds to those inner-city areas facing the greatest need. Of the 57 designated local authority areas which fall into this category, nine are 'partnership authorities', where the government has formed a close partnership with local authority agencies to tackle the problem of urban decay (e.g. Hackney, Liverpool, Manchester, Salford). The remaining 48 'programme authorities' (including Barnsley, Bolton, Sandwell, Wrekin) have no such partnership, but are eligible for government assistance for projects which contribute to the economic development of the inner area. In both cases, requests for funds must be submitted from or via the local authorities who assess the application and pay the grant for projects receiving official approval.

The current aim of the programme is to support projects which have job creation potential and/or environmental improvement aims, particularly if these projects are undertaken by the private sector. Amongst the funds available to private industry via the local authorities are:

- Loans or grants for environmental improvements or the provision of access roads and parking (including landscaping, treeplanting, painting or demolition of buildings).
- Grants for converting, extending, improving or modifying industrial and commercial buildings and for conversion of buildings into business premises.
- Loans for site preparation (e.g. sewers, roads, drains).
- Grants to support small-firm establishment, development and land acquisition.
- Loans or grants for co-operative ventures.
- Premises and managed workshops for new firms.

In 1991/92 the total funds available under the Urban Programme for projects of this kind was about £270 million.

Urban Development Corporations (UDCs)

Urban Development Corporations are independent development agencies, established by central government to oversee inner-city development within designated areas. The first two such areas were London Docklands and Merseyside which gained UDCs in 1980. Subsequently, Urban Development Corporations have been established in Trafford Park (Manchester), the Black Country (Birmingham and surrounding districts), Teesside, Tyne and Wear, Cardiff Bay, Central Manchester, Leeds, Sheffield and Bristol. These ten agencies – whose powers of development within their designated areas supersede those of the local authorities in their area – are scheduled to cease operation in 1995/96.

Using funds mainly provided by central government and employing around 500 permanent staff in total, the UDCs have the following objectives:

1 To bring land and buildings into effective use.

2 To encourage the development of industry and commerce.

3 To ensure housing and other social facilities are available in order to encourage people to live and work in the designated area.

To achieve these aims, corporations have been given wide powers to acquire, reclaim, assemble, develop, sell or lease land and to provide the necessary infrastructure. In addition they have powers to build houses for rent or sale and to renovate and re-use existing buildings. In short, they are the development control authorities for their areas.

A fundamental aspect of the UDC's role as an agency for urban regeneration has been its ability to act as a catalyst for encouraging private sector investment. Using public money to bring about environmental improvement and infrastructural development, corporations seek to attract private investors by removing some of the abnormal costs of development such as land clearance and servicing. This 'pump-priming' role cost the taxpayer over £500 million in the early 1990s, with the lion's share of the funds going to the London Docklands Development Corporation (LDDC), whose fortunes were considerably affected by the collapse in property prices in the late 1980s and early 1990s.

Enterprise Zones (EZs)

Like UDCs, Enterprise Zones were first established in the early 1980s with the first batch of 11 EZs being designated in 1981 with a planned life-span of ten years. By the late 1980s the number of EZs had risen to 27, though this has fluctuated recently as some of the original EZs (e.g. Corby) have been wound up and new ones have been announced in the wake of the closure of a large number of pits in the United Kingdom coal industry.

In essence, Enterprise Zones are small areas of territory within a locality where the government is seeking to encourage industrial and commercial activity by the removal of certain tax burdens and other impediments to enterprise (e.g. bureaucratic procedures). Amongst the principal benefits for firms located or locating in an EZ are:

- Exemption from rates on industrial and commercial property.
- Allowances of 100 per cent for corporation and income tax purposes on all capital expenditure related to industrial and commercial development.
- A greatly simplified planning regime.

In addition, businesses normally face fewer requests from public bodies for statistical information and are often exempt from other administrative procedures.

Whether EZs – which currently include Dudley, Wakefield, Isle of Dogs, Sunderland and Rotherham – have been successful in attracting enterprise and in creating significant numbers of jobs in inner-urban areas is open to dispute. Some evidence exists to suggest that the net job-creation effect has been relatively small and that many of the 'new' jobs are simply relocations by local businesses moving to take advantage of the benefits offered to firms within an EZ. To the extent that such 'displacement' effects tend to occur, it is likely to remain the case that the net cost per job created within an Enterprise Zone is significantly higher than through other forms of state intervention (e.g. subsidies).

City Action Teams (CATs)

City Action Teams are designed to bring together government departments, local authorities, local community groups, voluntary organisations and businesses working in inner-city areas. In addition to providing information and advice to any business working in or moving to an inner-city area, a CAT may help with funding for schemes which safeguard or create jobs, improve the environment, provide training places, or encourage enterprise and the growth of business. It also funds feasibility studies and assists with consultancy fees for local projects. The current locations with Action Teams are London, Nottingham/Derby/Leicester, Liverpool, Manchester, Birmingham, Newcastle upon Tyne, Leeds/Bradford and Cleveland.

City Challenge

This is a relatively new initiative designed to concentrate resources on key areas in the 1990s. Under the initiative, local authorities in partnership with the private sector, local organisations and the local community are asked to draw up detailed plans for solving the problems of their area and special government funds are allocated to acceptable projects. City Challenge areas currently in existence include Bradford, Lewisham, Liverpool, Manchester, Nottingham and Wolverhampton.

City Grant

City Grant is the descendant of the Urban Development Grant – an idea copied from the United States after the Toxteth and Brixton riots in the early 1980s. The aim of the grant is to support private sector capital projects which benefit local areas (e.g. bringing derelict land and buildings into use) by bridging any adverse gap between the estimated costs of a project and its expected market value, thus allowing a developer to make a reasonable profit on the venture. Large-scale projects that give rise to new jobs or housing and which improve the environment are the focus of the grant-aid, and priority is given to schemes within City Challenge areas before those from the 57 local authorities who are part of the Urban Programme.

Inner-City task forces

Task forces are composed of small teams of civil servants from various government departments and people on secondment from the private sector who work directly with local authorities and local businesses to stimulate economic development in inner-city areas. Their role is to co-ordinate and monitor the whole range of government initiatives within the designated area.

Freeports

Freeports are areas within selected ports or airports where imported goods are exempted from the payment of customs duties and VAT, unless the goods are subsequently removed from a freeport zone into the United Kingdom. Initially six areas – Liverpool port, Southampton port, Birmingham airport, Prestwick airport, Cardiff port and Belfast airport – were designated for freeport status in the mid-1980s in an attempt to attract business and investment into the zones. By 1990 only three remained in operation and these look likely to discontinue following the changes introduced under the Single European Market programme (see Chapter 13).

LOCAL GOVERNMENT AND BUSINESS IN THE UK

The basis of local economic development

As a major service provider, consumer, employer and landowner, local government has always played an important role in the economy and its influence on business activity at local level remains considerable. Large local authorities annually spend hundreds of millions of pounds, employ tens of thousands of workers and support many thousand additional jobs through the placement of contracts with local businesses. Further employment is also created through the 'multiplier effect', as local authority employees spend their income in the local economy and local citizens consume local authority services such as transport and leisure.

Not content with local economic conditions, many local authorities have actively intervened in the local economy by establishing economic development programmes which are designed to alleviate the familiar problems of unemployment, industrial decline and environmental decay. These programmes – often co-ordinated through an economic development unit within the local authority – are normally comprised of a range of initiatives designed to create or safeguard local jobs by supporting local businesses and encouraging enterprise in a variety of ways (see below). Whilst the origins of such initiatives can be traced back to the nineteenth century, the majority of measures have been introduced in the last twenty years and represent a move from a reactive to a proactive role by local authorities in local economic development.

The basis for such local authority intervention is partly legal and partly political. Under the law, local authorities in the United Kingdom can only engage in activities for which they have statutory authority, whether granted by public statute (i.e. applying to all authorities) or by private Act (i.e. applying to a specific authority). These statutes not only impose specific duties on local authorities to provide certain services (e.g. education, special housing, care in the community), but they may also grant both general and permissive powers which allow local government to engage in different forms of development activity such as the purchase and sale of land and other assets, the granting of financial assistance to industry, and the provision of promotional and advisory services. Coupled with this, many local authorities – particularly in Labour-controlled urban areas – have interpreted their responsibilities and powers in an interventionist way and have used some of their funds to support a range of measures designed to benefit the local community. Such interpretations have frequently brought local government into conflict with a Conservative-led central government whose philosophy of freeing markets and fiscal restraint runs counter to the notion of state intervention at local level.

It is worth noting that funds for local economic development come from local, national and supranational sources, though not all authorities qualify for all three. By far the largest contribution comes from locally generated income, which includes the

council tax, local authority reserves, and revenue derived from charging for local
authority services.

Central funding includes the government's block grant to support local authority
services, income from other centrally funded programmes (e.g. environment) and from
the various initiatives which are part of the government's regional and urban policy. In
the case of the latter, these are available to authorities within the assisted areas and/or
the Urban Programme areas, though some funds may be channelled through other
agencies (e.g. the Scottish and Welsh Development Agencies).

Supranational support from the European Community comes mainly from the ERDF
which is used in the assisted and Urban Programme areas to fund infrastructural
projects (e.g. Tyne and Wear Metro, Liverpool Ring Road). In addition, further funding
is also available under certain circumstances from the European Social Fund (e.g. for
training), the European Coal and Steel Community (e.g. for support for declining steel
and coal areas), the European Investment Bank (e.g. low-interest loans for
infrastructural investment) and a number of other sources. More often than not, these
funds are directed at those areas identified by the national government as areas of
greatest need – hence the decision by the United Kingdom government in the 1980s to
extend the number of authorities covered by its Urban Programme, thus qualifying
those added to the list for EC financial aid.

Types of intervention

Local authority aid to industry and commerce takes a wide variety of forms, but three
areas in particular are worth noting: help with land and buildings; financial assistance;
and the provision of information, advice and other support services. These were three
of the major priorities identified by local authorities in a survey carried out in the late
1980s by the chartered accountants Deloitte, Haskins & Sells.[1]

As far as land and buildings are concerned, local councils as planning authorities,
landowners and site developers clearly have an important role to play in industrial
development, and despite recent attempts by central government to reduce their
influence, their involvement in the local property market has generally grown over time.
Amongst the key activities undertaken by local government in this area have been:

1 The identification of land available for industrial use (e.g. local authority registers of
   vacant land and land use).
2 The provision of local-authority-owned land for industrial and commercial
   development.
3 The supply of on-site infrastructure (e.g. roads, drainage).
4 Land reclamation and site assembly.
5 Environmental improvement (including derelict land).
6 Advice and help to private sector developers.

In addition, local authorities have become increasingly involved in the provision and/or
conversion of premises for business use (including starter units, workshops and small
factories) and have encouraged the development of a number of science parks, often
working in conjunction with private companies and institutions of higher education.

Financial assistance has also been important in encouraging business activity, with local authorities often providing grants to firms seeking to move to new premises or to expand and/or convert existing buildings, particularly if additional jobs are likely to be created. Funds – mainly in the form of grants or loans – have also been made available to firms wishing to purchase new equipment or to establish certain types of enterprise (e.g. co-operatives) or to meet some of the costs of creating jobs for the unemployed or to cover rental charges. Added to this, some councils have established Enterprise Boards, which are essentially trading companies concerned with the provision of long-term development capital for investment in local businesses and property. Using funds from local sources, the boards have invested in local companies – usually by taking an equity stake – and have managed their portfolio of investments through a specially created company which is independent of the local authority. Through such investments the boards have sought to attract additional funds from financial institutions such as pension funds, thus creating a financial leverage which is designed to multiply the impact of the support from the public sector.[2]

To complement these direct forms of intervention, all local authorities have sought to encourage local economic development through their promotional and advisory activities which are aimed at both existing and would-be entrepreneurs. Many councils, for example, produce publicity material, booklets, leaflets, information packs and other types of promotional literature, extolling the advantages of their area for tourism or for industrial and commercial use; this can be one of the factors encouraging investment, including direct inward investment by multinational companies, particularly if it is supported by financial and/or other incentives offered by the local authority (e.g. the Toyota development at Burnaston near Derby) or under regional or urban assistance programmes (e.g. the Nissan plant near Sunderland).

Similarly, as active providers of information to businesses on matters such as vacant premises and sites, local labour market conditions, housing availability and sources of finance, local councils deliberately promote their respective areas and many make use of trade fairs or trade delegations to ensure that the 'message' is not restricted to a domestic audience but also reaches potential overseas investors. For the most part, these activities tend to be co-ordinated through the economic development unit or some other agency operating under the purview of an authority's chief executive officer. Significantly, however, an increasing number of authorities have established specialist Marketing departments in an effort to 'sell' their area to organisations and individuals who are likely to contribute to the regeneration of the local economy through investment in capital assets and through job creation.

Partnership with the private sector

Whilst local authorities acting alone can be an important agency for local economic development, their support for local businesses often occurs through some form of partnership with the private sector. Such partnerships – including the establishment of Local Enterprise Agencies – are increasingly seen as a vital element in effective economic regeneration in the SME sector at both local and regional level.

Local Enterprise Agencies (known as Enterprise Trusts in Scotland) date back to the early 1970s, but their main period of growth began a decade later with the number of agencies reaching around 300 by the end of the 1980s. Using funds provided by industry and commerce and by central and local government, LEAs act essentially as business development organisations assisting both new and existing enterprises. Their core activity is to provide information and business counselling (often referred to as 'signposting') which points individuals wishing to start a business to sources of help or assists those already running a business with specific problems. In addition most LEAs provide a number of other services, including business training, workspace, help with the preparation of business plans, provision of *ad hoc* services (e.g. solicitors), advice on marketing, taxation, personnel matters and help in locating premises.

Unlike Enterprise Boards which are essentially interventionist bodies established by local authorities, Enterprise Agencies are independent organisations which are either private sector initiatives or more regularly a partnership between the public and private sectors, operating through a board which is private sector led. Increasingly, LEAs are tending to work together to provide a more effective service to small businesses as exemplified by the formation of the Local Investment Networking Company (LINC) in 1987. LINC – which is run jointly by a number of LEAs located throughout the United Kingdom and sponsored by several large companies including BP and Lloyds Bank – was established to help small businesses seeking funding and additional managerial input to find suitable investors. The aim of the organisation is to help both small start-up and growing firms whose financial requirements tend to fall into an 'equity gap' (below £250,000) which may be difficult to bridge through conventional sources. It does this by bringing together private investors willing to invest in new or expanding small businesses and companies looking for such investment and/or additional management skills to aid their development.

Further encouragement to the creation of public and private sector partnerships comes from organisations such as Business in the Community (BITC), which also operates as an umbrella organisation for local enterprise agencies. BITC's main role is to encourage the involvement of the business community in a wide range of issues affecting local areas and in particular in economic development at local, sub-regional and regional levels. The assumption is not only that the business sector has a responsibility to the local community but also that it has the skills, experience, expertise, contacts and other resources which help to increase the chances of such economic development initiatives being successful.

Within the area of economic development and enterprise, BITC has been particularly active in encouraging community-based partnerships between businesses, government, local groups and individuals aimed at regenerating urban and rural communities, and in this it often works alongside national organisations such as the Action Resource Centre and the Civic Trust. In addition, through a range of initiatives on community enterprise, customised training, business support, innovation and partnership sourcing, the organisation has sought to develop closer links between firms and their local communities in the belief that such community involvement is a natural part of successful business practice, as well as a key influence on the quality and quantity of business activity at local level.

THE GROWTH OF CORPORATE COMMUNITY INVOLVEMENT

The active involvement of business in the development of local communities looks likely to be a significant feature of entrepreneurial activity in the 1990s. From a simple concern with the interests of traditional 'stakeholders' (e.g. employees, shareholders, customers), many businesses are coming to recognise that policies which enhance the well-being of the wider community (e.g. job creation, pollution control, welfare provision) can also benefit the organisation and increase its chances of success. This fundamental change in British corporate culture stems from a growing acceptance that corporate community involvement helps to contribute to local economic and social development, thus creating a more stable and prosperous environment within which firms operate. According to David Grayson – managing director of BITC's business strategy group – such involvement is one of the strategic management tools that is essential to any company which wants to thrive in the 1990s.[3]

Increased community involvement clearly benefits businesses in a variety of ways. Firms participating in community projects and campaigns can enhance their reputation and create goodwill in the local area, as well as increasing public awareness of their products and developing more effective networks with local individuals and organisations. Where these initiatives involve supporting education and training projects, improvements tend to occur in the quality of the workforce and in its attitude towards the organisation and its products. Similarly, through support for local economic development, businesses help to improve the physical environment and stimulate the growth of new businesses, thus helping to attract further financial investment and to boost the local economy upon which many of them depend for their long-term survival.

Whilst most of the initiatives in this area have tended to be associated with US businesses which have traditionally been community-minded, a growing number of UK-owned or based companies have embraced corporate community involvement. BAT Industries, for example, supported the Southampton Enterprise Agency as long ago as 1981 and has subsequently assisted the Brunswick Small Business Centre in Liverpool, Brixton Small Business Centre and the South London Business Initiative. In addition, BAT subsidiaries, such as Eagle Star, have been active in other areas of community support – including the Church Urban Fund which raises money for community projects in disadvantaged urban areas and in a project on local crime prevention in Gloucestershire.

All the signs are that such community involvement will increase substantially over the next decade as a combination of economic, social, political and consumer pressures force firms into becoming more socially aware and responsible and not simply concerned with increasing market share and profit margins. Moreover, with the development of global markets and the growth in overseas investment, the successful firms are likely to be those which accept that community concerns have an international content. Toyota, for example, claims that its activities are designed to meet local needs and to contribute to the economies and communities of the countries in which it operates. Accordingly the organisation has been involved in a range of cultural, educational, social and environmental projects in an effort to promote itself as a good corporate citizen.[4]

SPATIAL POLICIES: THE EUROPEAN DIMENSION

Government policies aimed at encouraging and supporting business activity at subnational level can be found throughout Europe and beyond and it is appropriate to consider just a few examples by way of comparison with practice in the United Kingdom. Students wishing to undertake a more comprehensive and detailed analysis will find Yuill and Allen's book *European Regional Incentives* a very useful source of information.[5]

As far as EC countries are concerned, it is worth re-emphasising that regional assistance is available to all Member States from the Community's structural funds, which are designed to support investment in infrastructure, industry and agriculture in the less-developed regions of Europe. As indicated above, these funds – described in more detail in Table 10.1 – are basically designed to provide a counterbalance to unequal development within the Community and to support declining areas, often with the help of additional special programmes tailored to alleviate specific problems or to meet certain needs (e.g. the RECHAR programmes in declining coal mining areas; the European Community Support for Women's Enterprise to encourage women to start their own businesses and to create full-time jobs for females). The amount available under EC structural funds for 1993 was around £10 billion.

Table 10.1 European Structural Funds

Fund	Main focus	Typical support
European Regional Development Fund	Redevelopment and structural adjustment of less-developed and declining industrial regions. Funds are concentrated in: (a) least-favoured regions; (Objective 1 areas); (b) regions/areas suffering industrial decline (Objective 2); (c) rural areas (Objective 5b).	Industrial investment Infrastructure Local initiatives Environmental
European Social Fund	Funding for organisations running vocational training schemes and job creation. Responsibility for implementing Objectives 3 and 4.	Schemes which have funding from a public authority.
European Agricultural Guidance and Guarantee Fund	Funding designed to guarantee farm incomes with the EC and to guide farm production.	Support for farm agricultural prices and to encourage farm rationalisation.

Within each country, national-based initiatives are determined by local conditions and are thus in a strict sense unique to the country concerned; in practice, however, many governments arrange spatial policies along broadly similar lines. In the EC, for example, virtually all countries designate areas for special assistance and target aid to these areas, primarily in the form of capital grants similar to those used in the United Kingdom. In addition, most EC governments use loan-related schemes, fiscal benefits and labour-based incentives to encourage entrepreneurial activity and to help create or maintain employment in areas of particular need. As in the United Kingdom, many of these schemes are aimed at supporting the growth and development of small and medium-sized enterprises in the belief that they are a key contributor to a healthy and competitive market economy.[6]

Across most of Europe responsibility for economic development tends to be devolved to regional and/or local authorities, often working in partnership with central government and the private sector. France, for instance, established 22 regional councils in the early 1980s with a view to increasing the involvement of the regions in economic and social planning. In Belgium an extension of the Devolution Act 1988 has meant that the three regions (Flanders, Wallonia, Brussels) are almost entirely responsible for regional and industrial policy, whilst in Germany, Austria and Switzerland, economic development is undertaken through national/regional partnerships that involve a considerable degree of devolved authority from the centre to the regions.

An interesting insight into practices in Europe at regional and local level is provided by a recent study that was undertaken on behalf of Business in the Community by a team under the chairmanship of John Bullock of Coopers & Lybrand (Europe).[7] Looking at four areas – Hamburg (Germany), Catalonia (Spain), Limburg (Netherlands) and Lombardia (Italy) – the team examined both the wider economic framework within which local agencies and businesses co-operate and the specific business support mechanisms which provide direct help to individual firms. In Hamburg, the team found a publicly funded and highly influential Business Development Corporation (HWF), staffed by senior businessmen, which was responsible for promoting the area and providing various forms of help and advice to businesses and the City State. In Limburg, it found business support delivered within an integrated organisational framework that provided clear roles for the chief players involved – namely, the Provincial Authority, the Regional Development Agency and the Chamber of Commerce, all three of whom worked together to develop the overall strategic plan.

The study's most significant finding was that whilst highly competent economic development and business support players existed within the United Kingdom, the European practice of forming partnerships for regional development was not sufficiently widespread and this needed to be urgently encouraged with the support of central government. Without this partnership of all key players in a locality – including the DTI, the local authorities, the CBI, the Chambers of Commerce, BITC, TECs and private companies – the team felt that a common purpose in economic development could not be achieved and this made existing initiatives less effective. It also threatened to place individual geographical areas of the UK at a significant competitive disadvantage, at a time when global competition between both countries and companies was intensifying.

BUSINESS AS INFLUENCE ON GOVERNMENT

Both individually and collectively, business organisations in a market economy are an important influence on government decision-making; they are an essential part of what has been termed the 'negotiated environment' in which individuals and groups bargain with one another and with governments over the form of regulation of the environment that a government may be seeking to impose.[8]

At an individual level, it tends to be large companies – and in particular multinational corporations – who are in the strongest position to influence government thinking, by dint of their economic and political power, and many of them have direct contacts with government ministers and officials for a variety of reasons (e.g. large defence contractors supply equipment to the Ministry of Defence). In addition, many large businesses use professional lobbyists or create their own specialists units whose role is to liaise directly with government agencies and to represent the interest of the organisation at national and/or supranational level (e.g. in Brussels), using the kind of techniques described in Chapter 3. Whilst such activities do not ensure that governments will abandon or amend their proposals or will pursue policies favourable to a particular company's position, they normally guarantee that the views of the organisation are considered alongside those of the other vested interests. Added weight tends to be given to these views when they are supported by all the leading firms in an industry (e.g. the tobacco lobby's fight against a complete ban on tobacco advertising).

The voice of business is also heard in political circles through various voluntary representative organisations such as Chambers of Commerce, employers' associations, trade associations and the Confederation of British Industry (CBI). Chambers of Commerce, for example, largely represent the views and interests of small businesses at local level, but also have a national organisation that lobbies in Whitehall and Brussels. In contrast, trade associations – which are sometimes combined with employers' associations – are usually organised on an industry basis (e.g. the Society of Motor Manufacturers and Traders) and handle consultations with appropriate government agencies, as well as providing information and advice to members about legislation and administration pertinent to the industry concerned.

The Confederation of British Industry (CBI)

The largest employer's association overall, representing thousands of companies employing millions of workers, is the CBI, whose members are drawn from businesses of all types and sizes and from all sectors, but especially manufacturing. Through its director-general and council – and supported by a permanent staff which has representation in Brussels – the organisation promotes the interests of the business community in discussions with governments and with national and international organisations, as well as seeking to shape public opinion. Part of its influence stems from its regular contacts with politicians, the media and leading academics and from the encouragement it gives to businesses to take a proactive approach to government legislation and policy. Additionally, through its authoritative publications – including the Industrial Trends Surveys and reports – the CBI has become an important part of the debate on government economic policy generally, as well as a central influence on legislation affecting the interests of its members.

Indicative of its more proactive approach in recent years has been its attempts to shape government thinking on environmental policy and to harmonise the work of both government and businesses in this area by promoting its own 'Action Plan' for the 1990s. To this end the CBI has established a group of staff dedicated specially to work on environmental issues of interest to business and has set up a policy unit and management unit to provide information, contacts and advice to the various parties involved. The policy unit monitors developments in legislation, liaises with government departments and enforcement agencies (e.g. the National Rivers Authority), lobbies government and other organisations, provides information and advice, and helps to formulate CBI policy on vital environmental issues. The management unit produces promotional literature for businesses, organises conferences and seminars on specific topics, conducts surveys and provides advice on financial and other assistance available to its members to help them develop good environmental management practices within their organisation.

Whilst it is impossible to say with any degree of certainty how influential industry is in shaping government policy, there is little doubt that the views of leading industrialists and their representative bodies and associations have received increased attention under recent Conservative administrations. Regular pronouncements by senior government ministers, including the Prime Minister and Chancellor of the Exchequer, frequently refer to the fact that a particular policy or piece of legislation has been framed 'with industry in mind'.

SYNOPSIS

State involvement in business activity takes many forms and can be seen as an attempt by government to tackle the problems caused by the operation of the free market. One such problem – regional imbalance – is normally the focus of a government's regional policy that seeks to correct economic disparities through spatially selective forms of assistance. Similarly, the adverse consequences associated with urbanisation and localised economic decay and decline have generally given rise to a range of government initiatives, often in partnership with the private sector, and involving different forms of state intervention at local, national and supranational level.

Local government, too, has been active in this sphere and has used a variety of means to encourage local economic development and to support the local business community, both as agent for central government and as sponsor in its own right. Many of its activities have involved direct collaboration with businesses and with the voluntary organisations which represent them and the private sector has remained a key influence on government policy at all spatial levels. Given the increasing emphasis on free market activity, the voice of business is destined to remain a key input into the process of economic decision-making in Britain and elsewhere for the foreseeable future.

CASE STUDY: SWAN HUNTER

As a maritime nation, Britain has had a history of shipbuilding stretching back for centuries. For much of the twentieth century, however, the British shipbuilding industry has been in decline, largely as a result of foreign competition. This decline has affected a number of famous shipbuilders and the communities they serve, including Swan Hunter at Wallsend on Tyneside which has been building ships for over 100 years.

Swan Hunter's problems are typical of those faced by other major British shipbuilders who are unable to compete with cheaper yards in the Far East, in a market where demand has fallen appreciably and where cost and delivery dates are critical. As the demand for merchant ships has declined, Swan Hunter has become more reliant on military work, including refitting and refurbishing frigates and other naval vessels and has looked to the government as a major customer to provide enough work to keep the shipyard in operation, albeit on a smaller scale than in the past. Consequently the announcement in 1993 that a naval order worth £180 million had been awarded to the rival VSEL yard at Barrow – whose tender price was £50 million less – came as a mortal blow to Swan Hunter and forced the company into receivership amidst considerable political controversy.

Given the British government's concern to control public expenditure and its emphasis on achieving value for money, the decision to place the order with VSEL was understandable and was greeted with delight in Barrow which had also been experiencing similar problems to those faced on Tyneside. From an economic and political point of view, however, the likely demise of Swan Hunter could prove very costly, which may yet help to save the yard from complete closure.

At the heart of the problem for the government is the importance of the company in the national and regional as well as the local economy. In an area which has traditionally suffered unemployment problems and which has recently seen a reduction in the numbers employed in local government, the offshore industry and the closure of Sunderland Shipbuilders, the contribution of Swan Hunter is vital. In addition to the 2,000 workers employed at the yard, another 4,500 local jobs could be lost if the company ceases operations, and other local businesses are likely to experience reduced turnover (e.g. pubs, cafés, shops). In addition, the company is also served by over 900 suppliers from all over the country, many of whom are dependent on Swan Hunter as their largest customer and a third of whom are located in Conservative constituencies. It also employs one of the highest-skilled manufacturing workforces in Europe – the loss of which would have national as well as regional implications.

Whilst some jobs have recently been created in the region through government-backed direct inward investment (e.g. Nissan at Sunderland), few believe that this will provide a permanent solution to the structural problems faced in the North East, where currently 43 people are chasing every job vacancy. Similarly, the government's proposal to create an enterprise zone in Wallsend is seen by many as a palliative that fails to address the underlying problem of regional imbalance. For some critics, the difficulties experienced by Swan Hunter are merely symptomatic of the problems faced by manufacturing industry as a whole and reflect the lack of assistance given to it by a government which has consistently emphasised the virtues of market forces. To this extent, the future of shipbuilding on the Tyne is regarded as a test of the current government's avowed intention to support British manufacturing and, where necessary, to intervene to help it to compete in world markets.

NOTES AND REFERENCES

1 Deloitte, Haskins & Sells, *Local Authority Assistance to Growing Businesses*, London, 1989.
2 Many Enterprise Boards were set up by Metropolitan County Councils. Their activities have generally continued, despite the abolition of these councils.
3 *The Guardian*, 14 April 1993, p. 14.
4 *Toyota Factfile*, April 1992.
5 Yuill, D. and Allen, K., (eds), *European Regional Incentives 1992–93*, Bowker Saur, London, 1992.
6 See Bachtler, J. and Downes, R. with Yuill, D., *The Devolution of Economic Development: Lessons from Germany*, The Scottish Foundation for Economic Research, Glasgow, 1993.

7 Coopers & Lybrand, *Lessons from Continental Europe: Promoting partnership for local economic development and business support in the UK*, July 1992.
8 See Thomas, R.E., *The Government of Business*, 3rd edition, Philip Allan, 1987.

REVIEW AND DISCUSSION QUESTIONS

1 Why should a government committed to the free market intervene in the working of the economy?

2 Using a range of current socio-economic indicators, comment on the notion that there is a North–South divide in the United Kingdom.

3 Why are some local authorities more interventionist than others?

4 Discuss the advantages and disadvantages of corporate community involvement.

ASSIGNMENTS

1 You are employed in the publicity and promotion unit of a local authority. Part of your work involves promoting the area as a suitable location for industrial and commercial activity. Your task is to produce a leaflet – for distribution to potential clients – indicating the advantages of locating within the area and the forms of assistance available.

2 You are the chairperson of the local Chamber of Commerce. The local authority has written to you concerning its plans to pedestrianise the town (or city) centre and asking for the reaction of local businesses. Your task is to produce a short report, for the next meeting of the Chamber, outlining the benefits and disadvantages to the local business community of such a scheme and indicating how the Chamber of Commerce could make its views known in political circles.

FURTHER READING

Hare, P. and Simpson, L., (eds), *British Economic Policy: A modern introduction,* Harvester, 1993.
Hasluck, C., *Urban Unemployment,* Longman, 1987.
Lever, W.F. (ed.), *Industrial Change in the United Kingdom,* Longman, 1987.

PART 4

Markets

CHAPTER 11

The market system

Chris Britton

As part of their normal production activity, businesses are involved in buying (inputs – like labour and raw materials) and selling (outputs – the finished product). Buying and selling takes place in markets and although there are many different types of markets the basic analysis remains the same.

OBJECTIVES

1 To understand the working of the market system.
2 To apply the theory to the real world.
3 To understand the importance of key concepts like elasticity to business.

INTRODUCTION

As indicated in Chapter 4, the market system is an economy in which all of the basic economic choices are made through the market. The market is a place where buyers and sellers of a product are brought together. The nature and location of the market depends on the product. For example, within your local town there is likely to be a vegetable market where you would go to buy vegetables. Here, buyers and sellers meet face to face in the same location, but this is not always the case. The market for used cars might be the local newspaper classified section; the sale of stocks and shares passes through a broker so that the buyer never meets the seller. There are many different types of market, involving different buyers and sellers. Firms sell goods and services they produce to households on the product markets, while in the factor markets firms are buying resources such as labour and raw materials. The discussion in this chapter will concentrate on the product markets but much of the analysis could also be applied to the factor markets.

A free market system is one in which the basic economic choices are made through the market, without any intervention by the government. In reality, markets are not completely free; governments intervene in markets for many reasons and in many different ways (see Chapter 14), but in this chapter such intervention will be ignored.

THE MARKET MECHANISM

In every market there will be a buyer and a seller, and somehow they have to be brought together so that a sale can take place. The market mechanism is the way in which this takes place in a market economy. In the product market, the buyer is the household and the seller is the firm. In economic language the household *demands* the good or service and the firm *supplies* the good or service. Each of these will be considered separately first and then brought together.

DEMAND

The quantity demanded refers to the quantity of a good or service that households are willing and able to purchase at a particular price. This definition shows that it is effective demand that is important; although many people would like to own a Rolls-Royce they could not afford it and so their demand is not effective on the market. The demand for a good or service depends on a number of factors, the most important of which are:

- the price of the good;
- the prices of other goods;
- disposable income; and
- tastes.

To begin with, the relationship between quantity demanded and price will be looked at, assuming that the other factors above remain the same. This assumption will be relaxed in the subsequent analysis.

Table 11.1 shows what happens to the quantity demanded of beer as the price per pint goes up. Note that demand is measured over some period of time. The information is then presented in a graphical form in Figure 11.1; the line joining the various combinations of price and quantity demanded is called a demand curve. The demand curve shows that if all of the other factors which influence demand are constant then as price goes up, quantity demanded goes down. This is commonly referred to as 'the law

Table 11.1 The demand for 'Real Brew' draught beer

Price (£ per pint)	Quantity demanded (000s of pints/week)
0.90	83
1.00	70
1.10	58
1.20	48
1.30	40
1.40	35
1.50	32

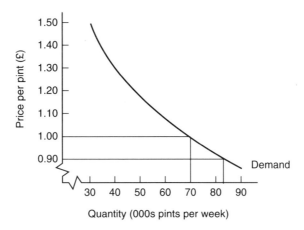

Fig. 11.1 A demand curve for 'Real Brew' draught beer

of demand'. What happens when price rises is that some individuals will cut down their consumption of beer and others may switch to other types of beer. There are some goods where this relationship might not hold:[1] for example, in the stock market where a rise in share prices might lead to the expectation of further price rises and therefore an increase in demand on the part of those wishing to make a capital gain. However, these exceptions are rare and it is therefore safe to assume that the law of demand holds.

If the price of beer changes, there is a movement along the demand curve. For example, if the price of beer goes up from 90p a pint to £1.00 a pint, the quantity demanded goes down from 83,000 pints per week to 70,000 pints per week. In drawing the demand curve the assumption was made that other factors affecting demand are constant. If this assumption is relaxed, what happens to the demand curve?

Price of other goods

The quantity of beer consumed will be affected by the prices of other goods. These other goods are likely to be substitutes or complements. A substitute for beer may be lager, and if the price of lager goes down, some individuals may switch from beer to lager; thus the demand for beer goes down. What happens to the demand curve is that at all prices levels, the demand for beer is now lower. Thus the demand curve shifts to the left, indicating that at £1.00 per pint only 60,000 pints of beer are demanded per week. If the price of a substitute goes up, there will be an increase in the demand for beer. The demand curve moves to the right. These movements are shown in Figure 11.2. The closer the goods are as substitutes and the greater the change in the price of the substitute, the greater will be the shift in the demand curve.

A complementary good is one which tends to be consumed with another good. For beer, it is possible that individuals eat crisps, or smoke cigarettes at the same time as drinking beer. The relationship is the opposite of that for substitutes. If the price of a complement goes up, individuals might be less likely to drink beer, and demand will fall. The demand curve moves to the left. If the price of a complement goes down, the

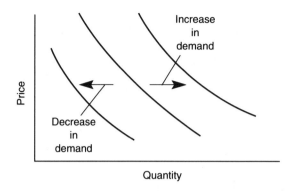

Fig. 11.2 Shifting demand curves

demand for beer will rise. Again the closer the goods are as complements, and the greater the price change of that complement, the greater will be the shift in the demand curve.

Disposable income

Changes in disposable income will clearly affect demand. If the economy moves into recession, then retail sales and the housing market might suffer. As incomes increase once the economy recovers, then such sectors will pick up again. Higher incomes will lead to increased consumption of most goods. If your income is boosted, how will this affect your consumption? You might buy more textbooks, and probably spend more money on leisure activities and clothes. Most students might also drink an extra pint of beer per week. Thus an increase in disposable income will lead to an increase in demand for these goods, indicated by a rightward shift in the demand curve. As incomes fall the demand for these goods will fall, indicated by a leftward shift in the demand curve. These type of goods are called normal goods.

There are goods, however, that experience a fall in demand as a result of income increases. These goods are called inferior goods. A good example is hard toilet paper; as individuals become richer, they are likely to substitute more expensive soft toilet paper, and thus the demand for hard toilet paper will fall.

Tastes

This includes attitudes and preferences of consumers, and will be affected by such things as fashion, and advertising campaigns by producers or by governments. For example, a successful advertising campaign by the government pointing out the effects of smoking would cause tastes to change and demand for cigarettes to fall.

The demand curve, then, is downward sloping, indicating that as the price of the good rises the quantity demanded by households falls, shown by a movement along the demand curve. Changes in the other determining factors lead to movements of the demand curve.

SUPPLY

The other side of the market is the supply side. In the market for goods and services it is the firm that is the supplier. The quantity supplied of a good is defined as the quantity that firms are willing and able to supply to the market at a particular price. Again notice the wording of the definition is such that it only includes effective supply and, as with demand, it is measured over a specific time period.

The quantity supplied to the market depends on a number of factors, the most important of which are:

- the price of the good;
- the prices of other goods;
- the prices of the resources used to produce the good;
- technology;
- expectations; and
- number of suppliers.

In the same way as for demand, all factors other than price will be assumed to be constant and the relationship between quantity supplied and price will be considered first.

Table 11.2 provides some information on price and quantity supplied of beer. The same information is represented graphically in Figure 11.3; the line joining the points together is called the supply curve. The upwards sloping curve illustrates the 'law of supply'. This states that as the price of a good rises the quantity that firms are willing to supply also rises. This is because if costs are constant as we have assumed, then higher prices must mean higher profits to the firm.

Table 11.2 The supply of 'Real Brew' draught beer

Price (£ per pint)	Quantity supplied (000s of units/week)
0.90	0
1.00	35
1.10	43
1.20	48
1.30	55
1.40	60
1.50	68

Note that there is no supply at a price below 90p per pint; this is the minimum price required by the producer to produce the beer. If the price per pint changes there is a movement along the supply curve in the same way as for demand. If any of the other factors listed above change there will be a movement of the supply curve.

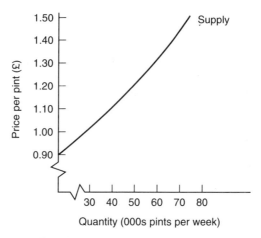

Fig. 11.3 A supply curve for 'Real Brew' draught beer

Other prices

The supply of one good can be influenced by the price of another. For example, if the brewery in which Real Brew beer is brewed is also producing lager, then an increase in the price of lager (with the price of beer remaining the same) will encourage the firm to produce less beer and more lager, as lager is now more profitable to produce. The supply curve for beer would shift to the left, indicating that at every possible price, less is now supplied than before. If the price of lager fell, the supply of beer would increase. This is shown by a rightward shift of the supply curve. The size of the shift would depend upon the degree to which the goods could be substituted for each other in production, and the size of the price change. These shifts are illustrated in Figure 11.4.

Goods can also be complements in their production process; for example, beef and leather hides. An increase in the price of beef would not only increase the supply of beef but also the supply of hides. There would be a corresponding shift in the supply curve for hides.

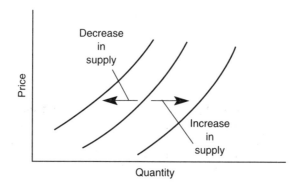

Fig. 11.4 Shifting supply curves

The prices of the resources used in the production of the good

If any of the costs of production (wages, rent, rate of interest, and so on) increased, then the profitability of that good at each price will fall and there would be a tendency for supply to be reduced. The supply curve would move to the left. If costs of production fall there would be an increase in supply and a rightward movement of the supply curve. The extent of the shift depends upon the size of the price change, the significance of that factor in production, and the degree to which the factor could be substituted for another factor.

Technology

As illustrated in Chapter 5, technical development in all aspects of production has lead to great improvements in output per worker. Such improvements generally result in either more being produced with the same resources, or the same being produced with fewer. In most cases it would also lead to a substitution of one factor of production for another. For example, car production becomes less labour intensive as robotic techniques take over. Even such a product as traditional British beer has benefited from significant technical improvements in production. The effect of such advances would result in increased supply at each price level and hence a movement of the supply curve to the right.

Business expectations

Expectations play a crucial role in the decision-making of firms. Good expectations of the future would encourage firms to invest in new plant and machinery, which would increase their productive potential. Chancellors of the Exchequer are occasionally accused of trying to 'talk the economy up': that is, they may paint a rosy picture of the current and future state of the economy in the hope that this will enhance business expectations, and help pull the economy out of recession. If business does become increasingly confident, or perhaps more inclined to take risks, then this would shift the supply curve to the right. The reverse would shift it to the left.

The number of suppliers

As the number of suppliers in a market increases the supply will rise; the supply curve shifts to the right. If suppliers leave the market, supply will fall and the supply curve moves to the left.

PRICE DETERMINATION

The market is the place where buyers and sellers meet and where demand and supply are brought together. The information on demand and supply is combined in Table 11.3 and presented graphically in Figure 11.5.

Table 11.3 The supply and demand for 'Real Brew' draught beer

Price (£ per pint)	Quantity demanded (000s/wk)	Quantity supplied (000s/wk)
0.90	83	0
1.00	70	35
1.10	58	43
1.20	48	48
1.30	40	55
1.40	35	60
1.50	32	68

The equilibrium price

At a price of £1.20, the quantity demanded is the same as the quantity supplied at 48,000 pints per week. At this price the amount that consumers wish to buy is the same as the amount that producers wish to sell. This price is called the equilibrium price and the quantity being bought and sold is called the equilibrium quantity. The point of equilibrium can be seen on the diagram at the point where the demand and supply curves cross.

At price levels above £1.20 the quantity that producers wish to supply is greater than the quantity consumers wish to buy. There is excess supply and the market is a 'buyers' market'. At prices less than £1.20 consumers wish to buy more than producers wish to supply. There is excess demand and the market is a 'sellers' market'.

In competitive markets, situations of excess demand or supply should not exist for long as forces are put into motion to move the market towards equilibrium. For example, if the price level is £1.30 per pint, there is excess supply and producers will be forced to reduce the price in order to sell their beer. Consumers may be aware that they are in a buyers' market and offer lower prices, which firms might accept. For one or both of these reasons, there will be a tendency for prices to be pushed back towards the

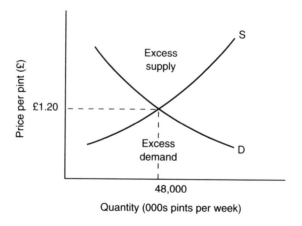

Fig. 11.5 The market for 'Real Brew' draught beer

equilibrium price. The opposite occurs at prices below equilibrium and price is pushed upwards towards equilibrium.

Shifts in demand and supply

So long as the demand and supply curves in any market remain stationary, the equilibrium price should be maintained. However, there are numerous factors that could shift either or both of these curves. If this were to happen, then the old equilibrium would be destroyed and the market should work to a new equilibrium. How does this happen?

In Figure 11.6 the original equilibrium price for Real Brew draught beer is P_1. Assume that the demand curve moves from D_1 to D_2. This increase in demand could be due to a variety of factors already mentioned. For example, the price of a rival drink may have increased; disposable income could have risen; or sales may have benefited from a successful advertising campaign. In any event, at the old equilibrium price there now exists an excess of demand over supply of Q_1Q_3. It is likely that price will be bid upwards in order to ration the shortage in supply. As price rises demand is choked off and supply exhausted. Eventually, there is a movement to a new equilibrium of P_2. At this new price both supply and demand at Q_2 are higher than they were at the previous equilibrium. If, alternatively, the demand curve had shifted to the left, then the process would have been reversed and the new equilibrium would have been at a level of demand and supply less than Q_1, with a price below P_1. Illustrate this process diagrammatically for yourself.

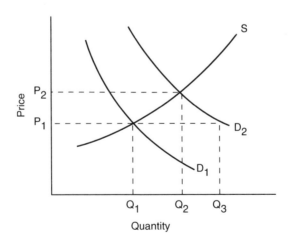

Fig. 11.6 A shift in the demand curve

In Figure 11.7 there is a shift in the supply curve from S_1 to S_2. Refer back in this chapter to envisage specific reasons for such a shift. At the original equilibrium price of P_1 there would now be an excess supply over demand of Q_1Q_3. Price would therefore fall in a free market. As it does, demand will be encouraged and supply diminished. Eventually there will be a new equilibrium at P_2 with a higher quantity demanded and

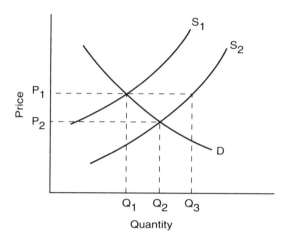

Fig. 11.7 A shift in the supply curve

supplied than at the previous equilibrium. If the supply curve had instead shifted to the left, then market forces would have resulted in a lower quantity supplied and demanded than before. Once again, illustrate this diagrammatically for yourself.

The analysis so far has been relatively straightforward; it has been assumed that either the demand or the supply curve moves alone. However, it is likely that in any given time period both curves could move in any direction and perhaps even more than once.

Given the many factors that may shift both the demand and the supply curves, it is easy to imagine that markets can be in a constant state of flux. Just as the market is moving towards a new equilibrium, some other factor may change, necessitating an adjustment in an opposite direction. Given that such adjustment is not immediate, and that market conditions are constantly changing, it may be the case that equilibrium is never actually attained. It is even possible that the very process of market adjustment can be destabilising.[2] The constant movement of price implied by the analysis may also be detrimental to business. The firm might prefer to keep price constant in the face of minor changes in demand and supply.

PRICE CONTROLS

Governments occasionally take the view that a particular equilibrium price is politically, socially or economically unacceptable. In such circumstances, one course of action is the imposition of price controls. This involves the institutional setting of prices at either above or below the true market equilibrium. For example, if it was felt that the equilibrium price of a good was too high, then the government might try to impose a lower price on the market. This would now be the maximum acceptable price or price ceiling. Price may not rise above this ceiling. Alternatively, the equilibrium price could be seen as too low. In this case, a higher price, or price floor is imposed, below which price should not fall.

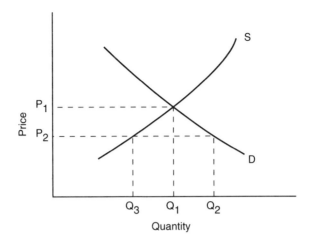

Fig. 11.8 Imposition of a price ceiling

Figure 11.8 illustrates the market for a basic foodstuff. Imagine that it is wartime and the disruption has shifted the supply curve to the left. This could be largely due to a movement of resources away from the production of this good and towards munitions. The free market price at P_1 is seen to be unacceptably high relative to the prewar price, and the decision is made to impose a price ceiling of P_2. It is hoped that such a ceiling will alleviate the problems of consumers who could not afford the free market price. The problem now is that at the price ceiling only Q_3 units will be supplied, whereas demand is for Q_2. The volume of output Q_3Q_2 therefore represents an excess of demand over supply. Many customers are frustrated in their desire to purchase that good. To help bring order to the situation, a system of rationing might be introduced. This could allocate the limited output between the many customers in a more orderly fashion than 'first come, first served'. For example, one unit could be allocated per person and priority could be given to the old and the sick. This does not solve the problem of excess demand. It is commonly found in such situations that illegal trading starts to emerge at a price above the ceiling. To obtain the good many would be willing to pay a higher price. This is commonly referred to as black market trading.

Figure 11.9 illustrates the market for a specific type of labour. The downward sloping demand curve indicates that at lower wages, employers will wish to take on additional workers. The supply curve shows how more people will offer themselves for work as wage rates increase. At the intersection of the curves, the market is in equilibrium. Imagine that this equilibrium wage is seen to be too low, and the authorities seek to impose a minimum wage of W_2. Employers are not permitted to pay any less than this amount. It is hoped that the policy will improve the welfare of workers by raising their living standards to some acceptable level.

At this minimum wage, employment becomes more attractive, and Q_3 persons seek employment. On the other hand, employers only wish to take on Q_2 workers. There is now a situation of excess supply. Only Q_2 find work, the remainder Q_2Q_3 are unsuccessful. The policy has actually reduced the level of employment from Q_1 to Q_2.

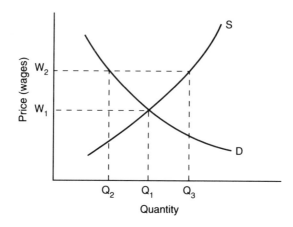

Fig. 11.9 Imposition of a price floor

In such a situation, there will be a temptation to flout the legislation. For example, unscrupulous employers, observing the ranks of unemployed would realise that many would willingly work at less than the minimum wage.

The above examples illustrate the problems that arise once price is imposed away from its equilibrium. Further examples of such price controls would include the guaranteed minimum prices to farmers within the common agricultural policy (CAP) of the European Community, and various postwar attempts to control the cost of rented accommodation at a price affordable to the low-paid. The former has been associated with overproduction and the need to control the mountains of excess supply, while the latter tended to result in landlords taking their properties off the rental market in order to seek more profitable returns. The success of such policies requires careful control and monitoring. In many circumstances, it might be better to consider alternative ways of achieving the policy goals.

ELASTICITY OF DEMAND

It has been shown that as long as other factors affecting demand remain constant, a decrease in price would be expected to increase the quantity demanded by consumers. This knowledge is obviously of importance to business, in that it implies that sales will expand as the good becomes more price competitive. It does not, however, say anything about the degree to which sales might increase. As prices change, will demand change by a large or a small amount? At the end of the day, will the extra sales bring in more or less total revenue? In short, a measure is needed of the responsiveness of demand to price changes. In the same way the responsiveness of quantity demanded to other factors like income or other prices can also be measured. It is also important to be aware of the responsiveness of supply to changes in prices. All of these are measured by the concept of elasticity.

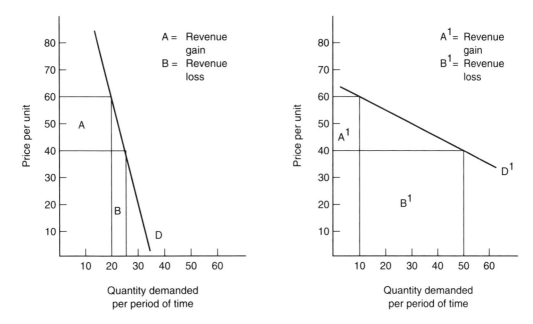

Fig. 11.10 Responsiveness of demand to a price change

Price elasticity of demand

Figure 11.10 illustrates two different-shaped demand curves and shows the effect of a price increase from 40p to 60p in each case. On the left-hand diagram, the increase in price causes demand to fall from 25 to 20 units. Total revenue received by the producer (i.e. price multiplied by the number of units sold) changes from £10.00 (40p × 25 units) to £12.00 (60p × 20 units). As illustrated, the area A represents the gain in revenue as a result of the price change, whilst B shows the loss of revenue. In this case there is a clear net gain. The reason for this is that the significance of the price rise is greater than the fall in demand. Compare this with the right-hand diagram. The same price rise now causes total revenue to fall from £20.00 (40p × 50 units) to £6.00 (60p × 10 units). The loss of revenue, area B′, is clearly greater than the gain in revenue, area A′. There is a net loss of revenue. This is a situation where the decrease in demand is of greater significance than the increase in price.

The traditional way of measuring the responsiveness of demand to a change in price is via the concept of price elasticity, the formula being:

$$\text{Price elasticity of demand (Ep)} = \frac{\text{Percentage change in quantity demanded}}{\text{Percentage change in price}}$$

$$Ep = \frac{\%\ \text{change QD}}{\%\ \text{change P}}$$

The significance of this formula lies in whether the value of price elasticity is greater or less than one. If it is greater, then the percentage change in quantity demanded is greater than the percentage change in price. Demand is referred to as being relatively elastic, or responsive to price changes. If, on the other hand, the percentage change in quantity demanded is less than the percentage change in price, then price elasticity will be less than one. Demand is now referred to as being relatively inelastic, and demand is not very responsive to price changes.

The higher or lower the value of price elasticity, the greater or lesser the responsiveness of demand to the price change. Table 11.4 demonstrates the connection between price elasticity and total revenue. It will be observed that if price elasticity is greater than one, then there is a negative relationship between price changes and total revenue. For example, an increase in price results in a decrease in total revenue. Whereas, if elasticity is less than one, then there is a positive relationship.

Table 11.4 Elasticity and total revenue

Elasticity	Price change	Change in total revenue
Elastic	Upward Downward	Downward Upward
Inelastic	Upward Downward	Upward Downward

Calculating elasticity

From the information portrayed in Figure 11.10, in the left-hand diagram price rose from 40p to 60p and demand fell from 25 to 20 units; thus:

$$Ep = \frac{\% \text{ change QD}}{\% \text{ change P}} = \frac{5/25 \times 100}{20/40 \times 100} = \frac{20\%}{50\%} = 0.4$$

This shows that demand is inelastic. One problem with this measurement is that if you measured elasticity when price fell from 60p to 40p the answer would be different:

$$Ep = \frac{\% \text{ change in QD}}{\% \text{ change in P}} = \frac{5/20 \times 100}{20/60 \times 100} = \frac{25\%}{33.3\%} = 0.75$$

The reason for this variation is that the percentage change in each case is being measured from a different base. When price rises from 20p to 40p, this is a 50 per cent rise. Yet when it falls from 60p to 40p this is only a 33.3 per cent fall. The value of elasticity therefore varies. To avoid this ambiguity, elasticity is measured as the percentage change from the average value of price and quantity before and after the change, that is:

$$\% \text{ change} = \frac{\text{Change in value} \times 100}{\text{Average value}}$$

The value of elasticity for the price increase and decrease must now be identical:

$$Ep = \frac{\% \text{ change QD}}{\% \text{ change P}} = \frac{5/22.5 \times 100}{20/50 \times 100} = \frac{22.2\%}{40\%} = 0.55$$

The determinants of elasticity

There are a number of factors which determine how responsive quantity demanded is to price changes. First, the nature of the good and how it is viewed by consumers. A good which is a necessity will have a low value of elasticity, as an increase in price will not have a very big impact on the quantity consumed. Goods like cigarettes will have inelastic demand because they are habit forming. The tastes of consumers will be important: whether they view a television, for example, as a necessity or a luxury will determine the value of elasticity. Another factor is whether substitutes are available for the good or not. If there is no substitute for a particular good and the household wishes to continue to consume it, an increase in price will have little effect on the level of demand. Other factors include the importance of the good in the household's total expenditure. The smaller the proportion of the household's budget which is spent on a particular good, the smaller will be the effect on demand of any change in price.

Income elasticity of demand

This is a measure of the responsiveness of quantity demanded to changes in income. It can be negative in the case of inferior goods, where an increase in income leads to a fall in the demand for a good, or positive in the case of a normal good, where an increase in income leads to an increase in demand. There is also a difference between luxuries and necessities. Luxuries will have positive income elasticities with values over 1. This means that an increase in income will cause an increase in demand for that good and that a 1 per cent increase in income will cause a more than 1 per cent increase in demand. A necessity on the other hand will also have a positive income elasticity but its value will lie somewhere between 0 and 1, showing that an increase in income of 1 per cent causes an increase in demand by less than 1 per cent.

Income elasticity is calculated in a similar way to price elasticity except that it is income which is changing rather than price of the good:

$$\text{Income elasticity} = \frac{\%\ \text{change in quantity demanded}}{\%\ \text{change in income}}$$

The effect of changes in income to the overall level of expenditure depends upon the type of the good being considered, as Table 11.5 shows.

Table 11.5 Income elasticity and total expenditure

Type of good	Income elasticity	Change in total expenditure brought about by an increase in income of 1%
Inferior	Negative	Downward
Normal	Positive	Upward
Luxury	Positive and above 1	Upward by more than 1%
Necessity	Positive between 0 and 1	Upward by less than 1%

Cross-price elasticity of demand

This is a measure of how the demand for one good is affected by changes in the prices of other goods. It is calculated with the formula:

$$\text{Cross price elasticity} = \frac{\text{\% change in quantity demanded of good X}}{\text{\% change in the price of good Y}}$$

Like income elasticity it can be positive or negative depending this time upon the nature of the relationship between the goods. If the goods are substitutes for one another, as the price of Y goes up, the quantity demanded of X will also rise, as consumers substitute the relatively cheaper good (e.g. margarine for butter). Therefore cross-price elasticity will be positive. If the goods are complements, as the price of Y rises the demand for X will fall and cross-price elasticity will be a negative value. The size will depend upon how closely the goods are related, either as substitutes or complements.

ELASTICITY OF SUPPLY

The concept of elasticity can be applied to supply as well as demand, and is a measurement of how responsive quantity supplied is to changes in the price of a good. Figure 11.11 illustrates two differently shaped supply curves and the effect of the same price change in each case.

Elasticity of supply is measured with the following formula:

$$\text{Elasticity of supply} = \frac{\text{\% change in quantity supplied}}{\text{\% change in price}}$$

The higher the numerical value, the more responsive is supply to changes in price.

The main determinants of the elasticity of supply for a good are the nature of the

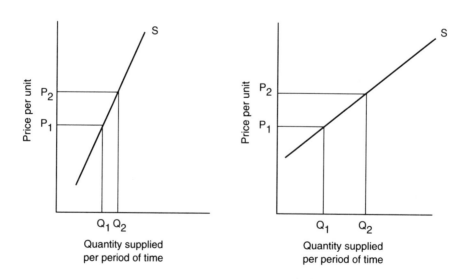

Fig. 11.11 Responsiveness of supply to a price change

production process and the time-scale in question. It may well be easier to increase the supply of manufactured goods than agricultural goods, given the nature of the production processes involved. Even agricultural goods can be increased in supply, given time to replant stock, so supply is more responsive to prices changes in the longer time period.

THE IMPORTANCE OF THE MARKET TO BUSINESS

All firms operate in markets, whether they are localised, national or international. Although firms might be able to influence the market conditions that face them, they need a knowledge of their own markets and how markets fit together in the market economy. Firms often have a range of products and they need to be aware of the differing conditions in each of their markets. They need a knowledge of the shape and position of the demand curve they face, including knowledge of the following aspects:

- The nature of the good they produce.
- The way in which it is viewed by consumers.
- The factors which affect the demand for their good.
- Any changes likely in the future which will affect the market.
- Any likely government intervention in the market.

Only through this information can the firm hope to retain markets, expand existing markets and move into new ones.

An understanding is also needed of the concept of elasticity of demand. Knowing how the demand for its product responds to changes in its price will help the firm in its pricing policy. Measures of income elasticity help the firms in forecasting the effects of changes in income on the demand for its products. Economic growth will affect markets with high income elasticities much more than markets with low income elasticities. This knowledge will also help the firm in developing its marketing strategy. For example, goods with low income elasticities could be marketed as 'economical', thus hopefully increasing the market share.

If the firm wishes to be successful in existing markets and to expand into new markets, as well as detailed knowledge of demand conditions, it also needs to know about its own supply curve and production process and the supply curves of other firms.

Although the economy in which the firm operates is not a totally free market economy (see Chapter 14), the businessman needs to know and understand the importance of market forces which form the basis of our economic system.

SYNOPSIS

In this chapter, the market has been examined in some detail. The determinants of demand and supply have been considered and the effects of changes in any of these factors shown on the market. The concept of elasticity has also been examined and calculated and the importance of all these issues has been demonstrated to business.

CASE STUDY: THE MARKET FOR RECORDED MUSIC

According to economic theory, market price is determined by the forces of demand and supply as outlined in this chapter. Consumers demand goods and services in order to maximise the satisfaction they derive from them. Firms, on the other hand, attempt to maximise the profits they earn from what they sell. Consumers and producers are supposed to act independently and for both, price is the prime consideration in their decision-making. A look at the real world, however, reveals that the true situation is much more complex than this.

The market for recorded music

The UK market for recorded music is dominated by seven large companies which together account for about 80 per cent of the market. These are Warner, Sony, EMI, Virgin, BMG, Polygram and MCA. The rest of the market is taken up by the small independent recording companies and groups themselves who are increasingly setting up their own recording companies (Dire Straits for example).

The industry produces recorded music in three main forms at present: vinyl LPs, cassettes and CDs. The total demand in the world for recorded music has increased and the industry forecasts a continued increase, as shown in Figure 11.12. However, there are marked differences in the sale of recorded music in the three different forms, as Figure 11.3 shows. These changes are due to both demand and supply factors. Over the last ten years, it seems that the market for LPs has all but disappeared, the market for cassettes has peaked and is falling and the market for CDs has experienced very rapid growth. The industry expects the market for CDs to peak before 1995 and the newly developed digital compact cassette (DCC) to have taken over from CDs by the year 2000.

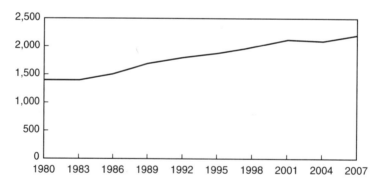

Fig. 11.12 Total world demand for recorded music (m. units)
Source: BPI

There has been much controversy in recent years over the prices charged for recorded music, in particular for CDs. There is a widespread belief that prices are too high. The industry was the subject of investigation by the Office of Fair Trading in 1992 and again in 1993 and the Consumers Association has asked MPs to take action to reduce the price of CDs.

There is a fairly uniform price for the three types of recorded music with little difference in the prices charged by the large record producers. The typical cost of an LP is around £9.00, a cassette is similar at around £8.50 while the cost of a CD is about £12 in the shops. There is some undercutting by the smaller independent companies, either artists marketing themselves or companies like NAXOS that offer lower prices in classical music by using eastern European musicians and singers.

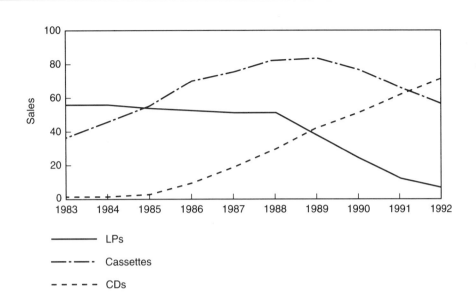

Fig. 11.13 Sales of LPs cassettes and CDs (m. units)
Source: BPI

Demand factors

As seen above, the total world demand for music has increased. It does, however, appear to be affected by economic conditions as it moves in a cyclical way over time. This is to be expected as recorded music is not a necessity and will be affected by factors like income levels.

The decline in the demand for the vinyl single market can be partly explained by demographic changes which have resulted in a smaller number of teenagers, who are the ones who buy singles. Added to this is the fact that there is now a much wider range of goods and services on which teenagers can spend their income. The decline in the demand for vinyl LPs can be partly explained by economic factors like high interest rates. But a basic explanation for the decline in both singles and LPs is technological change, as cassettes and more lately CDs, replace vinyl.

One constraining factor on the market for CDs is the availability of CD players in the home. At present only around one-third of households in the UK have CD players.

Supply factors

Added to these demand factors there are supply factors. Cost is one of the most important factors in the firm's decision about how much to supply. The cost of producing a CD was around £2.00 in 1983 and this has now fallen to about 70p due to fierce competition between the CD manufacturing plants. The cost of producing an LP is also around about 70p, so the difference in price is not due to differences in cost. The producers themselves have made conscious decisions to cut back the supply of LPs on the market. For example in the recent release of the new David Bowie album *Black Tie White Noise*, only 5 per cent of the release was done on vinyl LP. Because of the decline in the vinyl market, record producers in Japan and the United States have actually stopped producing LPs.

It is therefore difficult to separate out the demand and supply factors. Has the market for vinyl LPs declined because the consumer no longer demands them (as manufacturers claim) or has the market declined because the manufacturers have cut back on supply? The experience of the

Bowie release mentioned above implies it is a mixture of the two, as the 5 per cent issued in vinyl was an underestimate of demand and was quickly bought up despite the fact that many retailers such as W. H. Smiths and Our Price no longer stock LPs.

In the United States prices of CDs are about 50 per cent less than in the United Kingdom and although international comparisons are difficult to make the US industry does seem to have reacted to the demands of consumers for lower prices. In 1988 there was a 10 per cent reduction in the price of CDs by all the big record companies. As Table 11.6 shows, in comparison with the rest of Europe the United Kingdom fares better. In 1991 consumers in the the United States bought 15 CDs per CD player compared with eight in the United Kingdom. But it is difficult to say whether the sales of CDs are higher in United States because the prices are lower or whether prices are lower because sales are higher.

Table 11.6 Average price of a CD in selected countries

	(£)
United Kingdom	12.78
West Germany	13.14
Spain	14.50
France	14.51

The breakdown of the price of a typical CD with a selling price of £12.99 is shown in Table 11.7. To refute the claim that CDs are overpriced the record industry claim that a profit of £1.00 per CD is all that is made after all costs have been covered. The cost of research and development is actually for 'artists and repertoire' – that is, the search for and the development of new talent. The price of CDs was investigated in 1992 by the Office of Fair Trading, who found at that time that profit margins in the industry of 11 per cent were not excessive. However, the OFT has started another investigation and it is not certain when or whether the results will be published. One reason for the difference in prices between the United States and the United Kingdom is the copyright laws which make it difficult to import recorded music from countries where they are cheaper, and this is one area that the OFT is to concentrate on.

The record companies also argue that the size of the market in the United States allows the full benefits of economies of scale to be reaped. But this implies that the European markets are self-contained which is not the case.

The main difference in the price of LPs and CDs (according to the producers) is due to the willingness of the public to pay higher prices for CDs because of the higher quality and

Table 11.7 Breakdown of the price of a CD

	£
Cost of production of a CD	0.70
Paid to artist	1.50
Research and development	2.30
Marketing and packaging	2.10
Profit per CD	1.00
Wholesale price	7.60
Retail price	12.99

durability. The greater durability of CDs also means that the size of the replacement market for recorded music is smaller for the producers in the future.

Conclusion

What will happen to prices in the market for CDs depends upon many things like the basic demand and supply factors mentioned above, the force and weight of public feeling and the OFT investigation. It is clear that what happens in the market is not just the result of consumer sovereignty but also the result of producer power. It is not the case that consumers demand fewer LPs and therefore the producers react by supplying fewer; the producers have been proactive by cutting the supply so that consumers cannot buy LPs.

NOTES AND REFERENCES

1 In such cases the demand curve would be upward sloping, indicating that as price rises demand rises. Other examples include 'snob goods', which are consumed *because* their price is high and everyone knows that. Also antiques and valuable works of art may have upward-sloping demand curves.
2 In the markets described in this chapter there is an automatic tendency for the market to move back towards equilibrium once it is disturbed. However, it is possible for the demand and supply curves to be so shaped that once the market is disturbed it tends to move away from equilibrium rather than towards it. This is called the cobweb model. The interested reader should look at R. Lipsey, *An Introduction to Positive Economics*, Weidenfeld & Nicholson, 1989.

REVIEW AND DISCUSSION QUESTIONS

1 For the market for CDs show the effects of the following changes using demand and supply diagrams:
   (a) an increase in the number of people owning CD players;
   (b) a fall in the cost of producing CDs; and
   (c) a movement away from releasing music on LP and towards releasing music on CD.

2 Have your predicted changes actually happened in the real world? If not, why not?

3 Show the effects on the market for houses of the following:
   (a) a fall in average income levels;
   (b) a rise in the rate of interest; and
   (c) an increase in the supply of houses to the market.

4 The Halifax Building Society produces a list of regional house prices to show the difference in prices of an average three-bedroom semi-detached house in different parts of the country. Prices in the second quarter of 1993 were as follows:

Location	Price(£)
Greater London	128,850
Oxford	77,950
Bristol	63,600
Birmingham	59,400
Manchester	52,500
Rotherham	40,700
Belfast	38,300

What factors might account for these differences?

5 Is the market for houses a buyers' or sellers' market at the moment? Give reasons for your answer.

ASSIGNMENTS

1 You are a journalist on a local newspaper and have been asked to write an article on the price of houses in your locality. Identify the factors which influence house prices and explain why prices fluctuate over time. (You can use information from question 4 above.)

2 You work in the marketing department of a company that produces light bulbs. The company is considering increasing the price of its light bulbs by 20 per cent. At present a 100 watt light bulb costs 80p. The only information that is available is a survey carried out earlier in the year on the sensitivity of sales to price, the results of which are shown below:

Price	sales (m.)
80p	5800
100p	4000

Write a report for your manager on the likely effects of the proposed price increase, explaining the concept of elasticity of demand and the factors that are likely to affect it for this product.

FURTHER READING

Begg, D., Fischer, S. and Dornbusch R., *Economics*, McGraw-Hill, 1991.
Lipsey, R., *An Introduction to Positive Economics*, Weidenfeld & Nicholson, 1989.

CHAPTER 12

Market structure

Chris Britton

All businesses operate in a market which will be peculiar to that industry. Each market will have its own particular characteristics which depend upon many factors, and although it is not possible to have a model which describes every market, there are some economic models which provide some guidance to the kind of characteristics and behaviour that will be found in individual markets.

OBJECTIVES

1 To understand the market structures of perfect competition, monopoly, oligopoly and monopolistic competition and their implications for the behaviour of firms.
2 To appreciate the applicability of these predictions to the real world.
3 To understand the measurement of competition by concentration ratios.
4 To survey differences in industrial concentration between industries, countries and over time.
5 To recognise what determines market structure and what determines the behaviour of firms.

INTRODUCTION

In economics the behaviour and the performance of firms in an industry is thought to depend upon some basic structural characteristics. This view is exemplified by the structure–conduct–performance model, where structure determines conduct which in turn determines performance. The basic elements included under these headings are given in Table 12.1.

Although this model is open to criticism,[1] it provides a good framework for classifying and analysing an industry. A simple example of the process can be seen in the soap powder industry. Here the market is dominated by two large producers, Unilever and Procter & Gamble. This apparent lack of competition gives rise to certain behavioural characteristics like the massive amount of advertising, the existence of many brand names and fairly uniform prices. This process will be considered in more detail later in the chapter, but the example serves to indicate the relationship between the structure of the market and the behaviour and ultimately the performance of firms in an industry.

In this chapter, one of the structural characteristics will be considered in detail – the

Table 12.1 Structure – conduct – performance model

Structural factors

- Amount of actual competition: (a) seller concentration; and (b) buyer concentration.
- Existence of potential competition.
- Cost conditions.
- Demand conditions.
- Existence of barriers to entry.

Conduct factors

- Pricing policy.
- Amount of advertising.
- Merger behaviour.
- Product differentiation.

Performance factors

- Profitability.
- Technological innovation.

degree of actual competition, and two others will be considered briefly – the degree of potential competition and demand conditions.

'Market structure' refers to the amount of competition that exists in a market between producers. The degree of competition can be thought of as lying along a continuum with very competitive markets at one end and markets in which no competition exists at all at the other end. This chapter looks at the two extremes (perfect competition and monopoly), and the markets structures which exist between. The theory predicts the effects of market structure on behaviour and performance in those markets. However, as with the working of the market mechanism, the real world is often different from the theory and therefore this chapter will look at real markets and the relevance of the theory to the real world. In addition, it will also examine how the level of competition is measured in a market, how the level of competition varies between industries and countries and how this has changed over time, and will discuss the reasons why different market structures exist.

MARKET STRUCTURES – IN THEORY AND PRACTICE

As mentioned above, market structures can be thought of as lying along a continuum with perfect competition at one end and monopoly at the other (see Figure 12.1). Both of these market structures are unrealistic representations of the real world, but are useful as benchmarks in assessing the degree of competition in a market. Between these two extremes lie other market structures, which are more realistic. Two will be described, oligopoly and monopolistic competition.

Perfect competition

This is the most competitive market structure. A number of conditions need to be fulfilled before perfect competition is said to exist. These conditions are as follows:

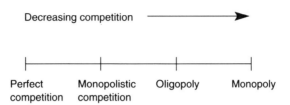

Fig. 12.1 Market structures

1 There are so many buyers and sellers in the market that no *one* of them can influence price through its activities.
2 The good being sold in the market is homogeneous (i.e. all units of the good are identical).
3 Perfect knowledge exists in the market. This means that producers have perfect knowledge of prices and costs of other producers and that consumers know the prices charged by all firms.
4 There exists perfect mobility of both the factors of production and consumers. This means that people, machines and land can be used for any purpose, and that consumers are free to purchase the good from any of the producers.
5 There are no barriers to entry or exit in the industry. There is nothing to prevent a new firm setting up production in the industry.

Naturally, this is a highly theoretical model and these conditions are unlikely to be all met in reality, but if they did, and the theory is followed through, the conclusion is that there will only be one price in the market for the good being sold. For example, if one firm is charging a higher price for the good than other firms, everyone on the market will know (because of perfect knowledge), and because the good is homogeneous and because of perfect mobility on the part of consumers, consumers will simply purchase the good from another firm. The firm that was charging a higher price will be forced to reduce the price of the good in order to sell it, or face mounting stocks of the good. There is therefore only one price for the good and this will be determined by *market* demand and supply – that is, total demand and total supply, no one consumer or producer having enough market power to influence the price. Accordingly, the firm is said to be a 'price taker'.

Price determination in perfect competition

Firms need to cover costs of production and to earn a certain level of profits in order to stay in business. This minimum level of profits is called 'normal profit', and profits over and above this level are called abnormal profits. If the firm is trying to maximise its profits it will decide what level of output to produce by setting the cost of producing the last unit of the good equal to the revenue gained from selling the last unit: in economic terminology, where marginal cost equals marginal revenue. Included in cost would be elements of wages, rent, rates, interest, raw materials *and* normal profits. If these cost are not being covered the firm will be making a loss.

As there is only one price in perfect competition, the revenue derived from selling the last unit must be equal to its price. Therefore, the price of the good depends on the level of marginal cost.

In the short run, individual firms can earn abnormal profits, but these are not sustainable in the longer term. If one firm is earning abnormal profits, given the assumption of perfect knowledge, everyone will know and, since freedom of entry exists, other firms will enter the market in order to earn abnormal profits. This means that there is an increase in market supply and price will fall back to a level where abnormal profits have been competed away. Similarly when losses are being made, freedom of exit means that supply will be reduced and price will rise again until normal profits have been regained.

The implications of perfect competition for market behaviour and performance are summarised in Table 12.2. Perfect competition involves very restrictive assumptions, which will rarely be fulfilled in the real world. The usefulness of the model lies in its role as an ideal market in which competition is at a maximum, rather than in its applicability to the real world.

Table 12.2 Implications of perfect competition for conduct and performance of firms in an industry

Extent of market power	The firm has no market power at all.
Price	There will only be one price for the good. The firm will be a 'price taker'.
Advertising	There will be no advertising, as all units of the good are the same and everyone knows this.
Profitability	There can be no abnormal profits, except possibly in the very short run if a producer reduces price and captures a larger share of the market.

An example of perfect competition?

The nearest example to perfect competition is probably the fruit and vegetable market in the centre of a large town. The goods will be fairly homogeneous, with perhaps slight variation in the quality. Knowledge will be almost perfect with respect to prices charged, as consumers could quickly walk around the market and ascertain the price of tomatoes, for example. Mobility of consumers is also high because the sellers are located in the same place. Thus the conditions for perfect competition nearly hold. The prediction is that there will be only one price for a particular good. Again this prediction is nearly fulfilled; the price of tomatoes tends to be rather similar across such a market, and when one trader reduces the price towards the end of the day, others tend to follow suit. Another market which is said to be close to perfect competition is the stock exchange, although with the increasing use of computers this is less likely to be true in the future.

Monopoly

Monopoly lies at the opposite end of the spectrum of competition. In its purest form a monopolistic market is one in which there is no competition at all; there is a single producer supplying the whole market. The monopolist has considerable market power and can determine price or quantity sold, but not both because he or she cannot control demand. The power of the monopolist depends on the availability of substitutes, and on the existence and height of barriers to entry. If there are no close substitutes for the good being produced, or if there are high barriers to entry, the power of the monopolist will be high and abnormal profits can be earned in the long run.

A monopolist could also be a group of producers acting together to control supply to the market: for example, a cartel such as OPEC (Organisation of Petroleum Exporting Countries).

In monopolistic markets the producer might be able to charge different prices for the same good: for example, on an aeroplane it is quite likely that there will be passengers sitting in the same class of seat having paid very different prices, depending upon where the tickets were bought. Essentially they are paying different prices for the same service, and the producer is said to be exercising price discrimination. Why is this possible? There are certain conditions that must hold for this type of price discrimination to occur. First, the market must be monopolistic and the producer must be able to control supply. Secondly, there must be groups of consumers with different demand conditions. For example, the demand for train travel by the commuter who works in London will be more inelastic than the demand of a student going to London for the day, who could use alternative forms of transport or even not go. This means that the willingness to pay amongst consumers will vary. The final condition necessary is that it must be possible to separate these groups in some way. For example, British Telecom is able to separate its markets by time so that it is cheaper to phone after 6 p.m.; British Rail separates groups by age for certain of its railcards.

The monopolist will maximise its profits by charging different prices in different markets. Price discrimination is often thought of as a bad thing as the monopolist is exploiting the consumer by charging different prices for the same good. But there are some advantages, in that it makes for better use of resources if cheap airline tickets are offered to fill an aeroplane which would otherwise have flown half full. It can also lead to a more equitable solution in that higher-income users pay a higher price than lower-income users. The main problems with the notion of price discrimination is not that it is always a bad thing, but that it is the monopolist who has the power to decide who is charged what price.

Again the effects of monopoly on the behaviour and performance of the firm can be predicted (see Table 12.3). Like perfect competition, this is a highly theoretical model and is mainly used as a comparison with perfect competition to show the effects of the lack of competition.

A comparison of perfect competition and monopoly

● It would be expected that price would be higher under monopoly than under perfect competition because of the absence of competition in the monopolistic market. It is

Table 12.3 Implications of monopoly for the conduct and performance of firms in an industry

Extent of market power	The firm has absolute market power.
Price	There will only be one price for the good, except in the case of price discrimination. The firm is a 'price maker'.
Advertising	There will be no need for advertising, as there is only one firm producing the good.
Profitability	Abnormal profits can exist in the long run as there is no competition which might erode them away.

argued, for example, that the large telephone companies (including BT) are overcharging the consumer. The benefits of the considerable technological advances that have been made in this area have not been passed on fully to the consumer. This can only be sustained by virtue of the monopolistic power of the companies.

- *But*, to counter this it could be argued that a monopolist is in a better position to reap the benefits of economies of scale, therefore it is possible that price might be lower.
- There might be less choice under monopoly since firms do not have to continually update their products in order to stay in business. *But*, it is also possible to think of examples where monopolies provide greater choice (e.g. in the case of radio stations), where under perfect competition all radio stations would cater for the biggest market which would be pop music. A monopolist, however, would be able to cover all tastes with a variety of stations.
- There is less incentive to innovate under monopoly, since they are subject to less competition. *But*, equally, a monopolist might have more incentive to innovate as they can reap the benefits in terms of higher profits. They may also have more resources to devote to innovation.

As can be seen there is not a clear set of arguments that imply that perfect competition is better than monopoly, and, as will be seen in Chapter 14, this is taken into account in British competition policy.

An example of monopoly?

Although it is easy to think of examples of industries where the dominant firm has a great deal of monopoly power, there is no such thing as a pure monopoly as substitutes exist for most goods. For example, British Rail has monopoly power in the market for rail travel, but there are many alternative forms of travel. The nearest examples of monopolies are the old public utilities, like gas, electricity, water, and so on, many of which have recently been privatised.

The government, in determining whether monopoly power exists in a market, has a working definition of what constitutes a monopoly. It is when 25 per cent of the market is accounted for by one firm or firms acting together. This would form grounds for investigation by the Monopolies and Mergers Commission. The process of British competition policy is discussed in Chapter 14 in more detail. The sources of monopoly power are the existence of barriers to entry and the availability of substitutes. Barriers to entry are any barriers which prevent or inhibit the entry of firms into the industry. There are several sources of barriers to entry.

Barriers to entry

Some industries are what are called 'natural monopolies' in that the production process is such that competition would be wasteful. The old public utilities are good examples of these, as it would be very wasteful for there to be two national grid systems in the electricity industry spanning the whole country.

Some production processes are subject to economies of scale. In other words, as the scale of production is increased, costs also increase but by less than the increase in output. As a result the average cost of production falls as output is increased. Economies of scale are fully considered later in this chapter, but it can be said at this stage that they are a very effective barrier to entry. If the incumbent firm in an industry has lower average cost as a result of economies of scale, it will be hard for a newcomer to compete effectively at a smaller scale of production. Gas, electricity and water are examples of this. The production processes of these goods are subject to economies of scale and it is therefore difficult for others to come into the market in competition with established firms. This is why such industries are called 'natural monopolies'.

Barriers to entry can also be legal ones, as in the case of patents and franchises which serve to restrict competition and prevent new firms from entering an industry. The effect of such barriers can be seen in the case of the artificial sweetener aspartame, where NutraSweet held the patent in the United States. The patent expired at the end of 1992, and the result was increased competition and as a result of this a fall in prices. The company restructured its workforce, laying off about 25 per cent of its employees.

Advertising and branding can also be barriers to entry, in that industries where brand names are well established are difficult to enter without massive expenditure on advertising.

Oligopoly

In both perfect competition and monopoly firms make independent decisions. In the case of monopoly there are no other firms in the industry to consider; in the case of perfect competition the firm has no power to affect the market at all. So for different reasons they act as though they have no rivals. This is not true in the case of oligopoly. Oligopoly is where a small number of producers supply a market in which the product is differentiated in some way. The characteristics of oligopoly are:

- A great deal of interdependence between the firms; each firm has to consider the likely actions of other firms when making its decisions.
- A lack of price competition in the market; firms are reluctant to increase their prices in case their competitors do not and they might lose market share. Firms are also reluctant to reduce their prices, in case other firms do the same and a price war results which reduces prices but leaves market share unchanged and so everyone is left worse off.[2] Price cutting has taken place in the cigarette industry recently in an attempt to maintain market share. Philip Morris, the leader in the American market

and producer of Marlboro, predicts that profits from cigarettes will be down by 40 per cent in 1993. As a result they are cutting the price of Marlboro, their leading brand, by as much as 20 cents. This will have serious repercussions on the rest of the firms in the industry.

● The lack of price competition means that different forms of non-price competition takes place such as branding or advertising. Oligopolists will sell their products not by reducing the price but through heavy advertising, brand names or special offers. An example of this that went wrong was the Hoover offer of two free flights to America when £100 was spent on a Hoover appliance in 1992/93. This was an attempt by Maytag (the parent company) to increase market share among a small number of domestic appliance producers. The offer, however, was not costed properly and the obstacles put in the way of customers made it practically impossible to take advantage of the offer. As a result there were many thousands of disgruntled customers and a market flooded with Hoovers. Table 12.4 shows the implications of oligopoly for conduct and performance of firms in an industry.

Table 12.4 Implications of oligopoly for conduct and performance of firms in an industry

Extent of market power	A great deal of market power.
Price	A stable price level. Prices set by price leadership or collusion.
Advertising	Much advertising and branding. Non-price competition is common.
Profitability	Abnormal profits can exist, their extent depends on the strength of competitors.

The way in which price is determined in an oligopolistic market is either through price leadership or some sort of collusion. Price leadership is where one firm takes the lead in setting prices and the others follow suit. The price leader is not necessarily the firm with the lowest cost, it depends upon the power of the firm. So price could be set at a higher level than in a competitive market. Collusion is an explicit or implicit agreement between firms on price, which serves to reduce the amount of competition between firms. Collusion is illegal in most countries as it is seen as a form of restrictive practice, but this does not mean that collusion does not take place. A cartel is a form of collusion where firms come together to exercise joint market power. Cartels are now illegal in most countries, but the most famous of all is OPEC (Organisation of Petroleum Exporting Countries) which has had a dramatic effect on the oil industry over the last thirty years. Collusive agreements, as well as possibly being harmful to the consumer, tend to be unstable as there is great temptation on the part of individual firms/countries to cheat. What is clear in the case of oligopoly is that once price is set there is a reluctance to change it. Therefore price competition is replaced by non-price competition of the sort mentioned above.

The most often quoted examples of oligopoly are the market for tobacco and the market for soap powder. Both of these markets are dominated by a very small number of producers and both exhibit the predicted characteristics. There is little price competition and price is fairly uniform in both markets. There is a high degree of non-price competition in both markets – high advertising, strong brand names and images, and the use of special offers or gifts at times in order to sell the goods.

Compared with monopoly and perfect competition, oligopoly is a much more realistic market structure, with many markets exhibiting the characteristics stated above. Table 12.5 gives a few examples.

Table 12.5 The top five firms' share of the market in the UK (1989) %

Industry	%
Sugar and sugar products	100
Tobacco	98
Cement	88
Brewing	73
Ice cream	63
Pharmaceutical products	35

Source: *Census of Production*, 1989

Monopolistic competition

This market structure exists when all of the conditions for perfect competition are met except for the existence of a homogeneous good, so that each firm has a monopoly over its own good but there is a great deal of competition in the market from other suppliers producing very similar products. In monopolistic competition the good is slightly differentiated in some way, either by advertising and branding or by local production. There does not have to be a technical difference between the two goods, they could be identical in composition, but there must be an 'economic difference' – that is, a difference in the way the goods are perceived by consumers. There is also some degree of consumer loyalty, so that if one firm reduces price, consumers might not necessarily move to that firm if they believe that the difference between the brands justifies the higher price. Abnormal profits can exist in the short run but cannot persist since new firms are free to enter the industry and compete away abnormal profit. (See Table 12.6.)

Table 12.6 Implications of monopolistic competition for the conduct and performance of firms in an industry

Extent of market power	The firm has little market power.
Price	There will be small differences in price.
Advertising	There will be heavy advertising and branding.
Profitability	Small abnormal profits can exist in the short run but will be competed away in the longer run.

An example of monopolistic competition?

There are many examples of this types of industry: for example, the paint industry where ICI are the only producers of Dulux but there are many other types of paint on the market.

How accurate is the theory?

The implications of the theory of market structures for the behaviour and performance of firms are summarised in Table 12.7.

Table 12.7 Implications of theory for behaviour of firms

	Market power	Price	Advertising	Profitability
Perfect competition	None	One price	None	Only normal profits
Monopoly	Absolute	Price discrimination possible	None	Abnormal profits
Oligopoly	High	One price	High	Abnormal profits
Monopolistic competition	Little	Small differences in price	High	Only normal profits in long run

As argued above, both perfect competition and pure monopoly tend to be based on assumptions that are somewhat unrealistic and should be regarded as 'ideal types' of market structure, in the sense that they establish the boundaries within which true markets exist and operate, and against which they can be analysed. In contrast, oligopoly and monopolistic competition are much nearer to the types of market structure which can be found in the real world, and economic theory does appear to explain and predict behaviour in these markets to a certain extent. In oligopolistic markets, for example, price tends to be 'sticky' and much of the competition between firms occurs in non-price ways, particularly branding, advertising and sales promotion (see Table 12.8). Occasionally, however, price wars do occur – as in the petrol market in the 1980s and more recently between the two biggest supermarkets, Tesco and Sainsburys – and this form of behaviour is difficult to predict.[3]

Table 12.8 Top advertisers in the United Kingdom in 1991

Rank[1] 1991	1990	Advertiser
1	1	Proctor & Gamble
2	2	Unilever/Lever Bros
3	3	Kelloggs Company
4	7	Ford
5	10	Proctor & Gamble (health and beauty)
6	20	Unilever (Elida Gibbs)
7	5	Mars
8	8	Nestlé
9	15	Vauxhall
10	6	Kraft General Foods

Note: [1]ranked according to advertising to sales ratios.
Source: *Advertising Statistics Yearbook*, 1992, NTC Publications Ltd

Table 12.8 shows the top advertisers in the United Kingdom ranked for 1991; their ranks in 1990 are also given. The names in the list are familiar and largely expected from the predictions: for example, Procter & Gamble and Unilever are the two companies who together account for around 90 per cent of the market for washing powder.

It is much more difficult to judge how accurate the behavioural implications are. Lack of data is one problem, as is the fact that only one structural characteristic has been considered here – the level of competition between producers. The other structural factors listed in Table 12.1 will also have an effect, like the level of demand, the degree of competition between the buyers and the degree of potential competition. Profitability, price and advertising, for instance, will be affected by the level of demand in the market.

Competition between buyers

So far this chapter has looked at the extent of competition between producers in a market, but the amount of competition between buyers will also have an impact on an industry. Markets will range from those where there are many buyers, as in the case of retailing, through markets where there are a small number of buyers, as in the case of car manufacturers and parts, to markets where there is only one buyer. This latter type of market is called a monopsony, and it is the buyer who has a great deal of market power rather than the seller. An example of this is the coal industry, where the majority of output goes to the electricity producers. Increasingly in retailing the giant retailers are exerting a great deal of power over the manufacturers. Toys 'R' Us, the world's largest toy retailer, is involved very early on by manufacturers in the design process for new toys and as a result gets many exclusives that are not available in other toy shops.

The level of buyer power could be measured in the same way as seller power (see later in this chapter), but no data is collected centrally on the level of buyer concentration. It is clear, however, that there are many markets in which powerful buyers can exert a great deal of control over suppliers, and this power is an important source of marketing economies of scale. It is possible to put together the level of competition between producers and consumers in order to predict behaviour. For example, a market which consists of a single buyer and a single seller will have quite different characteristics from a market which has many buyers and sellers. The existence of strong buyers might have beneficial effects on the market, as they could offset the power of strong producers, or it could lead to higher seller concentration as sellers come together to counteract the power of the buyer.

In markets where there are strong sellers and weak buyers, producer power can be offset by such things as Consumer Advice Centres or watch-dog bodies, as in the case of the public utilities.

Potential competition

It has been shown that market structure affects the behaviour of firms in an industry. But looking at the number of firms in an industry does not provide the whole picture. It is possible that firms in an oligopolistic market might act in a way consistent with perfect competition because of the threat of potential competition. This threat can affect the behaviour of firms even if it does not happen. The degree of potential competition is related to the existence and height of barriers to entry. A contestable market is one in which there are no barriers to entry or exit.[4] This means that all firms (even potential entrants) have access to the same technology and there are therefore no cost barriers to entry. It also means that there are no sunk or unrecoverable costs which would prevent a firm leaving the industry. It therefore follows that it is possible to ensure that firms behave in a competitive way, even if the market structure they operate in is imperfectly competitive, by ensuring that the market is contestable. What is regulating market behaviour, then, is not actual competition but potential competition.

Measuring the degree of actual competition in the market

In industrial economics the level of competition in a market is measured by concentration ratios. These measure the percentage of total output or employment that is produced by a stated number of the largest firms in the industry. The common numbers are three or five. The five-firm concentration ratio measures the percentage of employment or output accounted for by the five largest firms in the industry, and is reported in the *Annual Census of Production* produced by the government.

Table 12.9 Five-firm concentration ratios for selected industries in the UK (1989)

Industry	Employment (%)	Output (%)
Sugar and sugar by-products	100.0	100.0
Tobacco	98.1	98.8
Asbestos goods	94.1	93.6
Iron and steel industry	92.5	95.0
Mineral, oil processing	53.4	63.3
Footwear	37.8	38.6
Pharmaceutical products	34.6	40.0
Leather goods	11.4	13.3
Executive recruitment industry[1]	10.5	9.5

Note: [1] see L. C. Britton, T. A. R. Clark and D. F. Ball, 'Executive search and selection: imperfect theory or intractable industry?', *Service Industries Journal*, April 1992.
Source : *Census of Production PA 1002*, 1989, table 13

Although Table 12.9 only shows a small selection of industries, it does show that there is great variation in the degree of concentration across industries. Only one service industry is shown because of the unavailability of data relating to the services; most official data refer to manufacturing industry because of its relative historical importance. Generally services are less concentrated than manufacturing industries because of the nature of the production process and the fact that there is less scope for economies of scale.

Although it is relatively easy to compare the level of concentration in particular industries over time it is more difficult to make any conclusion about the 'average' level of concentration. Table 12.10 gives the percentage share of total employment and sales of the largest 100 firms in the United Kingdom from 1973 to 1989. Although these are not concentration ratios as such, the data does provide an indication of how concentration has changed over time in aggregate. The change in the Standard Industrial Classification during this period has only a small impact on the figures. Note how the level of 'average' concentration decreased slightly during the period, reversing the trend of the first half of this century where industrial concentration increased. The reason for the decrease is largely the process of privatisation and the growth in the small firm sector during the 1970s and 1980s.

Table 12.10 100 largest enterprise groups

Year	Percentage share of total	
	Employment	Sales
SIC(68)		
1973	35	42
1974	36	40
1975	36	40
1976	35	40
1977	35	39
1978	35	39
1979	35	38
SIC(80)		
1980	35	38
1981	34	38
1982	35	39
1983	34	40
1984	32	38
1985	32	36
1986	33	38
1987	30	36
1988	31	37
1989	30	37

Source : *Economic Trends*, April 1992

It is difficult to make comparisons between different countries because of this problem of 'averaging' concentration and because of national differences in the way in which data is collected and reported. Moreover official EC publications on industry have changed the way in which they report data, so comparisons over time are impossible. Available evidence suggests, however, that in the 1960s concentration increased in Europe and that this had stabilised by the 1970s before declining in the 1980s, as in the United Kingdom.[5]

Table 12.11 gives average concentration ratios for the EC, United States and Japan for 1986, suggesting that concentration in the EC is lower than in the United States or Japan. Within these figures there are differences between sectors, for example between 1975 and 1986 concentration in the automobile industry rose in the EC and USA but fell in Japan. Table 12.12 shows four-firm concentration ratios for two industries and

Table 12.11 Five-firm concentration ratios for manufacturing industry on a sales basis 1986

	%
European Community	6.8
United States	13.5
Japan	8.0

Source: Commission of European Communities, *European Economy* no. 40, May 1989. Reproduced with permission of the Commission of the European Communities

Table 12.12 Four-firm concentration ratios on a sales basis

	Food manufacturing and processing (1986)	Chemical industry (1985)
European Community	10.9	15.0
United States	9.9	13.8
Japan	8.9	12.4

Source: *18th EC Competition Policy Report*, 1989. Reproduced with permission of the Commission of the European Communities

illustrating that whilst 'average' concentration was lower in the EC in 1986, in the two sectors listed EC concentration was higher than in the two other countries.

The general view is that more recently concentration in the EC has risen as a result of increased merger activity (see Chapter 8) and a competition policy which is torn between promoting competition by preventing market domination and the need to establish European competitiveness by encouraging it.

Despite the difficulties in comparing concentration ratios, the general view of industrial economists is that concentration is greater in the United Kingdom than other member states.

Reasons for high concentration

Many industries in the United Kingdom are highly concentrated and it is believed that the United Kingdom has higher concentration ratios than other large industrial countries. Why are there different market structures between industries?

As firms grow in size, or as the scale of production increases, there are certain economies that occur which serve to reduce the average cost of production. These are called economies of scale. The scale of production can be increased in many ways: for example, by increasing the capacity of the existing plant, by increasing the number of plants or by increasing the product range. Figure 12.2 shows the how average cost of production changes as the scale of production changes. The downward sloping part of the curve shows falling average cost or economies of scale. The upward sloping part shows rising average cost or diseconomies of scale. Economies of scale reduce average

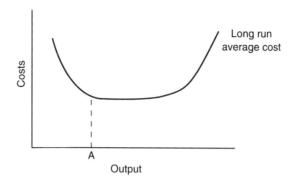

Fig. 12.2 A firm's average cost curve

cost and therefore benefit the producer and also the consumer if they are passed on in lower prices.

The sources of economies of scale are usually classified under three headings – technical; financial; and marketing:

1 *Technical economies* Technical economies come from increased specialisation and indivisibilities. The larger the scale of production the more the production process can be broken down into its component parts and the greater the gain from specialisation. There are certain indivisibilities involved in production which only large firms can benefit from. For example, a small firm cannot have half a production line as that is meaningless, but might not be big enough to use a whole production line. Another type of indivisibility in involved in the notion of fixed costs. Fixed costs – like the cost of rates or an accountant, for example – remain the same irrespective of the level of production. Therefore the greater the level of production, the lower will be the average cost of these items as their cost is being spread over a larger output.

2 *Marketing economies* Marketing economies come from spreading marketing costs over a larger output, so that average costs will be lower. The company can also take advantage of bulk-buying, and will probably have a specialised department devoted to marketing.

3 *Financial economies* Financial economies come from the fact that larger companies find it easier and often cheaper to borrow capital.

Added to these, risk diversification is possible with larger companies as they may well have interests in other industries. All of these economies of scale give rise to falling average cost and therefore explain the downward sloping part of the cost curve in Figure 12.2. The point at which the curve becomes horizontal (A in diagram) is called the minimum efficient scale of production or MES. It is the point at which all economies of scale have been reaped by the firm, and the point at which firms who wish to maximise their efficiency must operate.

The higher the MES relative to the total output of the industry, the fewer will be the number of firms operating in an industry and therefore the higher will be the level of concentration. For example, if the MES in an industry is half of the industry output, the industry could only support two firms, as smaller firms could not achieve low enough costs to compete with the large firms.

As the scale of production continues to increase, average costs eventually start to rise, this is due to diseconomies of scale, which are mostly attributed to managerial inefficiencies. These are the difficulties faced by management in controlling, co-ordinating and communicating in a large organisation.

Firms in every industry will face differing average cost curves and therefore market structures will be different. In services, for example, because of the nature of the product, the scope for economies of scale is small and, accordingly, the MES is small relative to the size of the total market and the industries tend to be unconcentrated. The level of concentration in manufacturing tends to be much higher because of the nature of the production process and the scope for economies of scale.

The size of the MES is not the only explanation of why there are different market structures. If it was, one might expect that the same industry would have similar levels of concentration in different countries, but this is not the case, as indicated above. Obviously government policy can influence the type of market structure, and this will differ between countries. It is also true that the significance of barriers to entry varies between countries. Empirical results from West Germany and the United Kingdom show that in both countries barriers to entry are high, but that in the United Kingdom advertising is the most important barrier, while in West Germany it is economies of scale.

SYNOPSIS

In this chapter, four different market structures were considered that embraced the whole spectrum of competition: perfect competition; monopoly; oligopoly; and monopolistic competition. Each of these market structures gives predictions about the behaviour of firms in those markets. Generally the more realistic of these market structures predict well what happens in the real world. As well as the level of actual competition in the industry, two other structural factors were considered, the level of demand and the level of potential competition.

The amount of competition in a market is measured using concentration ratios and evidence on concentration was examined both within the United Kingdom and between countries as far as that was possible. Finally the reasons for different market structures were examined, and these are further considered in Chapter 8 in the section concerned with the process of organisational growth.

CASE STUDY: GROCERY RETAILING

When looking at real markets in the economy, economic theory is often only useful as a measuring rod for the level of competition that exists in a market and the behaviour that is expected of firms. The four market structures described in this chapter are only four points along a continuum of competition; it is not possible to cover all possible market situations. Real markets will often exhibit behaviour different from that predicted by its market structure.

Grocery retailing

Structural characteristics of the market

Demand The demand for food has fallen as a proportion of income over the last 20 years. It was 33 per cent of total expenditure in 1970 and 25 per cent in 1990. Such a trend is to be expected because as incomes grow people change their spending habits and spend more on luxuries and less on necessities like food. There has also been a decline in population growth which has affected total expenditure on food.

Technology The scale of technological change and the impact it has had on the grocery industry has been immense over the last 20 years. Electronic cash registers were used for the first time in the mid-1970s in retailing, but then only by the large companies who could afford them. Since then new technology has become much more widely available and used. The electronic point of sales (EPOS) system and the bar-coding of goods has revolutionised retailing. It enables retailers to control and order stock more effectively and to respond to the wishes of consumers more quickly. EPOS can be operated by individual stores or can be controlled by a centralised computer for a number of branches. Electronic data interchange (EDI) even enables firms to be linked with suppliers so that the reordering of goods automatically takes place.

EPOS means that the service to the consumer can be improved as check-out times can be reduced, itemised receipts can be issued, and more staff time can be devoted to customers as their time spent on boring, repetitive tasks has also been reduced. Since the use of credit card and Switch cards are becoming more common, the development of electronic funds transfer at point of sale (EFTPOS) was a logical step. Another development which is more widespread in other European countries than the United Kingdom is tele-shopping, using cable TV networks or national data networks. However, this development is taking place in the non-food sector.

Economies of scale There are large economies of scale to be reaped in retailing and as a result there has been a trend towards larger-scale retailing establishments over the last 20 years, mainly due to the increased mobility of the consumer as a greater proportion of the population now owns a car. This has enabled retailers to open superstores in locations that serve a much larger area and therefore to reap the benefits of economies of scale. The smaller grocery retailers have reacted by setting up their own voluntary buying groups like Spar and VG, which provides them both with the ability to share some of the benefits of economies of scale (e.g. bulk buying) and with a ready-made image.

Concentration The retail industry in the United Kingdom is one which is dominated by the multiples, particularly where groceries are concerned. Multiples are retail companies operating a number of retail outlets. The number of branches could be as few as two or a great many more. In the United Kingdom, the multiples account for about 50 per cent of the retail market. This is much higher than other countries in the EC. Figure 12.3 shows the share of the market of the large grocery retailers in the United Kingdom over the last 10 years. As can be seen there has been a steady increase over the period. This level of concentration is much higher than in other European countries. For example the corresponding figure for Germany is around 50 per cent, for France around 45 per cent, for Spain about 20 per cent and Italy (the lowest of them all) about 10 per cent.

The top ten supermarkets in the United Kingdom by market share and their corresponding ranking by turnover are shown in Table 12.13. Tesco and J. Sainsbury are clear leaders whichever measure is used and there is fierce competition between these two. Together they account for less than 25 per cent of the market, and so the market is clearly not monopolistic or

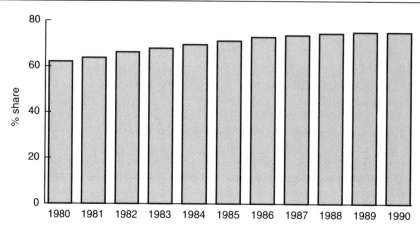

Fig. 12.3 Share of the large grocery retailers in UK groceries, 1980–1990
Source: *Economic Trends*

even oligopolistic as defined by economic theory, but the competition that exists between the two largest players would lead you to expect some of the behavioural characteristics that would be found in an oligopoly (e.g. high advertising and competition of both a price and a non-price nature).

Table 12.13 The top ten supermarkets in the UK

		Market share (%)[1]	Ranking by turnover (£m.)[2]
1	Tesco	12.3	2
2	J. Sainsbury	11.9	1
3	Asda	7.6	4
4	Safeway	6.3	5
5	Gateway	5.5	6
6	Marks & Spencer	3.7	7
7	Kwik Save	3.2	8
8	Presto/Low Cost	2.1	–
9	Waitrose	1.8	9
9	Morrison	1.8	–

Notes: [1]March 1991 to March 1992; [2] 1990.

Behavioural and performance characteristics of the retailers

Advertising Advertising expenditure is high in the food sector; in 1989 the sector was the largest spender on advertising in the United Kingdom in the press, TV and radio advertising. As well as the retailers this would include the food manufacturers who are very anxious to promote and maintain their brand images. In a ranking of spenders on advertising in the United Kingdom, five of the top ten are food manufacturers and include names like Mars, Kelloggs and Tesco.

Pricing policy A recent press campaign claims that 'Supermarkets Push British Food Prices to the Top of the League' (*The Sunday Times*, August 1992). The claims are that supermarkets are exploiting consumers by charging higher prices for basic foodstuffs than other European countries. This claim is based on a cross-country comparison of prices charged and profit margins. Prices are difficult to compare across countries because of differences in things like the exchange rate and taxation and because of cultural differences in consumption habits, but the profit margins of the British supermarkets are four times the European average and eight times as high as in the United States.

The claims made by the press were tested by the Consumer Association, who found that the evidence on prices was not clear cut and that, although profit margins were higher in the United Kingdom, this did not necessarily mean that consumers were being exploited. Among the reasons given by the supermarkets themselves for higher profit margins are: the introduction of own brand labels; increased efficiency; and the introduction of superstores. They argue that they compete on choice rather than on price. This has been supported by two recent surveys, one by Harris International Marketing and the other commissioned by Marketing.

The Harris International survey found that one-third of shoppers questioned outside supermarkets could not recall the prices of leading brand goods that they had just bought. The survey also found that attitudes had changed over the last 10 years away from price being the prime consideration towards other non-price features like packaging, convenience and brand image. In 1980, 65 per cent of those questioned said that price determined where they shopped; in 1988 65 per cent said that convenience was most important.

The survey for Marketing identified four different types of shopper who exhibited different buying patterns.

1 The *relaxed shopper* experiments with new products, shops slowly and is not particularly budget conscious.
2 The *controlled shopper* does not experiment very much at all. Most decisions are taken at home, but some minor decisions are made in the supermarket.
3 The *rigid by personality shopper* shops very quickly, nearly all decisions are made beforehand from detailed lists.
4 The *rigid by circumstance shopper* shops in the same way as the above but because of circumstances rather than any other reason (e.g. unemployment in the family which leads to lower income available for shopping).

These shoppers obviously shop in different ways and the layout of the store will reflect this. For example, relaxed shoppers will take a great interest in displays of goods in the supermarket, and many of their decisions will be made in such a way. Clearly the supermarket needs knowledge of the characteristics of its shoppers in order to tailor the supermarket to their needs and to encourage them to spend their money. The research confirmed that value rather than price was the main concern of shoppers. Only 9 per cent of the sample bought on the basis of the cheapest price, but 13 per cent bought special offers even if they had no use for them at the present time.

Own brands In the United Kingdom the supermarkets have been particularly successful in pushing their own brands, and own brand concentration has increased steadily over the last 30 years, as has the market share of the big multiples. This contrasts markedly with other European countries where market share is lower and own brand penetration is lower (see Figures 12.4 and 12.5).

There is a strong relationship between the power of the supermarkets and the level of own brand penetration, only Tesco and J. Sainsbury have been very successful. The advantage of own brand products is that they cost less to purchase and can therefore yield a greater profit margin even with lower prices. At the same time the presence of own brand goods curtails the power of the food manufacturers as it creates excess capacity in the market and prevents them charging higher prices. There are a few areas where own brand goods have not yet penetrated like coffee

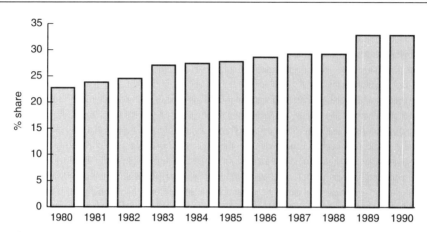

Fig. 12.4 Own brand penetration in the United Kingdom, 1980–1990
Source: *Economic Trends*

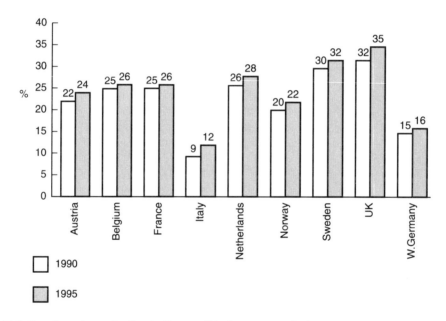

Fig. 12.5 Own brand penetration in Europe (% of grocery sales)
Source: *Book of European Forecasts*, 1991

and detergents; these markets are maintained by high levels of advertising expenditure. But even these areas are facing increased competition from the supermarkets.

Discounters The most recent happening in the food retailing business is the arrival of the discounters. These are companies which offer very limited choice in brands for goods but at a much lower price than the big supermarkets. In the United Kingdom the largest of these is Kwik Save. The number of discount stores is on the increase and has recently been joined by Aldi the German giant. Recent research compared the cost of a basket of goods, which in Aldi would have cost £27.85 and in J. Sainsbury would have cost £38.20. This is about a 30 per cent discount and although the service they offer the shopper is very different from that of the large food retailers, it will be interesting to watch the developments.

Price competition Although the large food retailers concentrate more on non-price competition, there are periodic bouts of price competition. In January 1993, J. Sainsbury reduced the prices of various basic food stuffs and ran a heavy advertising campaign to promote this. Many claimed, however, that the reductions were largely illusory.

Non-price competition The large food retailers have adopted strategies other than price reductions in order to encourage trade. For example, in 1992 J. Sainsbury launched a campaign offering discounts on flights with BA of 30 per cent for shopping at Sainsburys. All of the large retailers have moved into other areas, partly as a response to the decline in the food market and all of them (with the exception of Marks & Spencer) have flaunted the law to open on Sunday. In line with the increased environmental and health awareness of the general public, supermarket chains have promoted an environmentally friendly image and increased the amount of information that is available on food packaging about additives and nutritional value. The large retailers are busy establishing and promoting their own images by having things like their own magazines.

Conclusion

The grocery market is fairly competitive, the large retailers account for about 75 per cent of the market, but there are about 80 of them. The two largest, Tesco and J Sainsbury, both have around 12 per cent of the market each. Thus the market is not an oligopoly, but the fierce competition between the two means that the market does exhibit some of the characteristics expected in an oligopoly. There will not be complete independence in decision-making, as Tesco is unlikely to formulate policies without considering the possible reaction of Sainsburys and vice versa. The level of advertising is high and much of the competition that takes place is of a non-price nature. Claims that prices are too high are difficult to verify because of the problems of international comparisons. The level of concentration is high because of the existence of economies of scale and the level of concentration is much higher in the United Kingdom than in other EC countries, as too is the level of own brand penetration. These factors are interdependent. The industry performs well as measured by profitability.

NOTES AND REFERENCES

1 See Hay, D. A., and Morris, D. J., *Industrial Economics: Theory and Evidence,* 1979, for a summary of the criticisms which are beyond the scope of this book.
2 For a full discussion of the 'kinked demand curve', see Begg, D., Fischer, S., and Dornbusch, R., *Economics*, McGraw-Hill, 1991.
3 In this context students should note the use of game theory to model and predict the behaviour of firms in oligopolistic markets. For a simple introduction to this area, see Griffiths, A., and Wall, S., *Applied Economics*, 5th edition, Longman, 1993.
4 Baumol, W. J., Panzar, J. C. and Willig, R. D. *Contestable Markets and the Theory of Industry Structure,* 1988.
5 *18th EC Competition Policy Report,* 1989.

REVIEW AND DISCUSSION QUESTIONS

1 What economies of scale are likely to exist in retailing?

2 Why do you think that the food retailing market is more concentrated in the United Kingdom than in Italy?

3 Think of examples of a market which is very competitive and a market which is not very competitive. Does the behaviour of the firms in these markets comply with the predictions in Table 12.7?

4 Why are goods like washing powders and coffee advertised more heavily than goods like matches or bread?

ASSIGNMENTS

1 You are working in the local consumer advice centre which each week produces an information sheet giving the prices of a typical 'basket of goods' in local shops. Choose ten branded items (like Nescafé for example) to constitute your basket of goods and survey three types of retail outlet: a small corner shop, a mini-market on a local main road and a large supermarket. Design an information sheet and present the information you have gathered in the form of a table. Include a list of bullet points which might explain any differences in price.

2 You are working in the marketing department of a newspaper company whose main output is a tabloid newspaper that takes around 40 per cent of the market. It has one close competitor that takes around 30 per cent of the market. Your rival company has decided to cut the price of its newspaper by a half for one week in order to try to increase its market share. Your company is considering various strategies in retaliation to this: to do nothing and see what happens; to follow suit and cut its price by a half for one week; or to cut price by 20 per cent for a longer period than a week. Produce a report for your line manager pointing out the likely results of these strategies.

FURTHER READING

Begg, D., Fischer, S. and Dornbusch, R., *Economics*, McGraw-Hill, 1991.
Griffiths A. and Wall S., *Applied Economics: An introductory course*, 5th edition, Longman, 1993.
Jones T. T. and Cockerill T. A. J., *Structure and Performance of Industries*, Philip Allan, 1984.

CHAPTER 13

International markets

Chris Britton

The importance of international markets will vary between firms and industries but most businesses do not operate solely within national boundaries. Businesses which operate in the export market will obviously need an understanding of international markets but even the sole proprietor producing for a small local market may well use imported raw materials in the production process and so will be affected by changes that take place internationally.

OBJECTIVES

1 To understand why international trade takes place.
2 To look at the international organisations which serve to promote free trade.
3 To survey the balance of payments position in the United Kingdom.
4 To understand the working of the foreign exchange markets.

INTRODUCTION

International markets are important to most firms; even if they do not produce for the export market they may well be dependent upon raw materials which are imported and they will almost definitely be affected by movements in the exchange rate. Britain, like all other advanced industrial countries, is highly dependent upon international markets and that dependence has grown over the years. What makes international trade different from trade within a country is that the trade is taking place across national borders. Thus a system for international payments is needed. It is essential for businesses to have an understanding of international markets, exchange rates and the balance of payments.

INTERNATIONAL TRADE – WHY IT TAKES PLACE

Trade between countries takes place because resources are unevenly distributed through the world and the mobility of the factors of production is limited, consequently some countries are better at producing certain goods than others. Some countries could not actually produce a particular good: for example, Britain cannot produce minerals that are not indigenous or fruit that can only be grown in tropical weather conditions. If there is a demand for these goods in Britain, there are a number of possibilities: either the British could do without these goods; or an attempt could be made to grow them (in the case of the fruit) despite the climatic conditions; or Britain could buy the goods from other countries that can produce them. In other words it can trade for them.

It is easy to see that if country A can produce video cameras more cheaply than country B and B can produce wheat more cheaply than A, specialisation should occur and A should produce video cameras and B should produce wheat and they should trade with one another. Complete specialisation, however, is unlikely for strategic reasons. It is also true that even if country A can produce both goods more cheaply than country B there is scope for benefits from trade. As this may not be so easy to imagine, Table 13.1 gives a numerical example. Country A can produce 100 video cameras or 100 units of wheat using 100 workers. Country B can produce 20 video cameras or 40 units of wheat with the same number of workers. Country A can therefore produce both goods at lower cost than country B. To show that even in this situation trade will benefit the world, assume that both countries produce both goods and that they each devote half of their workforce to each good.

Table 13.1 Production of video cameras and wheat

	Number of units that 100 workers can produce	
	Video cameras	Wheat
Country A	100	100
Country B	20	40

The total output of video cameras is 60 and of wheat is 70 units. Country A is 5 times more efficient at producing video cameras than country B, but only 2.5 times more efficient than B in producing wheat (see Table 13.2). It would therefore benefit both countries if production was rearranged. If B specialised completely in wheat and A produced 35 units of wheat and 65 video cameras, world output would be as indicated in Table 13.3.

Table 13.2 Production of video cameras and wheat

	Video cameras	Wheat
Country A	50	50
Country B	10	20
	60	70

Table 13.3 Production of video cameras and wheat

	Video cameras	Wheat
Country A	65	35
Country B	0	40
	65	75

In short, world output has been increased and everyone is better off provided that trade takes place. This simplified example illustrates the basic argument for free trade. Free trade brings the advantages of higher world output and higher standards of living. Countries will produce the goods in which they have a cost advantage and trade with other countries for other goods. So countries can buy goods at lower prices than they could be produced at home. Where economies of scale are present, the savings as a result of specialisation can be immense.

Theoretically free trade brings most benefit; however, there are often restrictions to such trade and it is unlikely that complete specialisation will take place. Most countries would regard being totally dependent on another country for a particular good as a risky proposition.

RESTRICTIONS TO INTERNATIONAL TRADE

There are a number of things that governments do to restrict international trade. These restrictions include:

- *Quotas* A physical limitation on the import of certain goods into a country, sometimes by mutual agreement (e.g. voluntary export restraints).
- *Tariffs* A tax placed on imported goods.
- *Exchange controls* A limit to the amount of a currency that can be bought, which will limit the import of goods.
- *Subsidies* Payments made to domestic producers to reduce their costs and therefore make them more competitive on world markets.
- *Qualitative controls* Controls on the quality of goods rather than on quantity or price.

All of these serve to restrict international trade, and therefore reduce specialisation on a world level. They invite retaliation and could lead to inefficiencies. Import controls have a wide effect on industry. The 200 per cent tariffs that the Americans threatened to impose on French cheeses and wines at the end of 1992 if the GATT talks were not successful, would have impacted on many other industries like the bottle-making industry or the insurance industry. But there are powerful arguments used in support of import controls. For example, they can be used to protect industries, whether these industries are 'infant' industries or strategic industries. In the recent debate within the EC on bananas, it was argued by the African, Caribbean and Pacific countries who receive preferential treatment in the EC for their bananas that the relaxation of these preferential terms might lead to the complete devastation of their economies. Import controls can also be used to improve the balance of payments position in the case where a deficit exists.

The United Kingdom is a member of a number of international organisations who serve to promote free trade and control the restrictions to free trade.

THE EUROPEAN COMMUNITY (EC)

The EC was established in 1958 by the Treaty of Rome. The six original members, France, West Germany, Italy, Holland, Belgium and Luxembourg were joined in 1972 by the United Kingdom, Ireland and Denmark. Greece joined in 1981, followed by Spain and Portugal in 1986. These countries, along with the former East Germany, currently constitute the 12 Member States of the Community, a number which is likely to grow by the end of the decade.

The primary aim of the Treaty of Rome was to create a 'common market' in which Member States were encouraged to trade freely and to bring their economies closer together, ultimately culminating in the creation of a 'single market' within the Community. To bring this about, a protected free trade area or 'customs union' was established which involved the removal of tariff barriers between member states and the institution of a common external tariff (CET) on goods from outside the Community. Institutional structures (see Chapter 3) and Community policies – most notably the common agricultural policy (CAP) – also contributed to this end and to the creation of a trading bloc of immense proportions. Within this bloc, Member States were expected to gain numerous advantages including increased trade and investment, huge economies of scale and improvements in productivity and cost reductions. To support the goal of increased trade and co-operation between community members, a European Monetary System was established in 1979 in which a majority of Member States undertook to fix their exchange rates within agreed limits (see below).

A significant step towards the creation of a single market – capable of competing effectively with the United States and Japan – was taken in 1986 when the 12 community members signed the Single European Act. This Act established the 31 December 1992 as the target date for the creation of a Single European Market: an area (comprising the 12 EC countries) without internal frontiers, in which the free movement of goods, services, people and capital was to be ensured within the provisions contained in the Treaty. Amongst the measures for making the Single Market a reality were agreements on the following issues.

- The removal or reduction in obstacles to cross-border travel and trade (e.g. customs checks).
- The harmonisation or approximation of technical and safety standards on a large number of products.
- Closer approximation of excise duties and other fiscal barriers (e.g. VAT).
- The removal of legal obstacles to trade (e.g. discriminatory purchasing policies).
- The mutual recognition of qualifications.

In all, the overall programme has involved hundreds of changes to each country's national laws – a majority of which have now been introduced, though not always exactly as originally envisaged.

The benefits expected to flow from the creation of the Single Market can be viewed in both macro and micro terms. At the macro level, for instance, it has been suggested by the Cecchini Report that at the worst, the new measures would increase the EC's gross domestic product by 4.5 per cent and would create 1.8 million jobs – a prediction, which in the current recessionary climate in Europe, looks slightly ambitious.[1]

In micro terms, it is generally accepted that despite some additional costs for firms who have to implement the new requirements (e.g. safety standards), many businesses are likely to gain from increased trade and efficiency (e.g. through greater economies of scale), although this will vary between firms and across sectors within and between each Member State. Likely beneficiaries are those larger firms which have adopted a European approach to business development and have put in place structures and procedures to cope with the threats as well as the opportunities of the Single Market (e.g. by establishing joint ventures; by modifying personnel policies; by adapting marketing strategies; by modifying products). The sectors which arguably have the greatest potential are those where technical barriers are high or where a company has a distinct cost advantage over its rivals. In the United Kingdom, these would include the food and drink industry, pharmaceuticals, insurance and a number of other service industries.

Further steps in the development of the EC have come with the decision to establish a European Economic Area (EEA) – which would permit members of the European Free Trade Area (EFTA) to benefit from many of the Single Market measures – and, in particular, from the Treaty on European Union, agreed by the 12 Member States in December 1991 at Maastricht. Apart from the institutional changes mentioned in Chapter 3, the Maastricht Treaty contains provisions for:

- Increased economic and monetary union between Member States.
- A single currency.
- A social charter to protect workers' rights.
- A common foreign and security policy.
- Community citizenship.

These various measures are scheduled to be introduced over a number of years, although in some cases – most notably the United Kingdom – specially negotiated 'opt-out' clauses will mean that some provisions will not be implemented by all Member States (e.g. the single currency; the social charter). Added to this, the problems for the franc and a number of other currencies within the Exchange Rate Mechanism has called into question the timetable on a single European currency and on attempts to observe closer monetary co-operation. In short, the process of European union may yet be delayed into the next century – a situation likely to be presented by the UK politicians as a vindication for their gradualist approach.

GENERAL AGREEMENT ON TARIFFS AND TRADE (GATT)

As Chapter 4 indicated, GATT is a loose organisation with over 100 members. It meets periodically to discuss trade matters, and its primary aim is to reduce tariffs and other barriers to trade. Under its 'most favoured clause', every tariff concession agreed between any group of countries must be extended to all members of GATT. GATT allows the formation of customs unions such as the EC, even though this appears to contradict the notion of free trade.

THE BALANCE OF PAYMENTS

The balance of payments is a record of the United Kingdom's international trade with other countries over a period of time, usually a year. It records the flows of money rather than goods, so that an import will be recorded as a negative amount since the money is flowing out of the country to pay for the good, and an export is recorded as a positive amount. Money flows into and out of the United Kingdom for two basic reasons; first, in exchange for goods and services (current transactions), and secondly, for investment purposes (capital transactions). These two flows are recorded separately in the UK balance of payments accounts which are produced by the government.

Current transactions

The current account records the flows of money received and paid out in exchange for goods and services. It is subdivided into visible trade (the import and export of goods) and invisible trade (the import and export of services). Invisible trade includes:

1 Services like banking, insurance, tourism.
2 Interest, profits and dividends.
3 Transfers, which includes grants to developing countries, payments to the international organisations like the EC and private transfers such as gifts.

The balance of these flows on visible trade is called the balance of trade and the balance on the current account overall is called the current balance. It is one of these balances that newspapers and politicians are usually referring when they talk about the balance of payments. Table 13.4 shows the balance of payments for the United Kingdom in 1990, it can be seen that the balance of trade was –£18,809m, the invisible balance was +£1,778m. and the current balance was –£17,029m. More will be said later about the history of the balance of payments in the United Kingdom.

Capital transactions

As well as these current transactions there are flows of money for investment purposes. This includes funds from both the public and private sectors and long-term and short-term monetary movements.

Long-term capital transactions include:

● Overseas investment in the United Kingdom (e.g. purchase of shares, acquisition of real assets, purchase of government securities by non-residents).
● UK private investment overseas, where UK residents buy shares, acquire real assets, and so on, in overseas countries. The capital account does not include interest, dividends or profits but only flows of money for investment purposes. A capital

transaction can give rise to a current flow in the future. If a non-resident bought shares in a UK company the initial amount would appear on the capital account. The resulting flow of dividends paid in the future would be recorded as a flow on the invisible account.

● Official long-term capital (i.e. loans from the UK government to other governments).

Short-term transactions include:

● Trade credit – as goods are often not paid for as they are received the physical export and import of goods is not matched with an inflow or outflow of money. In order that the balance of payments balances these amounts would be included here as trade credit.
● Foreign currency borrowing and lending abroad by UK banks.
● Exchange reserves held by other countries and other organisations in sterling.
● Other external banking and money market liabilities in sterling.

These capital transactions are recorded in the UK balance of payments as changes from the previous year they are not a record of all the transactions that have taken place over time. If money is flowing into the United Kingdom for investment purposes there is an increase in the UK liabilities and these are shown as positive amounts on the balance of payments. If money is flowing out of the country there is an increase in the UK assets and these are shown as negative amounts in the balance of payments.

Until 1986 capital flows from/to the private sector and capital flows from/to the public sector were shown in two separate accounts. Now all capital transactions are recorded under the heading of 'UK transactions in external assets and liabilities'. The balance of this account is called 'net financial transactions'. In Table 13.4 it can be seen that transactions in external assets for 1990 was –£72,399m., transactions in external liabilities was +£87,035 and net financial transactions was +£14,636.

The short-term flows of capital are bank and other lending/borrowing. It is here that speculative flows would appear in the balance of payments. Portfolio investment is the purchasing of shares in companies, while direct investment is the setting up of subsidiaries. The difference between the inflow and outflow of funds in any one year is shown by the change in official reserves. An increase in official reserves is shown as a negative amount and a decrease is shown as a positive amount.

The balance of payments overall should balance as negative flows will be balanced by positive flows. As this is often hard to understand two examples will be given.

Example 1

If a UK resident buys foreign goods there will be a negative entry in the current account equal to the value of those goods. That individual has to pay for those goods in foreign currency and could do this by using money from a foreign currency bank account if he or she has one, or by borrowing the foreign currency from a bank in that country. Either way there is an increase in the amount of liabilities and the same amount would be shown as a positive amount in the capital account.

Table 13.4 UK balance of payments, 1990 (£m)

Visible trade balance		−18,675
Invisible trade		
Services	5,201	
Interest, profits and dividends	4,029	
Transfers	−4,935	
Invisible trade balance		4,295
Current account balance		−14,380
Transactions in external assets		
UK investment overseas		
Direct	−11,702	
Portfolio	−12,587	
Bank lending	−37,246	
Other lending	−9,462	
Official reserves	−77	
Other external assets of central government	−1,227	
Total	−72,301	
Transactions in external liabilities		
Overseas investment in UK		
Direct	18,997	
Portfolio	5,070	
Bank borrowing	46,179	
Other borrowing	12,977	
Other external liabilities of central government	1,159	
Total	84,382	
Net transactions		12,081
Balancing item		2,299

Source: *Annual Abstract of Statistics*, 1992 (CSO)

Example 2

If a foreign investor purchased shares in a UK company, there would be a positive amount recorded in the capital account. The investor might pay for these shares by using sterling from a sterling bank account and so there will be an equal negative amount shown in the capital account.

The balance of payments should therefore always balance but invariably fails to owing to errors and omissions in the recording process, and so a balancing item is included to ensure it balances. As can be seen from Tables 13.4 and 13.5 the balancing item can be very large, and this calls into question the accuracy of the figures.

Equilibrium in the balance of payments

If the balance of payments always balances how can there be a deficit on the balance of payments? The answer is that the media and politicians are referring to the current balance or the balance of trade rather than the overall balance of payments position. A balance of payments surplus on the current account is where the value of exports exceeds the value of imports. A deficit is where the value of imports exceeds the value of exports. As explained above, if there is a surplus on the current account, this will be matched by an outflow in the capital account, for example a reduction in the size of sterling bank balances, or an increase in official reserves. The opposite is true for a deficit. This implies that there can not be a balance of payments problem, however persistent surpluses or deficits on the current account are considered to be problematic. A persistent deficit has to be financed in some way, either through borrowing, to increase the external liabilities or by selling more of its assets. A deficit will also lead to pressure on the exchange rate, as will be shown later. A continued surplus is also a problem, since one country's surplus must mean that other countries are experiencing a deficit, and they will be faced with the problem of financing the deficit. Political pressure will be brought to bear, and there is the possibility of the introduction of tariffs or other import controls in order to reduce a deficit.

Methods of correcting balance of payments deficits

Since surpluses are not regarded as being such a problem as deficits, this section will concentrate on action needed to overcome a deficit, although the actions would be reversed for a surplus. When there is a current account deficit, the outflow of funds is greater than the inflow of funds from international trade. The authorities need to increase exports and/or reduce imports. Thus:

1 A fall in the exchange rate will have the double effect of making exports cheaper abroad and imports dearer at home, thus encouraging exports and discouraging imports. This will be explained fully later.
2 To increase exports British companies that produce for the export market could be subsidised. This would have the effect of reducing the price of UK goods abroad, making them more competitive.
3 Import controls could be imposed to restrict the level of imports coming in to the country.
4 A rise in the rate of interest would make Britain more attractive to investors and therefore increase capital flows into Britain and help offset the current account deficit.

THE HISTORY OF THE BALANCE OF PAYMENTS IN THE UNITED KINGDOM

Table 13.5 gives a summary of the balance of payments in the United Kingdom over the last five years. It can be seen that the current account has been in deficit since 1987. This hides underlying trends as the visible balance has been in deficit since 1983 and within this the non-oil balance has been in deficit since 1982. This latter deficit did not show in the overall current account figures until 1987 because of the offsetting effects of invisibles and oil. The United Kingdom's weakness on the current account comes from several sources:

Table 13.5 UK balance of payments (£m.)

	1986	1987	1988	1989	1990
Visible trade balance	−9,559	−11,582	−21,624	−24,589	−18,675
Invisible trade balance	9,747	7,423	6,103	4,195	4,295
Current account balance	187	−4,159	−15,520	−20,404	−14,380
Net financial transactions	−7,234	5,810	9,645	12,916	12,081
Balancing item	7,047	−1,651	5,875	7,488	2,299
Drawings on (+) or additions to (−) official reserves	−2,891	−12,012	−2,761	55,440	−77

Source: *Annual Abstract of Statistics*, 1992 (CSO)

1 Exports have risen but imports have risen faster. In the United Kingdom there is a high propensity to import goods.
2 The collapse of oil prices has reduced the value of the United Kingdom's oil exports.
3 The recession of the early 1980s left the UK manufacturing base in an extremely weak position. This means that it is difficult to produce enough goods for export or even to meet domestic demand, so the balance of payments has been hit from both directions. The changes in the structure of industry in the United Kingdom described in Chapter 9 have implications for the balance of payments, as services are less exportable than goods.
4 The consumer boom that occurred in the late 1980s after the Lawson budget of 1986 lead to an increase in the level of exports.
5 The impact of oil has been twofold. First, as the United Kingdom is now an oil exporting country it brings in revenue which will improve the balance of payments. Secondly, it has kept the exchange rate higher than it would have been, as will be shown in the next section, which makes UK goods less competitive in world markets and will therefore lead to a worsening of the balance of payments.

Patterns of trade

Over time, patterns of trade change for many reasons, Table 13.6 shows UK patterns of trade by destination/source and Table 13.7 shows UK trade by type of good. From these tables it is possible to look at how the country's patterns of trade have changed.

The most obvious change that can be seen in Table 13.6 is that trade with the EC has become more important over the last 20 years. More than a half of our imports in 1990 came from the EC and more than half of our exports went to the EC. Despite this, the United States is still important to Britain. There has been a decline in our trade with other developed countries, although the importance of Japan within that has increased, particularly with respect to imports. Our trade with the oil exporting countries has declined in importance – as too has our trade with other developing countries, which include much of the old Commonwealth countries. At one time these countries were our biggest markets.

Table 13.6 UK's imports and exports by destination/source (%)

	1970 Exports	Imports	1980 Exports	Imports	1990 Exports	Imports
European Community	32	32	46	44	53	52
Other W. Europe	13	12	12	12	9	13
United States	12	11	10	12	13	11
Other developed countries of which	11	10	6	7	5	7
Japan	2	2	1	4	2	6
Oil exporting countries	6	11	10	9	6	2
Other developing	18	14	12	11	10	10

Source: *Annual Abstract of Statistics*, 1992, 1982, 1972 (CSO)

Table 13.7 Pattern of trade by type of good (%)

	1970 Export	Import	1990 Export	Import
Food and animals	3	20	4	8
Beverages and tobacco	3	2	3	1
Crude materials except fuels	3	12	2	5
Minerals, fuels	3	14	8	7
Chemicals and related products	9	6	13	9
Manufactured goods	24	20	15	17
Machinery	43	19	41	38
Miscellaneous manufacturing	9	7	13	15
Total manufacturing	85	51	81	78
Others	3	2	2	1

Source: *Annual Abstract of Statistics*, 1992 (CSO)

Since 1970 the United Kingdom has been importing less food and animals for consumption. The impact of oil can be seen in Table 13.7, as the quantities of oil-related products imported into the United Kingdom has fallen over the period. Manufacturing is clearly the most important category of good as far as the balance of payments is concerned. Manufacturing has retained its importance for exports, accounting for 85 per cent of exports in 1970 and 81 per cent in 1990. As far as imports are concerned the percentage has increased a great deal over the last 20 years. The United Kingdom is now a net importer of manufactured goods. In 1990 the value of imported manufactured goods was £98,275.3m., whereas the value of exported manufactured goods was £84,505.9m. One reason for this is the increased import penetration in the United Kingdom. Table 13.8 shows import penetration in UK manufacturing for 1970, 1980 and 1990, from which it can be seen that this penetration has increased over this time period.

Table 13.8 Import penetration[1] in manufacturing in UK (%)

1970	1980	1990
16.6	26.2	36.7

Note:[1] measured as $\dfrac{\text{import value}}{\text{home demand}} \times 100$

Source: *Annual Abstract of Statistics*, 1972, 1982, 1992

EXCHANGE RATES

The exchange rate of a currency is the price of that currency in terms of other currencies. If each country has its own currency and international trade is to take place an exchange of currencies needs to occur. When a UK resident buys goods from France, these must be paid for in French francs. The individual will probably purchase francs from a bank in exchange for sterling in order to carry out the transaction. There must therefore be an exchange rate between sterling and francs. Likewise there will be exchange rates between sterling and all other currencies.

Basically speaking, there are two types of exchange rate: the floating exchange rate; and the fixed exchange rate. There are also hybrid exchange rate systems which combine the characteristics of the two main types.

The floating exchange rate

This type of exchange rate is determined within a free market, there is no government intervention, and the exchange rate is free to fluctuate according to market conditions. The exchange rate is determined by the demand for and the supply of the currency in question.

As far as sterling is concerned, the demand for the currency comes from exports – that is, overseas residents buying pounds either to buy British goods and services or for investment purposes. The supply of pounds comes from imports – that is, UK residents who are buying foreign currencies to purchase goods and services or for investment purposes and who are therefore at the same time supplying pounds to the market.

The market for sterling can then be drawn using simple demand and supply diagrams. In Figure 13.1, the price axis shows the price of £1 in terms of US dollars and the quantity axis shows the quantity of pounds being bought and sold. The equilibrium exchange rate is determined by the intersection of demand and supply at £1 = $2. As this is a totally free market, if any of the conditions in the market change the exchange rate will also change.

The demand for and supply of sterling, and therefore the exchange rate, is affected by:

1 Changes in the balance of payments.
2 Changes in investment flows.
3 Speculation in the foreign exchange markets.

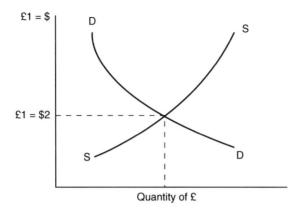

Fig. 13.1 **The determination of the exchange rate of £ for $**

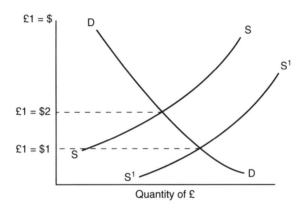

Fig. 13.2 **The effect of changes in the balance of payments on the exchange rate**

Changes in the balance of payments

Figure 13.2 show the effect on the exchange rate of changes in the balance of payments. The original demand curve is DD and the original supply curve is SS. At the equilibrium exchange rate of £1 = $2 the demand for pounds is equal to the supply of pounds. In other words if the demand for pounds comes from exports and the supply of pounds comes from imports, imports and exports are equal and the balance of payments is in equilibrium. Now it is assumed that a balance of payments deficit appears, caused by the level of imports rising while the level of exports stays the same. If exports remain the same there will be no change in the demand curve for pounds. As imports rise there will be a rise in the supply of pounds to the market, the supply curve moves to the right to S^1S^1. At the old exchange rate of £1 = $2, there is now excess supply of pounds, and as this is a free market there will be downward pressure on the value of the pound until equilibrium is re-established at the new lower exchange rate of

£1 = $1. At this exchange rate the demand for pounds is again equal to the increased supply of pounds and the balance between imports and exports is re-established.

How does this happen? When the value of the pound falls two things happen, the price of imports rises and the price of exports falls. Thus the level of imports falls and the level of exports rises and the deficit if eradicated. A simple numerical example illustrates this point:

At old exchange rate £1 = $2:

An American car which costs $20,000 in US costs £10,000 in UK.
A British car which costs £10,000 in UK costs $20,000 in US.

If the exchange rate falls to £1 = $1:

The American car still costs $20,000 in US but now costs £20,000 in UK.
The British car still costs £10,000 in UK but now costs $10,000 in US.

Therefore a depreciation in the exchange rate has made imports dearer (the American car) and exports cheaper (the British car). Thus a fall in the value of the pound helps to re-establish equilibrium in the balance of payments.

In the case of a surplus on the balance of payments, the exchange rate will rise, making exports more expensive and imports cheaper and thereby re-establishing equilibrium in the balance of payments. You should test your understanding of the working of the foreign exchange markets by working through what happens if a surplus develops.

A fall in the value of the pound in a free market is called a depreciation in the value of the pound, a rise in its value is called an appreciation.

Changes in investment flows

In Figure 13.3, the original equilibrium exchange rate is £1 = $2. If there is an increase in the level of investment in the UK from overseas, there will be an increase in the

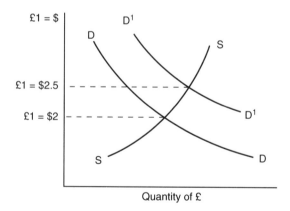

Fig. 13.3 **The effect of changes in the investment flows on the exchange rate**

demand for pounds. The demand curve moves to the right (to D^1D^1), and the exchange rate rises to £1 = \$2.5.

The effect of speculation

If the exchange rate of sterling is expected to rise, speculators will buy sterling in order to make a capital gain by selling the currency later at a higher exchange rate. There will be an increase in the demand for pounds and the exchange rate will rise. If the exchange rate is expected to fall, speculators will sell sterling in order to avoid a capital loss, there will be an increase in the supply of sterling and therefore a fall in the exchange rate. Illustrate these changes yourself using demand and supply diagrams.

The important thing about speculation is that it tends to be self-fulfilling. If enough people believe that the exchange rate is going to rise and act accordingly, the exchange rate will rise.

The main advantage of the floating exchange rate is the automatic mechanism it provides to overcome a balance of payments deficit or surplus. Theoretically, if a deficit develops, the exchange rate will fall and the balance of payments is brought back into equilibrium. The opposite occurs in the case of a surplus. Of course in reality it does not work as smoothly or as quickly as the theory suggests. A depreciation is supposed to work as demonstrated in Figure 13.4.

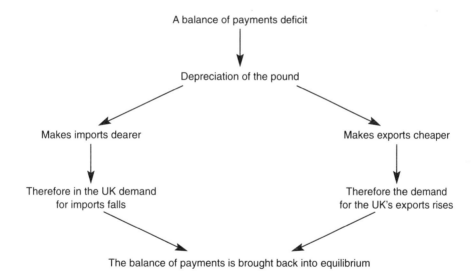

Fig. 13.4 The effect of depreciation

There are, however, a number of problems which may occur to prevent this self-correcting mechanism working properly. First, if in the United Kingdom the goods which are imported are necessities that cannot be produced at home, then even if their price goes up as a result of a depreciation, they will continue to be demanded. Thus not only will the balance of payments deficit not be automatically rectified, another economic problem will result, that of inflation. The United Kingdom will continue to buy the imported goods at the new higher price. A second problem occurs on the other side of the equation. It is assumed above that as the price of exports falls more exports are sold. This presupposes that in the United Kingdom the capacity is there to meet this increased demand, but this may not be the case, especially if the economy is fully employed already or if the export producing industries are not in a healthy enough state to produce more.

These problems give rise to what is called the 'J-curve effect'. A fall in the exchange rate may well lead to a deterioration in the balance of payments in the short term, until domestic production can be increased to meet the extra demand for exports and as substitutes for imported goods. Once this can be done there will be an improvement in the balance of payments, hence the J-curve effect pictured in Figure 13.5. The effect of a fall in the exchange rate is limited and the curve levels off after a certain time period. The depreciation in the value of the pound seen when Britain left the ERM did not have an immediate effect on the balance of payments and many argued that this was due to the J-curve effect.

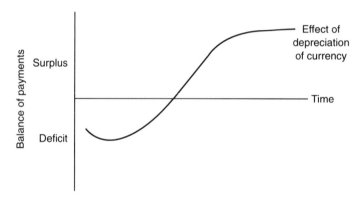

Fig. 13.5 J-curve

One big disadvantage of the floating exchange rate is that it introduces uncertainty into the market, and for firms that operate internationally, this introduces another variable which needs to be considered when planning. Moreover since the possibility of speculation exists with the floating exchange rate, this can be destabilising and unsettling to markets, something which businesses do not welcome.

The fixed exchange rate

The fixed exchange rate is one that is fixed and maintained by the government. An exchange rate can be fixed in terms of other currencies, gold or a basket of other currencies. In order to maintain a fixed exchange rate the government has actively to intervene in the market, either buying or selling currencies.

Figure 13.6 shows the action needed by the UK authorities in the case of downward pressure on the value of the pound. The exchange rate is fixed at £1 = $2, and the government wants to maintain that rate. If a balance of payments deficit develops, brought about by an increase in imports, exports remaining the same, there will be excess supply of pounds at the fixed exchange rate. In a free market the value of the pound would fall until the excess supply had disappeared. However, this is not a free market, and the government must buy up the excess supply of pounds in order to maintain the exchange rate at £1 = $2. Thus the demand curve moves to the right and the exchange rate has been maintained at the same level. Alternatively if there is excess demand for pounds, the government has to supply pounds to the market in order to maintain the fixed exchange rate.

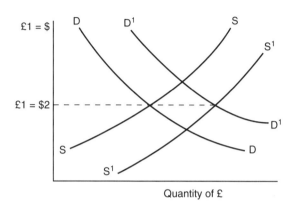

Fig. 13.6 **The effect of changes in the balance of payments on a fixed exchange rate**

A prime advantage of a fixed exchange rate is that there is less uncertainty in the market; everyone knows what the exchange rate will be in a year's time, and long-term planning is made easier. It also reduces the likelihood of speculation in the foreign exchange markets. One serious disadvantage, however, is that there is no longer an automatic mechanism for rectifying any balance of payments problems as there is in the case of the floating exchange rate and this means that government intervention is necessary not just to support the exchange rate, but also to overcome any balance of payments problems. Added to this, a fixed exchange rate is not sustainable in the case of persistent deficits or surpluses. In the event of a surplus, the government must supply pounds to the market and if the surplus persists then eventually the government will exhaust its reserves and might well have to revalue the pound (i.e. increase the exchange rate of the pound). In the case of a persistent deficit, the size of the government's reserves will be increasing over time and the government may have to devalue the pound to correct the problem.

There are, then, advantages and disadvantages to both types of exchange rate and there have been hybrid exchange rate systems which serve to combine the advantages of both systems. In such an exchange rate system the exchange rate is basically fixed but is allowed to fluctuate by a small amount either side of the central value. The Exchange Rate Mechanism (ERM) of the European Community is an example of this. When the United Kingdom entered the ERM the exchange rate was fixed against other member currencies but allowed to vary by 6 per cent either side of the central value before action was needed.

Over the years the United Kingdom has had a variety of different types of exchange rate. Before the First World War and for sometime between the wars, the exchange rate was fixed in terms of gold – the old gold standard. From the Second World War until 1972, the United Kingdom was part of the Bretton Woods system of fixed exchange rates, where the pound was fixed in terms of dollars. Then from 1972 to 1990, there was a floating exchange rate. In 1990, however, Britain joined the Exchange Rate Mechanism of the European Community, which was again a fixed exchange rate. In September 1992, the pound left the ERM and was allowed to float once more.

The Exchange Rate Mechanism

In October 1990, the United Kingdom joined the ERM, which is a system of fixed exchange rates. The currencies within the ERM are fixed against the European currency unit (ECU) and are therefore fixed against one another. The ECU is a weighted basket of EC currencies, designed to act as a unit of account and eventually as an international currency. When the pound entered, a variation of 6 per cent either side of the par value was allowed. Most other European countries were allowed only a 2.25 per cent fluctuation either side of their central values. The understanding was that the United Kingdom would eventually go to 2.25 per cent fluctuation and in the end all European currencies would be completely fixed against one another.

Table 13.9 Central exchange rates of the pound against other ERM currencies October 1990

	Exchange rate
Belgian francs	60.85
Danish kroner	11.25
French franc	9.89
German Deutschmark	2.95
Irish punt	1.10
Italian lira	2,207.25
Luxembourg franc	60.85
Dutch guilder	3.32
Spanish peseta	191.75

Note: Estimate of the pound's effective limits against Deutschmark: 2.77–3.13 DM.

The essence of the ERM is that it provides a means of stabilising the exchange rates of participating Member States. If the pound, for instance, strays too far from its central rate the Bank of England and other central banks of ERM members will buy or sell currencies in order to stabilise the exchange rate. Each member holds reserves in the European Co-operation Fund in order to settle debts between countries, and these funds can be used to stabilise currencies. Another thing that can be done to help an ailing currency is changing the domestic rate of interest. If the pound's exchange rate falls towards its lower limit, an increase in the rate of interest would make the United Kingdom a more attractive place for investors and therefore increase the demand for pounds. If both of these approaches fail, there could be a realignment of the currencies within the ERM. This has happened from time to time, but such realignments are

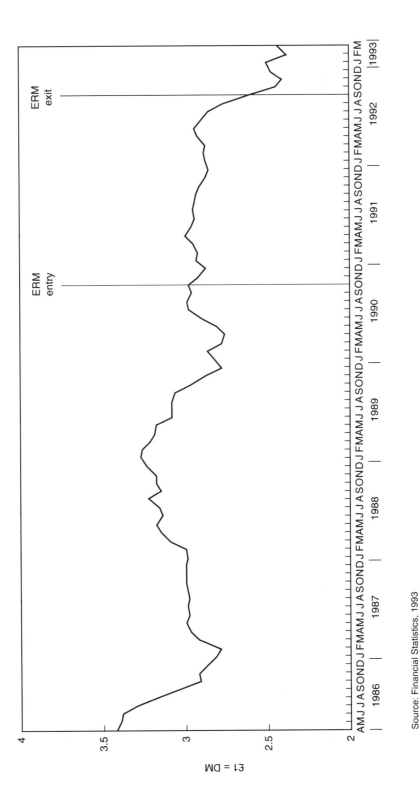

Source: Financial Statistics, 1993

Fig. 13.7 Exchange rate of sterling with the Deutschmark

against the spirit of the fixed exchange rate, and countries are expected to avoid this if possible.

Britain's reasons for entering the ERM in 1990 were as follows:

● To enjoy the benefits of fixed exchange rates, and in particular, less uncertainty and reduced speculation.
● As part of the government's anti-inflationary stance, since the discipline of the ERM would force the United Kingdom's rate of inflation towards the lower European average.
● As part of our commitment to Europe, the Maastricht Treaty and the Delors plan calling for economic and monetary union between the countries of the EC.

Figure 13.7 shows the fluctuations in sterling's exchange rate since joining the ERM. It is clear that the exchange rate of the pound has been much more stable since joining the mechanism, but sterling ran into problems in mid-1992, mainly as a result of speculation against the pound. The Bank of England intervened in the market but was unable to stop the fall in the value of the currency. An increase in interest rates was announced but then withdrawn very quickly because of political pressures and the effect such a move would have on UK industry in the midst of recession. In the end the pound was suspended from the ERM and allowed to float, and has since fallen in value sharply. The United Kingdom is expected to rejoin the ERM 'when the conditions are right'. At the time, most forecasters expected re-entry in late 1993 at a central rate of around DM 2.60, but this looks increasingly unlikely as other currencies have also run into difficulties within the ERM.

EXCHANGE RATES AND BUSINESS

Reference has already been made to the fact that changes in exchange rates can affect businesses in several ways. These would include:

● Making it easier or harder to export (as prices change).
● Making it easier or harder for foreign competitors to penetrate the domestic market (again through the price effect).
● Causing uncertainty in both trading and investment terms.
● Adding to or reducing the cost of imported raw materials and component parts.

In addition, if a falling exchange rate causes inflationary pressures within the economy, this could add to a firm's production costs (e.g. through higher wage bills) and could encourage the government to introduce counter-inflationary policies which might subsequently depress demand in the home market.

For businesses regularly involved in currency dealing and/or multinational activities, changing currency values can also bring other gains or losses. Shell and Allied Lyons, for example, lost over £100 million each on currency gambles in the early 1990s by entering into deals when the exchange rate between currencies was not fixed in advance. In contrast, Unilever's record profits for the financial year 1992/3 included substantial overseas earnings, some of which were the direct result of a weaker pound, which in turn, meant that remitted profits increased when converted back into sterling.

SYNOPSIS

This chapter has looked at the international marketplace and, in particular, the benefits that derive from international trade. Consideration has also been given to some of the restrictions that exist to free trade and the organisations that are active in promoting it. Patterns of trade in the United Kingdom have been examined, as well as a recent history of the balance of payments position. Finally, exchange rates were covered, including an analysis of how businesses are affected by changes in the value of currencies.

CASE STUDY: BREAKFAST CEREALS

The internationalisation of markets and the creation of the Single European Market has had a profound effect on the structure of all industries in Europe, not least in the food and drink industry. There is great diversity in European food and drink markets due to differences in culture and economic conditions. For example, consumers in the north of Europe eat far more meat than those in the south, who instead eat more fresh fruit and vegetables. There are, however, some factors at work that are likely to reduce the diversity. These are:

- An increased preference on the part of consumers for convenience foods and snack foods.
- A greater awareness of health and nutritional issues.
- Greater mobility leading to a greater willingness to try new foods (a relatively recent phenomenon is the advent of export markets for people on holiday).
- The spread of supermarkets through Europe has led to the introduction of new brands which might not previously have been available.

In the European food and drink industry two main corporate strategies can be identified: first, some companies are focusing their activities around one main product, as is common in the food and drink industry (e.g. Coca-Cola, Marlboro); and secondly, companies are expanding their range of products through acquisition and merger. There has been a number of important mergers and acquisitions over the last six years in the European food and drink manufacturing industries, and in terms of the value of mergers and acquisitions the sector was the seventh biggest in Europe in 1990 with a value of £4,089.6 million.

The removal of non-tariff barriers has had the further effects of allowing producers to use less expensive ingredients, reducing the costs of packaging and labelling, and the elimination of expensive bureaucratic restrictions on trade.

Breakfast cereals

All of these factors can be clearly seen at work in the market for breakfast cereals. As consumers become more affluent they typically spend less of their income on food and drink. This has happened in Europe as expenditure on food has fallen from 33 per cent of the consumers' income in the 1970s to 25 per cent in 1990. What has happened within this is that there has been a change in the pattern of spending. Greater affluence has led to a boost in the market for breakfast cereals in two ways: first, as more women work and more houses have microwaves there has been an increased demand for convenience foods (of which breakfast cereal is one); and secondly, increased affluence has led to greater foreign travel and hence exposure to and a willingness to try new varieties of food. This means that in addition to the extension of the market with new product lines through merger and acquisition, there has been an increase in the market geographically, as cultural barriers break down. Consumer habits and demands are continually changing, and the removal of barriers in Europe is contributing to this. Continental

Europeans are not seen as cereal eaters; the biggest markets are the United States and the United Kingdom. However, recent trends in the market show that the popularity of breakfast cereals is spreading into Europe. In 1990 the market grew by 9 per cent in value terms in both the United Kingdom and the United States, while in France, Germany and Italy the markets grew by 20 per cent. Other countries like Sweden, Denmark and Holland are following suit. Table 13.10 shows forecasts for growth in the value of breakfast cereals in selected countries between 1990 and 1995.

Table 13.10 Growth in the real value of sales of breakfast cereals between 1990 and 1995 (%)

	%
France	53
Germany	64
Italy	92
UK	10
USA	13

Source: *Euromonitor Market Direction*

The higher growth rate in Italy is due to its retailing structure, where retailing is not dominated by the large supermarkets as in other countries. This is likely to change as larger outlets are already being built.

The market for breakfast cereals is segmented; it is a product which is enjoyed by both children and adults alike. Cereals designed specifically for children account for about 22 per cent of the market, and children play an important part in the decision over which cereal to purchase. In the adult market there is a much greater awareness of health and nutritional issues and this has led to an increase in the popularity of cereals like muesli and bran or oat-based cereals. All of this is well recognised by the producers of breakfast cereals. Advertising is high in the food market generally, but is especially high in the market for breakfast cereal and it is clearly targeted at particular market segments. Corn Pops has recently been introduced by Kellogg's into the British market (although it was available in Germany, France and Spain before this) and it has been accompanied by a massive television advertising campaign. As well as the targeted advertising, there has been an advertising war between the two cereal giants in Europe, both attempting to capture part of a new and growing market. The two market leaders are Kellogg's and Cereal Partners Worldwide (CPW). CPW was formed as a joint venture between Nestlé and General Mills in 1989; General Mills is Kellogg's biggest competitor in the United States. In Europe, Kellogg's is the market leader, accounting for about 45 per cent of the market, but after a period of growth in the 1980s this percentage has stabilised and there is evidence that CPW is competing effectively.

There has also been an increase in the number of supermarkets and hypermarkets across Europe, which means that there is much more space available for the storage and display of products. This is particularly important for breakfast cereals which are large bulk products.

Despite these trends there remain some cultural differences. For example, in France there is a high demand for cereals with some chocolate input. This could be due to the higher amount of chocolate drinks that are consumed, particularly by children. Thus there is a proliferation of chocolate-based cereals in France.

In the United Kingdom there is competition to breakfast cereal coming from the opposite direction (i.e. from continental style breakfasts such as bread rolls and croissants). Despite this, it is unlikely that the market for breakfast cereals will decline because of the increased use of breakfast cereals as a snack food. It is estimated that about half of children in the United Kingdom have breakfast cereal as a snack in the evening.

Conclusion

The internationalisation of markets and companies is leading to a reduction in international diversity in many industries. This can clearly be seen in the market for breakfast cereals, where cultural differences are breaking down and new markets are opening up and growing. Manufacturers are quick to recognise these changes and reinforce them through heavy advertising, which serves to further reduce cultural diversity.

NOTES AND REFERENCES

1   Cecchini, P., *The European Challenge 1992: The benefits of a single market*, Widwood House: Aldershot, 1988.

REVIEW AND DISCUSSION QUESTIONS

1   Think of other markets where there are likely to be international differences and analyse the effects of the changes that will be brought about by the internationalisation of markets.

2   Using demand and supply diagrams show the effect on the market for foreign exchange of the following:
   (a)   a decreased level of imports;
   (b)   a fall in the rate of interest; and
   (c)   the development of a balance of payments surplus.

3   What is the likely effect on a system of fixed exchange rates of continued speculation on one of the member currencies?

4   Explain why businesses generally prefer fixed rather than floating rates of exchange.

ASSIGNMENTS

1   You work for a company that is considering expansion into Europe. Most of the high street banks have introduced new services related to the Single Market. Your departmental head has asked you to investigate and produce a report on the services offered by one of the high street banks. Produce such a report with supporting evidence.

2   You work for a trade union in the hosiery industry which strongly supports the use of import restrictions to protect its workers from competition from countries where wages rates are much lower. You have been asked to take part in a debate on the issue by the local Conservative MP, who is a champion of the free market. Present a set of arguments that will counter any points that your opponent is likely to make.

FURTHER READING

Griffiths, A. and Wall, S., *Applied Economics: An introductory course*, 5th edition, Longman, 1993.
Palmer, A. and Worthington, I., *The Business and Marketing Environment*, McGraw-Hill, 1992.

CHAPTER 14

Government and markets

Ian Worthington

The central role played by government in the operation of the economy and its markets has been a recurrent theme of this book. Paradoxically, many of the government's interventionist policies have been designed to remove existing barriers to the operations of free markets and to promote greater competition and choice. In some cases, the government's strategy has been to disengage the state from some of its involvement in the economy – as in the case of 'privatisation'. In other cases, policy changes and legislation have been deemed the appropriate course of action – as in the government's approach to competition policy and to the operation of the labour market.

OBJECTIVES

1 To outline the rationale underlying the government's approach to markets.
2 To analyse UK privatisation policy and give examples of privatisation in other countries.
3 To examine the changing nature of UK competition policy, including the legislative and institutional framework within which it operates.
4 To survey government initiatives on the labour market and, in particular, its approach to employment and trade union power.

INTRODUCTION

A belief in the virtue of competition and in the need to develop competitive markets remains a central tenet of government economic policy in capitalist states. At the heart of this belief lies the widely accepted view that competition provides the best means of improving economic efficiency and of encouraging wealth creation. Proponents of this view argue that competition:

● Ensures an efficient allocation of resources between competing uses, through the operation of the price system.
● Puts pressure on firms to perform as efficiently as possible.
● Provides a mechanism for flexible adjustment to change, whether in consumption or in the conditions of supply.
● Protects consumers from potential exploitation by producers, by offering alternative sources of purchase.

It follows that an absence or lack of competition in either the factor or product markets is seen as detrimental to the well-being of the economy as a whole and that governments have a responsibility for ensuring wherever possible that markets operate freely, with a minimum of state interference.

Much of the philosophical basis for this perspective can be traced to the 'monetarists' who have tended to dominate official thinking in Britain and elsewhere for over a decade. Broadly speaking, monetarists argue that levels of output and employment in the economy are supply-determined, in contrast to the 'Keynesian' view which emphasises the importance of demand in shaping economic activity. Accordingly, supply-side policies seek to improve the output responsiveness of the economy, by focusing on the workings of markets and in particular on removing the obstacles which prevent markets from functioning efficiently.

The influence of the supply-side approach to economic management can be seen in a number of key areas, and in particular, in the government's policy of privatisation and in the reforms in the labour market in the 1980s. Concerns over competition and potential abuses of market power also figure prominently in the government's approach to monopolies and mergers. These three aspects of government intervention in markets – privatisation, competition policy, and labour market reforms – are considered separately below and illustrate how state involvement can be a key influence in the environment of individual business organisations on both the input and output side.

PRIVATISATION POLICY

On privatisation

In its broadest sense, 'privatisation' involves the transfer of assets or different forms of economic activity from the public sector to the private sector. In the United Kingdom such transfers occurred throughout the 1980s and early 1990s and are set to continue in the foreseeable future with the planned sale of the coal industry and British Rail and with the disposal of the government's remaining shares in British Telecom.

In practice, the term privatisation has been applied to a range of activities that involve a measure of state disengagement from economic activity. Typically these have included:

- The sale of government-owned assets, especially nationalised industries (e.g. British Telecom, British Gas) or industries in which the government has a substantial shareholding (e.g. BP).
- The contracting out of services normally provided by the public sector (e.g. school meals, hospital cleaning).
- The deregulation or liberalisation of activities over which the state had previously placed some restriction (e.g. the deregulation of bus routes or postal services).
- The injection of private capital into areas traditionally financed by the public sector (e.g. the road system).
- The sale of local authority-owned property to private citizens or organisations (e.g. council houses, school playing fields).
- The privatisation of government agencies (e.g. Her Majesty's Inspectors for Education).

Of these, the sale of state assets – especially the public corporations and nationalised industries – has been the main plank of UK privatisation policy and the one which has captured the most public and media attention. For this reason, in the discussion below attention is focused on this aspect of the privatisation programme.

The scope of government asset sales in the period 1979–93 is indicated in Table 14.1. In the first phase, between 1979 and 1983, these tended to generate relatively small sums of money compared with later years and generally involved the sale of government shares in companies such as British Aerospace, Britoil, BP, ICL and Ferranti. Between 1983 and 1988, the government disposed of a number of its largest industrial and commercial undertakings, including British Telecom, British Gas and British Airways, along with Rolls-Royce and Jaguar. These were followed by the sale of British Steel, the Rover Group, the National Bus Company and, more significantly, by the Regional Water Authorities and the electricity industry in the late 1980s and early 1990s.[1]

Table 14.1 Major asset sales 1979-1993

Amersham International	Fairey Aviation
Associated British Ports	Ferranti
British Airports Authority	Forestry Commission
British Aerospace	Istel (Rover)
British Airways	Jaguar (British Leyland)
British Gas	National Bus Company
British Petroleum	National Enterprise Board Holding
British Rail Hotels	Rolls-Royce
British Steel	Rover Group
British Sugar Corporation	Royal Ordnance
British Telecom	Short Brothers
Britoil	Sealink (British Rail)
Cable and Wireless	Unipart (Rover)
Electricity industry	Water Authorities
Enterprise Oil	Wytch Farm onshore oil (British Gas)

In disposing of its assets the government used a number of different methods including selling shares to a single buyer, usually another company (e.g. the sale of Rover), selling shares to the company's management and workers (e.g. the management buyout of the National Freight Corporation), and selling shares on the open market for purchase by individuals and institutions (e.g. the stock market flotation of British Telecom). In some cases the process took place in several stages, as a proportion of shares was released onto the market over several years (e.g. BP); in other cases a one-off sale occurred, with investors invited to subscribe for the whole of the equity (e.g. British Steel). As Figure 14.1 indicates, proceeds from privatisation sales between 1979 and 1991 exceeded £34 billion, with the majority of the revenue being raised in the mid- to late 1980s.

Rationale

The roots of privatisation policy lie in the attempt by the Conservative government, under the leadership of Margaret Thatcher (1979–90) to tackle the perceived

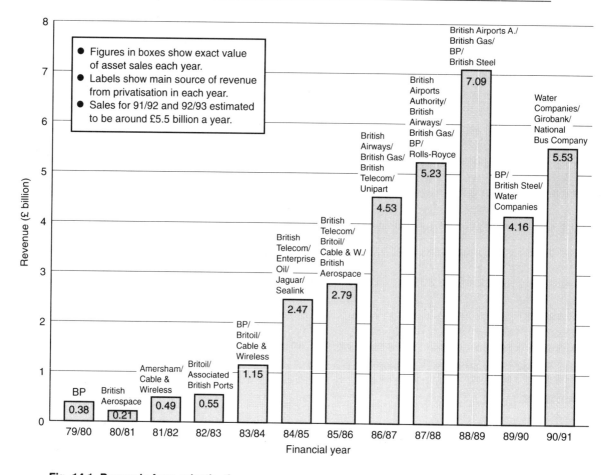

Fig. 14.1 Proceeds from privatisation

Source: Cook, G.C., *Privatisation in the 1980s and 1990s*, Hidcote Press, 1992

deficiencies in the supply side of the UK economy. Central to the government's philosophy was the belief that the free market was a superior method of allocating economic resources and that large-scale state involvement in business activity hampered economic progress. 'Rolling back the frontiers of the state' – by reducing the size of the public sector – was consequently seen as a key component in improving the country's economic performance at both national and international level.

The government's case for privatisation centred round the claim that the sale of state-owned businesses would improve their efficiency and general performance, and would give rise to increased competition that would broaden consumer choice. Under state control, it was argued that businesses had no incentive to strive for efficiency or to respond to consumer preferences, since many of them lacked any direct competition and all of them could turn to government for financial support, if revenue was insufficient to meet operating costs. In contrast, firms which were exposed to the 'test' of the market would have to satisfy both the consumer and the financial markets if they were to survive or to avoid take-over by more efficient and competitive organisations.[2]

Allied to this argument was the proposition that privatisation would improve the performance of an organisation's management and workers. Freed from the need to meet objectives laid down by government, management could concentrate on commercial goals such as profitability, improved productivity and cost reduction, and on encouraging greater flexibility and technical innovation within the organisation. Implicit in these claims was the acceptance that a considerable degree of restructuring would need to occur within each privatised company and that this was likely to act as an incentive to the workforce to improve its performance. Additional encouragement was also expected to derive from the use of employee share-ownership schemes, under which current employees within a newly privatised company were offered a proportion of the equity, thus giving them a vested interest in the organisation's fortunes.

The sale of shares to employees and to the public generally was also presented as a benefit of privatisation in that it helped to encourage wider share ownership and to create a 'share-owning democracy', with increased sympathies towards capitalist modes of production (and possibly the Conservative party!). Concomitantly, the sale of state assets also served to reduce the size of the public sector borrowing requirement – since revenue from sales was counted as negative public expenditure – and this helped to reduce the government's debt burden and to take some of the pressure off interest rates, as well as releasing funds for use by the private sector.

Criticisms of privatisation

Opponents of privatisation have likened the process to 'selling the family silver' – disposing of important national assets for short-term financial gains. Under privatisation, these assets, once owned by the general public, pass into the hands of those individuals and organisations able and willing to buy shares and this includes overseas buyers who could ultimately gain control of important parts of British industry, unless prevented from doing so by government action (e.g. through a 'golden share'). To add to this criticism, some observers claim that valuable assets, bought over many years by public funds, have been sold off too cheaply to private investors who will reap the benefit at the expense of the general public. Only industries which are not attractive to the stock market are likely to remain in public ownership and this will mean that the taxpayer has to pay the bill to support their continued existence.

Further criticisms include the loss of future government revenue from the sale of profitable state-owned businesses and the problem of ensuring that commercial goals are not allowed to displace completely the broader economic goals once pursued by nationalised industries (e.g. the possible closure of unprofitable rural telephone boxes or railway lines under privatisation). In essence, the fear is that once freed from government regulation, privatised companies will tend to replace the loss-making 'public service' element of their former activities with products or services that offer the greatest levels of profit. Whilst this will benefit some consumers, the cost is likely to be borne by other buyers who have limited market power and, in some cases, no alternative product to turn to.

This problem of lack of choice is particularly acute where the privatisation of a state monopoly has given rise to a private monopoly, as in the case of British Gas, British Telecom and the electricity and water companies. Despite the establishment of 'regulators' to oversee the operations of some of the newly privatised concerns (see Table 14.2), many opponents feel that the interest of consumers is not fully protected under the current arrangements and that the new private companies can exploit their monopoly position through higher prices. Recent reports of increased profits for many of the former public utilities – despite a recession – has only served to add fuel to the critics' fire and to strengthen the demand that government should find meaningful ways of encouraging competition in industries which have traditionally been regarded as natural monopolies.

Table 14.2 Regulatory bodies for key privatised utilities

Name	Date established	Main activities
Office of Tele-communications (OFTEL)	1984	Regulates BT – especially line rentals, inland calls, overseas calls; provides conditions for new entrants; licenses new forms of service; regulates equipment market.
Office of Gas Supply (OFGAS)	1986	Regulates gas supplies to domestic users – including average price per therm.
Office of Water (OFWAT)	1989	Regulates domestic and non-domestic supply by water and sewerage companies. Regulates price increases to customers.
Office of Electricity Regulation (OFFER)	1990	Regulates prices of transmission distribution and supply to regional electricity companies and overall electricity costs for smaller customers.

Privatisation overseas

Before offering an assessment of privatisation in the United Kingdom, it is worth noting that many other states have embarked on similar experiments and that these have embraced a large number of countries of differing size, ideology and level of economic development, including China, Japan, Spain, France, Hong Kong, Jamaica and South Africa. By 1989 it was estimated that worldwide sales of state assets to the private sector exceeded $25 billion or about £14,000 million. With planned privatisations in eastern Europe and elsewhere, this figure is likely to continue rising for much of the 1990s and is expected to exceed £40 billion in Europe alone in the period 1993–5.[3]

Whilst few countries have been as active in this sphere as the United Kingdom, numerous examples exist of privatisation, some of which are outlined below:

● Spain has sold numerous publicly owned businesses, including its majority stake in the vehicle manufacturer Seat, which has been purchased by Volkswagen. In the June 1993 general election, the People's Party – the main opposition party to the ruling Socialists – announced plans for an £11 billion privatisation programme, including the sale of the telephone monopoly Telefonica and the electricity utility Endesa.
● In France and Italy the sale of a number of smaller companies and subsidiaries of state-owned business has occurred, along with the sale of government-owned shares in larger private companies. The new French and Italian governments have plans for

further wide-ranging sales of state assets, as part of an attempt to improve the state of public finances.[4]

- In Holland, state shareholding in a number of companies, including ECM (an airline), have been reduced.
- In Japan, Nippon Telephone and Telegraph was floated on the Tokyo Stock Exchange in 1986 and 1987 and contracting out of public sector services has been popular.
- In Jamaica, a number of companies have been privatised including the Caribbean Cement Company and the National Commercial Bank.

Arguably the most dramatic and exciting experiments in privatisation are currently taking place in eastern Europe, with the demise of communism and the move towards private enterprise. In the newly unified Germany, for example, the federal government has established a special privatisation agency (Treuhand) to oversee and assist in the large scale privatisation of former East German state industries and firms, and other governments (including those in Hungary, Poland and Czechoslovakia) have committed themselves to similar programmes of rolling privatisation. Whilst it is too early to predict whether such schemes will be successful, it is clear that the political and economic obstacles to reform remain formidable, as Russia's President Yeltsin has found. As long as such obstacles exist, western investors are likely to prove cautious and this is certain to delay the privatisation process in most eastern European economies.

Assessment

Measured against some of the UK government's stated objectives, there is little doubt that privatisation has proved successful. Apart from the fact that many other national governments have sought to emulate Britain's approach to asset sales, the privatisation programme appears to have been popular with large sections of the British public – if general election results and share dealings are anything to go by. In 1979 only 7 per cent of adults owned shares in public companies; by 1991 this figure had risen to 25 per cent or 11 million individual shareholders, many of whom bought shares for the first time in the 1980s with the sale of the big public utilities.

This significant growth in the number of ordinary shareholders can be explained in a number of ways. For a start, most stock market flotations were accompanied by extensive and costly advertising campaigns and these helped to raise public awareness and to attract investors (e.g. British Gas's 'Tell Sid' campaign). Added to this, investors in public utilities were often offered special incentives to buy shares in businesses they dealt with on a regular basis (e.g. cheaper telephone bills) or in which some of them worked and therefore had a vested interest. Perhaps most importantly, and with the benefit of hindsight, some privatisation stock appears to have been sold at substantially lower prices than the market would bear and this guaranteed quick profits for people who bought and then sold immediately as prices rose. In the circumstances it is not surprising that many flotations were hugely over-subscribed – a fact which led to criticism that some privatisation stock had been considerably undervalued.

Many shareholders who invested for longer-term capital gains also benefited from under-pricing of share issues and in some cases received free additional shares and other benefits (including annual dividends) by holding on to their investment. An analysis by Gary Cook of the share performance of privatised companies shows that some of the earlier privatisations have produced spectacular long-term gains, though some privatised company shares performed less well.[5] Cable and Wireless Shares, for example, were issued at an average price of 56 pence in the early 1980s and were trading at 588 pence by August 1991. Similarly, BT's initial issue price of 130 pence in 1984/5 had risen to 391 pence by the same date, a threefold increase despite the Stock Market crash in 1987.

Whatever the reason for the growth in share ownership, it is clear that privatisation, along with the sale of council houses, has helped the government to claim that it has encouraged the growth of a 'property owning democracy' in which an increasing number of citizens have a stake in the success of the economy and therefore in the performance of the private sector. That said, it is still the case that the majority of shares in public companies are held by individuals in better paid professional and managerial occupations and that overall the percentage of *all* UK shares owned by individuals has fallen dramatically over the last 30 years. In contrast, the holdings of institutional investors (such as insurance companies and pension funds) has risen rapidly – a fact which not only gives them significant influence over the future of many public companies, but which also suggests that the claim of wider share ownership has to be treated with a degree of caution.[6]

Notwithstanding this latter point, the government's relative success in selling state assets also helped it initially to achieve another one of its objectives – that of reducing the size of the PSBR. From the early 1980s onwards, public expenditure as a percentage of GDP fell substantially – partly as a result of the revenues from the privatisation programme – and by the latter part of the decade the government had a budget surplus (or public sector debt repayment) as revenue exceeded spending. Once again, however, this apparent benefit needs to be seen in context. For a start, much of the improvement in public finances during this period was a result of the government's restraint on public spending, rather than the effects of privatisation, though the receipts clearly helped the government to balance its books. Added to this, by the early 1990s, as the recession took hold, public spending rapidly began to outstrip the amounts raised in revenue, causing a dramatic growth in the size of government borrowing, despite a decade of privatisation receipts. Understandably, some critics have asked whether the sale of valuable state assets has been in vain and has distracted the government from addressing some of the underlying structural weaknesses in the British economy.

With regard to privatisation as a spur to greater organisational efficiency and performance, this is an area in which assessment is particularly problematical. Part of the difficulty arises from the fact that direct comparisons between state and privatised companies are often impossible, since some goods and services are not provided by both the public and private sector simultaneously (e.g. railways). In addition, even where such provision occurs (e.g. the health service), the public sector usually has to pursue a number of non-commercial objectives laid down by politicians and this makes direct comparisons somewhat unfair, particularly if profitability alone is taken as a measure of performance.

One way of approaching some of these 'problems' is to attempt a comparison between the performance of an organisation before privatisation and after it has become part of the private sector – using measures such as relative profitability, productivity, or levels of service. Yet, once again, significant methodological difficulties exist which call into question the validity of many of the conclusions. Industries such as British Gas and British Telecom, for instance, have always been profitable and profits have tended to grow since privatisation; but this could as easily reflect the benefits of monopoly price rises as improvements in efficiency resulting from a change in ownership. Conversely, the recent decline in the fortunes of the once publicly-owned British Steel Corporation could be interpreted as a decline in efficiency and/or performance under privatisation, when in fact a combination of over-capacity in the world steel industry and the impact of the recession have clearly been the main culprits.

Comparisons of productivity can also be misleading and usually fail to take into account the substantial 'economic' costs of privatisation (e.g. large-scale redundancies). Many state industries were substantially restructured prior to flotation in order to attract investors, and the resulting job loss – invariably at the taxpayer's expense – helped many newly privatised businesses to claim substantial productivity gains in their first few years of trading. Perhaps ironically, the greatest improvements in productivity in the period 1984–91 often occurred amongst nationalised industries – such as British Coal and British Rail – whose massive redundancy programmes helped them to outpace the productivity gains of manufacturing industry by anything up to three times, according to Treasury figures. In such circumstances, it would be easy – though probably unreasonable – to conclude that whilst being privatised was good for productivity, it was not as good as not being privatised!

Further complications arise when comparing the performance of privatised companies which have remained monopolies with those which have consistently operated under competitive market conditions. Writing in *The Guardian* on 3 March 1993, Victor Keegan argued that the recent fortunes of companies such as British Steel, Rolls-Royce and Rover had been seriously affected by the sort of violent cyclical disturbances which had previously driven them into the public sector and that this had significantly influenced their attractiveness to private investors. In comparison, businesses facing little effective competition in some areas of the market (e.g. Cable and Wireless, British Airways) and those facing none (e.g. the water companies, British Gas) had invariably performed well for their shareholders; though the price of this success had frequently been paid by customers (in the form of inflated charges) and workers (in the form of redundancy).

Keegan's conclusion, that it is competition rather than ownership which acts as a spur to increased efficiency, is one that is widely held and underlies some of the recent attempts by government and by the regulatory bodies to identify ways of reducing the monopoly power of the privatised public utilities. The proposition is that under a more competitive market structure the commercial pressures of the marketplace force management to seek ways of improving organisational efficiency and performance, for fear of the consequences if they fail to meet the needs of the consumer and the investor. If left to their own devices, the large utilities are unlikely to put themselves to such 'tests' voluntarily, and this approach would presumably find favour with shareholders who have a vested interest in maximising revenue. Paradoxically, in order to improve the position of the consumer, government may be forced to intervene more aggressively and imaginatively in the marketplace, in order to promote greater competition amongst producers and increased choice for the consumer. Such intervention could easily be justified under current competition policy.

COMPETITION POLICY

Whereas privatisation has focused on the balance between public and private provision within the overall economy, UK government competition policy has largely been concerned with regulating market behaviour and in particular with controlling potential abuses of market power by firms acting singly or in concert in specific markets. To achieve these aims, successive British governments have relied mainly on legislation, as well as on a measure of self-regulation and persuasion, and have generally taken a more liberal view of market structures than in the United States, where monopolies have been deemed illegal for over a century. This legislative framework to regulate market activity, and the institutional arrangements established to support it, are considered immediately below.

The legislative framework

Official attempts to control market behaviour through statutory means date back to the late 1940s with the passage of the Monopolies and Restrictive Practices Act 1948. This Act, which established the Monopolies Commission (now the Monopolies and Mergers Commission), empowered it to investigate industries in which any single firm (a unitary monopoly), or a group of firms acting together, could restrict competition by controlling at least one-third of the market. Following such an investigation, the Commission would publish a report which was either factual or advisory and it was then the responsibility of the relevant government department to decide what course of action, if any, to take to remove practices regarded as contrary to the public interest. In the event, the majority of the Commission's recommendations tended to be ignored, though it did have some success in highlighting the extent of monopoly power in the United Kingdom in the early postwar period.

In 1956 investigations into unitary monopolies were separated from those into restrictive practices operated by a group of firms, with the enactment of the Restrictive Trade Practices Act. This Act, which outlawed the widespread custom of manufacturers jointly enforcing the retail prices at which their products could be sold, also required firms to register any form of restrictive agreement that they were operating (e.g. concerning prices, sales, production) with the Registrar of Restrictive Practices. It was the latter's responsibility to bring such agreements before the Restrictive Practices Court and they were automatically deemed 'against the public interest', unless they could be justified in one of a number of ways (e.g. benefiting consumers, employment, exports). Further extensions to the Act in 1968 (to cover 'information agreements') and in 1973 (to cover services) were ultimately consolidated in the Restrictive Practices Act 1976. This new Act vested the responsibility for bringing restrictive practices before the court in the recently established Director General of Fair Trading (see below).

A further extension of legislative control came with the passage of the Monopolies and Mergers Act 1965, which allowed the Monopolies Commission to investigate actual or proposed mergers or acquisitions which looked likely to enhance monopoly power and which involved at that time the take-over of assets in excess of £5m. The aim of this Act was to provide a means of regulating activities which threatened to be contrary to the public interest, by permitting government to decide which mergers and acquisitions should be prohibited and which should be allowed to proceed and, if necessary, under what terms. Additional steps in this direction were taken with the passage of the Fair Trading Act 1973 and the Competition Act 1980, and together these form the basis of current legislation on monopolies and mergers within the United Kingdom.

The main provisions of these two Acts can be summarised as follows:

1 A unitary monopoly exists where at least 25 per cent of a market is controlled by a single buyer or seller and this can be applied to sales at local as well as national level and can include monopolies resulting from nationalisation.
2 Investigations can occur when two related companies (e.g. a parent and a subsidiary) control 25 per cent of a market or when two separate companies operate to restrict competition even without a formal agreement (e.g. tacit collusion).
3 Mergers involving gross assets over £30m. or a market share over 25 per cent can be investigated.
4 Responsibility for overseeing consumer affairs, and competition policy generally, lies with the Director General of Fair Trading (DGFT), operating from the newly created Office of Fair Trading (OFT). The DGFT has the power to make monopoly references to the renamed Monopolies and Mergers Commission (MMC) and to advise the relevant government minister on whether merger proposals should be investigated by the MMC.

In the latter context, it is worth noting that whilst there is no legal obligation on companies to inform OFT of their merger plans, the Companies Act 1989 introduced a formal procedure enabling them to pre-notify the DGFT of merger proposals, in the expectation that such pre-notification would enhance the prospects for rapid clearance in cases which are deemed straightforward.

Whilst the question of market share still remains an important influence on official attitudes to proposed mergers or take-overs, there is no doubt that in recent years increasing attention has focused on anti-competitive practices and under the Competition Act 1980 such practices by individuals or firms – as opposed to whole markets – can be referred to the MMC for investigation. In addition the Act allows the Commission to scrutinise the work of certain public sector agencies and to consider the efficiency and costs of the service they provide and any possible abuses of monopoly power, and similar references can also be made in the case of public utilities which have been privatised (e.g. under the Telecommunication Act 1984, the Gas Act 1986, the Water Industry Act 1991).

Additional statutory control also comes in the form of EC legislation governing activities which have cross-border implications. Article 85 of the Treaty of Rome prohibits agreements between enterprises which result in a restriction or distortion in competition within the Community (e.g. price fixing, market sharing). Article 86 prohibits a dominant firm, or group of firms, from using their market power to exploit consumers; whilst Articles 92–4 prohibit the provision of government subsidies if they distort, or threaten to distort, competition between industries or individual firms.

More recently – under Regulation 4064/89 – which came into force in September 1990, concentrations or mergers which have a 'Community dimension' have become the subject of exclusive jurisdiction by the European Commission. Broadly speaking, this means that mergers involving firms with a combined worldwide turnover of more than 5 billion Ecu are subject to Commission control, provided that the EC turnover of each of at least two companies involved exceeds 250 million Ecu and the companies concerned do not have more than two-thirds of their EC turnover within one and the same Member State. Mergers which do not qualify under the regulation remain, of course, subject to national competition law.

The institutional framework

The formulation and implementation of UK competition policy involves a variety of agencies including the Department of Trade and Industry, the Office of Fair Trading, the Monopolies and Mergers Commission and the Mergers Panel. Of these, the MMC and OFT deserve special attention.

Since its foundation in 1948, the Monopolies and Mergers Commission has remained a statutory body, independent of government both in the conduct of its inquiries and in its conclusions which are published in report form. Funded by the DTI, the Commission has a full-time chairman, and around 35 other part-time members, three of whom are deputy chairmen and all of whom are appointed by the Secretary of State for Trade and Industry. Such appointments normally last for three years at the outset and include individuals drawn from business, the professions, the trade unions and the universities. To support the work of the appointed members, the Commission has a staff of about 100 officials, two-thirds of whom it employs directly, with the remainder being on loan from government departments (especially the DTI) and increasingly from the private sector.

It is important to note that the Commission has no legal power to initiate its own investigations; instead, references – requests for it to carry out particular inquiries – come from either the Secretary of State for Trade and Industry, the Director General of Fair Trading, or from the appropriate regulator in the case of privatised industries and the broadcasting media. Where a possible merger reference is concerned, the initial evaluation of a proposal is made by a panel of civil servants (the Mergers Panel) who consider whether the merger should be referred to the MMC for further consideration. The decision then rests with the Secretary of State, who takes advice from the Director General of Fair Trading before deciding whether the proposal should be investigated or should be allowed to proceed.

Under current legislation, references to the Commission can be made on a number of grounds. As indicated above, these include not only monopoly and merger references but also references concerned with the performance of public sector bodies, privatised industries and with anti-competitive practices by individual firms (i.e. competition references). In addition, the Commission is empowered to consider general references, (involving practices in industry), restrictive labour practices and references under the Broadcasting Act 1990, as well as questions of proposed newspaper mergers, where special provisions apply.

On receipt of a reference, the Commission's chairman appoints a small group of members to carry out the relevant inquiry and to report on whether the company (or companies) concerned is operating – or may be expected to operate – against the public interest. Supported by a team of officials, and in some cases including members appointed to specialist panels (e.g. newspaper, telecommunications, water and electricity), the investigating group gathers a wide range of written and oral evidence from both the party (parties) concerned and from others likely to have an interest in the outcome of the inquiry. In reaching its conclusions, which tend to take several months or more, the group must take into account the 'public interest', as defined under Section 84 of the Fair Trading Act 1973, which stresses the importance of competition, the protection of consumer interests and the need to consider issues related to employment, trade and the overall industrial structure. Whilst in most references, issues relating to competition are the primary concern, the Commission may take wider public interest issues into account and may rule in favour of a proposal on these grounds, even if the measure appears anti-competitive.

The culmination of the Commission's enquiry is its report which, in most cases, is submitted to the Secretary of State for consideration and is normally laid before Parliament, where it may form the basis of a debate or parliamentary questions. In the case of monopoly references judged to be against the public interest, the Secretary of State – with the advice of the DGFT – decides on an appropriate course of action and this could involve an order to prevent or remedy the particular adverse effects identified by the Commission. In the case of merger references, a similar procedure occurs in the event of an adverse judgement by the Commission. The Secretary of State, however, is not bound to accept the Commission's recommendations; nor is he or she able to overrule the conclusion that a merger does not operate, or may be expected not to operate, against the public interest.

As a final comment, it is important to note that at all stages of this multi-stage process, a considerable degree of lobbying occurs by the various interested parties, either in an attempt to influence the outcome of the investigations or the subsequent course of action decided upon. Moreover considerable pressure tends to occur, even before a decision has been taken as to whether or not to make a reference to the MMC. As a number of recent cases have shown, lobbying *against* a reference can represent a key step in justifying a proposed merger. By the same token, lobbying *for* a reference has tended to become an important weapon used by companies wishing to resist an unwelcome take-over, particularly where matters of public interest appear paramount.

Turning more briefly to the Office of Fair Trading, this is a non-ministerial government department headed by a Director General, who is appointed by the Secretary of State for Trade and Industry. Under the Fair Trading Act 1973, the DGFT was given the responsibility of overseeing consumer affairs as well as competition policy and this includes administering various pieces of consumer legislation, including the Consumer Credit Act 1974 and the Estate Agents Act 1979. In carrying out his or her responsibilities in both these areas, the Director General is supported by a team of administrative, legal, economic and accountancy staff and has a Mergers Secretariat to co-ordinate the Office's work in this field.

With regard to competition policy, the OFT's duties are governed primarily by the Fair Trading Act and the Competition Act 1980; in addition, under the Restrictive

Practices Act 1976 the Director General has responsibility for bringing cases of restrictive practices before the Restrictive Practices Court. In the case of monopolies the DGFT has the legislative authority to refer these directly to the MMC, although references can also be made by government ministers without the involvement of the Director General. In contrast, in the case of actual or proposed mergers, references to the Commission come from the Secretary of State on the advice of OFT, usually following a meeting of the Mergers Panel which comprises officials drawn from the Office and from other government departments and chaired by the Director General.

It is worth stressing that only a small percentage of mergers are referred to the MMC for investigation and most of these tend to be on competition grounds. Moreover, in the case of other anti-competitive practices, preliminary discussions between the OFT and the company concerned frequently permit a resolution to the problem, without the need to involve the Commission. Should a reference proceed, the DGFT advises the Secretary of State on what action to take following a report by the MMC and he or she may be asked to seek an undertaking from the party (parties) involved to remedy or prevent any practice deemed to be anti-competitive. Equally, the Director General may be asked to keep under review any undertakings given or orders made in respect of mergers and to advise the Secretary of State if any further action seems necessary.

Some recent cases

Since it was established in 1948, the Monopolies and Mergers Commission has produced over 300 reports, covering a wide range of issues and affecting firms of different sizes in a variety of markets. At the outset most of its enquiries concerned monopolies – reflecting its initial role as the Monopolies Commission. In more recent years, its work has embraced not only mergers, which have tended to be its major pre-occupation, but also nationalised industries and, more recently, the work of the privatised large utilities. Figure 14.2 indicates the distribution of the Commission's work up to 1989.

The examples below provide a good insight into the Commission's role in competition policy and its relationship with the Office of Fair Trading. Students wishing to investigate a particular case in more detail should consult the appropriate report, a full list of which can be obtained from the Commission's library in London.

TI Raleigh Industries 1981

This concerned the supply of bicycles by Raleigh, the recognised market leader. The firm was operating a selective distribution policy and was refusing to supply some multiple retailers, on the grounds that the standard of after-sales service was not of the level desired. The DGFT concluded that the firm's behaviour was anti-competitive and referred the case to the MMC. The MMC agreed with this conclusion and held Raleigh's behaviour to be against the public interest, but recommended that the firm should be able to attach certain conditions in making supplies available to retailers.

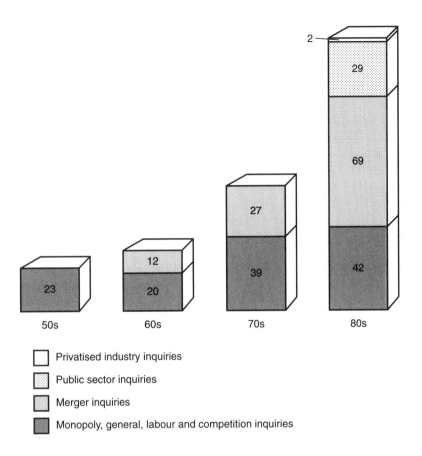

Fig. 14.2 MMC reports published
Source: Monopolies and Mergers Commission

Nestlé 1991

This concerned the claim that the Swiss-based foods group was using its monopoly on the supply of instant coffee in the United Kingdom to keep prices high. Concerned that the company was being slow to pass on to consumers the benefits of a fall in the price of raw coffee beans, the DGFT asked the MMC to investigate the instant coffee market. Following a nine-month investigation, the Commission concluded that whilst the company supplied more than 47 per cent (by volume) of the United Kingdom's instant coffee, there was still effective competition in the market and a wide degree of consumer choice, with more than 200 brands available (in 1989) and the leading supermarkets stocking on average 30 brands. Despite higher levels of profitability than its main competitors, and a tendency for branded coffees generally to respond less quickly than own brands to reductions in input prices, the Commission concluded that Nestlé's monopoly did not operate against the public interest. The DGFT indicated, however, that the operation of the soluble coffee market should be kept under review to ensure that it remained competitive.

British Gas 1992

This involves two parallel references to the Commission by both the President of the Board of Trade (under the terms of the Fair Trading Act) and the Director General of Gas Supply (under the Gas Act 1986). The first asks the Commission to investigate the supply of gas through pipes to both tariff and non-tariff customers; the second to investigate the supply of gas conveyance and gas storage facilities. According to the Office of Fair Trading, very little competition exists in the gas industry, since 17 million domestic household customers have no alternative source of supply and BG's control over storage and transmission facilities inhibits true competition in the industrial market where, theoretically, industrial customers can buy from other suppliers.[7] In the Commission's report published in August 1993, the MMC called for British Gas to lose its monopoly of supply to domestic households by no later than 2002 and for the privatised utility to be split into two separately owned companies.

Midland Bank 1992

This concerned two bids for the Midland Bank, made by Lloyds Bank and the Hong Kong and Shanghai Banking Corporation and illustrates the question of split jurisdiction between the United Kingdom and the EC. Lloyds bid fell within the United Kingdom's jurisdiction and was referred to the MMC as raising potential competition issues – a course of action which caused Lloyds to abandon its proposed merger. In contrast, the HSBC bid was deemed to be of wider concern and was referred to the competition authorities in Brussels. Following clearance by the EC, the HSBC proceeded with its bid and this was accepted by Lloyds shareholders.

Compact Disc Prices 1993

This concerns the claim that record companies and retailers are colluding to exploit consumers by charging excessive prices for CDs. This claim – by the House of Commons Select Committee on National Heritage, following an investigation involving a number of leading rock groups, record labels and main retailers – was relayed to the Office of Fair Trading. At the time of writing, a full investigation of CD prices by the MMC looks inevitable.

GOVERNMENT AND THE LABOUR MARKET

Government involvement in the labour market takes a variety of forms, and its influence on market conditions can be direct or indirect and can operate at different spatial levels. Many of the government initiatives mentioned in Chapter 10, for example, seek to affect employment prospects in the regions or in local economies and thus clearly have labour market implications. Similarly, in its general management of the economy through fiscal and monetary means (see Chapter 4), the government will influence the overall demand for labour which is derived from the demand for the products that labour produces. Some of that demand, of course, will come from the government itself, as a central provider of goods and services and hence a key employer of labour, and its attitude to pay settlements will affect wage levels throughout the public sector. This, in turn, can spill over to the wage bargaining process in the private sector and on occasions may even involve the use of statutory or voluntary restrictions on wage rises that invariably interfere with the operations of the free market (e.g. incomes policies).

Whilst all of these areas would need to be considered in any detailed analysis of labour market policies, in the brief discussion below attention is focused on government initiatives to improve employment prospects and training opportunities for the unemployed, and on the government's efforts to curb the power of the trade unions. Both of these approaches are particularly pertinent to the discussion on how government has sought to improve the efficiency of markets as part of its supply-side approach to economic management – using, in this case, a combination of policy and legislation to achieve its objectives.

Curbing trade union power

As a major force in the labour market, representing the interests of millions of workers, trade unions have been seen as an obstacle to the operation of market forces and as a cause of high wage costs and low labour productivity in the United Kingdom. Consequently, the government's approach since 1979 has been to curb the influence of the trade unions through legislative means, in the belief that a more 'flexible' labour market would develop and that this would benefit businesses seeking to respond to competition and change. To assist further in this direction, the UK government – with the general support of industry – has abolished the Wages Councils (which were set up to protect the interests of the lower-paid) and has refused to participate in the Social Chapter of the Maastricht Treaty (which includes a provision for minimum wage levels across the Community and the principle of equal pay for male and female workers for equal work).

The government's step-by-step approach to reducing the influence of trade unions is demonstrated by the following legislative measures, enacted in the period 1980–90.

The Employment Act 1980

This Act gave employers legal remedies against secondary picketing and most other types of secondary action. It also provided for all new 'closed shops' to be approved by four-fifths of the workforce and for public funds to made available to encourage unions to hold postal ballots.

The Employment Act 1982

This Act further tightened the law on closed shops and outlawed union-labour-only contracts. Employers were given legal remedies against 'political' strikes and trade unions were made liable for damages, if they instigated unlawful industrial action (e.g. 'secondary' action).

The Trade Union Act 1984

This Act sought to strengthen internal union democracy. Unions were required to hold a secret ballot every ten years if they wished to keep a political fund and union executives had to submit themselves for re-election by secret ballot every five years. In addition, pre-strike ballots were required if unions wished to retain their immunity from civil action for damages in the event of a strike.

The Employment Act 1988

This Act strengthened the rights of individual union members. Unions were banned from disciplining members who refused to support strike action; all senior union officials had to be elected by secret ballot; workers were permitted to apply for court orders instructing unions to repudiate industrial action organised without a secret ballot. Moreover strikes in defence of the closed shop lost all legal protection.

The Employment Act 1990

This Act made unions legally liable for 'wildcat' strikes called by shop stewards without a proper ballot. Pre-entry closed shops were banned and so individuals could not be refused a job for not belonging to a trade union prior to appointment.

In its Green Paper *Industrial Relations in the 1990s*, published in mid-1991, the government announced its intentions of continuing the process of reducing union power.[8] Amongst its main proposals were the right for an individual to join the union of his or her choice, the need for seven days' notice of any industrial action and the right for workers not to have union deductions made from their pay without their individual consent, together with a number of measures to provide for greater scrutiny of the administration of trade union affairs (including financial matters). These proposals formed the basis of an Act which was put before Parliament in the 1992/3 session and which is expected to become law before the summer recess in 1993.

Whilst there is no doubt that such legislation has altered the balance of power between employee and employer and has significantly weakened the power of the trade unions, this has been only one influence, and arguably not the most important. Apart from the fact that union membership has fallen significantly over the last decade, weakening their financial position and making them less able to sustain union action, the unions have had to operate in a market severely affected by changes in the economic cycle. Gone are the days when governments aspired to full employment and were willing to use fiscal and monetary means to achieve this objective. In the new climate of substantial and persistent unemployment, the influence of organised labour in the economy has inevitably been reduced and has been replaced, to some degree, by the pursuit of individual self-interest.

Employment policies

Employment policies are targeted specifically at the unemployed and include a wide range of measures designed to assist individuals to prepare themselves for employment and to gain a job. Many of the schemes seek to give a limited amount of work experience and/or to improve vocational training, and in recent years increasing emphasis has been given to the problem of skills shortages in the economy and to matching the needs of labour with the requirements of firms. Additionally, as the following examples illustrate, government has sought to promote the idea of 'self-help' amongst the unemployed and to encourage the growth of self-employment, in the hope that an expanding small firms' sector will generate a large number of jobs, to replace those lost in medium and larger-sized enterprises.

Restart

This scheme was introduced in 1986 and requires anyone drawing unemployment benefit for over six months to see a Restart counsellor in order to try to identify possible routes back into employment (e.g. by joining a Job Club to help with job applications).

Youth Training (YT)

This scheme replaced the Youth Training Scheme in 1990 and is designed to be more flexible than YTS. Under the scheme any person under 18 who is unemployed is guaranteed a YT place (excluding students, young people on ET, overseas nationals and those at school), where the emphasis tends to be on output rather than on the training process. Programmes can be tailored to meet different requirements (including local labour market needs) and can combine training and education, allowing individuals to achieve nationally recognised qualifications (e.g. NVQs).

Employment Training (ET)

This programme was introduced in 1988 as a means of relieving skills shortages and reducing unemployment simultaneously by 'training the workers without jobs for the jobs with workers'. Under the scheme, everyone aged between 18 and 24 who has been unemployed for between six and twelve months is guaranteed a training place on ET or an alternative. The scheme also includes a job interview guarantee to improve an individual's job application and interview techniques.

The New Business Scheme

This scheme is the successor to the Enterprise Allowance Scheme and is designed to help unemployed individuals to establish their own business. Most individuals over the age of 18 who have been unemployed for 6 months or more, have £1,000 to invest in a business in the first 12 months, and agree to work full-time in the enterprise, are eligible for financial support for the first year of operations.

Training credits

This initiative was announced in March 1990 and was designed to expand and improve the training of young people. The credits are issued by TECs (see below) or local education authorities and are redeemable by an employer who is able to provide training of the right standard. Credits may be used to purchase training from a range of providers, including LEA colleges of further education.

Local schemes

These schemes have taken a variety of forms including interest-free loans for individuals wishing to set up a local business (e.g. Sir Thomas Whyte Charity in Leicester), local training awards to stimulate interest amongst local employers or individuals (e.g. Bedfordshire TEC), programmes for groups with specific training needs such as women returners (e.g. Calderdale and Kirklees TEC), and partnerships with local companies to part-fund new training initiatives (e.g. Birmingham TEC's Skills Investment Programme).

As a final comment it is important to note that the government's national training programme is now run by a system of local Training and Enterprise Councils (TECs) which are responsible for providing training schemes for the unemployed and school leavers and for administering various business enterprise schemes, including the New Business Scheme referred to above. Funded by central government and run by a board of directors drawn predominantly from industry, the TECs (known as Local Enterprise Councils in Scotland) have control of the training funds for existing training programmes and have the wider role of encouraging training and enterprise in the economy, including supporting initiatives aimed at promoting local economic development. To this end the TECs are expected to work closely with local employers in both the public and private sector and to improve the quality and effectiveness of training in their locality, by identifying priorities and needs within the local community. The expectation is that funds generated from selling their services to local employers – who require training schemes – will be used to supplement the relatively modest contributions the TECs currently receive from central government.

SYNOPSIS

In market-based economies, governments exercise considerable influence over the structure and functioning of markets, not only through their own economic activities but also through their legislative and policy preferences. Privatisation policy seeks to reduce the role of the state in the workings of the economy through the sale of government-owned assets, in the belief that this will improve the operation of the free market. Competition policy tends to focus on the use of legal and institutional changes to curb the growth of monopoly power and to regulate market behaviour in a manner felt to be conducive to the public interest.

In both these areas the focus of government attention is essentially on the supply side of the economy and this parallels its approach to the operation of the labour market. Through a variety of legislative and administrative changes, the government has sought to create a more 'flexible' market for labour through the introduction of initiatives on training and employment and through its attempts to curb the power of the trade unions through statutory means.

CASE STUDY: THE UK BREWING INDUSTRY*

The 1980s was a difficult decade for the UK beer brewing industry – one of the country's oldest industries. Between 1979 and 1989 annual consumption per head of the population fell from 217 pints to 195 pints and, despite a significant increase in beer prices during this period, real consumer expenditure declined by almost £900 million at 1985 prices. This change in demand was accompanied by a reduction of output of about 7 per cent, and as a consequence of this – and the introduction of new technology – employment on the brewing side of the industry fell by one-third. Nevertheless, as figures produced by the Brewers' Society indicate, by the late 1980s the United Kingdom was still the world's third largest beer producer (after the United States and West Germany), with annual sales of around £10 billion or 2 per cent of the country's gross domestic product.

On the supply side, beer (ale and lager) was being produced by over 200 brewers, operating at local or regional or national level. The vast majority of it was consumed in public houses, clubs and other licensed premises and was predominantly draught beer, with lager constituting about 50 per cent of total consumption. A prominent feature of the industry was the high degree of vertical integration, with the large brewing companies not only brewing beer but also wholesaling and retailing it, the latter through their own public houses (i.e.'tied houses'). The Monopolies and Mergers Commission (MMC), for example, estimated that the brewers owned about 75 per cent of the country's pubs and operated them either as 'managed houses' (where the manager was an employee of the brewing company) or as 'tenanted houses' (where the tenant was self-employed, paid the brewery a rent for the premises and made a living from retailing beer and other products). In both cases, the brewery owning the pub specified which beers could be sold (invariably the brewer's own), where they were to be purchased and – in managed houses – the retail price to be charged. Of the remaining 25 per cent or so 'free houses' – which, in theory, could sell any beers the owner chose – about 50 per cent were 'loan-tied', that is, the owner having borrowed money from one of the brewers at preferential rates of interest, in return for a commitment to sell a guaranteed minimum level of the brewer's own beers.

To the Conservative government of the day – which was keen to promote competition – the structure of the brewing industry was a cause of concern, particularly since in both production and retailing the UK beer market was dominated by just a handful of very large companies. Figures produced by Marketing Intelligence (MINTEL), for instance, showed that by 1988 six national groups effectively controlled the market for all types of beer (Bass, Allied, Whitbread, Grand Metropolitan, Scottish and Newcastle, and Courage) and this market domination applied not only to different types of beer, but also across a range of retail outlets, including the so-called free trade.

Under mounting criticism from consumer groups, the government referred the issue of beer supply to the MMC, which was asked to investigate whether a monopoly existed in relation to the supply of beer for retail sale in the United Kingdom. The Commission's report, entitled *The Supply of Beer*, was published in March 1989.

The MMC's main finding was that, with regard to the supply of beer to the UK retail market, a complex monopoly existed in favour of those large national brewers with tied estates and loan ties. The domination of the market – and the restriction it caused on competition at all levels – served to keep 'the big brewers big and the smaller brewers small' and, in the process, to reduce consumer choice. The Commission argued that, as a result of the lack of competition, the market exhibited a number of unacceptable features, all of which tended to operate to the disadvantage of the consumer. These included:

*This is a revised version of a case study which originally appeared in G. C. Cook, *Business Studies Update 1992*, Hidcote Press, 1992.

- Significant (often excessive) regional variations in the wholesale price of beer.
- Higher prices for lager than could be justified by production costs.
- Annual increases in beer prices substantially above the rate of inflation.
- Restriction on competition in soft drinks, cider and other non-beer products.
- Substantial barriers to entry for smaller brewers and wholesalers of beer.

In order to achieve a more competitive market, the MMC suggested a number of important changes to the present system. Its main recommendations were:

- A ceiling of 2,000 on-licensed premises which any brewer could own (this would have meant the sale of over 20,000 pubs by the national brewers).
- The elimination of loan ties.
- The right of tenants to buy at least one 'guest beer' from a supplier other than the landlord.
- The freedom to buy non-beer products from any source.
- Changes in the contractual relationship between landlord and tenant to provide for a better balance of negotiating power.

Through the introduction of these changes, the Commission believed that beer prices could be reduced, new entrants attracted into the industry and consumer choice widened, whilst at the same time preserving the basic features of beer production and consumption in the United Kingdom.

Despite Lord Young's (Secretary of State for Trade and Industry) initial assertion that he was 'minded to implement the recommendations', a sustained multimillion pound defensive campaign by the large brewers and their representative organisations (e.g. the Brewers' Society) persuaded the government to modify the MMC's proposals. Under an order issued in December 1989 brewers with over 2,000 tied pubs were required:

- By 1 November 1992, to dispose of either their brewery business or the excess of licensed premises or to release the ties on 50 per cent of the excess (in the latter case the brewer was required either to sell the premises or let them at a market rent).
- From 1 May 1990, to allow their tied houses to sell a draught cask-conditioned beer supplied by someone else and to remove the tie relating to non-alcohol beers (NABs), low-alcohol beers (LABs) and non-beer drinks (e.g. wines, spirits, cider).

Under these regulations, brewers were able to avoid the conditions imposed, provided either that they were no longer brewers, or that they no longer held an interest in more than 2,000 licensed premises. In addition, the government agreed to give tenants the protection of the Landlord and Tenant Act, allowing the industry until 1 June 1992 to introduce this new-found security for tenants.

In the period since the government announced its changes to the brewing industry, a number of significant developments have occurred:

1   Scottish and Newcastle – which had just over 2,000 licensed premises – has reduced its estate to 2,000 in order to avoid having to introduce a guest beer.
2   Other large brewers have sold a proportion of their excess of licensed premises (often to regional brewers) and have released the tie on the remainder.
3   Some smaller brewers have given up brewing and have concentrated on other activities, including beer retailing.
4   Grand Metropolitan and Courage have undertaken a pubs-for-breweries swap, with Grand Met transferring its breweries to Elders (who own Courage) and the two companies merging their public houses in a joint venture called 'Inntrepreneur Estates'.
5   A number of breweries have established reciprocal arrangements to supply guest beers.

6   Carlsberg and Tetley (part of Allied) have merged.
7   Some brewers have sold or leased pubs to a new management company which then agrees a 'sweetheart' deal to buy all or most of its beer from the brewer.
8   Some tenants have faced substantial increases in rents and have been forced to sign long leases and to agree to other changes in their contract (e.g. paying for repairs) in order to keep their leases.

The net effect of these and other developments appears to have been to strengthen the grip of the big brewers on the supply of beer. By 1992 it was estimated that the Big Five brewers (formerly six) had increased their market share from 77 per cent (in the late 1980s) to 82 per cent, and critics claimed that the government's hopes of a better deal for the consumer had been frustrated by the actions of the big companies. Commenting on the changes to the industry, the Agriculture Select Committee in its report in May 1993 said that the government's attempts to break the large brewers' stronghold on pubs had been an expensive failure and had helped in some cases to tighten local and regional monopolies. It remains to be seen whether other changes – including recent developments in the wholesale market – will eventually help to reduce the oligopoly power of the large companies and thereby give the consumer a better choice of beer at a reasonable price as the Monopolies and Mergers Commission had envisaged.

NOTES AND REFERENCES

1   Numerous books and articles exist on privatisation within the United Kingdom. An excellent starting point for students wishing to study UK policy is G. C. Cook's *Privatisation in the 1980s and 1990s*, Hidcote Press, 1992.
2   The concept of 'market testing' is increasingly being applied to all parts of the public service, including the civil service, with some civil servants being required to compete with the private sector for their jobs.
3   *The Guardian*, 10 May 1993.
4   In May 1993, France's new centre-right government announced a FFr 300 billion (£35 billion) plan to privatise some of the country's biggest banks and blue-chip companies, including Air France, Credit Lyonnaise, Banque Nationale de Paris, Elf, Total and Aerospatiale (see *The Guardian*, 27 May 1993).
5   Cook, *op. cit.* pp. 23–4.
6   In a sense, however, individuals invest indirectly in shares through their pension funds, insurance policies, unit trusts and bank accounts.
7   In a submission to the MMC, Ofgas has argued for British Gas to be split into as many as 17 separate companies, including 12 competing regional gas suppliers. Other proposals include allowing independent gas suppliers access to the domestic market.
8   See *The Independent*, 25 July 1991.

REVIEW AND DISCUSSION QUESTIONS

1   Explain the paradox that government needs to intervene in the economy to allow markets to work more freely. What forms does this intervention take?

2   Why is privatisation felt to be a spur to greater efficiency in the major utilities? How would you measure such efficiency 'gains'?

3   In what ways is the government's policy on privatisation related to its policy on competition.

4   Examine the basis of the government's attempts to reform the labour market. How far do you think its reforms have been successful?

ASSIGNMENTS

1 You are employed as a research assistant by your local Member of Parliament. As a member of the ruling party, your MP has been asked to address the students at the local further education college on the government's proposals for privatising British Rail. Using a range of contemporary sources, draft a set of notes which he or she can use when addressing a meeting of the students. Your notes should indicate clearly the government's scheme for the privatisation of BR and the rationale underlying it.

2 Imagine you are employed by the Monopolies and Mergers Commission as an information officer. With regard to the case study, draft a press release explaining the basis of the Commission's findings on the UK beer market. Restrict your statement to 400 words maximum.

FURTHER READING

Cook, G.C., *Privatisation in the 1980s and 1990s*, Hidcote Press, 1992.
Price Waterhouse, *Privatisation: Learning the lessons from the UK experience*, 1989.

PART 5

Issues

CHAPTER 15

Corporate responsibility and the environment

Dean Patton

There is a growing body of opinion which holds to the view that businesses have a duty to fulfil objectives that stretch beyond the simple well-being of the organisation to the promotion of greater corporate social responsibility, particularly with regard to the natural environment. This chapter looks at the reasons which lie behind this perspective and speculates on how businesses can be encouraged to accommodate environmental policies into their strategic management techniques.

OBJECTIVES

1 To investigate the involvement that business has with other elements of society.
2 To identify a corporation's primary and secondary stakeholders.
3 To define the meaning of corporate social responsibility and determine the actions that are required in order to be considered socially responsible.
4 To estimate the benefits that are available to business from following a strategy of corporate social responsibility.

INTRODUCTION

Historically, economic development and growth through business activity have been portrayed as beneficial to the well-being of a society and as an important influence on the quality of life of its citizens. Accordingly, organisational practices and processes designed to increase production and consumption have generally been encouraged and welcomed, even though their detrimental effects on the natural environment have been recognised for some time.

Whilst growth invariably remains an objective of governments, its environmental impact has become part of the political agenda at both national and international level, where particular concern has been expressed about the extent of ecological degradation, the rate at which limited resources are being depleted, and the frequency and scale of accidents caused as a result of business practice. Pessimists have argued that in the pursuit of growth many countries may have already surpassed levels of usage of essential resources and sustainable levels of pollution, and have blighted future generations for the sake of present consumption. The more optimistic view is that individual and collective action can give rise to sustainable development which allows for present requirements to be met without compromising the ability of successive generations to meet their own needs. The concept of scarcity and choice is not new, but the way in which human needs are to be met while not seeking to compromise the future is the practical challenge that will face society and therefore all business organisations.

It is the philosophy of sustainable development that many argue is the only way forward for the world economy. The problem of environmental degradation is closely related to the issue of economic growth and both industry and society need to balance environmental protection with economic development. The difficulties in finding an appropriate balance lie not just in the need to reconcile a range of conflicting interests but also in the relative lack of information on the relationship between economic development and its long-term impact on the natural environment.

The seriousness of the situation and its potentially disastrous consequences suggest that an environmental revolution is needed which may require a dramatic change in the behaviour of society and industry as both consumers and producers. Much attention has, of course, been focused on political initiatives, such as the summits at Rio and at Maastricht and both are testimony to the widely accepted view that environmental policy needs to be formalised and co-ordinated at international level if it is to be effective in tackling the salient issues. 'Top-down' approaches, however, can only be part of the overall solution and much depends on the actions of firms and individuals in the marketplace and on their willingness to accept responsibility for their own behaviour and its consequences. In short, concern for the environment needs to be expressed through the actions of a myriad of actors, and for a revolution in environmental responsibility to be successful it must permeate all levels of society.

CORPORATE RESPONSIBILITY AND BUSINESS OBJECTIVES

Whether organisations should undertake greater corporate responsibility is a matter for discussion. The debate revolves around the purpose of business and the knowledge/abilities of those that run the organisation. If the sole responsibility of business is to the provider of capital, then all the resources of such an organisation should be devoted to making profit and any deviation from this by the managers of a firm's resources is contrary to the objectives of the organisation. Furthermore it can be argued that individuals who are given the task of running a business are not equipped to decide what actions are of a corporately responsible nature, and as such should simply operate within the rules established by the elected representatives of the people.[1] This is not, however, a view that is shared by all, and although most commentators would agree that business will not generally behave in a socially responsible manner out of altruism, it is acknowledged that there are benefits to be gained by business by at least making some efforts towards corporate responsibility.[2]

Some entrepreneurs and industrialists such as Roddick, Carey and Clement-Jones have taken the view that a change in business culture may be a more successful strategy. An alternative perception to the environmental responsibility of business has been put forward whereby business can make a contribution by facing up to moral choices concerning profits as opposed to social responsibilities. Roddick has commented that the Body Shop continues to espouse its values in the hope that one day the cosmetics industry will wake up and realise that the potential threat of the Body Shop is not so much economic as simply the threat of good example. The Body Shop, for many, represents an alternative view of how business might be run.

To summarise, there is a range of opinion over how business should interact with its environment and therefore how best to incorporate concern for the environment within corporate policy. However, if the majority of firms do not perceive the sea change necessary in business culture to promote sustainable development then external influences must ensure the protection of wider interests. Indeed one school of thought would argue that such control is the prerogative of elected representatives and that the attempts of business to develop social programmes independent of this would be to undermine the democratic process.

In essence, the stimulus behind organisational developments in the environmental management of business process and practice lies on some continuum between the need to operate in the confines of what is legally acceptable and the desire to create a business that is sustainable.

STAKEHOLDER THEORY

As indicated in Chapter 7, stakeholders are all the groups affected by a corporation's decisions, policies and operations. The number of stakeholders and the variety of interests that a company's management must consider when setting its aims and objectives can make decision-making a complex process. The amount of influence would depend upon the amount of power each group of stakeholders could wield and this will tend to vary over time.

Stakeholder theory suggests that there are a number of groups that a business is answerable to when pursuing stated aims and objectives. Traditionally it has been held that these will be the shareholders, customers and employees of the business – a very narrow definition that concentrates on those groups involved directly with the organisation. This assumption is being called increasingly into question and the incidents at Perrier and more recently Vauxhall have shown the influence that the wider society can bring to business practice.[3] It is often argued that businesses and organisations should be seen as tools for providing goods and services to satisfy the wants and needs of society. Such a definition deals with the purpose of business as a servant to society rather than simply a servant to a narrow set of groups involved directly with the business. This represents an important distinction. Organisations pervade all our lives to an ever-increasing extent; if they are to accept responsibility for the environment, then there is a need to integrate an 'environmental perspective' into the formulation and implementation of corporate policies. This is a necessary step in converting concern into actual behaviour. Accordingly, it could be suggested that the extension of stakeholders to include groups that are not directly involved in the business induces a more corporately responsible business culture.

BUSINESS RESPONSE TO ENVIRONMENTAL CONCERNS

Corporately responsible actions and/or expenditure have a trade-off cost: the alternatives that the money, resources, time and effort could have been put into if they had not been devoted to more socially oriented goals. This is generally known as the idea of 'opportunity cost', the notion that in a world of finite resources, whatever a business chooses to do it does so at the expense of something else, the opportunity forgone. As a result, the timing of returns is a critical factor in the decision-making process. The returns to investment in greater environmental responsibility are, however, likely to be of a long-term nature, an eventuality which may offer little comfort to firms, particularly small businesses that are fighting for survival and need short-term returns. Thus whilst business in general may therefore want to provide a more environmentally responsible policy – particularly if their stakeholders are forcing them to look to the wider concerns of business practice and process – the implementation of such a policy may only occur if it is deemed to be in the best interests of the business: that is, where the resources are used in an optimum way to provide sufficient reward for the hierarchy of stakeholders.

Business culture at present is still driven by short-term profit and the stakeholder that generally holds most influence is the provider of financial capital, the shareholders or owners of the business. In order to develop greater environmental awareness in business it is necessary to change the way organisations prioritise objectives, thus ensuring that the question of sustainable development is brought on to the corporate agenda. The willingness and/or ability of firms to be corporately responsible for their own sake has no precedent in current business practice; organisational policy is far more dependent upon the business environment in which they work. All business, by definition, involves some environmental damage and the best a business can achieve is to clear up its own mess while searching hard for ways to reduce its impact on the environment.

It is, therefore, impossible to expect the type of business environment not to influence the level of corporate responsibility, and the degree of change, the intensity of competition and the scale of complexity will all be factors in the creation of policy, whether this be to increase market share or to reduce the levels of air emissions.

If firms are to provide a greater level of corporate responsibility, does society have to resort to the use of laws and government regulation, or will business perceive the change in societal expectations and decide voluntarily to act more responsibly towards the general environment? The answer probably lies somewhere between the two, but there is obviously a close correlation between the level of legislative impact upon a firm and the degree of perceived impact the organisation would expect to have upon the environment that may lead to the implementation of environmental management systems. Sethi puts forward a threefold typology:[4]

1 *Social obligation* A situation where the organisation uses legal and economic criteria to control corporate behaviour. The strategy is, therefore reactive and dependent upon change instigated by the market or through legislation. The organisation exhibits an exploitative strategy, giving in to environmental concerns only when it can obtain direct benefit. The principal stakeholder in this type of organisation is the shareholder and the pursuit of profit the primary objective.

2 *Social responsibility* This type of organisation tries to go beyond the criteria prescribed by law and instead seeks to conform to the current values and norms of society. The organisation will, therefore, accept responsibility for solving current environmental problems and will attempt to maintain current standards of both the social and physical environment. In order to achieve this the organisation must be accountable to a range of stakeholders and this assumes that profit, although the dominant motive, is not the only one.

3 *Social responsiveness* This organisation exhibits a proactive strategy, actively seeking future social change. The policies of the organisation are followed with a fervent zeal, the business seeks to lead the field in terms of promoting a corporately responsible attitude. It accepts public evaluation of its policies and procedures and is prepared to impinge upon profit to maintain the high profile it has established through its corporately responsible actions.

The concept that business will be purely socially responsible must come from an ethical position, a standpoint which is difficult to envisage within the British economy but one to which the Body Shop must offer a close approximation. Businesses, however, may actually follow a socially responsible approach as a result of the possible advantages it might afford the organisation. In general the hypothesis can be supported that a better society produces a better environment for business. Further, it often makes sound investment sense, leading to increases in market share, a lowering of costs through energy and material savings and finally an improvement in the 'corporate image'.[5] Provision for responsible behaviour is therefore financially good for the business. A further possible impetus for implementing environmental management systems could come from political rather than economic sources. In simple terms, organisations that instigate their own environmental policies and/or regulations tend to face a reduced threat from external regulatory bodies and this improves company image while reducing possible checks upon corporate practices and processes.

In essence, the conclusions reached highlight the fact that organisations will not normally pursue a proactive role in the development of corporately responsible policies. The initial short-run costs are prohibitive when the payback is generally assumed to be over the long term. What might be required is a re-education of those involved in the decision-making process so that they understand the benefit of a longer-term view and can identify policies that offer a sustainable competitive advantage over time. This is true for all strategy and is therefore applicable to the implementation of environmental policies.

THE INTERACTION OF BUSINESS AND SOCIETY

In assuming that business needs to be more aware of its social consequences, society as a whole is expressing a dissatisfaction with existing performance. The method by which a group or individual may come to this decision could be very subjective, based upon value judgements and experience. To add weight to any argument there needs to be a more scientific measurement of performance that is based upon criteria other than those that can be easily assigned a monetary value.

Cost/benefit analysis is one technique which attempts to set out and evaluate the social cost and benefits of an action. The essential difference between cost/benefit analysis and ordinary investment appraisal methods used by firms is the stress on the social costs and benefits, and such an approach can prove problematical. Two specific difficulties arise:

1 The measurement of physical units such as improvements or otherwise in the quality of life.
2 The complexity involved in reducing all costs and benefits to some common unit of account in order to offer a degree of comparison. Since the unit of account most commonly used is money, this means that values must be attached to environmental degradation, resource usage and in some instances human life.

The main reasons why it is important to place a monetary valuation on environmental gains and losses is that it offers a measurement of society's preference. Placing a value upon environmental degradation allows ordinal ranking of preferences between the desire to have goods and services against the desire to maintain the environment and reduce the use of scarce resources. Monetary values offer a direct and more tangible comparison. Cost/benefit analysis, therefore, allows careful itemisation of all relevant classes of costs and benefits, the exclusion of irrelevant transfer payments, quantification of what can reasonably be quantified and a full specification of the complete set of alternatives to the action under consideration. This is said to provide a sounder basis for the decision and, most importantly, to permit an estimate of the implicit money values that must be attached to particular non-monetary benefits and costs in order to justify a particular action. Thus cost/benefit analysis can be viewed as a means of making the best possible information available to the decision-makers.

METHODS OF ENCOURAGING ENVIRONMENTAL CONCERN WITHIN BUSINESS

The quality of the existing environment and improvements in it would be regarded by economists as a form of public good. This is a good for which the principle of exclusion does not apply; it can be jointly consumed by many individuals simultaneously, at no additional cost and with no reduction in the quality or quantity of the public good consumed by any citizen.

The fact that the principle of exclusion does not apply creates the 'free-rider' problem because some groups will believe that others will take on the burden of paying for the public good: in this case the extra cost incurred to improve the quality of the environment. Historically, the government has taken charge of public goods (e.g. the fire and police services or the provision of street lighting) in order to ensure that they are provided and not left to the vagaries of the market. Recent events suggest, however, that state intervention in the future cannot be taken for granted, particularly in areas where market solutions appear possible.

Government intervention

Direct action by government within the business sector has not led to improved corporate responsibility. Nationalised industries have not been the bastions of the ecological environment and in some instances in the United Kingdom (e.g. the 'tall stacks' policy) have appeared to disregard the environmental degradation that they created. Indirect action through regulation or legislation may be more effective, but this is not in keeping with the general policy of *laissez-faire* which has operated in the United Kingdom under the current Conservative government.

Furthermore there are a number of dangers associated with a reliance solely upon a regulatory system as a means of control. Laws tend to be reactive and there may be significant differences between the letter and spirit of the law. Industry may hold a monopoly of expertise, making government regulation ineffective. Finally, transnational issues, (e.g. leaks from nuclear power stations, global warming, acid rain) are far too multifarious and intricate to resolve through regulation. This is not to say that the legal system is always ineffectual, but simply that it is not a precise means of control, often providing the unscrupulous with much scope to act as they please.

Indeed, regulation has become an increasingly complex tool to control business practice. The globalisation of business means that organisations are having to deal with different legislative controls and requirements in different countries. In some instances, company policies change from country to country to meet the lowest standards possible. The Bhopal tragedy illustrated how the multinational organisation Union Carbide was willing to accept lower standards of safety in a Third World plant than would have been deemed appropriate for a domestic plant. It pursued a policy of satisfying the law or regulatory frameworks of the individual host country, and similar arguments can be made for the many shipping organisations registering under flags of convenience which allow cost reductions.

Alternatively, to sell in all markets may require working to the highest common denominator. A current example is the enforced practice in Germany whereby responsibility for recycling 80 per cent of packaging is placed with retailers and manufacturers. Companies wishing to export to Germany must take action to facilitate conformity with this legislation or risk damaging their competitive position within that market. Conforming to the stringent requirements of certain markets may improve the competitive position of firms in other markets, as the recent experience of AEG and VW would suggest.

Proposed or possible regulation may also persuade organisations to consider the impact of their activities, particularly if in future more stringent legislation looks likely as governments accept the principle of the polluter paying for any environmental damage caused. To judge by recent American experience, it is possible that retrospective action may be taken, with companies penalised for decisions taken years previously.[6]

For some organisations legal compliance is an end itself, for others regulations form a minimum standard of behaviour. The culture of the organisation, within obvious cost constraints, will determine the level of behaviour above the law. For the organisation that sees its responsibilities over and above the law, there may be some additional benefits. Those organisations that develop environmentally sensitive processes and systems first will have greater experience than those slower to react who may find themselves overtaken by the quickening rate of new legislation. There is, however, a danger that organisations view the use of environmental management tools as a one-off measure. Like any business plan, such a process must be regularly reviewed in order to take account of our increasing knowledge of this subject and the changing needs of the organisation.

To summarise, legislation and regulation do have an important role to play in improving the environmental performance of business overall; this is most evident when governments have the relevant information concerning business practice and process. Frequently, however, business possesses the necessary information and the government has to incur a significant resource cost to acquire the relevant knowledge, suggesting that other tools of control are necessary to instil within business the required corporate responsibility. A strong argument can be made for providing greater information concerning products to the consumer, thereby offering the opportunity to individuals to make more informed decisions about which products to consume. Such a policy would reduce the level of government involvement and help to educate individuals as to the part they play in creating environmental hazards and damage.

Market mechanisms

The increased level of environmental awareness by the population – owing to the easier availability of information – has already led to more informed choices being made by various stakeholder groups that interact with business.[7] Customers, suppliers, employees and investors are all more aware of their responsibilities to the environment, and there are various ways in which their considered decisions can influence the overall objectives of business and ensure that the organisation is corporately responsible for its actions.

Increasingly, discerning consumers offer a powerful inducement to firms and despite the lack of perfect information some product-switching is already occurring. Firms seeking to maintain current market share or looking for new opportunities, must be aware of these changes. The European Community's new Eco-label should enter the shops in 1993. The label identifies the products which EC Commissioners believe to have the least impact upon the environment in their particular class. The Blue Angel – probably the best established Eco-labelling scheme – already operates successfully in Germany. Established in 1978 it now has over 3,600 products carrying the label and claims to be known in at least 80 per cent of households. Business, although initially sceptical of the scheme, is now an active supporter, viewing the label as an essential tool both to defend markets and to win new market share. The new Eco-label is expected to follow on from the success of the Blue Angel and establish a minimum environmental performance level in the market. Its effect will be felt throughout the supply chain, becoming a specification laid down by government departments and business alike. Most importantly, businesses that wish to apply for the label will have to provide proof of environmental performance from their suppliers to qualify. In this way products will be evaluated using life-cycle analysis, a cradle-to-grave assessment of a product's impact upon the environment.

Further emphasis upon the environment has been created with the instigation of the British Standard 7750 in Environmental Management systems. The new standard has followed the same basic approach of BS 5750 for Quality Systems and it is expected that organisations operating to BS 5750 will be able to extend their management systems to conform to BS 7750, although it is not a prerequisite. BS 7750 will, therefore, continue to emphasise business responsibility to the environment and it is likely that, as with BS 5750, organisations which fail or do not attempt registration will encounter a more difficult business environment. This theme is highlighted by the actions of the Body Shop which demanded that Peter Lane, the organisation chosen to distribute its stock, had satisfactorily to pass an environmental audit before being given the contract. This point is further supported by the actions of B&Q, a UK chain of hardware stores, whose recognition of voter concerns, in the Green Party vote in the 1989 Euro elections, provided the stimulus to act. The company audited not only its own products but those of its suppliers. These audits were the precursor of implemented 'environmental' policies, including the delisting of a large peat supplier who refused to desist from sourcing from Sites of Special Scientific Interest. It seems safe to argue that business will in future face greater pressures to meet new demands from the more discerning customer, be they individuals or other businesses.

It is interesting to note that premiums paid to insurance companies have increased in line with losses incurred for environmental damage caused by normal business activity. In the same way that householders who can demonstrate increased security measures in their homes are rewarded with lower premiums, companies which demonstrate evidence of environmental safeguards may also reap such rewards. More critically, failure to demonstrate extensive environmental management systems may lead to a refusal to offer insurance cover or loans. Similarly, lending institutions may not wish to be associated with 'poorly safeguarded' organisations. In the United States, a further development in legislation means that lending institutions may be held liable for environmental damage caused by plant held as collateral for loans. As a result there has been a significant tightening in the flow of funds to polluting industries such as scrap merchants, businesses dealing with hazard waste, pulp and paper mills and petrol filling stations. Similar trends are evident in the United Kingdom, where banks have become increasingly careful about loans made to small business that have any conceivable environmental risk potential. Therefore, finance that is already limited is being further reduced not because of the viability of the business but because of the environmental liability hanging over them. Thus, while the United Kingdom is yet to see this type of legislation, banks and other lending institutions are already very aware of their environmental responsibilities and this is increasingly encapsulated in their lending policies.

External pressure

There has been a considerable amount of pressure from external groups upon business; these have ranged from *ad hoc* groups formed in local communities to large transnational organisations like Greenpeace. The size and scale of the groups may be diverse but their objectives are similar; to use whatever power they have at their disposal to influence the decision-making process and there have been a number of notable successes. For many groups, however, this does not go far enough and accordingly the calls for increased democratisation of the decision-making process to include wider stakeholder groups are becoming more frequent and vociferous.

Effective democratisation assumes greater stakeholder access with attendant changes in structure and culture; the depth of access and the magnitude of change depends upon the degree to which democratisation is embraced. Participatory democracy may be the most effective form, if yet a largely untested philosophy; however, the success of such a scheme will require not only involvement in the decision making processes, but also access to information and expert knowledge which provide the basis for effective power and influence. Significantly, this approach has still to be culturally accepted by the majority of businesses in the United Kingdom.

A good example of this need for access to knowledge and expertise is the two environmental audits carried out on IBM in 1992.[8] The first was one commissioned by IBM and conducted by SustainAbility, an external environmental consultancy. The fact that this independent report was published unedited and in full is a factor that is to be applauded and should represent an example of good practice. However, an internal and parallel report was conducted by IBM which has remained unpublished, but which cast doubts over the validity of the independent report. The reason offered by IBM for the dual report is that SustainAbility was asked only to investigate the company's management processes. IBM did not consider it qualified to judge the company's technical environmental record and therefore opted to conduct its own internal investigation in this area.

Finally, there are the dangers of companies burying their heads in the sand in the hope that the 'new environmentalism' is the latest management fad. The costs, however, of a late response and the possible threat of legal action as well as punitive fines could be critical for those who are slow to develop environmentally sensitive policies. Organisations must realise that the stakes are high and that the costs of getting it wrong (e.g. a serious incident causing environmental damage) are significant in terms of company image, fines, lost production, lost sales, insurance premiums and customer loyalty.

Self-regulation

As noted previously, industry is frequently the holder of the information and expertise required for the effective and efficient implementation of regulation. To regulate, the government has to acquire that information, an expensive process. However, if industry were to self-regulate and adopt environmental controls without waiting for the government, then this process of information gathering is avoided. There are obvious drawbacks to this type of approach. Mintzberg has pointed out that often the implementation of self-regulation is a response by business to attempt to offset on-coming regulation. This has two very positive outcomes for the business sector. First, it offers credibility with society that as a sector it has the interests of the environment in mind when conducting business. Secondly, it provides a convenient smoke screen for practices which may be regarded as dubious by an external body. It is, therefore, inherent in the idea of self-regulation that the organisation can be trusted to fulfil the environmental requirements of the rest of society.

Growing public awareness of the environmental issues and the subsequent regulation of business activities have demonstrated that society is not prepared to allow business to be conducted without restriction or without consideration of its impact upon the environment. The assumption that organisations will abide by the rules and norms of their society has been seen to be misplaced. If society is to trust managers of businesses, it must ask by whose social norms they are controlling their organisations. Evidence from any daily newspaper would indicate that a large number of organisations cannot be trusted, completely. Governments are, therefore, likely to be forced to continue to monitor self-regulatory systems and to retain the power to enforce environmental objectives.

THE BENEFITS TO BUSINESS FROM THE IMPLEMENTATION OF ENVIRONMENTAL POLICIES

The previous section has indicated that industry is being driven to develop more environmentally friendly policies. The implication is that organisations would revert back to previous policies, if the forces driving environmentalism were negated. This assumption fails to take account of the benefits that the implementation of corporately responsible policies has brought some organisations. The drive for greater corporate responsibility has emanated from North America where companies are increasingly expected to draw up their own plans for meeting environmental obligations, putting a premium on having accurate knowledge about their own performance. Business strategists within North America are convinced that the 1990s will see environmentalism at the cutting edge of social reform and therefore one of the most important areas for business. This is supported by the commitment from some of the larger more successful companies of the 1980s. Thus:

- ICI increased its environmental spending from £50m. in 1985 to approximately £125m. in 1990 and has a planned expenditure of £200m. a year up to 1995, more than 20 per cent of the group's total expenditure.
- Du Pont is pulling out of a $750m. a year business because it may harm the earth's atmosphere.
- McDonald's, which produces vast amounts of paper and plastic waste annually, has become a crusading proponent of recycling, and aims to become one of America's leading educators about environmental issues.
- 3M is investing in a myriad of pollution controls for its manufacturing facilities, beyond that which the law requires.
- Procter & Gamble is moving to cast all its products in an environmental light.
- B&Q, British Telecom, IBM UK, and Scott have all sought to reduce the environmental impact of the goods and services they buy via pressure exerted on the supply chain.
- Mobil has produced a 16-page report for its shareholders, signed by the chairman, which states that protecting the environment is one of the important issues of the day facing business and goes on to identify the environment as a primary concern facing the company and industry in the years ahead.

Whilst the commitment of industry is being developed, many UK companies appear to be lagging behind. There needs to be an increase in information and training, not simply about the environmental consequences, but also concerning the benefits that are being obtained by organisations that are adopting greater corporate responsibility.

Efficiency of factor inputs

Business strategists as well as organisations have already generated a considerable amount of pro-environmental jargon; PPP, (Pollution Prevention Pays), WOW (Wipe Out Waste) and WRAP (Waste Reduction Always Pays) are some of the better-known acronyms. The obvious message is that more efficient use of materials and energy will reduce cost, provide a positive effect on the company's accounts and improve the 'bottom line'. 3M, for example, announced savings of approximately £200 million in 1986 mainly due to energy and material cost reductions under its PPP policy. Barclays Bank has had an energy efficiency audit operating since 1979, during which time it estimates it has saved the bank £11m. The Body Shop also commissioned an energy audit, where savings of £23,000 per annum were realised immediately through 'small investments' and further potential savings of £28,700 per annum were also identified as available with further investment. The message that businesses are beginning to receive is that too much attention has been extended to labour and capital costs at the expense of material and energy costs and the new environmental management systems are highlighting this issue.

Improved market image

The image that organisations portray to the rest of society is increasingly important, owing to the development of rapid information flows. Creating this image can be expensive and resources may be wasted as a result of a careless action or remark. A good example of this was the claim by Gerald Ratner that the jewellery sold in his stores was 'crap', a comment which was quickly communicated through the media. As a result Ratner lost his position on the board of directors and the share value of the company went into freefall. The image of quality jewellery at a cheap price was lost and it seems likely that consumers will remain sceptical for some time. In a similar vein a chance remark by a BP representative concerning the oil spillage from the *Braer* tanker in the Shetlands has been used in an advertising campaign by Greenpeace to illustrate the lack of responsibility shown by large corporations. BP has recently spent an undisclosed sum promoting and implementing a green strategy in order to project the image of an organisation that cares. It can be assumed that the Greenpeace advert will have at the very least reduced the effectiveness of this campaign.

Given the current climate of public opinion, organisations which are seen to be improving their levels of corporate responsibility and are able to communicate this to the consumer are likely to improve their market share and to develop customer loyalty (e.g. Varta's development of technology which reduced the heavy metal content of its consumer batteries). The image that a company portrays could also affect the quality of human resources available. Increasingly employees are taking into account an organisation's record on corporate responsibility when deciding upon future employment.

The claims of companies must, however, be supported by actions that can be readily communicated and understood by the consumer. New initiatives such as the Eco-label and BS 7750 will assist in providing clear statements of intent that provide better information for a more informed purchase.

Providing new market niches

The clear message from the market is that there is a growing number of consumers who are prepared to be more discerning about the type of goods they buy and, by doing so, taking into account the impact their purchases have upon the environment. As a result, a number of market niches have developed and these have proved attractive to business, given that consumers are prepared to pay extra for a product that is less harmful to the environment. In many cases this means that margins can be increased, a factor which is contrary to current market trends.

In addition to this, there are other market opportunities that result from the need to take action to improve the degree of corporate responsibility. Levels of environmental expenditure are increasing, as the ICI example indicates, and this extra expenditure must be generating revenue for those organisations providing the right type of product or service. There are significant market opportunities available, for example, in pollution reduction, energy saving and waste control technologies, and if it is assumed that the push towards more sustainable development will continue, then there will be further opportunities for firms in the field of product and process design.

Proactive legislative compliance

The legislative framework within which businesses operate involves a growing number of regulatory bodies. As indicated in previous chapters, legislation from the UK government is supported and often surpassed by EC directives, and organisations seeking to operate successfully in the Single Market must demonstrate compliance if they wish to compete. Regulations which were once confined to product and process now often extend to the way in which decisions are made within organisations and it seems more likely that the recent Cadbury report on corporate governance has started a process of increased democratisation of the decision-making process which businesses will have difficulty in preventing. Past organisational performance on environmental issues has not instilled confidence and trust, and it is unlikely that mere rhetoric will calm the calls for more accountability. In future it seems more likely that the demand will be for a socially responsive organisation that accepts full public evaluation of its activities and makes itself accountable to all interested parties; in short, an organisation which is proactive in developing greater corporate responsibility and which is committed in practice as well as in principle to the concept of sustainable development.

Corporate responsibility without intervention?

Many businesses at present appear to be taking up the challenge of corporate responsibility, if only out of the slow realisation that it is in their own interest – that is, to avoid regulation, to increase market share and/or to reduce costs. In its purest form, corporate responsibility could be supported for its own sake as representing a noble way for corporations to behave and such a stance can be closely associated with a business attitude of social responsiveness. Since this approach can conflict with a key objective of business – namely, profit maximisation – the question is whether the two are mutually exclusive or if a way can be found to combine profitability and corporate responsibility. Many observers believe that a business environment which is allowed to operate without government intervention seems unlikely to engender corporately responsible organisations. By the same token, legislation on its own cannot be expected to oversee all aspects of business, including the impact that firms have on the natural environment.

Arguably what is required is that a tone is set, through both legislation and societal norms and values, that provides clear signals to businesses; it will then be up to organisations to interpret these signals and to transmit them into policies which provide for the wants of society and at the same time satisfy the requirements of legislation. In this way corporate responsibility will tend to be seen as essential to competitive advantage and will become an integral part of the strategic management process. In short, the pursuit of a philosophy of sustainable development can be instilled into business practice without the excessive use of intervention that so often impinges upon the entrepreneurial flair of organisations. Businesses, however, need to play their part.

SYNOPSIS

Organisational change is one of the most important themes to have come out of the study of business policy in the 1980s and the failure of business, especially in the United Kingdom, to respond to increasingly dynamic and complex markets is often given as a reason for the country's poor industrial performance and its relatively low record of economic growth. One of the most significant areas of change in recent years has been the growing demand for businesses to behave in a socially responsible manner and this has become an important aspect of the strategic decision-making process in a growing number of organisations. Corporate social responsibility can be defined as the obligation a business has to seek socially beneficial results along with the economically beneficial results from its actions. This obligation may be imposed on firms by outside pressures or it may result from decisions within the organisation. Either way, it seems likely that businesses which accept it will find that the benefits ultimately outweigh the costs.

CASE STUDY: THE *BRAER* OIL TANKER DISASTER

Introduction

The *Braer* was built by Oshima Shipbuilding in Nagasaki in 1975; it was a single-engined vessel, 241.5 m long, with a dead weight of 89,730 tons. It was registered with the Norwegian classification society Det Norske Veritas (DNV) in 1985 and according to that particular institution had an exceptional record. The ship was required to undergo rigorous surveys every five years and an annual inspection; the last periodic survey was carried out in July 1989 whilst the last annual inspection occurred in May 1992. Records show that neither of these inspections found anything that could improve seaworthiness and DNV regarded the *Braer* as a very good ship. The vessel itself had not previously been involved in a shipping casualty and Skuld Protection and Indemnity, the insurers of the ship, stated that in their opinion it was a sound ship managed by a sound and responsible company.

The emergency began at about 5.30 a.m. on 5 January 1993 when the tanker, carrying 85,000 tons of light crude oil from Norway to Quebec was passing through the 22-mile gap between

Shetland and the Fair Isle. The storm force seas had somehow managed to drive seawater into the fuel tank and by 6 a.m. the *Braer* was without power and drifting sideways towards Shetland. The first tug was dispatched from Lerwick harbour, 30 miles from the incident, at approximately 7.30 a.m., a crucial delay of at least 90 minutes from the time the engines failed. Despite the efforts of the salvage crews, the tanker hit the rocks at 11.30 a.m.; by 3 p.m. there were already reports of large oil slicks, with its subsequent effects on wildlife in the area.

Consequences of the oil spillage

The environmental impact of the wrecked *Braer* oil tanker near Sumburgh Head in Shetland was described by the World Wide Fund for Nature as 'potentially catastrophic'. The site of the disaster is a region of high cliffs and sheltered coves teeming with wildlife all year round. Sumburgh Head was due to be designated a special protection area under the European Community birds directive. The oil coating the rocks settled on plants and fish in the intertidal zone and moved through the food chain, poisoning the feeding sea birds and threatening both the otter and seal population which have a stronghold in the area. A spokesperson for the Wildfowl and Wetlands Trust stated that they were particularly worried about the spillage in light of a previous incident in 1979 when the *Esso Bernicia* spilled 1,174 tonnes of fuel oil at Sullem Voe. This spillage had been fatal for all the ducks in the immediate area and the general population declined 25 to 30 per cent.

While many Shetlanders were dismayed by the threat to the birds and sealife caused by the pollution, their main concern was the economic threat to the fishing and fish farming industries. In spite of oil wealth, Shetland still earned much of its living from fish. Almost a third of the islands' 10,000 strong labour force worked in the fish industry, including fishermen, fish processors and salmon farmers. A spokesperson for the Shetlands Fishermen Association stated that 'the Shetlands were more dependent on fish than any other part of the EC'. Without fishing the future of the community appeared doubtful. The Shetland salmon industry alone was worth approximately £35m. of the £80m. turnover of the islands' fishing industry. Although the ship's cargo was largely harmless to fish because the oil floats upon the surface, the chemical dispersants employed against the oil slick produce an oily emulsion that could kill fish as it sinks to the sea bed. The combination of dispersant and oil was known to be more toxic than oil alone.

Historical precedent

The *Braer* disaster is simply the last in a long line of tankers that have come to grief on the seas. In 1967 the *Torrey Canyon* disaster released 30,000 tons of oil in a 35-mile-long slick off Cornwall. It was the first and remains the largest oil disaster in the United Kingdom. At the time one senior government official claimed that it had created 'an oil pollution problem of unparalleled magnitude'. There has been a regular stream of similar occurrences since this date:

1970	*Pacific Glory*, 3,500 tons of oil
1978	*Eleni V*, 5,000 tons of oil
	Amoco Cadiz, 223,000 tons of oil
1979	*Atlantic Empress* and *Aegean Captain*, 1.2m. barrels of oil
1987	*Exxon Valdez* 240,000 barrels of oil
1990	*American Trader*, 7,600 barrels of oil
1992	*Aegean Sea*, 24m. gallons of oil

From July 1993, under anti-pollution rules negotiated by the International Maritime Organisation, all new tankers must be constructed with a double-skinned hull. In two years' time existing vessels will have to meet the more stringent standards, which in practice means sending many older ships to the scrapyard because they will not be worth the cost of rebuilding. However, as a spokesperson for the IMO has indicated, ships built in the 1970s are now regarded as technically out of date, but, in the present climate, would be retained to meet the demand for oil. With 136 governments involved and a world tanker fleet of 2,900 ships, it was accepted that change could not happen overnight. In the meanwhile, the world's apparently insatiable demand for oil inevitably carries with it increased risk of environmental pollution.

The issues of corporate responsibility

The ship's course

Environmental experts initially found it difficult to understand why the captain of the *Braer* had followed a course that took it so close to the Shetland coastline. The waters around the Shetland Isles are classified as 'an area to be avoided' and this was confirmed by the International Maritime Organisation. Furthermore, International Collision Regulations say a 10-mile protection zone is necessary to avoid the risk of oil pollution and severe damage to the environment and the economy of Shetland. The regulations stipulate that all shipping of more than 5,000 gross tons should avoid the area. The main reason offered for the presence of the *Braer* in the area was the extreme bad weather, which may have led the captain to put the safety of the crew before any risk to the environment. Weather forecasts can, however, be brought into the equation, since the vast majority of crews rely on three-day forecasts rather than the longer 10-day forecasts that are available. In effect the dependence on the shorter prediction means that the crew is committed to a route as soon as a vessel leaves port. Paul Roberts, a representative of Oceanroutes, which advises the shipping industry on weather conditions along prime trading routes stated that oil tankers did not have standard routes: 'From Norway it is fairly natural for tankers to go around the top of Britain. If conditions are horrendous we might recommend the Channel, but extra miles means extra days means lots of bucks.'

Safety standards and flags of convenience

There has been a gradual acceleration over the years in owners cutting costs by registering ships under overseas 'flags of convenience'. At a time of worldwide recession, owners burdened by ageing fleets have adopted the lower safety standards of countries such as Cyprus, Panama and Liberia, whose flag was carried by the *Braer*. The Merchant Navy Officers union, NUMAST, said it had warned the government about the dangers of allowing so-called coffin ships to carry dangerous goods around Britain's coast. More than 60 per cent of foreign ships checked in British ports 1991 were found to have defects. The union's general secretary, John Newman, said a disaster was inevitable given the increasing amounts of hazardous cargoes being carried by vessels with 'safety records up to 100 times worse than British vessels'.

The structure of the ship's hull

US legislation, in response to the *Exxon Valdez* disaster, has concentrated on the introduction over the next 15 years of double-hulled tankers and the phasing out of the older oil carriers with a single-skinned hull. This stance has been incorporated into new international law and all new tankers must be constructed using the double-hull technique. This belated response hides a number of issues. First, this legislation does not indicate what should happen to the vessels built before 1993 but which are still very much in use. Secondly, it has been cogently argued by Joe Nichols, technical manager at the International Tanker Owners Pollution Federation, that the double-hull would not necessarily have prevented either the *Braer* or the *Exxon Valdez* disaster. Moreover the double-hull design itself may cause problems through the build-up of gasses and new so-called mid-deck designs may yet prove superior. Legislation may not be sufficiently flexible to accommodate all the necessary safety requirements.

The level and quality of training offered to the crew

The concentration upon the technical and safety requirements of the tanker has meant that an important issue has been overlooked. Approximately 80 per cent of oil spills are caused by human error, which indicates an urgent need to harmonise training procedures throughout the seafaring world. Although tanker crew members must have internationally recognised certificates of training, it is notoriously difficult to obtain uniformity within the awarding bodies. Possibly of more concern is the incidence of such certificates being purchased from markets in the Far East. According to a director of the International Shipping Federation 'there are indications that the overall world training standards have diminished'.

The depressed costs of chartering vessels

Training problems may be a symptom of the very low charter rates for oil tankers caused by an over-capacity in the industry. A company that invests in an up-to-date tanker with the necessary pollution control measures would need to make approximately $60,000 a day on charter rates. The rate at present due to the hard bargaining of oil companies is close to $15,000 a day. At present, therefore, charterers are not prepared to pay for quality shipping and indirectly sponsor the continuation of substandard shipping.

The delayed request for assistance

Comparison has been made between the *Braer* and the *Amoco Cadiz* (1978) disasters given the critical delay by the *Braer*'s captain in acknowledging the fact that the tanker was in extreme danger and in need of salvage under Lloyds 'open form'. The *Braer*'s captain may have felt in no imminent danger as the ship was lying roughly midway between the islands when the power failed, and he may have assumed that the tanker had a good chance of making it through the channel to relative safety. With the benefit of hindsight, it is difficult to understand how someone in such a position could make a rational decision based upon some form of cost/benefit analysis, given that the intangible costs of ecological and environmental damage and the secondary effects of lost income and quality of life would at the time be unquantifiable.

Conclusion

The *Braer* built in 1975 is owned by B & H Ship Management of New York. The pollution protection of the company is in keeping with other businesses with interests in shipping: B & H has contributed to a 'protection and indemnity' club under the management of Skuld in Oslo. These clubs are groups of like-minded shipowners which were formed at the turn of the century to provide for areas not covered by conventional policies. The cover they offer is compulsory for ships carrying 2,000 tonnes or more of crude oil to or from UK ports. If this is not enough, the state-supported International Oil Pollution Compensation Fund, administered by the International Maritime Organisation, will come into force providing a ceiling of £662 per tonne of ship. In the case of the *Braer* this would be £54.63m. Both schemes come under UK law. In effect, shipowners become liable for damage caused by the spillage itself, for the clean-up costs, and any damage caused by the clean-up measures. Skuld provides a standard $500m.-worth of coverage which in this case was never going to be enough once the full scale of the disaster was known, and this has led to renewed calls for raising minimum levels of compensation paid on oil spills. These calls have been consistently thwarted by tanker owners who face rising premiums and other costs. It is widely accepted that the compensation levels are set too low now and that delays in paying out compensation are far too long.

NOTES AND REFERENCES

1 Freidman, M., 'The social responsibility of business is to increase its profits', *New York Times Magazine*, 13 September 1970, pp. 7–13.
2 Mintzberg, H., 'Who should control the organisation', *California Management Review*, Autumn, 1984.
3 A reference to the problems that have faced both companies as a result of faults in the product's make-up. In the case of Perrier it was the issue of small amounts of benzene contained in the natural spring water source, while at Vauxhall it was the siting of the petrol tank within the vehicle design.
4 Sethi, S.P., 'Dimensions of corporate social performance: an analytical framework', *California Management Review*, Spring, 1975.
5 Mintzberg, *op. cit.*.
6 Simon, B., 'Sharks in the water', *Financial Times*, 27 November 1991.
7 Peattie, K., *Green Marketing*, Pitman, 1992.
8 *Environment Business*, 9 September 1992.

REVIEW AND DISCUSSION QUESTIONS

1 In the *Braer* case who are the stakeholders, what are their interests and how might they influence future decisions to avoid further environmental incidents such as the tanker disaster?

2 To what extent are governments responsible for establishing the parameters by which organisations conduct business? Should a business be free to decide its own level of corporate responsibility?

3 Consider the case for greater democracy in the decision process of firms. To what extent is it feasible for businesses to implement the recommendations of the Cadbury Report?

4 Writers have argued that the only objective of business is to make profit, within the boundaries established by government. Do you agree?

ASSIGNMENTS

1 As a group, select an environmental issue (e.g. business or natural feature) and write a report to the leader of a local pressure group which details an environmental impact assessment of the issue. The report should make clear reference to:
   (a) a cost/benefit analysis, carried out by the group, of the salient factors;
   (b) any legislation/regulation that concerns the case; and
   (c) the provision of a stakeholder map that illustrates who the stakeholders are, their importance to the case and their ability to affect future decisions.

2 As a newly appointed trainee manager you have been asked to look afresh at the business, with particular reference to the implementation of an environmental management system. Your immediate superior has asked you to write a report. Accordingly, you are required to:
   (a) consult the available literature and identify what you consider to be the necessary processes and procedures that would comprise an environmental management system;
   (b) indicate the areas within the organisation that need to be addressed; and
   (c) explain how such a policy should be implemented within the organisation.

FURTHER READING

Frederick, W. C., Post, J. E. and Davis, K., *Business and Society: Corporate strategy, public policy, ethics*, 7th edition, McGraw-Hill, 1992.

International Chamber of Commerce, *The Business Charter for Sustainable Development*, ICC, Paris, 1990.

Pearce, D. W. and Turner, R. K., *Economics of Natural Resources and the Environment*, Harvester Wheatsheaf, 1990.

Smith, D., *Business Strategy in the Environment*, Chapman, 1993.

Welford, R. and Gouldson, A., *Environmental Management and Business Strategy*, Pitman, 1993.

CHAPTER 16

Monitoring change

Ian Worthington

Business organisations operate within a changing and often uncertain environment. To ensure that corporate resources are used effectively in pursuit of organisational objectives, firms need ideally to examine the external influences upon them and, where possible, to anticipate the nature and extent of environmental change. The study and practice of strategic management and decision-making has provided a number of useful approaches in this area and has generated a variety of techniques for analysing the business environment. These techniques rely on the generation of data and information, much of which is in the public domain. Accessing this information has become significantly easier with improvements in computer technology and in collecting and collating material from both national and international sources.

OBJECTIVES

1 To demonstrate the need to monitor the changing business environment.
2 To examine broad approaches to environmental analysis.
3 To analyse a range of qualitative and quantitative techniques used by business organisations as an aid to decision-making.
4 To provide a comprehensive review of national and international sources of information and data useful to both students and practitioners of business.

INTRODUCTION

Few companies have been so universally admired as International Business Machines (IBM) – nicknamed 'Big Blue' after the colour of its packaging. For most of the postwar period it has completely dominated the world computer industry, becoming market leader in mainframe computers and the widely accepted industry standard in its field of technology. Investing huge sums in research and development, IBM has grown into the largest hi-tech company in America and Europe and one of the biggest in Japan, and has served as a model for other global firms. Its reputation for protecting the interests of its stakeholders – including its employees who have been offered lifetime employment and opportunities for education and training – is legendary and has helped to enhance its reputation not only in business circles, but also in the wider community, where it has been an important sponsor of sporting and cultural events.

In its quest for excellence, IBM has traditionally been a customer-driven organisation with a marketing and sales orientation in every part of the company and this has been a critical factor in its success. With a worldwide workforce of over 400,000 in the mid-1980s, IBM achieved operating profits of more than $10 billion. Buoyed by a booming world economy and a seemingly inexorable demand for its products, including its personal computers, IBM recorded the largest earnings in its history and this boosted its share price to record levels. At the time, senior executives confidently predicted that by 1990 sales would reach $100 billion and would stand at $185 billion by 1994 – figures which few inside or outside the industry dared challenge given the company's performance and apparently invincible position.

In the event these predictions proved woefully inaccurate. Pre-tax losses in 1992 amounted to $9 billion (about £5.84 billion) – the biggest loss in American corporate history and this followed a net loss the previous year of almost $3 billion, the first loss in the company's history, on sales that had fallen for the first time since 1946. By mid-January 1993, IBM's stock market value stood at only $27 billion and its shares were worth less than a third of their peak price in 1987. On the employment side, the company proposed a 25,000 cut in the workforce in 1993, and this came on top of the 40,000 jobs axed the previous year which had reduced the number of employees to 300,000 and which had involved the company in huge restructuring costs that had helped to plunge it into the red. The announcement by John Akers, the company chairman, that IBM might have to abandon two of its most cherished principles – no compulsory redundancies and no dividend cuts – only served to emphasise the depth to which the organisation had descended in such a relatively short time.

What went wrong? The answer in simple terms is that IBM failed to pay sufficient heed to the technological and commercial trends in the business environment in which it was operating. Improvements in 'chip' technology had given rise to the development of ever more powerful and flexible personal computers and IBM's decision to enter this market helped to legitimise the product. Unfortunately for the company, it also opened the doors to a multitude of new competitors who made use of the same off-the-shelf technology to build machines to the same standards and capable of running the same software, but at a fraction of the prices charged by IBM. At first this did little to affect IBM's mainframe business and the company continued to keep faith with its 'cash cow'. But as technological improvements occurred, mainframes came increasingly to be challenged by a new variety of extra powerful desktop machines called 'workstations' which could be linked together in 'networks' and could be designed to customer specifications at highly competitive prices.

The twin threats of technological change and vigorous competition seem to have been largely ignored at first by IBM's senior executives, whose minds seemed set on the belief that success in the industry was related to selling large pieces of hardware to corporate customers. Rapidly changing market conditions, however, brought about by technological advances and the aggressive behaviour of the cheap clone-makers, and further exacerbated by the world recession, have caused the company to reconsider its position and to institute a series of organisational and other changes designed to overcome its present difficulties. Whilst these changes – which include the replacement of senior executives, a restructuring of the organisation, a reduction in the workforce and a shift of resources from mainframes to the growth segments of the computer market – have largely been welcomed by investors, it is too early to predict if they will help the company to recapture its past position. Nevertheless, they clearly illustrate the problems which can be faced by businesses which take a reactive rather than a proactive approach to changes in the business environment and which fail to ask critical questions about markets and competitors until a crisis occurs.

THE NEED TO MONITOR CHANGE

IBM's experiences underline the need for business organisations to consider the environment in which they are operating and, wherever possible, to anticipate changes that can affect their position. Ideally, a firm's management should regularly monitor the external context in order to identify the potential threats and opportunities it poses for the enterprise and should fashion its decisions accordingly. As the previous chapters have indicated, this context comprises not only those groups and individuals affected directly by the organisation's primary operations, such as its customers, competitors and other stakeholders, but also the broader societal environment in which these operations take place.

Undertaking some form of environmental analysis (see below) inevitably implies the need to commit human and financial resources, which some organisations may be unable or unwilling to contemplate, particularly when the returns in terms of opportunities gained or threats avoided are difficult to calculate. Whilst such a view might be understandable, especially amongst smaller organisations operating in markets which appear relatively stable (e.g. undertakers), it may be misguided for at least two basic reasons. First, the resource cost of such an analysis need not necessarily be prohibitive, since a considerable amount of relevant data and information is available within both the organisation and the public domain at little or no cost to the enterprise. Secondly, the price paid for not investing resources in even a rudimentary form of environmental scanning may prove substantial and can range from lost opportunities to the ultimate failure of the organisation or its demise as an independent enterprise.

Problems of environmental complexity, uncertainty and the large number of external variables may prove a further disincentive to organisations seeking to monitor actual or potential changes in the business environment, and undoubtedly help to explain why many firms adopt either a 'do nothing' or reactive approach. Alternatively, the existence of these problems may be used as a convenient excuse by managers, who for one reason or another prefer to focus their attention on the day-to-day operations of the enterprise and to treat environmental influences as either irrelevant or peripheral to the processes of production. Whilst such a view may be sustainable in the short term, as a strategic approach it can prove highly risky, particularly if one's competitors take a more enlightened stance. It also indicates a lack of appreciation of the extent to which the internal and external environments are interdependent and of the need for management to achieve a 'strategic fit' between what the environment requires and the organisation can offer, as well as what the enterprise needs and the environment can provide.

ANALYSING THE BUSINESS ENVIRONMENT: BROAD APPROACHES

Environmental analysis or scanning should be seen as part of the process of strategic management and a prerequisite to the formulation and implementation of organisational strategies (see Figure 16.1).[1] It involves the monitoring and evaluation of information from the firm's internal and external environments and the dissemination of this information to key individuals within the enterprise for whom the internal strengths and weaknesses and external opportunities and threats are of critical significance in decision-making. As implied above, accurate forecasting of changing elements in a firm's environment not only reduces the danger that it will be taken by surprise by environment changes, but it may also give the firm a competitive advantage within its industry, especially if its rivals are less proactive in this sphere.

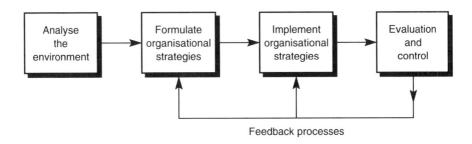

Feedback processes

Fig. 16.1 The strategic management process

Much of the process of environmental scanning can, of course, be undertaken on an informal and individual basis and the information can be gleaned from a variety of sources including suppliers, customers, consultants, financial institutions, pressure groups, local organisations (e.g. Chambers of Commerce) and government. Larger organisations, however, may feel the need to supplement this approach by a more formalised system of information-gathering and analysis, involving the use of a range of techniques – some of which are described below.

In broad terms, these more deliberate approaches to environmental scanning tend to focus on the firm's societal and task environments. PEST or STEP analysis, for example, looks at likely changes in political, economic, socio-cultural and technological factors and seeks to predict the extent to which change is likely to occur and its possible consequences for the organisation (e.g. as more women have returned to work in the United States, Avon has shifted its emphasis from selling its cosmetics at home to selling them at the office during the lunch break). In contrast, industry-based approaches focus on firms producing the same or similar products and on the key features of their competitive environment, including the relative power of buyers and suppliers and the actual or potential threats from rival organisations.

In this context, Porter's 5-forces model of competition provides a useful framework for analysis.[2] In essence Porter argues that an organisation's environment is predominantly conditioned by the intensity of competition in the industry or industries within which it is operating and that this is a critical influence not only on the competitive rules of the game, but also on the strategies potentially available to the firm. This competition is determined by five basic competitive forces – illustrated in Figure 16.2 – and it is the collective strength of these forces which determines the ultimate profit potential in the industry, measured in terms of long-run return on capital invested.

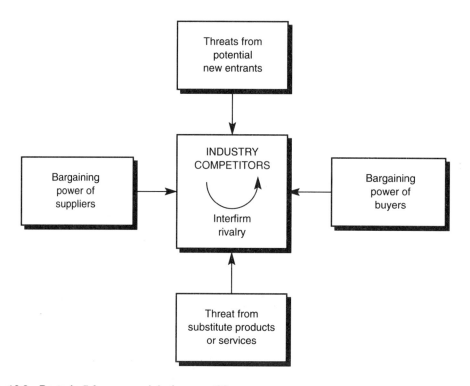

Fig. 16.2 Porter's 5-forces model of competition
Source: adapted from M. E. Porter, *Competitive Strategy*, reprinted with the permission of The Free Press, a Division of Macmillan, Inc., copyright © 1980 by The Free Press

Whilst not denying that a range of short-term factors may influence a firm's profitability (e.g. strikes, sudden increases in demand), Porter's contention is that any meaningful structural analysis must be based on an identification of the underlying characteristics of an industry which are rooted in its economics and technology, and it is these which are critical to the strengths of each competitive force. Foremost amongst these characteristics would be entry barriers to new firms, the intensity of rivalry among existing competitors, the pressure from substitute products, the relative bargaining power of buyers and suppliers, and the importance of government in influencing competition.

TECHNIQUES

To assist in an analysis of the business environment, organisations can make use of a wide variety of techniques, ranging from those involving quantitative measurements and predictions to the more qualitative or judgemental approaches associated with opinion canvassing. In practice the choice of technique(s) used will tend to be conditioned by a variety of factors, including the type of information required, the extent and accuracy of data available, the time factor, resource constraints and the perceived importance of the forecast to the process of organisational decision-making.

Trend extrapolation

As its name suggests, trend extrapolation is essentially a technique for predicting the future based on an analysis of the past. Implicit in this is the assumption that, in the short run at least, most factors tend to remain fairly constant and critical changes in the key variables are unlikely to occur. Accordingly, extending present trends into the future is seen as a useful means of anticipating forthcoming events and tends to be one of the techniques most frequently used by business organisations seeking a relatively simple and inexpensive means of forecasting.

At its simplest level, trend analysis tends to be used to predict changes over time (e.g. in the likely demand for a product), a process which can sometimes prove relatively accurate where there are sufficient historical data to allow seasonal and cyclical fluctuations to be taken into consideration. The analysis can also be refined to examine an observed relationship between one factor (e.g. sales) and another (e.g. levels of disposable income) and can even be extended to the simultaneous consideration of several variables felt to influence the subject under consideration (e.g. by using multiple regression techniques). In addition, techniques also exist to investigate causal or explanatory factors that link two or more time series together (e.g. statistical modelling techniques) and to consider the likely impact on forecasted trends of a range of factors, identified by analysts as likely both to occur and to have an effect on the predicted outcome. The latter technique is generally known as 'trend–impact analysis' and is sometimes used by large companies in conjunction with other methods of forecasting, including the Delphi approach and opinion canvassing (see below).

The fundamental drawback in the use of trend analysis as a forecasting tool is that there is no guarantee that the trends identified from historic patterns will continue in the future; sudden discontinuities – such as the United Kingdom's decision to leave the ERM – can invalidate or undermine the existing assumptions on which a trend was predicted. In a majority of cases, trends are based on a series of patterns or relationships among a wide range of variables, a change in any one of which can drastically alter the future course of events. These variables are not always easy to identify and the interactions between them are not necessarily fully understood. Attempts to link a simple cause with a simple effect run the danger of underestimating the complexities of the business environment.

Scenario writing

Scenario writing is essentially an attempt to paint a picture of the future; it is designed to provide a realistic description of possible future developments within the environment and/or an industry and to consider their likely impact on the organisation should they occur. This technique – which often includes 'best case', 'worst case', 'most likely case' predictions – helps organisational decision-makers to anticipate potential changes in the environment and to consider appropriate responses should such changes occur; as such it can be a useful stimulus to risk analysis and contingency planning in a corporate context.

In practical terms, organisational approaches to scenario writing can vary quite considerably. In some cases the technique – if used at all – is likely to be no more than a general prediction of the future based on relatively informal discussions between senior management, and will accordingly tend to be conditioned by the subjective judgements of the individuals concerned and by the influences upon them. In other cases, a more complex analysis of the future may occur, using a range of techniques which may include canvassing the views of individuals outside the organisation with no vested interest in its fortunes (see below).

Whilst scenario building is appropriate to all types and sizes of organisations and at all stages of their existence, Porter has argued that it is a particularly useful tool for emerging industries, where uncertainty tends to be considerable and where the only certainty is that change will occur. Through a structured analysis of possible developments in product/technology, markets and competition and their likely consequences, Porter claims that firms in an emergent industry will be in a position to examine where they stand and how they can behave strategically should one or other predicted scenarios occur. For some firms, such an analysis will provide a means of establishing the key events which will signal whether one scenario or another is actually occurring, and this can guide their actions. For others, with sufficient resources, it may encourage them to direct their efforts towards causing the most advantageous scenario to occur and, in doing so, will strengthen their ultimate position within the industry.

Expert opinion: the Delphi method

To predict future developments or to build likely scenarios, some organisations turn to experts, an increasing number of whom work as consultants. These experts often operate as a group to produce an analysis which is presented to management in the form of a report or which emanates from a discursive technique known as 'brainstorming'. Alternatively, the organisation may prefer to canvass the views of an anonymous panel of experts, using a technique known as the Delphi method, which was originally developed by the Rank Corporation in the United States to forecast likely military events.

In essence the Delphi approach involves eliciting opinions from a group of experts who operate individually, and anonymously, unaware of the other members of the group. Each expert is asked to respond to an initial set of questions and the answers are clarified and tabulated by a neutral investigator who uses them to generate a more refined set of questions that are then put to the experts. Following their replies, further revisions may occur and the respondents may be asked again to provide another set of predictions that take into account the information provided in the earlier replies. This process may continue for several rounds until a measure of convergence occurs between the views of the panel and a form of consensus is reached on likely future developments. As a technique the Delphi method tends to be expensive and time-consuming and there is no guarantee that a clear view will emerge. It can, however, be used to investigate any aspect of a firm's environment and to identify not only the effects of predicted changes, but also their causes, and this information may be incorporated into other forms of environmental analysis of both a qualitative and quantitative kind.

Cross-impact matrices

The cross-impact matrix provides a more complex means of assessing and forecasting environmental change than some of the other methods previously described. Under this approach, analysts identify a set of events that are forecast to occur within a given time period, and specify not only the expected timing of each event but also its probability of occurrence. By arranging these events in anticipated chronological order in rows and columns of a matrix (see Figure 16.3), attention is focused on the interaction between the events and, in particular, on the extent to which one may influence the timing or likely occurrence of another.

Probability and timing	Event 1	Event 2	Event 3	Event 4	Event 5
Event 1 (probability/ timing)					
Event 2 (probability/ timing)					
Event 3 (probability/ timing)					
Event 4 (probability/ timing)					
Event 5 (probability/ timing)					

Fig. 16.3 A simple cross-input matrix

As a means of predicting likely interactions between anticipated future developments, cross-impact analysis serves at least two significant purposes. First, it can be used to check the consistency of the various forecasts which go into it – such as the prediction of events and their relationships – given that inconsistencies will become apparent from an analysis of the results. Secondly, it provides a means of identifying events and trends that will have the greatest impact on subsequent developments, whether they be in individual segments of the environment or across a range of segments, as in the case of interactions between economic, technological, social and political factors.

'SWOT' or 'TOWS' analysis

It is widely accepted that corporate performance is influenced by a combination of internal and external factors. These factors can be characterised as the organisation's internal 'strengths' and 'weaknesses' and its external 'opportunities' and 'threats'. Systematically analysing these factors as an aid to strategic decision-making represents a form of situational analysis known commonly by the acronym 'SWOT' (or 'TOWS').

The starting point for a SWOT analysis is usually a review of the organisation's internal strengths and weaknesses, which may be undertaken by management or by external consultants brought in to provide a more objective view. The identified factors having been listed may then be given scores to indicate their importance, with the more significant issues receiving a larger score. This process is then repeated for the firm's external opportunities and threats in order to highlight those external factors which are likely to occur and which are expected to have an impact on the organisation's future position. The resultant SWOT grid can then be used to focus attention on the key environment influences faced by the organisation and to consider how far current strategy is relevant to the changes taking place in the business environment.

It is worth pointing out that the analysis of opportunities and threats cannot be absolute, since what might at first appear to be an opportunity may not be so when viewed against the organisation's resources or its culture or the expectations of its stakeholders. Moreover, the true value of the SWOT approach lies not in the listing of influences but in their contribution to the formulation of appropriate organisation strategies. One means of focusing attention on the latter is to produce a SWOT (TOWS) matrix which matches the firm's opportunities and threats against its internal strengths and weaknesses (see Figure 16.4). The result is four sets of possible strategic alternatives – termed SO, ST, WO and WT strategies – which range from the positive exploitation of strengths in order to take advantage of opportunities to the essentially defensive strategy of minimising weaknesses and avoiding anticipated threats.

LIMITATIONS TO ENVIRONMENTAL ANALYSIS

The techniques described above represent some of the ways in which organisations can examine the changing business environment in an attempt to understand what changes are likely to occur, how these may affect the organisation and what responses would be appropriate in the circumstances. In short, the value of such analysis lies not only in the information provided but also in the process of gathering and evaluating it and in applying it to the task of strategic management.

Despite its potential value as a tool of decision-making, environmental analysis is not without its limitations and these need to be taken into account. For a start, analysing the business environment is not a precise science and does not eliminate uncertainty for an organisation, caused, for instance, by unanticipated events which do not follow the normal pattern. Nor should it be regarded by managers as a means of foretelling the future, allowing them to avoid their responsibilities as strategic planners and decision-makers by blaming problems on a deficiency in the application of a particular technique or on inaccuracies in the data provided.

Added to this, environmental analysis of itself is by no means a guarantee of

		Strengths (S)	Weaknesses (W)
INTERNAL ASPECTS EXTERNAL ASPECTS		List major organisational strengths (e.g. quality products)	List major organisational weaknesses (e.g. poor distribution)
Opportunities (O) List major organisational opportunities (e.g. new markets)		SO strategies	WO strategies
Threats (T) List major organisational threats (e.g. competition)		ST strategies	WT strategies

Fig. 16.4 A SWOT matrix

organisational effectiveness, and can sometimes complicate the decision-making process by providing information which calls into question the intuitive feeling of experienced managers. The danger is that the analysis may become an end in itself and may obscure information and data coming from other sources, rather than being used in conjunction with them. Accordingly, its value in strategic thinking and strategic decision-making may not be exploited to its full potential and this may represent a lost opportunity to the organisation, as well as an inefficient and ineffective use of resources.

INFORMATION SOURCES

Researching the business environment can be a daunting task, given the extensive amount of information and statistical data available. To help in this direction the final section of this chapter outlines some of the key national and international information sources which are readily accessible to both students and businesses. Whilst the list is by the means exhaustive, it gives a good indication of the wide range of assistance available to researchers and of the different formats in which information is published by government and non-government sources for different purposes. It is worth noting that in recent years much of this information has become available in an electronic as well as a published format and can be accessed using computerised databases such as CD-ROM.

Statistical sources

Statistical information is an important component of business research and students need to be aware of what is available, particularly as some data turns up in the most unexpected places. Three key guides in locating statistical information are:

1 *Guide to Official Statistics* Published by the Central Statistical Office and an important starting point in any search for statistical sources of information. The *Guide* covers all official UK government statistics and some important non-official sources and provides broad descriptions of these and access through an alphabetical subject index.

2 *Sources of Unofficial UK Statistics* Compiled by Warwick University Library and providing details of a large number of unofficial statistical publications from a wide variety of organisations (e.g. pressure groups, trade unions, professional associations).

3 *The International Directory of Non-Official Statistical Sources* Published by Euromonitor and a key guide to non-official sources in selected countries outside western Europe, the latter being covered by the *European Directory of Non-Official Statistical Sources*. The *Directory* concentrates particularly on sources dealing with consumer goods, consumer trends, key industries and national economic and business trends. It has a subject and a geographical index.

Some of the main statistical sources, arranged in alphabetical order, are discussed below:

4 *Annual Abstract of Statistics* Published by the government's Central Statistical Office (CSO), this is an authoritative source of official statistics arranged under 18 headings, which include population, production, energy, transport, trade and public services. Figures usually cover a ten-year period and are presented in tabulated form. There is a detailed alphabetical index at the end.

5 *Basic Statistics of the Community* A pocket guide of comparative statistics on the EC, together with the United States, Canada, Japan and a number of other countries. Published by Eurostat, the annual guide covers areas such as population, finance, trade, environment and the economy and the data sometimes spans several years.

6 *Business Briefing* A weekly journal produced by the British Chambers of Commerce and containing a variety of comment, information and statistical data useful to business.

7 *Business Bulletins* Regularly issued bulletins from the CSO covering a wide variety of information, including data on company finance, cross-border acquisitions and mergers, overseas direct investment and company profitability. The data normally covers several years and sometimes has attached commentary.

8 *Business Monitor* A detailed source of summary information on the annual censuses of production. Data cover a range of aspects, including output, employment and costs.

9 *Consumer Europe* Produced by Euromonitor, this is a pan-European source of marketing statistics with the emphasis on consumer goods and consumer trends. The information which is updated at yearly or two-yearly intervals examines the

main product groups and includes predictions on future levels of consumption. A *Consumer Eastern Europe* has recently been added to the series.

10 *Economic Survey of Europe* Published annually by the United Nations (UN). The survey includes data in various forms on individual countries and on geographical groupings in Europe and identifies trends in areas such as agriculture, industry, investment and trade. Tables and charts include written commentary.

11 *Economic Trends* A monthly publication by the CSO and a key guide to the current economic indicators (e.g. prices, unemployment, trade, interest rates, exchange rates). The figures span several years, as well as the latest month or quarter, and tables and charts are provided. A quarterly supplement covering the balance of payments and the national accounts was added in March 1993.

12 *Employment Gazette* A monthly publication by the Department of Employment which covers a range of labour market data including employment, unemployment, vacancies and earnings. The *Gazette* includes news briefings and special feature articles and is the official source of information on the Retail Prices Index.

13 *European Economy* Published twice a year by the European Commission and concerned with the economic situation and other developments. The journal includes data on economic trends and business indicators and provides a statistical appendix on long-term macroeconomic indicators within Europe.

14 *European Marketing Data and Statistics* An annual publication by Euromonitor providing statistical information on the countries of western and eastern Europe. The data cover a wide range of market aspects – including demographic trends, economic indicators, trade, consumer expenditure, retailing – and often show trends over a fourteen- or fifteen-year period. The information is provided primarily in a spreadsheet format and there is an alphabetical index.

15 *Family Expenditure Survey* A comprehensive breakdown of data on households, including income, expenditure and other aspects of finance. The survey has very detailed tables and charts – mostly for the latest year – and some regional analysis is provided.

16 *Financial Statistics* A monthly publication by the CSO on a wide range of financial aspects including the accounts of the public and non-public sectors of the economy. Figures cover the latest month or quarter together with those of previous years.

17 *General Household Survey* A continuous sample survey of the general population produced by the Office of Population Censuses and Surveys. The survey spans a wide range of household-related aspects – including housing, health, education and employment – and is widely used as a source of background information for central government decisions on resource allocation.

18 *International Marketing Data and Statistics* An international compendium of statistical information on the Americas, Asia, Africa and Oceania published annually by Euromonitor. Information on demographics, economic trends, finance, trade, consumer expenditure and many other areas usually covers a thirteen- or fourteen-year period and an alphabetical index is provided.

19 *Monthly Digest of Statistics* The key source of current information on national income and expenditure, population, employment, trade, prices and a range of other areas. Previous as well as current data are provided.

20 *New Earnings Survey* An annual publication in parts from the Department of Employment. It contains detailed statistical information on earnings by industry, occupation, region, country and age group.

21 *National Income and Expenditure* Known as the Blue Book. Published annually by the CSO, it contains data on domestic and national output, income and expenditure, and includes a sector-by-sector analysis. Figures often cover ten years or more and an alphabetical index is provided.

22 *OECD Economic Outlook* A periodic assessment of economic trends, policies and prospects in OECD countries. Published twice a year, the *Outlook* includes articles as well as figures, tables, charts and short-term projections and looks at developments on a country-by-country basis.

23 *OECD Economic Surveys* An annual publication by the OECD providing individual country reports of the world's advanced industrial economies.

24 *Overseas Trade Statistics of the United Kingdom* A detailed analysis of current UK trade produced by the CSO. Data are produced on a country, area and commodity basis for both imports and exports and some cross-tabulation occurs.

25 *Regional Trends* An annual CSO publication providing a wide range of information on social, demographic and economic aspects of the United Kingdom's standard planning regions, together with some data on the sub-regions and on the EC. The guide includes a subject index.

26 *Social Trends* Another annual CSO publication, in this case looking at different aspects of British society, including population, education, environment, housing, leisure and transport. It provides a more detailed analysis of data produced for the *Annual Abstract of Statistics* and includes a large number of charts and diagrams. Information often spans a fifteen- to twenty-year period and an alphabetical subject index is included.

27 *United Kingdom Balance of Payments* Known as the Pink Book. It is a comprehensive guide to the United Kingdom's external trade performance and contains a wide range of statistics covering a ten-year period.

28 *United Nations Statistical Yearbook* Written in both English and French, the *Yearbook* is a detailed international comparative analysis of UN member countries. Data cover a wide variety of topics, including international finance, transport and communications, population, trade and wages, and a World Statistical Summary is provided at the beginning.

29 *World Economic Survey* Another UN publication produced every two years and examining fluctuations in the world economy, by individual countries and by groups of countries and using a variety of economic indicators.

30 *World Outlook* Produced by the Economist Intelligence Unit and forecasting political and economic trends for the current year in over 165 countries.

Information sources

Information on the different aspects of the business environment can be found in a variety of sources, including books, newspapers and periodicals. These often provide a wealth of contemporary data and commentary which can be located relatively easily in most cases, using indexes and other reference works designed to assist the researcher.

Some key sources in this area are discussed below:

1 *Anbar* Comprising six separate abstracting services covering fields such as accounting and finance, marketing and distribution and personnel and training. Each service is issued twelve times a year and is published in association with the appropriate professional body. All six services are subsequently published as the *Complete Anbar.*

2 *British Humanities Index* A comprehensive guide to over 300 current periodicals, *BHI* is published quarterly and contains a number of areas relevant to students of business. Sources are arranged in alphabetical sequence and there is an author index.

3 *British National Bibliography* A record of all books published in the United Kingdom and deposited in the British Library. The subject catalogue lists books in subject order in keeping with the Dewey Classification Scheme and hence is a good source of reference on business and management.

4 *Catalogue of Official Publications Not Published by HMSO* A bi-monthly publication listing sources from a range of public bodies (e.g. quangos) but not published by HMSO. The catalogue has a subject index and is arranged in order of department or organisation.

5 *Clover Newspaper Index* A monthly publication covering all the main quality dailies as well as the Sunday papers. The list of articles is arranged in alphabetical order by subject and provides a readily accessible means of tracing topics of current interest.

6 *Current Technology Index* A companion publication to the *British Humanities Index* providing an alphabetical subject index of articles relating to industry and technology.

7 *Extel* A detailed company information service for British and overseas companies provided by Extel Financial Limited. The service is in the form of information cards which are regularly updated and cover companies of various types, including quoted and unquoted business.

8 *Guardian Index* A monthly publication which provides a detailed index to articles appearing in *The Guardian* newspaper.

9 *HMSO Annual Catalogue* A list of all HMSO publications during a particular year. The catalogue is arranged in departmental order and has a subject index at the end.

10 *Lambda* A detailed and comprehensive guide to articles on marketing compiled by the Department of Marketing at Lancaster University.

11 *Monthly Index to the Financial Times* An index to all the articles listed by subject and by author that have appeared in the *FT* during the period concerned. The *Monthly Index* cumulates as the *Annual Index to the Financial Times* and both are an invaluable reference source on business matters.

12 *Publications of the European Community* An annual catalogue of all the publications, including periodicals, issued by EC institutions during the year.

13 *Research Index* A regularly published index to articles appearing in the commercial and industrial press and in periodicals. The *Index* provides references to industries and subject areas and to companies by name.

14 *Scimp* The selective co-operative index to management periodicals (hence 'scimp'), published ten times a year and a useful source of information on European publications on management issues.

15 *The Times Index* A monthly index, dedicated to *The Times* and its associated publications (excluding the *FT*). The index is arranged alphabetically by subject heading and by author and provides a list of the dates and the pages of the relevant publication.

16 *Whitaker's Books in Print* A list of all the titles currently available in the United Kingdom.

Other useful sources

1 *Bank of England Quarterly Bulletin* An assessment of economic developments in the United Kingdom and the rest of the world. It includes articles and speeches, together with general commentary on the economy.

2 *Bank Reviews* Quarterly publications by some of the leading clearing banks and often available free on request. These include *Barclays Review, Lloyds Bank Review, National Westminster Quarterly Bank Review* and *The Royal Bank of Scotland Review*.

3 *British Economic Survey* A twice-yearly update on the current state of the British economy, published by Longman.

4 *Business Update* Published annually by Hidcote Press and a very useful source of discussion on contemporary business issues.

5 *CBI Industrial Trends Survey* A quarterly guide to the state of UK manufacturing industry based on questionnaire responses by businesses. It provides a useful insight into business prospects and an indicator to future changes.

6 *Company Annual Reports* Available on request from all public companies and some private ones.

7 *Economic Briefing* Published three times a year by the CSO and replacing the *Economic Progress Report*.

8 *Economics Update* Another annual publication by Hidcote Press and designed to provide a review and discussion of contemporary issues relevant to students of economics and business.

9 *European Business Review* A pan-European journal published by MCB University Press. It includes articles, editorial comment, news reports and a discussion of recent publications. The journal also incorporates the *New European* which looks at the more cultural, political and environmental developments within Europe.

10 *European Journal of Marketing* Another publication by MCB University Press, relevant particularly to students of international marketing. It includes abstracts in French and German.

11 *European Trends* Published by the Economist Intelligence Unit, it is a quarterly review of key issues and business developments in a European context.

12 *Hambro Company Guide* A quarterly publication providing financial data drawn predominantly from the reports and accounts of UK companies. Each issue also includes feature articles.

13 *Income Data Services* A regular series of studies and reports on pay and other

labour-market issues (e.g. teamworking, childcare, redundancy), containing valuable up-to-date information and some statistical analysis.

14 *Journal of Marketing* A quarterly publication by the American Marketing Association and comprising articles together with recent book reviews in the field of marketing.

15 *Kelly's Business Directory* A substantial volume giving details of the address and main products of UK businesses.

16 *Key British Enterprises* A multi-volume compendium giving details of Britain's top 50,000 companies. Companies are listed alphabetically and are also indexed by trade, product and by geographical location.

17 *Kompass UK* A multi-volume directory produced in association with the CBI and providing details on UK companies, including names, addresses, products, number of employees, and so forth. Directories for other countries are also available.

18 *Lloyds Bank Economic Bulletin* A monthly publication covering a topic of current interest in an easily accessible form.

19 *Marketing* A weekly source of facts and articles on various aspects of marketing, presented in a journalistic style.

20 *Marketing in Europe* A monthly publication from the Economist Intelligence Unit containing detailed studies of the markets for consumer products in leading European countries. A comprehensive annual index, updated monthly, is available to subscribers.

21 *Marketing Intelligence* Formerly known as *MINTEL* and an invaluable source of information and statistics on a wide range of products. Reports cover market factors, trends, market share, the supply structure and consumer characteristics, and frequently include forecasts of future prospects.

22 *Sell's Directory: Products and Services* A useful directory in three main sections listing products and services, company details and trade names.

23 *The Economist* A standard reference source, published weekly and examining economic and political events throughout the world. It is an invaluable publication for business students and regularly contains features on specific business-related topics. It has a useful update on basic economic indicators.

24 *The Times 1000* Essentially a league table of UK top companies, with information on profitability, capital employed and other matters. Additional information is also provided on the monetary sector and on leading companies in other OECD countries.

25 *Who Owns Whom* An annual publication which identifies parent companies and their subsidiaries. It is a very useful source of information for examining the pattern of corporate ownership in the United Kingdom. Companion volumes are also available covering other parts of the world.

SYNOPSIS

IBM's recent experiences graphically illustrate the need for business organisations to monitor the environment in which they exist and operate and, where possible, to anticipate changes which are likely to affect the enterprise. Rather than being an optional extra, environmental analysis or scanning should be seen as an intrinsic part of strategic management and should ideally provide data and information that are used to guide the decision-making process. Much of this data and information already exists in published form and/or can be easily gathered from both literary and electronic sources on a national and international basis. Analysing it is also possible, using a range of techniques which have been developed by businesses and academics over a considerable number of years.

CASE STUDY: EAST MIDLANDS ELECTRICITY PLC

As previous case studies have illustrated, the privatisation of the electricity industry led to the formation of a number of private companies responsible for the generation and distribution of electricity within the United Kingdom. As far as distribution was concerned, this was placed in the hands of 12 regional electricity companies (RECs) which were the successors to the old electricity boards that had operated under the system of public ownership. In the East Midlands area – covering all of Leicestershire, most of Derbyshire, Lincolnshire, Northamptonshire, Nottinghamshire and Warwickshire, and parts of Bedfordshire, Buckinghamshire, Cambridgeshire, South Yorkshire, Oxfordshire and Staffordshire – distribution to commercial, industrial and domestic users was vested in East Midlands Electricity PLC (EME), operating from its headquarters in Nottingham. Like all other RECs, EME also retained the right to retail electrical appliances through its own shops and to provide electrical contracting services to its various customers.

Like many other large private sector companies, EME recognises the importance of gathering information about the environment in which it is operating. In pursuit of its mission to be 'simply the best electricity company in the United Kingdom', EME has developed a marketing plan which is used to examine the market environment in which the Electricity Division of the organisation operates. This marketing plan moves via a step-by-step approach from consideration of the company's corporate objectives, through an audit of the internal and external factors likely to affect the organisation's performance in the coming year, to the formulation of marketing plans and their subsequent evaluation and review (see Figure 16.5). This plan is then used to direct the activities of the company's marketing and sales teams in the year ahead.

A key step in the process is the use of a SWOT analysis which draws on information and data collected during the market audit. As Figure 16.6 illustrates, the focus of attention is on both internal and external factors and these provide a valuable input into the formulation of marketing objectives and strategies. The aim of such an analysis, in essence, is to identify ways in which to exploit the organisation's strengths or capabilities and to maximise the opportunities offered by the market, whilst addressing corporate weaknesses and minimising external threats. As the example clearly demonstrates, not all factors identified by the analysis are within the control of the organisation and some are of more immediate concern than others. Nevertheless they provide a valuable input into the process of organisational decision-making and help to contribute to the company's understanding of its marketplace.

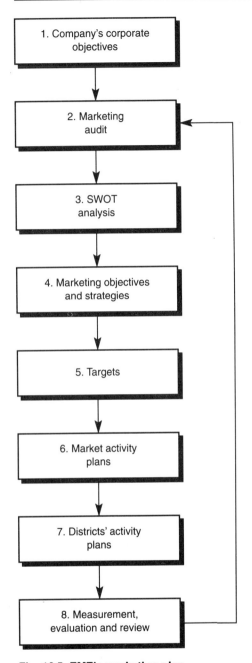

Fig. 16.5 **EME's marketing plan**

INTERNAL TO THE COMPANY	
Strengths	**Weaknesses**
● Tariff development	● Low profitability of certain tariff
● New product development	● Perceived high cost of electricity
● Dedicated sales force	● Customers perceive vulnerability in single fuel source
● Capital cost advantage	

EXTERNAL TO THE COMPANY	
Opportunities	**Threats**
● Net increase in population	● Slow recovery from recession predicted
● Possible Building Regulations review 1993/94	● Aggressive competitive activity
● Growing 1–2 bed house sector	● Gas dominance in the home heating systems

Fig. 16.6 **A SWOT analysis of the domestic electricity market**

NOTES AND REFERENCES

1 For a useful introduction to the subject see Fahey, L. and Narayanan, V.K., *Macroenvironmental Analysis for Strategic Management*, West Publishing, 1986.
2 Porter, M.E., *Competitive Strategy: Techniques for analysing industries and competitors*, Free Press, 1980.

REVIEW AND DISCUSSION QUESTIONS

1 Discuss the costs and benefits to businesses of the introduction of a system for monitoring and analysing the changing external environment in which they operate.

2 To what extent do you agree with the proposition that only large firms should or can make use of the various techniques of environmental analysis.

3 Using a firm or organisation of your choice, attempt a 'SWOT' analysis (e.g. can you apply such an analysis to the organisation in which you work or study?).

4 Using the information sources discussed above, and any others with which you are familiar, provide a comparative analysis of consumer markets in at least eight leading European countries (including eastern Europe).

ASSIGNMENTS

1 You work for a medium-sized private company in the UK fashion industry (it can be either on the production or retailing side). As a personal assistant to the manager director, your brief is to provide help and advice on various aspects of the firm's operations. You have recently become concerned about the lack of a system for monitoring changes in the business environment and have agreed to produce a report on the issue for the board of directors. In producing this report, you are required to identify both the costs and benefits to the business of implementing a system of environmental scanning.

2 As a librarian in a college (or university) library, with responsibility for help and advice to students on business studies courses, you are frequently asked for guidance on how to access information and data on a particular company. Choosing any well-known company you wish, produce a diagrammatic representation (e.g. flow chart) of the steps you would advise students to undertake to get the information they require. At each step, indicate what type of information is available and how and from where it can be obtained.

FURTHER READING

Cooke, S. and Slack, N., *Making Management Decisions*, 2nd edition, Prentice Hall, 1991.
Fahey, L. and Narayanan, V.K., *Macroenvironmental Analysis for Strategic Management*, West Publishing, 1986.
Palmer, A. and Worthington, I., *The Marketing and Business Environment*, McGraw-Hill, 1992.
Weihrich, H., 'Daimler-Benz's move towards the next century with the TOWS matrix', *European Business Review*, 93(1), 1993, pp. 4–11.

INDEX